# SHAPING CHINA'S SECURITY ENVIRONMENT: THE ROLE OF THE PEOPLE'S LIBERATION ARMY

Edited by

**Andrew Scobell**
**Larry M. Wortzel**

October 2006

\*\*\*\*\*

The views expressed in this report are those of the authors and do not necessarily reflect the official policy or position of the Department of the Army, the Department of Defense, or the U.S. Government. This report is cleared for public release; distribution is unlimited.

\*\*\*\*\*

Comments pertaining to this report are invited and should be forwarded to: Director, Strategic Studies Institute, U.S. Army War College, 122 Forbes Ave, Carlisle, PA 17013-5244.

\*\*\*\*\*

All Strategic Studies Institute (SSI) publications are available on the SSI homepage for electronic dissemination. Hard copies of this report also may be ordered from our homepage. SSI's homepage address is: *www.StrategicStudiesInstitute.army.mil.*

\*\*\*\*\*

The Strategic Studies Institute publishes a monthly e-mail newsletter to update the national security community on the research of our analysts, recent and forthcoming publications, and upcoming conferences sponsored by the Institute. Each newsletter also provides a strategic commentary by one of our research analysts. If you are interested in receiving this newsletter, please subscribe on our homepage at *www.StrategicStudiesInstitute.army.mil/newsletter/.*

ISBN 1-58487-251-9

# CONTENTS

# FOREWORD

This is the eighth volume on the People's Liberation Army (PLA) to be published by the Strategic Studies Institute. It is the product of a conference held at Carlisle Barracks, Pennsylvania, from September 23-25, 2005, to examine the PLA and the global security environment in which it operates. This gathering was the 18th in a series of annual conferences on China's PLA. I have been privileged to be involved with and/or attend most of these gatherings over the years. At the 2005 conference, I was honored to deliver the keynote address in which I offered some of my insights and observations about China derived from a lifetime of living in or working on the Middle Kingdom. More than 50 experts on China participating in this conference provided critical comments and guidance on the initial drafts of the chapters included in this volume.

These contributions contained herein address the role of the Chinese military in shaping its country's security environment. Of course, the PLA itself is shaped and molded by both domestic and foreign influences. In the first decade of the 21st century, the PLA is not a central actor in China's foreign policy the way it was just a few decades ago.

Nevertheless, the significance of the PLA must be understood. The military remains a player that seeks to play a role and influence China's policy towards the such countries and regions as United States, Japan, the Koreas, Southeast Asia, South Asia, and, of course, Taiwan. It is important not to overlook that, in times of crisis or conflict, the role and influence of the PLA rise significantly. Indeed, this was one of the findings of last year's volume (*Chinese National Security Decisionmaking Under Stress*) in this series of annual edited volumes published by the U.S. Army War College.

The 2005 conference was one of the best because of the vigorous and spirited exchanges, the revelation of interesting facts such as the PLA using target models of U.S. planes in its exercises, and the participation of top China scholars, such as Andy Nathan and Tom Christensen, who added depth and fresh insights into the process.

I commend to you this latest contribution to enhance our knowledge about the PLA and Chinese national security thinking. I know a careful examination of this volume will provide readers with important insights and a greater understanding of Chinese military and strategy.

Ambassador James R. Lilley
Senior Fellow
American Enterprise Institute

# CHAPTER 1
# INTRODUCTION

## Andrew Scobell
## Larry M. Wortzel

For 2 decades after the People's Republic of China (PRC) was established, there was no question that the People's Liberation Army (PLA) had a central role in shaping China's security and foreign policy. Indeed, the PLA also was a major actor in domestic policy. The new leaders that took over China in 1949 all came from the military or Communist Party cadre who fought the Nationalists from 1927 through the Anti-Japanese War, and then fought the final battles of the civil war. At the local, provincial, and national level, the Party, the Army, and the government were almost synonymous. The PLA's influence in national policy declined in subsequent decades, however. Today, one must carefully count the number of senior leaders with military connections in the Communist Party Politburo to debate the extent of PLA influence in China.

In 1950, when the Chinese forces poured across the border into the Korean War, there was no doubt that the PLA was a principal actor in shaping the security environment in China. The same is true of the PLA's actions in the Sino-Indian War and in the Cultural Revolution, when the military restored order. In Africa, PLA Railway Engineer Corps troops advanced China's interests with projects like the Tan-Zam Railway. During the American involvement in Vietnam, some 50,000 PLA troops deployed to North Vietnam and Laos in support of China's political and security interests. In 1979 and again in 1989, the generation of PLA veterans in the central Chinese government turned to the military. The numbers of military personnel in the National People's Congress and the leading bodies of the Communist Party today, however, are far lower than they were in the first few decades of the PRC's existence. This volume is an attempt to characterize the way that the PLA shapes, and is used by the government to shape, China's security environment. The military clearly is not as central an actor as it was in the past. The editors and the authors attempted in this volume to characterize the extent to which the PLA shapes the domestic, regional, or global security environment to meet China's interests.

We asked each of the contributing authors to examine a series of questions as he or she addressed the topic:

- How does the PLA function as an actor in China's security and foreign policies?

- Is the PLA the principal actor in policy formulation, or does it provide support for foreign policy and security initiatives?

- At what point in the policy process does the PLA interact with the various central Party and government "leading groups" that decide foreign and security policies?

- Is the PLA shaping the security environment through such mechanisms as defense exchanges, arms sales, visits by senior officers, student officer exchanges, or military exercises?

- Is there a clear security or foreign policy agenda in specific geographic regions attributable to the PLA?

The short answer to these questions is that the PLA remains an important actor and factor in shaping the international and domestic security environment for the central leadership. Clearly, the military is not the central player that it once was. Rather, the PLA is one of a number of foreign policy and security actors, and it responds to the Politburo Standing Committee and Central Military Commission, whose members are no longer almost exclusively military veterans.

This book is not all inclusive of the world, or all of the international activities by the PLA. The authors cover the domestic landscape in China and the state of civil-military relations. The book also explores how the PLA assesses U.S. military actions, the strength of the U.S. military, and the situation in and around the Taiwan Strait. For Asia, the book assesses the PLA's posture with respect to South Asia, Southeast Asia, Japan, and Korea. Clearly, the PLA also is active and a factor in China's security related interests in Latin America, the Middle East, Central Asia, and Africa. This volume does not cover these regions. However, we believe that the way that the authors have characterized the PLA's interests and activities is a good guide to the way that it is used, and behaves, as a security actor in other parts of the world.

In chapter 2, Frank Miller examines civil-military relations in China. The relationship between the populace and the military is in flux and evolving in response to Beijing's own domestic reforms and the changing international environment. The influx of western investment and business, broadened educational opportunities, generally higher standards of living, and greater freedom to travel all have created alternatives to military service, which once was an attractive way to gain some social mobility in Communist China. These new opportunities have created serious competition to the PLA in its traditional support and recruiting base. China's One-Child Policy, higher educational standards for the military, and efforts to stem corruption also have had a significant effect on the recruiting base from which the PLA can select. That said, rising nationalism has helped PLA recruiting and increased the interest of youth in anything military. The PLA has respect and support from the majority of Chinese citizens.

The General Political Department's (GPD) challenge is to fill the PLA's rolls with qualified and motivated youth who are loyal to the Party and the military. Miller makes the point that the PLA is examining personnel and recruiting systems in other modern militaries, in particular the United States, Russia, and India. The rise of nationalism in China also is a factor in civil-military relations. It has created increased interest in military service among China's youth. The PLA also has offered incentives to attract young people to military life, including tuition assistance, and a guaranteed technical assignment.

Miller concludes that the PLA is not as close to the people as it once was, and its claims of a close relationship to the people are exaggerated. That the PLA is searching for new ways to recruit and retain is an indication that the PLA is no longer seen as a good opportunity, and the rise of nationalism, by itself, is not enough to aid recruitment. The changing environment of civil-military relations is an aspect of China's overall social modernization and its emergence as a regional and global power. Recruitment issues provide a window into the PLA's relations with the people, the government, and the party. The bigger long-term question is whether the PLA retains its unique position in Chinese society as the unquestioning defender of the Communist Party, or becomes a professional military more motivated by affairs of the state.

In chapter 3, Ellis Joffe reminds the reader that there is widespread agreement that the Chinese armed forces have made remarkable, even surprising, progress in modernizing. Although the PLA is no match for the U.S. military, the fast growth of Chinese military capacity and the PLA's ability to use the weapons systems it has fielded have become serious considerations in U.S. Government assessments of China.

Joffe believes that the long-term objectives of China's military modernization reach far beyond settling the issue of Taiwan. In his view, Beijing's long-term plans are to provide the military underpinning for China's goals of rising to great power status. China's leaders have opted for slow and incremental military advances rather than for major but unrealistic attempts to modernize rapidly.

The near-term goal for the PLA is to be capable of conquering Taiwan and coping with U.S. intervention. Over the past decade, a concerted effort to acquire this capability was the strategic focus of China's military buildup. Specifically, China wants to be able to overrun Taiwan rapidly, preferably before the United States intervenes; to deter the United States by raising the costs of intervention; to deny U.S. forces access to the theatre of operations, primarily by improving China's naval capabilities; and, if all else fails, to defeat the United States in combat around Taiwan.

In the future, without Taiwan as the driving force, the scope and pace of the buildup might be reduced. The buildup also will be influenced by the continued availability of Russian weapons. The state of China's economy also will affect the future military buildup. Joffe thinks that if rural and urban unrest increase, the leadership might try to reduce increases in military appropriations in order to divert funds to other sectors. Nonetheless, according to Joffe, the dominant factor shaping civil-military relations will be the common objective of building up China's military power for the sake of objectives arising out of an assertive nationalism.

Susan Puska, like Frank Miller, is a former military attaché in China. In chapter 4, Puska tell us that, while overall bilateral U.S.-China ties moved in a more positive direction after September 11, 2001 (9/11), both the Chinese and American militaries remained mutually wary and cautious. The U.S. Secretary of Defense did not choose to make his first official visit to China until October 2005. When he was in Singapore in June of that year, he asked the pointed question about the ultimate goals of China's military buildup.

During the October 2001 Asia-Pacific Economic Cooperation (APEC) meeting, President Jiang Zemin expressed strong opposition to terrorism. He said China supported military operations in Afghanistan, but it was not open-ended support, and he cautioned that Afghanistan's sovereignty and independence must be ensured. The APEC meeting was an opportunity for China and the United States to begin counterterrorism intelligence cooperation. In addition, China generally acquiesced to the U.S. military intervention in Afghanistan, as well as U.S. cooperation with Pakistan and Central Asia. Puska says that, whereas they were cautiously supportive of operations in Afghanistan against the Taliban, China's collective leadership was skeptical of U.S. intentions to resort to military action in Iraq to remove Saddam Hussein.

Strategic level examinations of the motives and objectives of U.S. military interventions in Afghanistan and Iraq are discussed freely in official civilian press reports in China. These can be found in the *People's Daily* and *People's Liberation Daily*, as well as academic journals. The talking points are highly formulaic and reinforce one another through repetition. There also are operational and tactical assessments of the coalition effort in Iraq in technical and academic journals, both civilian and military. The articles tend to be straightforward discussions of U.S. capabilities, but they imply that the PLA also must have these capabilities as part of its own modernization efforts. With respect to operational doctrine and procedures, the PLA emphasizes operational and tactical logistics, high-technology weapons and equipment, information technology, and psychological operations. China's military contacts have widened in recent years, but China's central military relationship will likely remain with Russia for the foreseeable future. This military cooperation, which began largely as a marriage of convenience after the end of the Cold War, continues to mature in ways beyond arms sales of second-string Russian products and tentative cooperation.

Finally, Puska tells us that China's perception of the threat to its sovereignty posed by Taiwan independence and U.S. intervention provides urgency to China's military modernization. She thinks that, if China is to gain great power status, it must further develop its military in all components of power—land, sea, and air. China cannot afford and likely does not want to achieve parity with the U.S. military because the cost to China's overall national development would be destabilizing. However, China recognizes it must possess a credible military deterrent to protect China's national interests in the post-9/11, post-Iraq War era.

In Chapter 5, Lonnie Henley, former Defense Intelligence Officer for East Asia, examines how the PLA fits into the Chinese security establishment in managing conflicts and conflict escalation. Defining the issue, Henley reminds us "war control is the deliberate actions of war leaders to limit or restrain the outbreak, development, scale, intensity, and aftermath of war." The measures that may be taken include arms control, crisis control, and control of the scale of conflict.

According to Henley, Chinese military writings focus on how to prevent unwanted escalation of a crisis or conflict and how to ensure that military operations are controlled and modulated to serve broader political objectives. A central insight from Henley's review of books and papers from the PLA Academy of Military Science and the National Defense University is that PLA military academics have begun formal consideration of the issue only in the past 5 years. He believes that the concepts will continue to evolve over the next decade.

Preventing the unintended escalation of a political crisis into a military conflict, or a small-scale conflict into a major war, is part of a broader Chinese concept known as "containment of war" or "war control." China's military literature treats this as an activity involving all elements of national power designed to shape the international environment. The PLA's goals are to reduce the risk of war, manage crises, and prevent unintended escalation. Ultimately, the PLA seeks to adopt measures that will put China in a favorable position if war occurs and ensure military operations serve larger political objectives. PLA literature emphasizes that a principal contribution the military can make to control a fast-developing crisis is to be a highly visible and capable force obviously ready to take action.

There is a growing body of work in the field available in China, but it often is not examined in the English-speaking world.

Henley believes that a vigorous effort should examine Chinese-language sources and incorporate them into our understanding of PLA modernization efforts. Henley calls for greater exploration of Chinese concepts of nuclear escalation and war control in general. The discussion of crisis management, containment, escalation, and war control in Chinese military writing is a blend of classical Chinese strategic thought, practical considerations common to all modern militaries, sophisticated assessment of the political and military challenges the PLA would face in a crisis, and optimism about China's ability to mold the situation and control the course of events. There is a distinctively Chinese perspective that may have a significant influence on Beijing's behavior in a crisis, to include a potential conflict in the Taiwan Strait.

Paul Godwin, a veteran analyst of the PLA who taught for years at the National Defense University, looks at U.S. assessments of the implications of China's military modernization in Chapter 6. In the United States, the improving capabilities of the Chinese PLA are perceived as a potential threat to U.S. strategic interests in the West Pacific. China's intent to develop a self-sustaining military industrial complex also is a target of American concern.

China has broadened its foreign policy approach to pursue positive relations with the world. It has reached beyond its earlier concentration on Asian neighbors. Beijing seeks to work closely with the European Union and to extend its diplomatic influence into Latin America, the Middle East, and Africa. Godwin argues that much of China's diplomacy is to ensure access to the energy supplies, but it also is designed to reinforce Beijing's status as an influential player on the world scene. Although the strategy has made China richer and more influential, Godwin does not think that Beijing's defense policy reflects the confidence one might expect. Instead, Godwin sees a fundamental apprehension of U.S. power and military presence both globally and in the Asia-Pacific region.

Neither China nor the United States accept the legitimacy of each other's defense policies and strategies, according to Godwin. Instead, they are locked in "strategic distrust." Godwin thinks that Washington and Beijing must concentrate at senior levels on programs and contacts to ease mutual apprehension. Ultimately, however, Godwin argues that both sides must agree on mutually acceptable roles in Asia. Beijing and Washington cannot escape from some level of political and economic competition, but they must seek reciprocal acceptance of their military security policies.

John Tkacik, of The Heritage Foundation, assesses how the PLA views North Korea in chapter 7. Tkacik tells us that in 1950, at the start of the Korean War, senior Chinese military commanders did not think that North Korea was worth a war. At the time, the whole Politburo had military experience in one form or another, since China had just emerged from the war against Japan and its own civil war. Military commanders knew relatively little about North Korea then, and the ultimate decision to go in was forced by Mao Zedong, who believed that "when one's neighbors are on fire, we (China) cannot sit around crying about it." The decisionmaking process was something of a mystery then, according to Tkacik.

Tkacik tells us that things today are not much different. The Chinese Navy seems to be providing basing for North Korean special operations vessels. China facilitated the North Korean nuclear program by ensuring that transports from Pakistan could transit Chinese airspace carrying equipment to North Korea. In return for the nuclear help, North Korea sent back a *Nodong* ballistic missile to Pakistan after a refueling stop at a Chinese air base. Thus, the "support thy neighbor" analogy still seems to apply today. The PLA is quite concerned that the Korean Peninsula historically has been a corridor for aggression against China. Certainly, Japan took advantage of this route over a number of centuries. Thus, the Chinese military does not want to see North Korea collapse, but still defends the border to ensure that millions of North Koreans do not stream into Manchuria.

Robert Sutter, a former National Intelligence Officer for East Asia, looks at Japan's defense posture vis-à-vis China in Chapter 8. Sutter opines that a series of political and historical issues have molded the political climate in China in such a way that China and Japan face the most serious deterioration in Sino-Japanese relations since they established diplomatic relations over 30 years ago. Looking at the PLA, Sutter thinks that its priorities reflected in recent Chinese National Defense White Papers reflect a general worsening of security relations with Japan across a number of key national security issues in recent years.

To a certain extent, Japan's policies toward Taiwan affect PLA priorities about Tokyo. Moreover, China's emphasis on territorial integrity, as well as the goal of securing strategic resources such as oil and gas, makes Japanese forces a focus of PLA planning. In the year or so leading up to the October 2005 conference where Sutter's analysis was presented, PLA naval forces deployed in ways that exacerbated tensions with Japan, worsening relations.

Despite concerns over Taiwan, sovereignty, and contested maritime claims, Sutter sees "powerful reasons why Chinese leaders, as well as Japanese leaders, will seek to avoid further deterioration and restore more businesslike relations." One of the chief reasons for Beijing to moderate its own behavior is China's drive to project around the region an image that it is a leader in Asia, a benign good neighbor, and one that will show flexibility in accommodating the interests of regional partners.

Sutter points to tension among U.S. specialists on Asia over the outlook for China-Japan relations. Some U.S. specialists argue that the Sino-Japanese friction is against U.S. interests, and the United States should take concrete measures to reduce tensions. People advocating this approach suggest that the United States should discourage Japanese prime ministerial visits to the controversial Yasukuni war memorial. The same people believe that the United States should push the Japanese government officials to be more forthright in accepting responsibility for Japanese aggression in the Pacific War. The other side of the debate in the United States, Sutter says, are those specialists who see Sino-Japanese relations as unlikely to deteriorate substantially. They believe that it is in American interests to avoid actions that would offset Sino-Japanese tensions.

Sutter believes that the national security priorities of the PLA suggest that PLA leaders will focus less on economic and diplomatic consequences of escalating disputes in Sino-Japanese relations and more on security and historical aspects of relations. Thus, PLA concerns will serve as a drag on efforts by Chinese leaders to manage relations with Japan.

South Asia has not been the principal focus of China's attention over the last 5 decades. This is not to say that it has been overlooked: China fought a war with India in 1962, assisted Bangladesh and Pakistan in its sovereignty efforts, and has been a major military and foreign assistance supplier to both of the latter countries. The PLA was a major actor in all of these matters. However, the PLA's attention in the recent period generally has been on the eastern seaboard of the country, specifically towards Taiwan, Japan, Korea, and the South China Sea. The Soviet Union and its successor states, including Russia, also drew strong attention from China.

In chapter 9, Srikanth Kondapalli interprets the PLA's perspectives on South Asia. In a review of Chinese scholarship on the region, Kondapalli notes that China focuses on the major problems between the two countries such as the Tibet issue, the 1962 war, and relative configurations of power in Asia, including China-Pakistan relations. PLA scholars recognize that the domain of policy perspectives on South Asia is principally that of the foreign ministry. The PLA does not challenge this primacy. The same is true of areas including arms control.

The PLA's views on South Asia at times have differed from those of the civilian leadership. The primary differences have involved India, while there has been a coincidence of views of both the PLA and the civilian leadership regarding other South Asian countries. Kondapalli notes that although confidence-building measures (CBMs) have increased between India and China, some in the PLA have argued for "encircling" India. PLA scholars have suggested it would be a good idea to help other South Asian countries as a hedge against India and to curb its "regional hegemony" or chances of becoming a "great power."

The PLA's strategy of confronting India has become more nuanced in recent years. Still, in Indian military circles, China's actions were seen as an attempt by the PLA at "strategic encirclement" or "marginalization" of India. China's late 1985 PLA naval visits to Chittagong, Colombo, and Karachi (skipping Indian ports) are read this way, as are the continuing arms transfers to Pakistan and Bangladesh.

Overall, in Kondapalli's assessment, the PLA sees South Asia as a region dominated by India. The Chinese reaction is to develop closer relations with Pakistan and Bangladesh. While there is still PLA military cooperation with Pakistan, Bangladesh, Nepal, and Myanmar, the PLA has been expanding its contacts with the Indian military forces in terms of preventive CBMs and exchanges. While there has never been a military alliance between China and Pakistan or with Bangladesh, these states are being courted extensively for their value in countering India, besides being sources of raw materials and markets for Chinese low technology arms.

In chapter 10, Larry Wortzel assesses China's successful diplomacy and increasing influence in Southeast Asia. Wortzel thinks that the PRC has undertaken a diplomatic strategy of moderation and reassurance in Southeast Asia over the past decade, with the objectives of easing fears of China as a military threat to the region, building influence, working with multilateral organizations, and lessening U.S. influence in the region. The PLA has influenced and supported this strategy, but has not been the major actor in articulating the strategy.

Beijing uses its "comprehensive national power" to advance political, economic, military, and other security goals in Southeast Asia. The Foreign Ministry and the Chinese Communist Party, including its liaison and propaganda organs, have been major architects of the strategy and agents of its articulation. China's military organs have played a supporting role in articulating the strategy, but a role that has been clearly subordinate to the Foreign Ministry. However, unlike the situation in the 1960s and 1970s, there is no strong ideological component in today's strategy. Even though the Chinese Communist Party maintains friendly party-to-party relations with the Communist parties in the region, especially those of Vietnam and Laos, the Foreign Ministry plays the main role in articulating the strategy.

Still, Wortzel argues that, while the PLA is not the major instrument through which China addresses its goals in the region, it has an important role in advancing China's interests. The PLA provides the backdrop of military power that makes the nations in the region consider China's security interests as a factor in their policies. Southeast Asian nations, meanwhile, hedge their security interests. The nations in Southeast Asia maintain good relations with China, but want the United States and Australia present and active in the region. However, Southeast Asian nations would not "buy into" an American-led containment policy against China. China's public diplomacy is successful, but its military power is enough of a latent threat that Southeast Asian nations still hedge their security.

Wortzel argues that there has been a strong security component to all relationships in the region. The growing military power of China, and its increased ability to send its Navy around the region, have been factors in ensuring good relations. Thus, the PLA may not be leading in all relations, but it can certainly see itself as a major factor behind China's improved standing in Southeast Asia.

In summary, the authors have painted a picture that shows a part for the PLA in China's foreign and security policies, but not the leading part. Whether in domestic policy or foreign policy, the PLA is a major actor, but it is clearly subordinate to the dictates of the Ministry of Foreign Affairs and the domestic policy organs, respectively. China's foreign policies today are nuanced, with the PLA playing a prescribed role. That said, in domestic policy, it is still the military that is the ultimate guarantor of party control and stability.

# PART I:

## WHAT'S SHAPING THE PLA?

# CHAPTER 2

## CHANGING THE LANDSCAPE OF CIVIL-MILITARY RELATIONS IN CHINA: THE PLA RESPONDS TO RECRUITING AND RETENTION CHALLENGES

### Frank Miller

A lawsuit was filed in Guangzhou earlier this year claiming damages by the Ministry of National Defense' Tri-Service Honor Guard for the image of several of its soldiers being used without permission by a Chinese toymaker. The Shenzhen-based company was directed to remove all advertising featuring the servicemen, issue a public apology and pay RMB 100,000 Yuan (US$12,3300) in compensation.[1]

The PLA is the army of the CPC and of the country and of the people[2]

There is no doubt that the Civil-Military Relationship within the People's Republic of China (PRC) is evolving in response to many factors resulting both from Beijing's reforms and the changing international environment. The influx of western investment and business, broadened educational opportunities, generally higher standards of living, and greater freedom to travel all have created serious competition to the People's Liberation Army's (PLA) traditional support and recruiting base. To compound the situation, China's One-Child Policy, higher educational standards, and efforts to stem corruption also have had a significant effect on the recruiting base from which the PLA can select. To its favor, the PLA can count on the benefits of rising nationalism, increased interest by the youth in anything military, and a growing level of respect and support by the majority of Chinese citizens.

None of these benefits, however, translate directly into recruiting numbers, and actions are being taken to identify and solve the problem. The General Political Department's (GPD) Cadre Department is studying hard how to fill the PLA's rolls with qualified, motivated, and loyal (to both the Party and the job) youth. Their task in many ways is very similar to that of U.S. recruiters under strong economic conditions. Concurrent with the GPD's efforts is that of the General

Staff Department (GSD), which is trying to professionalize the PLA's professional military education (PME) system to reflect the needs of an informationalized military in a high-tech world.

The PLA is treading on new ground here, and they know it. To help them understand the problem they face, both the GPD and GSD are *seeking truth from fact* by researching the personnel systems of modern militaries, in particular the United States, Russia, and India (all of which have greater than a million personnel under arms) and the United Kingdom. While they have reached out to these countries for direct assistance in answering specific issues, the two responsible organizations have not integrated their strategies, and often are competing with each other for time with the foreign interlocutor.[3] Major conferences are being convened and study tours arranged to each of the above countries to gain ground truth (and, according to one PLA officer, to open the travelers' eyes to the need to change), while relationships with each other and with the foreign militaries are being subordinated to the search for a "Holy Grail" in personnel policies.

The desire to change their personnel policies is very real and can be attributed to their awareness that much of their modernization goals depend on getting it right. What is still at issue, though, is whether they have instituted a basic change in their principles regarding their role in society. Is the PLA changing its core values or just its façade? Are these attempts to make a military career more attractive to its dwindling recruitment base enough to overcome traditional Chinese norms, which are growing in importance as the strength of Cold War ideologies subside? And can they retool their educational system to match the industrial retooling that is equipping more and more of their combat units? Perhaps more accurately, can the PLA create a benefits package that attracts the tech-savvy talent already being trained in China's civilian institutions? And if they do build it, will anyone come? Will the PLA ever again be able to attract good iron to make its nails? Or must it create a system that builds on what it can get, stressing an independent system of education and advancement that is realistic in assessing its place in society? This question is the dilemma and source of divergence in the approaches taken by the GSD and GPD. It also is reflective of a changing relationship between the PLA and the people it claims to represent. On a larger scale, this change also represents a shift in personal loyalties of the average citizen in China. In the end, this change has the potential to be profound, leading observers to watch closely for the direction taken by the PLA. As the concept of a People's Army fades into the reality of the modern world, will the "P," which stands for "People," come to really mean "Party" or "Professional"? The path taken could be a harbinger of the larger political transition, and while it certainly needs to be watched, is arguably also worth attempting to influence.

## CLAUSEWITZ, WITH CHINESE CHARACTERISTICS

This chapter attempts to introduce two areas in which the search for a new personnel policy has highlighted a change in relationships to which the PLA must find a way to adjust. At the strategic level, the PLA is facing a significant change in its relations with both the Chinese people and with the government/party. This section seeks to identify and dissect the relations of the PLA as an institution with its main constituents — the PRC government, the Communist Party of China (CPC), and the Chinese people themselves. In Clausewitzean terms, the PLA sits comfortably in one corner of a double-summit "trinity," with a singular loyalty to the people and dual loyalties to the government and the party. As shown in Figure 1, the duality of governance in China allows for two seemingly congruous organs — the Party and the Government — shown separately in the Chinese version of Clausewitz's trinity model. The placement in the model is purposeful, to show that the Government is closer to and therefore more influential on the daily lives of the people, while it is the Party that has the greater influence on the PLA. Conversely, the influence of the government on the PLA and of the Party on the people is more indirect and usually through the actions of the other governing organ. The reality of this model is somewhat hidden by the convenience of having the national leadership hold concurrent positions in both organs, leading the casual observer to see a model that peaks at the Politburo, or more accurately its Standing Committee (PBSC) (See Figure 2.) In the model depicted below, the national leadership operates *in extremis* to both organs of power, with the ability to choose the route of influence based on the current situation and goals.

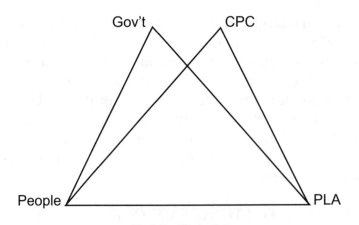

Public Relations

**Figure 1. Clausewitz in China.**

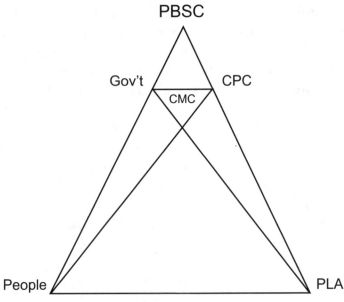

**Figure 2. The Reality.**

To the people, the PLA's current relationship is as an employer, a protector, and — at least among the youth — a growing source of pride. The growing professionalism of the PLA speaks to its relationship as an arm of the Chinese government, while the career aspirations of PLA officers are more closely linked to the PLA's relationship to the Communist Party. A recent article in the Chinese Academy of Military Science's monthly journal highlights the historical duality of PLA relationships with the government and with the people. The author, writing from the PLA's perspective, seems to imply the PLA's relationship with each has room to improve, and that the PLA's sacrifices over the years obligates the others to work harder to better support the PLA. By its absence of consideration, however, the author has demonstrated the relative closeness of the PLA to the Party.[4]

At a lower level, the incongruence in the PLA's parallel approach to personnel policy modernization has placed the General Staff and General Political Departments in competition with each other—with each major stakeholder stressing the area in which it is familiar. The GPD is trying to understand the mind of the Chinese youth in an attempt to develop benefit packages that will not only attract new blood, but that then keeps them in the military for the full term. The GSD is struggling to reform a backbone PME infrastructure that allows them on the one hand to prepare officers for each stage in their career, while on the other being itself the enticement needed to keep the officer on the rolls until retirement. In this search, the GSD actually is trying to sell its PME as part of a benefits package—and in so doing has become a competitor of GPD. This position on the part of the GSD seems to imply a pessimistic view of the Party and GPD's ability to attract quality recruits.

The GPD is responsible for ensuring Party loyalty through political education, promotions, assignments and overseeing the PLA's civil-military relations.[5] The latter is key to understanding the PLA's ability to give itself a makeover. The PLA sees itself as having three distinct roles in Chinese society. It is a key part of the PRC's national security apparatus, both at the tactical and operational level—following Mao's declaration that it be first and foremost a combat team[6]— and at the strategic level as an integral part of the Chinese policymaking apparatus. It is therefore an institution of the Chinese government that demands a great deal of respect from both foreign and domestic entities wishing to deal with Beijing. To Chinese society, the PLA also is used as an employer and as an educator, the latter role being especially important to the Communist Party, which continuously calls on the PLA to be the "model" in whatever political campaign is currently being undertaken.

## ROLES

### The Institution.

The PLA considers itself one of the founding members of the PRC, and as such, takes a great interest in its role in preserving the viability of the nation. At the same time, it seeks to preserve its traditionally deep connection with the people, and to maintain its stake in the central leadership of the nation and of the party. In many ways, these two relations are different and can be at odds with one another. The PLA is still considered a Party Army. Constitutionally, however, the PLA is linked to the National People's Congress (NPC) and State Council through the Central Military Commission (CMC), though this linkage is limited. The CMC is in Jiang Jingsong's seminal English-language work on the National People's Congress a "distinct state institution," though he later admits that only through its dual role in the CPC can the CMC exert direct power on the military. Additionally, Jiang points out that the CMC is unique as a state institution by not having any responsibility to the NPC. Only the Chairman of the CMC is constitutionally responsible to the NPC, though how he is accountable to the NPC is a question left unanswered by Jiang.[7] Despite not being accountable to the NPC, the PLA receives special consideration by the NPC for its own allotment of NPC Deputies[8] and authority (through the CMC) to introduce bills or reports to the NPC Standing Committee directly.[9] The result of this arrangement is a military that is significantly closer to the Party than the Government. The PLA has learned to use this double peak to its advantage, playing one off the other as the situation requires. Such advantage has created a semi-autonomous sub-group within the greater Chinese society that, while not able to fully govern itself, is able to ensure its equities are taken into account with all matters of state.

**The Employer.**

The PLA, even after this year's 200,000-man reduction, is still the largest army in the world, employing 2.3 million active duty and reserve troops and over 10 million militia.[10] The People's Armed Police, also a sector of China's armed forces, brings in another one million plus, for a total of about 14 million under arms. Much of this number consists of 2-year conscripts, with each new year offering another 13 million males who reach conscription age. In a country of 1.3 billion, with a birth ratio of 1.12 males to every female — created by the 25-year-old one-child policy — one would expect these numbers to be easy to maintain. It seems, however, that this is not the case, as the PLA recently announced a decision to hire civilians to fill many of the roles traditionally held by officers.[11]

Conscription is not really a problem for the PLA. First, it is legislated by law.[12] Second, the potential pool of conscripts is not going to dwindle anytime soon. The PLA is, for many young kids in the countryside, a chance to escape the drudgeries of near-subsistence farming. Rural families are normally supportive of filling a quota if they have a son, less so if they have a daughter. Urban families are more constrained by the one-child policy and are starting to lose the allure for letting their only child join the army.

In the case of one PLA women's sport team, the recruitment typically occurs at the age of 12-13, at which time the girls are sent to special schools to train and study, so that when they are old enough to join the PLA legally (18 years old), they have already mastered their sport. This allows the girls to complete their service obligation of 6 years (to pay for school) by the age of 24-25, leaving them still culturally eligible for marriage.[13] Girls selected for the various PLA Song and Dance Troupes are sent to special schools as early as age 5,[14] which can be witnessed on any televised variety stage show sponsored by or for the PLA.

The story is different for officer accessions. As an employer, the PLA is finding itself in stiff competition with the much higher paying high-tech industrial base, which is rapidly expanding in China. The need to modernize into a high-tech force capable of fighting on the 21st century battlefield means the PLA is seeking to hire officers from the very same pool of candidates from which Lenovo, Haier, AVIC, and a whole host of foreign companies are recruiting. At present, the PLA is able to meet their goals because of the vast economic disparity across China. The fact that the PLA operates its own college-level institutions allows them to recruit promising high school students from the villages of economically backward areas. The recruitment of these students is assisted by the presence of military departments at all levels of government. This is a recruiting support system that no other institution, with the obvious exception of the Communist Party itself, can claim.

This advantage is doomed to be lost as the economic growth expands domestically to include the harder to reach inner provinces. What today is an army led by coastal citizens and populated by Han Chinese from "upriver," will soon find itself led by those upriver-sourced officers and populated by an ever-decreasing pool of economic recruits (those who join for economic reasons) and an increasing percentage of non-Hans. This will require the PLA to change its relationship significantly with the people, to give it a greater attraction among the growing middle class and among the ethnic minorities. This is a task the PLA recognizes as essential, and it is working hard to figure out how to accomplish this transition. A recent briefing by the Xinjiang Military District Command noted that the PLA now has five ethnic Uighur and one Kazakh general officers. This comment was intended to show that the PLA values the contributions of China's ethnic minorities, but was followed by the realization that these numbers lagged far behind the civilian government numbers and will have to grow.[15]

**The Educator.**

I have already mentioned a key advantage of the PLA over other major employers in China — its own system of colleges and academies. This system is antiquated, however, and is no longer considered capable of preparing the number of junior officers, technicians, and conscripts needed to field an army under the high-tech conditions of the 21st century. In 2004, the ability to teach warfighting skills was enhanced by rotating former field commanders into teaching positions at the PLA's National Defense University.[16] In contrast, a recent CMC decision has approved a plan to hire contract civilians to handle nonwarfighting jobs in support of the military. While details of just which jobs fall under this category are unavailable,[17] it shows a recognition by the military leadership that it can no longer afford to recruit, educate, train, and retain qualified uniformed personnel for all of its required activities. It must, therefore, outsource certain jobs to civilian companies who can better recruit from the increasingly mobile population. This decision provides some insight into the limitations of the support provided to the PLA by the nation's civilian leadership. This concern is strong enough to have made it into the toast presented to the PLA and foreign military attachés at the annual PLA Birthday celebration.[18] In the same venue, the Minister of Defense also stressed the PLA's leadership role as a model for ideological education.

## PATH TO PARTY MEMBERSHIP

An unspoken role of the PLA is as a quick path to Party Membership. Current membership figures for the Communist Party are around 65 million, with the PLA-based membership always over one million. Approximately 95 percent of all Army officers are Party Members, while only 20 percent of enlisted have joined—or been allowed to join—the Party.[19] These numbers are more reflective of a limitation the Party places on its members than of desires by its members. The author has met dozens of PLA officers over the years who will admit their Party Membership was more a job benefit than a personal goal. It is a necessary criterion for advancement beyond the rank of major, and for key assignments and prestige. But it does not garner any more pay; better housing, or other direct perks for the member, making several junior officers question its immediate benefit to them.[20]

In early 2004, a new revision of the rules for Party recruitment was implemented which, according to the *PLA Daily*, drew on the experiences of recent recruiting drives. The article assures the reader that the original principles for membership have been retained, but the fact that they see a requirement to update the rules in order to "maintain progressiveness . . . of the CPC" demonstrates recognition of a changing recruiting base.[21] So how does the PLA recruit its future generation of officers? While details of the recruiting "plan" are not available to the author, much can be derived by asking the young officer candidates why they joined.

## WHY JOIN THE PLA?

In discussions with National Defense Students (Guo Fang Sheng), roughly equivalent to the U.S. ROTC program, the majority stated that someone in their family had been or was in the military, and that they had been a major influence in convincing the students to join the program. Of 10 students interviewed at Nanjing University, two had parents currently in the military, while another four had either grandparents or uncles that had been PLA. One of the remaining four claims to have always dreamed of being a soldier. All 10 agreed the money paid toward tuition helped their decision to join. These percentages generally are reflective of other conversations the author has had with military cadets around the country, indicating a major source of officer recruiting is by portraying the army as a family business. Other reasons offered in discussions with school cadre and students are discussed below.

### Quota.

Each military region is responsible for recruiting within its area of responsibility (AOR). They are given quotas from GSD, but the actual recruiting is decentralized from the Military Regions to the Districts, who work with the relative Provincial Military Headquarters.

### Incentives/enticement.

National Defense Students are provided tuition assistance. In return, they incur a service obligation following graduation.

### Sense of Duty (Nationalism).

Nationalism in China is reaching fervor. This extends well beyond those who actually join the military. Chatrooms and blogs are filled with pro-China and anti-everyone else rhetoric.[22]

Combined with a rising interest in anything military, nationalism is creating a generation more aware of China's role in the world and the importance of building a strong military to support this new role. When I asked a group of students who had accepted the National Defense scholarship how the recruiters had convinced them to decide so early to join the military, nationalism and patriotism was the number one response. One student went so far as to list the logic used to sign him, saying:

1. The recruiters persuaded us to work for the motherland.

2. They convinced us that the military provides a platform in which we could pursue our career goals (he was studying to be a computer engineer).

3. They assured us the PLA could provide a relatively good and stable quality of life.

In a follow-up with the school recruiter (a PLA Captain), he admitted that problems still exist with this technique—that it is not effective enough for the academically highest students. The students the author met with all had scores in the high 500s to low 600s on the national college entrance exams, good enough to gain entrance into Nanjing University, which is typically ranked around fifth in the nation.[23]

## CIVIL-MILITARY RELATIONS CHANGING OVER TIME?

Traditionally, the Chinese peasant feared the army. Seeing an approaching army on the horizon was never good news. Typically, the sons were conscripted on the spot, while the crops were destroyed in the fields or stolen from the cribs. This relationship, such as it was, existed into the Nationalist Army period and was a critical component for the success of Mao's Red Army in earning the respect of the peasants among which it hid during the fight against the Japanese and later against Chiang Kai-shek's ruling Kuomintang (KMT). The PLA's propaganda apparatus was very effective in promulgating the difference of the PLA by emphasizing the closeness to the people.[24] This theme has somewhat changed since the end of the honeymoon on June 4, 1989. The PLA has become more professional over its 78 years of history. Today, posters calling for the people's support to the nation's defense do not exalt the PLA as much as the more abstract responsibility to love and defend the country.[25] Even Minister of Defense General Cao Gangchuan openly admits the need to place a renewed emphasis on building reserve forces and strengthening the National Defense Mobilization Committees.[26]

By the time of Deng Xiaoping's Openness and Reform Period, the PLA had inculcated itself into society by consolidating gains made in the Cultural Revolution. Utilities that were "nationalized" were incorporated into local units, and Garrison Commanders became virtual warlords of their areas. This practice apparently was allowed to continue so long as it did not get out of hand. By the late 1980s, Deng's Four Modernizations placed economic development squarely ahead of defense issues, forcing an even greater commitment of a unit's time in nondefense-related activities. Units were forced to make up for themselves a budget share that could not maintain a decent quality of life, much less provide for ample training. In the mid 1990s, however, the need to modernize both the economy and the military signaled an end to the decentralization of quality-of-life budgeting. All division-level units and below were ordered to divest themselves of their businesses and get back into the training areas. This decision, in turn, required a steep increase in the central budget dedicated for defense issues, but since too much would have been destabilizing, much of the front-end research and development (R&D) and procurement lines were moved out of the MND and consolidated into the newly reorganized Committee on Science Technology and Industry for the National Defense (COSTIND). This divergence helps account for the consistent reduction of defense spending as a percentage of the overall state expenditures from 17.37 percent in 1979 to 7.6 percent in 2004.[27]

**Post-Tiananmen**.

The PLA's relationship with the people probably was never lower than in the years following the actions of late May and early June 1989, though the author doubts there was a corresponding drop in recruiting numbers. The PLA suffered not only from the general populace due to its obvious association with the hardliners in the

26

Politburo Standing Committee who had directed it to take action against the people, but also from within its own ranks. To date, this internal debate apparently is not entirely over, as witnessed by the astounding call of Dr. Jiang Yanyong in 2004 for the CPC to admit its errors that night 15 years earlier. Ironically, Dr. Jiang also played a major part in part of the PLA's major come-back roles — taking charge in stopping the severe acute respiratory syndrome (SARS) outbreak from reaching epidemic proportions. This action by the PLA, when other government agencies were denying a problem existed, helped convince skeptics that the major flood relief efforts of 1998 were not an anomaly; that the PLA was once again the People's Army.

Currently, the PLA enjoys a widespread and growing recognition for its service to the nation. The corruptive practices of the 1980s have been dealt with, and the distrust from June 1989 into the early 1990s have faded with time. For the PLA's part, it took stock of its floundering relationships and actively campaigned to restore its reputation. By the turn of the century, the PLA was well on its way, taking advantage, at the same time, of a new passion for youth video games.[28] The more popular games in the exploding number of on-line gaming centers required knowledge of military tactics and weapons, fuelling a surge in the interest of China's "Generation Y" for anything military related. Websites and chat rooms were created that specialized in everything from Military Doctrine and Strategy to the specific characteristics of the various types of military ammunition.[29] Fashions discovered camouflage and cargo pockets, and no wardrobe is complete without some sort of unit patch-bearing muslin or rip-stop nylon. The military motif of a popular new nightclub in Beijing is advertised as one of its drawing points.[30]

That being said, playing army and joining the army are two entirely different things, which the PLA is finding out to its chagrin. The kids who can afford to play these games, join the clubs, spend hours on the internet, and wear the latest fashions also can afford to avoid the lure of a free education in exchange for a 10-year commitment. They are the new urbanites from relatively wealthy double-income families who can send them to good high schools. They score relatively high on the entrance exams and therefore can get into the more prestigious universities. They are not, in the words of Howard Krawitz, "politically dependable members [of]

Chinese society most willing to accept the party's authority and most susceptible to manipulation through propaganda."[31] Those who do not get accepted to the top schools often are sent overseas to attend university, for to accept a lower-end degree in China is to limit the wage-earning potential of the family's only chance for a successful future — the only child.

## THE ONE-CHILD POLICY

The one-child policy has had a tremendous effect on PLA recruiting and retention, especially among the growing population of females. A retired colonel who coached one of the PLA's national sports teams explained that, with only one child, parents are reluctant to allow them to join the army. In the past, this was not the case, though the army typically would get the second or third child from families with a business background. For those already in the military, the effect of the one-child policy on their benefits has been positive. They are now allowed one trip home per year, vice the previous allowance of once every other year. According to a PLA squad leader, this change is attributable directly to complaints from parents under the one-child policy who were missing the traditional family observances with their only son or daughter deployed with the PLA.[32]

The problem is common to societies whose economies are coming of age and whose members see a rosy future. How do you get intelligent, computer-savvy youth who will be needed to operate or command the operators of an army's future high-tech equipment to give up the chance for a high-paying job and benefits to join the army? How do you get a college graduate — who traditionally could earn enough to hire a gardener if desired — to willingly waddle in the mud and rain, freeze at night, and bake during the day, just so he can lead a platoon of peasant conscripts in digging out irrigation ditches in *momo cun* [nowheresville] China? Worse yet, how do you get the increasingly computer savvy peasant conscripts to dig that ditch? This is essentially the question directed to the commandant of the U.S. Army Infantry Center during a senior level visit of PLA officers in 2004. The visitors were astounded that the students were college graduates, were volunteers [for the Infantry], and were conducting field training like privates. The head of the delegation invited the Commandant to visit China and explain to Chinese academy leaders how he motivates American lieutenants to "get down in the dirt and practice the drills."[33]

Efforts to find and fix this problem have been ongoing for several years. A study of the world's other large militaries focuses primarily on those with over a million in uniform; the United States, Russia, and India. This effort has demonstrated perhaps the clearest split in the PLA since Tiananmen. From the author's participation in many of the meetings to hear how the United States can help in professionalizing the PLA, several areas clearly are not agreed to by all within the PLA. While the author cannot always point to a specific reason, the body language, refusal to even sit in on sessions by certain staffs, and times when previous meetings were maligned by a member of another staff section, all point to an ongoing internal conflict on how best to modernize the personnel management system of the PLA — from recruitment through retirement and everything in between. To the author, it is clear that the GSD is not willing to trust that the GPD's recruiting strategy will succeed.

## NATIONALISM

Of interest is a simultaneous rise in nationalism within China. This rise corresponds with the same phenomenon throughout all of Northeast Asia, but combined with the increased interest in the military, one cannot help but speculate that at least some in the government and military condone the trend. Incentives also have risen to convince some to commit early to a military life, including tuition assistance, and a guaranteed technical assignment. In other words, the PLA will teach you a skill and pay you while you both learn and apprentice. And finally, when your commitment is over, the PLA's commitment is not, as it is tasked to "demobilize" all of its officers into appropriate jobs. In many cases, this means finding an appropriate-level management position in a state-owned enterprise, but more recently, private and international corporations are being successfully contacted.[34] A significant amount of the 2005 Defense Budget's announced growth of 12 percent over the previous year apparently is dedicated to the costs of demobilization.[35]

# CONCLUSION

The actions taken in response to the changing recruitment pool indicates a split for the PLA at two distinct levels. First, the PLA is not as close to the people as it once was and still claims to be. That the PLA is searching for new ways to recruit and retain is an indication not only that the PLA is no longer seen as a good opportunity (relative to others), but that even the rise of nationalism is not enough to aid recruitment without internal adjustments by the PLA. Second is within the PLA itself, particularly between the GSD and GPD, over how to make the needed adjustments. The GSD is working to fix its training base to not only better prepare its officers for a changing environment, but also as a recruiting incentive to attract the better candidate to enter their training pipeline. The GPD is working to adjust promotions, pay systems, and assignments issues.

Both reflect a desire to recruit and retain through retirement the best officers. Both agree that what defines "best" in an officer is changing with the Revolution in Military Affairs and other ongoing changes within the PLA, and both are faced with the same pressures that competition for resources creates.

The difference in how to overcome these pressures, however, is the potential source of inter-staff competition. If the GSD creates a system of Education and Training that is based on getting what it gets (in qualitative terms) and then polishing a diamond from the rough, it may find itself in competition with the GPD's ideas of increasing the quality of recruits at accession. This combination could also run counter to the GSD's own goals by not providing a challenging enough academic environment for the increasingly smart youth being recruited out of the high schools and universities. On the other hand, if they build a system of PME institutions based on the GPD's plan to entice higher quality recruits, they risk a mismatch in needed prerequisite knowledge should the GPD plan fail. If the two staffs get the combination right, however, each staff's adjustments will have a synergistic improvement over the current system. This is an area to watch.

Another area to watch is the demographics of PLA recruitment. In much the same way that the University of Michigan's Lee and Campbell Group[36] is researching family relationships in Liaoning, the issue of a shifting recruit pool needs to be studied in depth. Where are regional quotas being filled by actual volunteers, vice selections from an unwilling population? And from where are the officer candidates recruited? Are there demographic similarities that support analysis of a shifting recruitment pool? Can this pool be linked to economic conditions or academic opportunities? Is there a pattern geographically or in terms of economic opportunities that can be detected? And perhaps much can be deduced by asking the young members of China's growing high-tech industries why they did not consider a career in the military. The PLA also will need to answer all of these questions in the coming years to determine if their reforms are having the desired impact.

The changing environment of the PLA's civil-military relations is an important aspect of China's overall social modernization and emergence as a regional and global power. Recruitment issues provide a good window into the PLA's relations with the people, the government, and even the party. Further study is necessary to determine if the anecdotes presented in this chapter become trend lines. The outcome of this transition will determine whether the PLA retains its unique position in Chinese society as the unquestioning defender of the Communist Party, or as a professional military more motivated by affairs of the state. The future is fraught with contradictions. Ironically, the latter case is a possibility should the GPD succeed in its goal of attracting highly educated urban recruits, especially if they have the opportunity for overseas study before their PLA-sponsored political indoctrination. On the other hand, a more professional military — one that is closer to the government than to the party — also moves closer to the people, a long-time goal of the post-Tiananmen PLA.

Areas for further study include the use of nationalism as a recruiting tool, especially among the minorities, and whether the technologically growing PLA also is acquiring the requisite moral, ethical and legal bases for managing their personnel. As the PLA's weaponry becomes more lethal, the failure to instill a sense of professionalism in their future leadership will create a danger to itself and to the region. It is for this reason that foreign scholars and governments alike should pay particular attention to this sector of the PLA's transformation.

# ENDNOTES – CHAPTER 2

1. The PLA unit initially was not identified. See Liu Li, "PLA has Toymaker in its Sights," *China Daily*, May 25, 2005, p. B1. For the verdict and further details on the case, see Liu Li, "PLA Guard Defends its Honour in Court," *China Daily*, November 30, 2005, p. A3. No mention was made of who was to receive the compensation.

2. Mao Zedong, as quoted by Major General Yao Youzhi, Academy of Military Sciences, in "People's Liberation Army and Contemporary China," a presentation given to the Beijing Military Attaché Corps, Beijing, China, May 18, 2005.

3. The author witnessed this dynamic while escorting a senior Army officer through China in June 2005. Meetings with the General Staff and Political Departments would occur sequentially, even though the topic covered was identical. In each case, the senior representative from one would attempt to play up the focus of his department at the expense of the other.

4. See Xu Genchu, "Establishing Army-Government and Army-People Relations in a Harmonious Society," *China Military Science*, Vol. 81, No. 4, Beijing: Academy of Military Sciences (AMS), 4th quarter 2005, pp. 103-107. Xu is a Lieutenant General and Deputy Commandant of AMS.

5. James C. Mulvenon and Andrew N.D. Yang, eds., *The People's Liberation Army as Organization: Reference Volume v1.0*, Santa Monica, CA: RAND, CF-182-NSRD, 2002.

6. Yao.

7. Jiang Jingsong, *The National People's Congress of China*, Beijing, PRC: Foreign Languages Press, 2003, pp. 137-140.

8. *Ibid.*, p. 89.

9. *Ibid.*, p. 165.

10. The statistics in this section are compiled from China's 2004 *Defense White Paper*, the *Annual Report to Congress on the Military Power of the People's Republic of China*, and the *Central Intelligence Agency (CIA) World Fact Book* online at *www.cia.gov/cia/publications/factbook/geos/ch.html*. The Militia figures are for "primary" militia only, defined as under 35 years of age. The International Institute for Strategic Studies *Military Balance* separates the reserves from the active duty, adding another 800,000 reservists to the total. The active duty figure includes an unknown number of PLA uniformed civilians (*Wenzhi Ganbu*). I am indebted to Dennis Blasko for the above information on reserve and civilian numbers.

11. The high point of the PLA manpower roles was 1951, when they had 6.27 Million on active duty. The decision to undergo the latest cuts was made in September 2003. See "PLA on Course to Cut 200,000 Personnel," *China Daily*, July 15, 2005, p. 1.

12. The Military Service Act was promulgated during the 2d Session of the 6th NPC, May 1984. See Jiang, p. 176.

13. From author's conversation with the former coach of the Chinese Women's Sport Parachute Team, Beijing, July 14, 2005.

14. Interview with unnamed PLA dancers, Urumqi, August 31, 2005.

15. Briefing to Beijing–based Foreign Army Attachés, Urumqi, September 1, 2005. As June Teufel-Dreyer correctly pointed out during discussions of this chapter's draft, there is virtually no difference between Han, Manchu, Korean, and Zhuang ethnicities in Chinese society. Any discussion of ethnic makeup of the PLA can be skewed if too much credit is given to these latter groups as minorities.

16. Although the policy was decided upon in 2003, the officers did not begin teaching until the term beginning after the Spring Festival in 2004. See "Senior Commanders to Teach in University," *PLA Daily*, September 2, 2003.

17. One known example is the canteen service for the Ministry of National Defense Foreign Affairs Office. Judging from the comments that the canteen is now more expensive and less flexible in its hours, the PLA will probably go through the same growing pains of dealing with contractors as the U.S. military.

18. General Cao Gangchuan, "We must do still a better job in ensuring mutual support between the PLA and the government . . . so as to consolidate the solidarity between the military on the one hand and the government and the people on the other." Toast at the Reception Marking the 78th Anniversary of the Founding of the Chinese People's Liberation Army, Beijing, July 31, 2005.

19. Yao, offered during the question and answer section of his presentation.

20. This is a consistent theme the author has heard since the early 1990s.

21. Tang Wu and Sai Zongbao, "New Rules on Recruiting CPC Members in the Military Promulgated," *PLA Daily Online*, February 27, 2004. See *http://english. chinamil.com.cn/english/pladaily/2004/02/27/20040227001021_TodayHeadlines.html* In one reported case during the same timeframe, party membership played a role in four demobilized NCOs finding work as policemen in Shanghai. See Ming Jie and Fang Hongxiang, "Demobilized Soldiers Engaged as Civil Servants," *PLA Daily Online*, February 12, 2004. Both articles accessed on August 27, 2005. See *http://english.chinamil.com.cn/english/pladaily/2004/02/12/20040212001032_China MilitaryNews.html*

22. For a detailed discussion of the origins and dangers of this rise in nationalism, see Peter Hays Gries, "*China's New Nationalism: Pride, Politics and Diplomacy*," Berkeley, CA: University of California Press, 2004.

23. Interview with Nanjing University National Defense Student Unit, Nanjing, June 8, 2005.

24. Thousands of posters, sayings, writings, movies, and plays were authored with this theme. See, for example, Hu Ko, "*Steeled in Battle*," Peking, PRC: Foreign Languages Press, 1955. See also Xu, p. 105.

25. These posters are posted around major cities in China by the local National Defense Support Unit and the People's Civil Defense Corps.

26. Cao, Bayi Toast, July 31, 2005.

27. Major General Ge Tiede, Deputy Commander, Lanzhou Military Region, Briefing to the Beijing-based Army Attachés, Dunhuang, PRC, August 30, 2005. The *CIA Factbook* Online estimates the 2004 military expenditure as a percentage of gross domestic product (GDP) to be 4.3 percent.

28. The video games also are seen by the PLA as a means to simulate combat in the training of its junior officers and NCOs. The author has been approached on numerous occasions while in uniform by young PLA officers who want to know the differences between U.S. Army Rangers and Special Forces, so that they would know better how to play to their strengths in their unit gaming sessions. At the institutional level, every Army academy the author has visited has built a simulations center to help train their cadets.

29. For more on websites in China dedicated to studying the PLA, see James C. Mulvenon and Andrew N. D. Yang, eds., *A Poverty of Riches: New Challenges and Opportunities in PLA Research,* Santa Monica, CA: RAND: CF-189-NSRD, 2003.

30. Haidian District's The Nameless Highland ". . . caters to a younger crowd and with its military décor, blends in well with the nascent live music in Beijing." See "City Weekend," November 24-December 7, 2005, p. E16. Also available Online at *www.cityweekend.com.cn.*

31. Howard M. Krawitz, "Modernizing China's Military: A High-stakes Gamble?" Strategic Forum Paper No. 204, National Defense University Institute for National Strategic Studies, December 2003, p. 3. Elsewhere, he describes the PLA's traditional population base as "members of a politically acceptable class with historically low levels of education, readily susceptible to political indoctrination." See Krawitz, p. 4.

32. Interview with a Third Class NCO, Urumqi, September 1, 2005. This NCO had a wife and daughter in Qingdao, but used his annual leave to visit his parents. His own family joined him at that time, but was also able to visit him in Xinjiang during school breaks.

33. Author's notes while escorting a senior PLA officer, Ft. Benning, GA, September 2005.

34. Author's discussions with a senior PLA officer in Bejing, April 16, 2005.

35. *Ibid.* This rise in the demobilization share of the budget does not, however, include retirement pay, which is not included in the Defense Budget.

36. The University of Michigan's Lee-Campbell Resarch Group is a collection of Ph.D. candidates, researchers, consultants, and technical staff under the leadership of faculty members James Lee and Cameron Campbell. They conduct long-term research on family relationships, demographics, and population behavior in Asia and Europe. For more information on this group and their on-going projects, see their website at *http://michigan.ccast.ac.cn/leegroup/index.htm.*

# CHAPTER 3

## CHINA'S MILITARY BUILDUP:
## BEYOND TAIWAN?

### Ellis Joffe

Although specialists on the Chinese military are divided as to the ramifications of China's military modernization, there is widespread agreement that in the past few years the Chinese armed forces have made remarkable and unexpected progress. Even though the conventional wisdom only a few years ago was that the Chinese army was no match for the U.S. military and that the gap would widen, the surprising growth of Chinese military power clearly has become a serious consideration in U.S. Government assessments of China's behaviour in its vicinity and beyond.

This growth was considered substantial enough by 2005 to have elicited expressions of concern, if not alarm, by top U.S. Government and intelligence officials over China's military buildup. Its extent and implications were detailed in the report on China's Military Power submitted to Congress by the Department of Defense (DoD) in July 2005,[1] which asserts that, although China does not face a direct threat from another country, it continues to increase its military buildup.

What, then, have been the objectives of China's military buildup? How have they shaped its course and content? What does the buildup indicate about the possible use of China's military power, and where is it headed?

### The Objectives of China's Military Buildup.

Although China's military buildup began at the start of the 1980s, there is no doubt that the catalyst for its acceleration and for the acquisition of advanced capabilities from the late 1990s has been the emergence of the Taiwan issue in a form that is unacceptable to the Chinese — unacceptable because Taiwan leaders reject the "one China" principle and are intent on moving toward separation from

China. However, a broader look at the process shows that, despite the supreme significance of this issue, the process began in earnest before its emergence, and presumably will not end even if tensions over Taiwan will be reduced substantially, if not resolved.

The long-term objectives of China's military modernization are more far-reaching than the Taiwan issue: they are to provide the military underpinning for China's coveted rise to great power status, beginning with the attainment of regional preeminence backed by military power. However, China's leaders realized from the outset that the enormous gap between their capabilities and whatever capabilities were commensurate with their long-range objectives was unbridgeable for a long time due to the appalling backwardness of the People's Liberation Army (PLA) and the low level of China's economic and technological development. China's leaders therefore opted for slow and incremental military advances rather than for major but unrealistic attempts to modernize rapidly.

In the meantime, their long-term objectives remained dormant and did not influence the course of military modernization for more than a decade. During this decade, modernization proceeded unevenly: following a successful spurt in the early 1980s, it slowed down until the end of the period. However, this spurt was limited largely to the nontechnological aspects of the army's combat capabilities and was marked mainly by the upgrading of old weapons rather than the acquisition of new ones.

The turning point occurred in the early 1990s with the appearance of several factors conducive to military modernization. The fortuitous combination of these factors convinced Chinese leaders that their long-term objectives did not have to remain dormant any longer, and enabled them to begin the long process of building up military forces that are essential for a rising power. From then on, these objectives have provided the broad strategic impetus to the step up of China's military buildup.

The first factor was the Gulf War. The vast array of modern weapons that demolished the Iraqi army demonstrated dramatically to the Chinese military that, despite a decade of modernization, their armed forces were still generations behind those of the United States.[2] Not that this was news to them, but knowing something theoretically was one thing, seeing it on their screens, quite another. And what they saw convinced the Chinese that they had to initiate sweeping changes that would begin to pull the PLA out of its backwardness and prepare it for a different kind of war: "limited war under high technology conditions." These changes encompassed operational doctrines and training, but the most pressing need was for new weapons.

Meeting this need was beyond the capacity of China's military industries that were mired in technological backwardness and bureaucratic incompetence. Although the Chinese also began to initiate reforms in these industries, it was clear that this would be a long process, the success of which was not guaranteed. In the meantime, the Chinese surely would have been unable to move ahead if not for the second factor that worked in their favor: the collapse of the Soviet Union and the availability from 1992 of advanced weapons from Russia. In turning to Russia, the Chinese broke two of their own rules against large imports of new weapons: the desire not to become dependent on foreign suppliers and the difficulty of absorbing such weapons. The readiness of the Chinese to do this, and the timing of the arms deals, which began several years before the Taiwan crisis, was a clear indication of China's desire to push ahead with military modernization independent of specific contingencies.

The third factor was economic. Modern weapons are expensive. China is estimated to have spent about $20 billion on imports from Russia alone, with some $12 billion worth of weapons and equipment delivered by 2004. High cost was the chief reason for the small quantities of weapons that the Chinese had bought until then, and it was the strongest rationale of the Deng Xiaoping leadership for rejecting military demands for more money. Its argument was that economic development had to precede military advances. By the early 1990s, this argument began to weaken. After a brief recession due to leadership differences that followed the suppression of the Tiananmen demonstrations, the Chinese economy began to move ahead rapidly. Deng's 1992 "southern tour," during which he castigated conservative leaders who opposed China's transition to a market economy, broke the logjam and released the enormous energies that have powered China's subsequent economic surge. The new party leader, Jiang Zemin, could no longer hold off the financial demands of the generals by telling them that they had to wait for the expansion of the economy.

Jiang could not hold them off for political reasons as well. Lacking the political authority and military stature of his predecessors, Jiang could not rely on the automatic support of the military, as they could. Although his rise had been sanctioned by Deng, Jiang had to win over the generals by being receptive to their needs. Foremost among these was money. In addition, Jiang genuinely seemed to be committed to modernizing the armed forces not only for internal political reasons, but also because he was fully aware both of their backwardness and of their importance for advancing China's external aims.

Despite the push that this combination of factors gave to military modernization in the interest of far-off objectives, progress still was relatively slow until the second half of the 1990s precisely because the objectives were far off. What the endeavor lacked was a strategic focus that would give it a clearly defined target and a sense of urgency. This much-needed focus was provided by the emergence of the Taiwan issue.

**Taiwan and China's Military Buildup.**

The Taiwan issue first emerged in a new and, from China's standpoint, provocative form as a result of Taiwan President Lee Teng-hui's trip to the United States in 1995, which sparked a crisis that intensified for nearly a year and reached a climax during the spring of 1996 in the run-up to elections in Taiwan. In the end, the crisis brought two U.S. carrier groups into the vicinity of Taiwan, and forced a humiliating Chinese retreat from missile firing exercises. Tensions remained high in the following years and were further exacerbated by Lee Teng-hui's 1999 enunciation of the "two state" theory. As his successor, Chen Shui-bian, continued to push for the de facto separation of Taiwan from China, the Taiwan issue remained deadlocked.

After the 1995-96 crisis, the Chinese began to prepare for military action in order to prevent separation. There is no doubt that from the outset of their preparations the Chinese considered such action to be only a means of last resort, not only because of the uncertainty of the outcome, but also because of the enormous political and economic damage that it would wreak on a rising China. At the same time, there also is hardly any doubt that in the event of a formal declaration of independence by Taiwan, concern for national honor, international credibility, and internal politics would leave the Chinese little choice except to make good on their threat of war. Nonetheless, their preparations were designed first of all to deter war, not to wage it.

Not that militarily the Chinese had much choice. The gap between their capability and an effective warfighting one was evidently still too wide for the Chinese to contemplate seriously an invasion of the island, even without the possibility of American intervention. Their initial steps, therefore, were directed at increasing and improving their missiles opposite Taiwan on the apparent assumption that the threat of a missile strike would deter the Taiwanese from pushing for separation too far.[3]

Whether at this time the Chinese already were certain of an American counterattack if they struck Taiwan with missiles is not clear, but given the dispatch of carrier groups in 1996 and the U.S. policy of "strategic ambiguity" toward the Taiwan issue, they must have taken such a possibility into account. In any case, missiles alone could only be an interim solution for the Chinese. First, because there was always the possibility that a missile attack, while crippling Taiwan, might not bring about its capitulation, leaving Taiwan defiant and China without the option of following up its attack with an invasion. Such a failure would cause China an enormous loss of national face. It would damage severely China's relations with the United States, even if the United States refrained from military action. And it would harm China's economy, international posture, and regional relations. The Chinese surely could settle for nothing less than Taiwan's surrender.

Similar calculations presumably came into effect in case China tried to subjugate Taiwan by imposing a naval blockade. A blockade — the forms of which could range from marking shipping lanes for missile strikes, through physical stopping of ships, to submarine attacks — could presumably undermine Taiwan's economy, or even destroy it if imposed over a long period. However, this, too, was an unsure option due to uncertainty about its results, as well as doubts about China's ability to enforce it, the possibility of U.S. intervention, and international pressure.

This left only one certain option—a successful invasion and occupation of Taiwan. However, in the second half of the 1990s, China was woefully unprepared to undertake such an invasion. Its weapons were still far from adequate, new ones were still in the process of absorption, and indigenous acquisition programs begun several years previously—especially of naval vessels—was still in early stages. Chinese troops, moreover, apparently were still not ready for complex operations.

At the same time, by the end of the decade the possibility of U.S. intervention became, for the Chinese, a certainty. The "U.S.-led" North Atlantic Treaty Organization (NATO) bombardment of Yugoslavia during the Kosovo crisis was viewed by the Chinese as reflecting U.S. readiness to bully other nations in order to impose its will. Foremost among America's adversaries, as the Chinese saw it, was China, whose rise to great power status the United States was determined to block.

The conclusion was clear to the Chinese: their armed forces had to be capable of conquering Taiwan and coping with U.S. intervention. A concerted effort to acquire this capability therefore became the strategic focus of China's accelerated military buildup. Its specific aims have been to enable China's armed forces to overrun Taiwan rapidly, preferably before the United States intervenes; to deter the United States by raising the costs of intervention; to deny U.S. forces access to the theatre of operations, primarily by improving China's naval capabilities; and, if all else fails, to defeat the United States in combat around Taiwan.

China's weapons acquisition and troop preparations have both been oriented toward these aims. Foremost among the new or improved weapons have been ballistic and cruise missiles; submarines and surface vessels armed with advanced attack and defense systems; sea lift capabilities; advanced aircraft, new air refueling capabilities, and early warning and control aircraft; and new air defense systems. For the ground forces, the emphasis has been on improved armor and artillery, helicopters, amphibious capabilities, and joint service operations. Command, control, communications, and computer systems also were improved, as well as logistics and the use of information technology.[4]

Although it is clear that, as a result of these efforts, the Chinese have increased greatly the quality and quantity of weapons and equipment, it is not at all clear what progress they have made in the professionalism and proficiency that are required to make effective use of their new acquisitions. The extent of such progress is uncertain. Even though the Chinese have increased slightly the transparency of their armed forces, this has not contributed much to facilitating an assessment of their combat capability. Nonetheless, there can be little doubt that the proven quality of Chinese soldiers and basic-level leaders, combined with new weapons and extensive preparations, have increased greatly the reach and effectiveness of the PLA.

How does this increase relate to the objectives of their buildup? The Pentagon report is vague on this question. It states that "the cross-Strait balance of power is shifting toward Beijing" and notes that China's "attempt to hold at risk U.S. naval forces . . . approaching the Taiwan Strait" potentially poses "a credible threat to modern militaries operating in the region." At the same time, it notes major defects in interservice coordination, joint operations, and operational experience, and states that "China's ability to project conventional military beyond its periphery remains limited." Nevertheless, the bottom line seems to be that an acceleration of China's military modernization threatens stability in the Taiwan Straits and the safety of U.S. personnel.

Top U.S. naval experts take exception to this view of China's threat on the seas. According to one, all of China's outstanding strategic problems are maritime, so it is not surprising that it is building up its naval forces. China is not building a huge navy for sea control but is aiming at sea denial with submarines, land-based aircraft, and ballistic missiles. To achieve this, the Chinese need a highly sophisticated targeting network that would not be vulnerable to disruption. This is a very ambitious objective, and China still has a long way to go. The U.S. Navy will have time to take appropriate action to make sure that U.S. forces are not denied access to the region.[5]

Do the Chinese think they are on the way to achieving this objective with respect to Taiwan? Obviously this is not a subject that they tend to discuss openly, and their occasional public statements are marked by bravado and confidence. However, during an internal debate on China's security several years ago, some Chinese analysts candidly acknowledged U.S. military superiority over China in a Taiwan conflict.[6] Although China has made much progress since then, so has the United States, and it is doubtful whether Chinese strategists now consider the Chinese armed forces capable of stopping or defeating the United States in a Taiwan conflict.

One clue to their thinking in 2005 inadvertently may have been given by a Chinese general known for his outspoken views. Responding to a reporter's question about China's ability to defend itself against U.S. intervention (especially with aircraft carriers) in a Taiwan conflict, he replied that China is the weak side, and the balance of power between the United States and China is such that China has no capability to wage a conventional war against the United States. In the event of war, therefore, China will have to respond with nuclear weapons.[7] Although his preposterous conclusion was presumably a silly attempt at weakening American resolve over Taiwan, his admission of China's inferiority probably reflects a realistic appraisal that is widespread among the Chinese military.

In conclusion, China may be able to invade and occupy Taiwan, and it may be able to inflict damage on U.S. forces approaching the battle zone. But it clearly does not have the ability to deny access to these forces. Since this is one of China's main objectives in the event of war, it will continue to build up its forces to that end as long as the Taiwan issue remains unresolved. But is this the only objective driving China's military buildup?

**Beyond Taiwan?**

This is a difficult question because China's accelerated buildup has "dual-use" possibilities. Even if the strategic focus and fuel for the buildup has been provided by the Taiwan issue, the new weapons and improved combat skills acquired for that purpose already have given China a capability that it can use for limited purposes beyond Taiwan. For example, the penetration of an advanced Chinese submarine into Japanese waters in November 2004 may have been a response to rising tensions with Japan, especially due to Japan's strengthening of strategic ties with the United States. And in another show of force, five Chinese naval vessels, including a missile destroyer and two missile frigates, were spotted by the Japanese in September 2005 in the vicinity of a disputed undersea exploration site.

Since China's purpose is to disable U.S. forces as far from Taiwan as possible, it will continue to develop naval and air capabilities that increase its regional reach. As these capabilities develop, China might be inclined to use them against other countries in the region as backup for its diplomatic or economic interests.[8] As long as the Taiwan issue continues to generate tensions, the military buildup increasingly will provide China with "dual-use" capabilities. But what if both sides settle on a stable status quo and tensions are vastly reduced?

It is a safe bet that the military buildup will continue. Just as in the early 1990s China's leaders took initial steps toward developing the armed forces appropriate for a rising power unrelated to Taiwan, so they view the continuation of this development as an essential component of China's ascent. China's stunning surge in the world economy and the concurrent rise in its international stature can only have strengthened this view. The necessity of acquiring this component is underlined by the concern of China's leaders over the impact of U.S. power on the global situation, and on China's security as a result of its military presence and its alliances, most notably with Japan, in the region.[9] It also is underlined by their concern for protecting China's sea lines of communication, especially in view of its thirst for oil. If the Chinese continue on their current trajectory, it is possible that they will present a substantial military challenge to U.S. preeminance in the Western Pacific in a couple of decades.

However, without Taiwan as the driving force, the scope and pace of the future buildup might be reduced. The buildup also will be influenced by some of the same factors that started it in the first place. First, although the continued availability of Russian weapons is not ensured, given the unease of some Russian generals with the building up of China's armed forces, China's improving military industry presumably will be able to fill many of China's needs.

More important will be the future state of China's economy. If it continues to develop at similar levels, it will be difficult for the political leaders to make big cuts in the military budget on economic grounds. Even so, if rural and urban unrest increases due to widespread disaffection, a leadership worried about instability might try to reduce increases in military appropriations in order to divert funds to these sectors. However, if the economic fault lines identified by many observers cause a serious economic slowdown, if not worse, the military undoubtedly will be under pressure to reduce expenses.

How competing economic and military demands balance out will depend largely on civil-military relations. Almost a year after Hu Jintao replaced Jiang Zemin as head of the military establishment, his relations with the generals seem to be correct but cool. The military's expressions of support for Hu are sparse and lukewarm; his public presence on the military scene is low key, if not elusive; and Hu's statements of support for military modernization are perfunctory.

This coolness presumably reflects the increasing separation between a development-oriented civil leadership and an increasingly insular professional military. If Hu succeeds in consolidating his control over the generals—primarily by using his vast institutional powers of appointment and dismissal—he should have no difficulty in keeping down the military budget in the event of an economic slowdown. If not, his attempt to do this presumably will cause friction. Nonetheless, the dominant factor shaping civil-military relations will be the common objective of building up China's military power for the sake of objectives arising out of an assertive nationalism.

## ENDNOTES – CHAPTER 3

1. "The Military Power of the People's Republic of China 2005," *Annual Report to Congress*, Washington, DC: Office of the Secretary of Defense, July 2005.

2. David Shambaugh, *Modernizing China's Military: Progress, Problems, and Prospects*, Berkeley, CA: University of California Press, 2002, pp. 69-74.

3. On China's options, see Shambaugh, pp. 311-327.

4. Paul H. B. Godwin, "China as a Major Asian Power: The Implications of Its Military Modernization," unpublished paper, 2005.

5. *Inside the Navy*, July 25, 2005.

6. David M. Finkelstein, "Chinese Perceptions of the Cost of a Conflict," in Andrew Scobell, ed., *The Costs of Conflict: The Impact on China of a Future War*, Carlisle, PA: Strategic Studies Institute, U.S. Army War College, 2001, pp. 9-27.

7. *The New York Times*, July 15, 2005.

8. Godwin.

9. *Ibid.*

# PART II

# WAR AND DEFENSE MODERNIZATION

# CHAPTER 4

## ASSESSING AMERICA AT WAR: IMPLICATIONS FOR CHINA'S MILITARY MODERNIZATION AND NATIONAL SECURITY[1]

### Susan M. Puska

## INTRODUCTION

The September 11, 2001 (9/11), terrorist attacks on America provided a strategic opening for China and the United States to rebuild bilateral relations most recently damaged by the April 2001 EP-3 Incident.[2] President Jiang Zemin, watching the unfolding events on CNN, wasted little time in contacting President Bush to express his condolences personally.[3] The following month, President Bush attended the Asia Pacific Economic Cooperation (APEC) forum hosted by the Chinese in Shanghai. Meeting President Jiang for the first time, President Bush cautiously began to reenergize the bilateral relationship. With top-down authority on both sides, relations shifted to a more positive and constructive approach that have continued to grow over the last 5 years.

While overall bilateral ties moved in a more positive direction after 9/11, both the Chinese and American militaries remained mutually wary and cautious. The U.S. Secretary of Defense, for example, did not choose to make his first official visit to China until October 2005, 5 years after assuming office, and 4 years after President Bush told Jiang Zemin in October 2001 that military-to-military ties were an important part of bilateral relations and should be resumed.[4] While bilateral military activity has increased gradually since 9/11, with promises for more contacts in 2006, they remain uncertain and vulnerable to recurring cancellations and postponements.

During the October 2001 APEC meeting, President Jiang Zemin expressed strong opposition to terrorism. He said China supported military operations in Afghanistan, but it was not open-ended support, and he cautioned that Afghanistan's sovereignty and

49

independence must be ensured. The APEC meeting, nonetheless, led the way for U.S.-China counterterrorism intelligence cooperation[5] and China's general acquiescence to the U.S. military intervention in Afghanistan, as well as U.S. cooperation with Pakistan and Central Asia.

Whereas they were more cautiously supportive of operations in Afghanistan against the Taliban as a direct response to 9/11, China's collective leadership was far less supportive of U.S. intentions to resort to military action in Iraq to remove Saddam Hussein, although they were not capable of stopping military action. In general, Chinese leaders put a priority on maintaining stable relations with post-9/11 America, while asserting China's fundamental foreign policy principles (expressed in the Five Principles of Peaceful Coexistence), which provide a counterpoint to U.S. priorities and international action since 9/11. At the same time, China's leaders used the mechanisms of influence available to them, such as the Shanghai Cooperation Organization (SCO), to protect and promote China's national interests along China's periphery from India and Pakistan to Central Asia and Russia, often in reaction to U.S. initiatives to support Afghanistan operations and the wider war on terrorism.

In the summer of 2002, China's official press began to question U.S. motives toward Iraq, particularly after President Bush's West Point commencement address in which he implied that the United States would use preemptive and unilateral force. Chinese military interlocutors in Beijing at the time expressed surprise and frustration with the "Bush Doctrine." Some in the official press attributed this "shift" in U.S. policy to America's global dominance, which stimulated "hegemony."[6] The polemic analysis in civilian and military press in response to the Bush Doctrine sidestepped any recognition that any country, including China during its 1979 unilateral and preemptive intervention in Vietnam, reserves the unstated right to resort to preemptive military action against national threats. These criticisms of the United States were largely masked behind the "personal opinions" of the writers, which avoided damaging bilateral relations with more direct official criticisms.

Yuan Jing-dong, a Chinese national security academic writing for a Western audience succinctly characterized China's complicated policy toward U.S. military intervention in Iraq based on three often contradictory considerations: (1) China's principle of sovereignty and nonintervention, (2) U.S.-China relations in the post-9/11 era, and (3) "[China's] growing concern over the implications for [China's] security [within the context] of an expanding campaign against terrorism."[7] Chinese civilian leaders and the military worried what implications U.S. preemptive action could have on China's national security.[8] In particular, the Bush Doctrine raised old and new worries about whether or not the United States might be more inclined to intervene on Taiwan's behalf. After the 2002 State of the Union address, they also faced the prospect that the United States might attack North Korea militarily, which the President had identified as a member of an "axis of evil." Lacking sufficient power to persuade the superpower, and also prudently assessing that confrontation would only undermine China's long-term national interests, especially economic development, the Chinese leadership sought nonconfrontational and new indirect ways to promote Chinese interests. Consequently, China's post-9/11 national security strategy has given more weight to diplomatic cooperation with the United States. At the same time, China has sought to enhance its image as a positive force for peace and economic development within the Asia-Pacific and the rest of the world.

As a result of a more cooperative approach to the United States, the general arch of U.S. China bilateral relations since 2001 has been relatively positive and cooperative, dominated by diplomatic cooperation under the purview of the Ministry of Foreign Affairs (MFA). The People's Liberation Army (PLA), for the time being, is taking a back seat on national security policy. Since 2003, China's leadership has taken greater initiative, such as its work to ease tensions on the Korean Peninsula, which has enhanced bilateral ties and raised China's stature in the Asia-Pacific region and globally.[9]

While the possibility of an American intervention in East Asia was raised by the Bush Doctrine, which required delicate handling, China nonetheless also has benefited from the strategic breathing room of a distracted and aggressive United States. Particularly since 2003, the United States remains intensely focused on achieving complete "victory" in Iraq stabilization and reconstruction. Extensive work also remains unfinished in Afghanistan, while the vital mission to protect the U.S. homeland against terrorist attacks has been unfulfilled in key areas. Beyond security issues directly arising from America's global war on terrorism, domestic challenges, such as the need for extensive domestic recovery and reconstruction in the wake of the Katrina disaster, weigh heavily on the attention of leaders at all levels of government and national resources. Combined with the U.S. intent to reduce its military footprint in Asia, the U.S. focus on Iraq provides China with an opportunity to strengthen its own influence among Asia neighbors.

But beneath the relatively positive political atmospherics and targeted bilateral cooperation, the foundation of U.S.-China ties remains unstable and vulnerable to disruption during the next bilateral crisis. As China's confidence and military capabilities mature, and issues that are essential to China's national security, such as Taiwan reunification, remain unresolved, the U.S. preoccupation allows China to reshape its regional presence. Core issues of potential conflict in the bilateral relationship merely have been papered over. Resolution of explosive issues, such as Taiwan, remain perpetually deferred to an undetermined future, when it may be too late to negotiate peaceful solutions. Mutual threat perceptions, distrust, and even underlying hostility, particularly between the militaries and other influential national security actors in each country, are potential tinder to the overall relationship.

Despite cosmetic improvements since the EP-3 incident, the bilateral military relationship continues to be treated as an expendable facet of bilateral relations, or a stick with which to beat the other side to demonstrate distrust and suspicion. Within national security and military circles on both sides of the Pacific, it is now common to entertain the likelihood of conflict between China and the United States as an inevitable outcome.[10] Some even cavalierly welcome the prospects of a conflict between the United States and China, too easily disregarding the potential costs of such a confrontation or what end-state such a war could achieve. Consequently, the next bilateral crisis easily could wipe away this recent positive trend, but this time the consequences to regional stability could be quite high, and the ability for both sides to recover may prove elusive.

Within this complex and contradictory civil-military context, an examination of China's ongoing national security assessment and adjustments to a post-9/11 America may provide a more realistic, if

52

sober, view of mid to long-term U.S.-China relations than the current rosy picture provides. At a time of post-9/11 global military activism, U.S. operations in Iraq and Afghanistan, as well as its antiterror operations in other countries, have been of particular interest and concern to Chinese leaders, academics, diplomats, and military observers, causing China to adjust its national security posture in Central Asia, for example, as well as its bilateral relationship with Russia. Below the strategic level, the Chinese military plays a role in assessing operational capabilities that the Chinese military may have to fight or employ itself in the future as its military develops modern informational military capabilities. Having been at peace internationally since the 1979 intervention in Vietnam, the PLA lacks any modern military wartime experience. Consequently, observations of America at war in Afghanistan and Iraq provide proxy experience for study, evaluation, and adaptation to the PLA modernization.

This chapter examines overall analytical trends in both civilian and military writings on the U.S. war in Iraq and Afghanistan. Civilian writings tend to focus on the strategic level and overall foreign policy issues that address why the United States intervened and what it hopes to achieve internationally and in terms of U.S. national security. Military writings concentrate on how the military has carried out its operations and the tactics employed.

This is not intended to be an exhaustive study of all Chinese writings, but rather draws on a representative sample. Many of the Chinese writings (civilian and military) heavily exploit Western (especially American) writings on the war. The use of indirection, particularly when criticizing the United States, has been strong in Chinese open source writings, so the author has attempted to filter out original Chinese viewpoints, rather than regurgitate Western writings.

The chapter addresses the following strategic questions:

- Why, according to Chinese assessments, did the United States militarily intervene in Iraq and Afghanistan? What are its long-terms goals as they affect China? What are the implications of U.S. military intervention on China's national security?

- How has China's threat assessment of the United States been effected by the Iraq and Afghanistan military operations?

- What strategic opportunities do the U.S. interventions in Iraq and Afghanistan provide China and how are the Chinese exploiting these?

- Has China's assessment of America's comprehensive strength and influence, as well as its military, changed since 9/11?

At the operational and tactical level, the chapter will identify some of the PLA's main areas of interest and discuss how the PLA is using these American operations to promote its own interests and enhance their own military modernization.

## THE ROLE OF THE PLA IN NATIONAL SECURITY DECISIONMAKING

The PLA has enjoyed a monopoly over military matters in China during much of the reform era since 1979. Loose civilian oversight depended upon key personalities at the highest levels, such as Deng Xiaoping, who possessed Long March military credentials, or Jiang Zemin, who tried to follow the Deng model despite his lack of military experience. Jiang worked assiduously to buttress his position as Deng's heir by developing special links to military leaders through promotions and intense courting.

Over time the PLA's role and influence on central politics declined in relative terms. In national security affairs where Chinese policies toward the United States remain centrally and tightly controlled, the PLA plays a subordinate role, but it still can influence policy by advocating certain positions. It can also shape policy through its management of military information.

Military influence on national policy is not unique to China. The U.S. Department of Defense (DoD) influences national policy and public threat perceptions of China when it emphasizes particular aspects of Chinese military modernization in the Annual Report to Congress, or when Secretary of Defense Donald Rumsfeld pointedly questions Chinese intentions for acquiring certain military capabilities and declaring that China has no threats that justify these, for examples. Although the PLA has come to play a more "normal" role as one of many interest groups in Chinese politics, it still is unique in the amount of control and compartmentalization it exercises over military information. Further, the PLA's special relationship to the Chinese Communist Party (CCP) through its officer corps, all ostensibly embedded Party members, assures the PLA will have special influence over foreign policy, although not necessarily decisive. In bilateral military relations, as an example of PLA power and influence, the PLA is often a check on greater openness and transparency in the name of protecting "state secrets," which may inhibit the scope of bilateral relations. In the case of the EP-3, the PLA could not resolve the international crisis with the United States, which was the responsibility of the MFA to resolve, but they could inhibit resolution through withholding of information and general foot dragging, which complicated MFA negotiations. The PLA also withheld health information during the severe acute respiratory syndrome (SARS) crisis, for example, which could have helped the central authorities respond quicker to the crisis.

## ASSESSING AMERICA'S MILITARY OPERATIONS

The Chinese view of the U.S. military's performance in Afghanistan and Iraq can be found openly in the official press, as well as military and civilian works published throughout China. Relatively well-informed academics and journalists, who interviewed named and unnamed military experts, have written extensively on various aspects of the operations. Writers also have depended on Western sources, quoting Americans at length. While many reports are long quotes of Western media and government statements, others pick and choose criticisms, which allow the Chinese official press to criticize the United States, using Western reporting.

In general, strategic level discussions of the motives and objectives of U.S. military interventions in Afghanistan and Iraq are discussed freely in official civilian press reports such as *People's Daily* and *People's Liberation Daily* and academic journals. The talking points are highly disciplined and reinforce one another through repetition. Operational and tactical assessments can be found in technical and academic journals, both civilian and military. At the operational and tactical level, Chinese writings on Iraq and Afghanistan are more technical. These technically oriented assessments address capabilities. The articles tend to be straightforward discussions of U.S. capacity, sometimes without comment of the implications for PLA modernization. At other times, however, the articles imply that the PLA also must have these capabilities as part of its modernization effort, if it hopes to provide a viable deterrent capability or will have to fight the U.S. military in the near future. Countermeasures generally are not discussed directly in open sources publications; however, mistakes and miscalculations that the U.S. military makes often are discussed in some detail. The needs of the PLA in terms of doctrine and procedures, as well as capabilities, are also discussed in general terms, with emphasis on operational and tactical logistics, high-technology weapons and equipment, information technology, and psychological operations.

With some exceptions, Chinese civilian and military observers of the 21-day military campaign to topple Saddam Hussein viewed U.S. military operations with admiration for the speed of offensive operations and the employment of high–technology weapons and equipment. The U.S. arsenal of military precision-guided weapons, high-tech communications, and modern throughput logistics system performance were praised in broad, sometimes unrealistic, terms. Many compared these capabilities to the Gulf War, and noted how far the U.S. military capability had developed as a fully informational force. The brevity of the military campaign reinforced the view of some Chinese analysts that the PLA must acquire modern weapons and equipment faster to develop into an effective force. Although peer military capability with the United States is judged to be far beyond China's reach for the near to mid-term, some analysts argued that China must possess high-technology weaponry and equipment in the information age to deter a preemptive attack on China's territory. Some writers charged that the dramatic mismatch between the Iraqi military and U.S. forces demeaned the value of the U.S. defeat of Iraqi forces, but many Chinese observers remained focused on the methods and results of American high-technology and its information age military.

Professor Qiao Xinsheng of the Zhongshan University of Finance, Economy, Political Science, and Law writes an example of an academic, nontechnical piece focused on a polemic criticism of the

U.S. war in Iraq,[11] including an examination of several "paradoxes" of the war. He wrote, for example, that the Iraq War was a "real war," in which two powerful armies met in battle, but it also was an "unreal war," in which one side (Iraqi military) melted away into the general population, rather than defend its positions or take effective measures to delay the advancing U.S. Army, such as destroying bridges.[12]

Qiao said Iraq was a "just war," because a hated dictator was disposed. But it also was an "evil war" because it lacked clear international legal authority and caused untold suffering for the Iraqi people. The American goal to liberate the Iraqi people, who had suffered for years under a ruthless dictator and 12 years of sanctions, was undermined, Qiao wrote, by the number of civilian casualties and damage to property that the U.S. military operation caused.[13]

Qiao observed that although the war seemed to be prepared carefully, with advance assembly of forces and materiel over a period of months, it also was launched hastily without the support of Turkey and lacking an effective plan for reconstruction.[14] Writing prior to the insurgency in the summer 2003, Qia wrote that the American "victory" in battle did not justify the use of force. He thought that the Iraq War provided an "impressive display" of American military capability, but in the end, he wrote, "the most modern military in the world could only defeat an underdeveloped Iraqi military, which easily allowed the Americans to decapitate the Iraqi regime."[15]

Further, Qiao saw the Iraq War primarily as "America's war." Unlike the 1991 Gulf War, which had a powerful coalition force that shared a large portion of the costs of that war, the Iraq War had a small coalition of the willing and depended largely on a preponderance of American forces, equipment, weapons, and financing.[16]

Several commentaries concentrated on the miscalculations of the Iraq War, in particular. For example, a commentary by Lin Bo of the National Defense University Strategic Studies Research Institute on March 27, 2003, analyzed military miscalculations during the first week of the conflict. He wrote that the "myth of the U.S. military's "zero casualties" (more a reflections of Chinese beliefs that the United States would shrink away from escalating American casualties). He argued that the strategy of "no contact" (stand off) war, created in the 1990s, had been "demolished."[17] Lin assessed that the Iraq War could not be fought, let alone won, merely through air and precision guided attacks. He echoed what many retired American soldiers would also conclude—only land power can seize and hold terrain and ferret out a hidden enemy and command structure.

Lin also noted several "lessons" from the war, such as the "taboo" of making last minute changes during battle preparations because of the "failure" to get Turkey to support a northern route of advance, which left the 4th Infantry Division on board ships in the Mediterranean. According to Lin, this caused a shortfall in U.S. ground forces, which led to problems during the battle. Lin's focus on the plan and a failure to follow the script is more of a political comment on U.S.-Turkey relations than a military assessment, despite any debate of whether or not the United States has ever provided sufficient troops to accomplish the mission in Iraq. Lin's attention on the plan also reflects a difference between Chinese and American military planners. Chinese planning tends to be rigidly developed from the top to the bottom. Chinese military planners stress the importance of "the plan" and executing it to the letter. American military planners and commanders, on the other hand, value advance planning, but also flexibility to adjust to the conditions on the ground, according to the situation and relying on the initiative of officers and soldiers alike.

Among the other lessons Lin identified, he anticipated problems to come when he predicted: "Once the war gets into the stage of urban warfare and guerrilla fighting, it will be difficult for the United States to bring its advantages to bear, and its casualties [will mount]."[18] He assessed that the use of outdated U.S. equipment in some units would cause higher casualties, a situation that would hurt some units that lacked sufficient body armor and hardened vehicles. He also said problems in the military information system would lead to friendly fire and misdirected attacks.

In terms of the overall shortcomings of U.S. forces, Lin wrote that the war against Iraq exposed numerous problems in the U.S. military information systems. He noted that U.S. guided missiles hit a British [jet] fighter because the enemy identification systems analysis was "not stable." He also wrote that numerous incidents of "impeded signals" also occurred, which disrupted operations. In the battle of Umm Qasr, for example, Lin noted that the United States and Iraqis fought for 5 hours while ground support aircraft took a very long time arriving—a delay he attributed to communications system problems.

Lin found that the U.S. military global positioning system (GPS) experienced interference and, consequently, precision bombing effectiveness was not as good as "publicized." Additionally, he said, U.S. fighters violated Iranian airspace and launched a number of missiles into Iranian territory, which resulted in Iranian casualties.[19]

Although Lin's comments also were reflected in Western analysis before and after the war, they nonetheless present a view of Chinese modernization priorities and concerns, such as communications, precision bombing, close air support, use of GPS, etc. Such comments also could serve to caution a domestic audience in the PLA leadership that may be inclined to overemphasize acquisition of high-technology as the magic weapon for PLA modernization. Lin's assessment does not reflect any appreciation of the softer elements of military power, such as training, nor the battlefield complications that can degrade the effectiveness of weapons and equipment for any informational era army, including a modernized PLA.

Another report in *People's Liberation Daily* directly questioned whether U.S. forces intended to remain in Iraq "because, in the global strategy of the United States, having troops stationed in Iraq is of major strategic significance." The commentary of this author, Yu Zi, was consistent with other civilian commentaries that claimed the United States seeks control over Middle East oil, while others see the U.S. role to be a more expansive objective to unilaterally shape the world in America's favor. Yu noted that, although the United States said it would withdraw when "the conditions are right," the United States likely would only "withdraw its forces from Iraq in a limited, controlled, and gradual manner." He added that the United States would concurrently, "ask the UN [United Nations] to send international peacekeeping forces (which actually may quite possibly still be mainly U.S. forces) to Iraq in order to ensure the military presence and dominant position of the United States there."[20]

In an otherwise admiring report on the Internet version of *People's Daily* by Li Xuejiang,[21] the author wrote: "While the United States spent nearly a year to prepare for it, when it came the time to start it, it was launched in a hurry," which echoed other criticisms. Li added, "the advance [to Baghdad] was met with repeated resistance, eventually the quick end came with the surprisingly easy capture of the capital . . . the victory was won after all in only 3 weeks. A war myth was thus created," which he suspected had less to do with the ability of the American forces and more to do with the voluntary collapse of Iraqi forces.

"In all fairness," he continued, "the U.S. military is really good and laudable for many of its innovations in strategy and tactics." First, he said, the "decapitation operation" was effective. The U.S. military persistently and continuously used its absolute domination of the air and superiority in precision guidance technology to "track-bomb" Saddam and his senior officials. As a result, he said, the Iraqi army lost its commander-in-chief and became disorganized like a group of "headless flies."[22]

Second, the "theory of shock and awe" was applied successfully, Li wrote. "With its air superiority," it was like "entering an unpeopled land," as the United States carried out an unprecedented large-scale bombing of the Iraqi capital. The strategy overwhelmed Iraqi commanders, disintegrating and demoralizing the army, and the Iraqis soon realized that it was impossible to fight the superior U.S. military, he wrote. Consequently, the Iraqi military reached the "pessimistic conclusion" that to put up a desperate resistance would be "like hitting an egg against a rock," and they fled or surrendered.[23]

Third, Li judged, the most noteworthy point was the "bold strategy" of a "direct thrust into the heart." The thrust could be separated into a major and minor round. During the first round, the British army nibbled away at such cities like Umm Qasr and Basra, while the U.S. main force advanced unchecked toward Baghdad. This was a risky move, Li thought, since an insufficient number of American troops were stretched thinly in exposed positions along over 500 kilometers of supply lines.[24] For a time, this overextension was a "fatal flank," which compelled the Pentagon, Li wrote, to adjust its strategy and dispatch another 120,000 troops.[25]

The second round opened on April 5 and 7, when armored detachments were ordered into the center of Baghdad. "Fortunately," Li said, "the Iraqi command in the city had already been paralyzed."

Consequently, the Iraqi troops had no leaders. The Republican Guards collapsed into "stragglers and disbanded soldiers," with no possibility to organize any "meaningful resistance," he wrote.[26]

In Li's assessment, the Iraqi forces should have and could have done much more to counter the U.S. invasion, such as bomb out bridges, dig deep defensive ditches, construct high forts, and deploy large number of troops to protect the capital. Li assessed that the Iraqi army's defensive strategy was a complete "blunder," but the "foolishness and impropriety [of military commanders] obviously contributed" to Iraq's defeat. "The easy capture of Baghdad [by U.S. forces] was due half to good planning and half to luck. In the annals of war, it can be regarded only as an "exception and not a model," he wrote.[27]

Finally, Li wrote, the most significant characteristic of the war was the unprecedented disparity in the balance of strength of the U.S. and Iraqi forces, a comment echoed by other commentaries. The U.S. superpower, he said, defeated a "tired and weak country" that had not yet recovered from the Gulf War. The Iraq War, consequently, was a confrontation between a modern army equipped with 21st century high technology against a "motley force" that lacked discipline and was poorly equipped with the outdated arms and equipment from the 1970s and 1980s. As a result, the circumstances of the Iraq War "were really like . . . a falcon catching a rabbit, there is no chance of a miss," Li said.[28]

Wu Liming and Liao Lei, writers for the Hong Kong Xinhua service, marveled at the ability of the United States to send aircraft into the region without the need of forward operational bases. They also expressed admiration for air operations, including "the U.S. forces' B-2 bomber [which] took off from the continental United States, stopped and reorganized at a U.S. military base in the Indian Ocean after completing its mission, and then returned to the United States."[29] The ability of the United States to project air and naval power from the continental United States to Afghanistan and Iraq impressed Chinese observers, but, so far, has not tipped the balance to support investment in a comparable Chinese capability. It has stimulated the China military, however, to find lower cost ways to counter aircraft carrier power, while also looking to what will replace the carrier battle group in the future.

## Psychological Warfare Assessment.

Several Chinese writers extensively examined the role and effectiveness of U.S. psychological operations and informational warfare during the Iraq War.[30] They assessed that the United States had a considerable advantage over Iraqi forces because the United States has psychological assets within its force structure, including special psychological warfare units.[31] The use of over 400 news media from different countries that were embedded in U.S. forces, but strictly controlled, was praised as an effective means for U.S. troops to maintain the initiative in propaganda.[32]

The U.S. military also was praised for being able to carry out "electronic interference" over the Iraqi media, as well as use the exploitation of more traditional propaganda means, such as distributing flyers by air. "Secret agents" and "special troops" also were praised for their ability to "instigate rebellion" within Iraqi forces effectively, as they did during the Gulf War, which resulted in over 80,000 troops surrendering at that time, according to one Chinese report.[33]

U.S. forces were lauded by the Chinese for their stress on disinformation (rumor and information fed to news media) to carry out "soft killing" to shake popular support for the regime and military morale.[34] The American forces, practiced resourceful "deception to create confusion . . . giving the impression that there is indeed someone inside the Iraqi Government passing information" to U.S. forces, according to one report.[35]

Despite their achievements in psychological warfare in Iraq, however, the American forces were found to be less effective than they could have been. Sowing rumors and false information, as well as dropping pamphlets, for example, were not as effective in the Iraq War as in the earlier Gulf War because some were discredited quickly. Further, the U.S. military did not suppress Iraqi radio and television completely. As a result, pictures of civilians being bombed, U.S. prisoners of war, and downed U.S. aircraft were broadcast nationwide, boosting the morale of the Iraqi forces.[36]

Nonetheless, according to Chinese assessments, the U.S. operation in Iraq showed that "modern psychological warfare" plays an increasingly important role in information warfare. "The present war in Iraq could mark a turning point in the development of this warfare as it moved from the backstage to the front stage to play a more important role in battle," according to one article.[37] Through its reliance on its "military superiority" and the application of extensive "modern high technological means," the United States carried out "the most extensive and most complex psychological warfare against Iraq since the Vietnam War."[38]

The Chinese military, which has its own long history in the effective application of propaganda, seemed to learn or reinforce much from the American experience in the Iraq War during the 21-day campaign. Chinese analysts assessed that propaganda is even more important in the information age. Control over the media and other electronic means must be ensured early and thoroughly, as the U.S. military did, to ensure success. The campaign reinforced that the propaganda message also must be controlled, while consistency and repetition must be ensured. Bluff, intimidation, and deception remain effective means to force your adversary and the population to give up or give in to your wishes, but advanced technology is essential to maintaining command and control over the message.

If the psychological warfare lessons of the Iraq War discussed above prove influential on China's military modernization, we can expect the PLA to put greater emphasis on psychological operations as a wartime specialization, rather than simply a means to maintain good order and discipline, and ensure subordination of the military to the Party, which appears to be the primary mission of PLA propaganda departments at present. The commissar system likely would be changed by greater emphasis on wartime propaganda in the information age. If we see greater professionalism within the wartime propaganda function, we also should expect to see some reorganization of propaganda entities into special psychological warfare units, similar to U.S. PSYOPS units.

Psychological warfare and the lessons of the U.S. experience in the Iraq War likely would be most relevant to Chinese ongoing training and military modernization to execute a Taiwan contingency operation. During such an event, however unlikely, the Chinese military could be expected to attempt to avoid giving the appearance that they are attacking "Chinese people" in Taiwan. Hence, Operation IRAQI FREEDOM as a war of liberation may provide some useful lessons to the PLA for a possible Taiwan contingency. As a cautionary tale, however, Iraq also is useful in demonstrating the limits of propaganda and good works. The Iraqi insurgency demonstrates how a relatively small number of nonbelievers can wreak havoc, disrupting even the most modern and powerful army in the world as it tries to stabilize an area after a military victory. Although the PLA likely would dismiss the lesson of the liberation of Iraq as it applies to Taiwan because the latter is filled with welcoming compatriots, it should not be lost on the Chinese that even if a small number of people on Taiwan were to resist the PLA after a successful liberation (with or without the use of force), it could be very costly and disruptive to post conflict stabilization, reconstruction, and political consolidation.

**Insurgency Assessment.**

The role and effectiveness of the post-conflict insurgency in Iraq has received less attention that one would expect from Chinese civilian and military writers, given China's history in guerrilla warfare and the enshrinement of people's war within its national strategy. Several writers prematurely anticipated the United States becoming ensnared in an insurgency. Wu Liming and Liao Lei, for example, wrote: "The entire nation in arms is another 'assassin's mace' (*sha shou jian*) of Iraq's." The authors cited reports that Iraq had sent out "tens of thousands of assault rifles to more than 2,000 clans" in advance of the war to prepare for guerrilla war and ambushes. They wrote that Iraq's large tribes resolutely would resist the U.S. force's invasion."[39] Although these and other writers were wrong about guerrilla tactics being used against the U.S. forces as they advanced through Iraq, they eventually were proven right after the end of major combat. Nonetheless, authors have not dwelled on the effectiveness of guerrilla warfare to disrupt and terrorize, and potentially influence political decisions on the ground. This oversight perhaps reflects a view among PLA analysts that information war and military modernization is more important for the PLA's future than its historic reliance on guerrilla warfare. China's military may still straddle the old and new, but the PLA clearly wants to move in a direction that takes it into a modern future, rather than its historic past.

## Logistics Assessment.

U.S. military logistics operations during the Iraq War were of particular interest to civilian and military observers. Assessments of U.S. military logistics in the Iraq War focused on modern logistics trends, such as large-scale operations, integration, accuracy, and specialization. They reflect a trend toward greater professionalism within integrated joint logistics planning and advance preparation, and a greater recognition of the importance logistics plays in modern warfare.

Since 2003, numerous articles[40] have been published in Chinese technical journals that analyze U.S. logistical support during the war. Several articles proposed that China expend greater energy researching modern military logistics operations that can be applied to the PLA's modernization. Although some analysts criticized the American military's long logistics lines, which were vulnerable to disruption in Iraq, they also recognized the lesson for China. Even in peacetime, China's military operations are spread widely over a complicated topography slightly larger than the United States. Already stretched by domestic operations, in a contingency, the PLA also would face the challenges of protecting stretched lines of communications, which would be exacerbated if and when China's military force is projected outside continental China.

## High-technology Assessment.

Among the topics of greatest interest regarding American high-technology application during the Iraq War and Afghanistan, Chinese observers have shown special interest in America's Integrated Joint Battlefield Intelligence, Surveillance, and Reconnaissance System (in Afghanistan),[41] use of the GPS,[42] and Unmanned Aerial Vehicles (UAVs),[43] among others.

China's military modernization can be expected to continue, even accelerate, opportunities to exploit off-the-shelf purchases and other military acquisitions of advanced military weapons and equipment.

**Afghanistan Assessment.**

With the exception of the article mentioned on battlefield intelligence, much of the writing on Afghanistan military operations has concentrated on the political-military consequences of a long-term U.S. military presence in Central Asia, how this intrusion promotes U.S. long-term national interests in control over Eurasia's heartland, and how this challenges, not only China, but also Russia.

One author's criticism of the lingering presence of U.S. military in Afghanistan is typical: "After the end of the Afghanistan War, the United States said it would be even harder to predict whether or not it could capture the leaders of the al-Qa'ida organization. Consequently, it has kept on sending military personnel to Central Asia, which has made the anti-terrorism war more complicated. Think about it this way: (According to the U.S. media) the United States clearly understands how . . . the leaders of the al-Qa'ida organization enter and exit the country. Therefore, people have reason to doubt whether or not the United States will lose the reason for the continued establishment of its military bases in Central Asia, as well as for the maintenance of its military forward deployment there."[44]

Although the military, in particular, was very suspicious of the long-term intentions of the U.S. presence in Central Asia to support Afghanistan operations after 9/11, they were not in a position to resist U.S. intervention and, in fact, were not inclined to protect the Taliban, in any case. Still, they resisted participation in the U.S.-led coalition. Some military representatives at the time said the PLA was considering sending PLA engineers, whom they had also provided to Cambodia, but they expressed concern over their ability to provide their own force protection and logistics support. China's primary response to the U.S. intervention in Afghanistan and its ongoing presence in Central Asia has been at the diplomatic level, where they have over time been able to reenergize the Shanghai Cooperation Organization (SCO) and promote Chinese perspectives within the collective body. Economic development and the quest for greater energy security also have guided China's post-9/11 priorities in Central Asia, which over time has proven more effective than a confrontation with the United States over its military presence in Central Asia.

On the military and security side, military diplomacy and multilateral exercises have supported diplomatic moves. Additionally, the attack on Islamic extremism on China's testy western border has helped the PLA and internal security forces step up operations to suppress Islamic extremism in Xinjiang Province, all in the name of fighting the global war on terrorism,[45] Han migration, infrastructure improvements, and economic development also were accelerated after 9/11 as a means to stabilize the area.

While the United States remains engaged in Afghanistan but primarily concentrating on operations in Iraq, China may find increasing opportunities to fill a void and promote its own interests in Afghanistan, but diplomatic and economic development, rather than military involvement, remain at the top of their strategy.

**Some Lessons for Chinese Military Modernization.**

The Iraq War, and to a lesser extent the Afghanistan War, have reinforced the necessity of advanced technology, professionalism, and specialization to develop a modern military, which is the ultimate guarantor of national security. Chinese observations of America at war, combined with a perceived propensity for post-9/11 America to use preemptive force unilaterally throughout the world, added urgency to China's military modernization, but the primary response has been at the diplomatic level, which the Chinese have reinforced by continuing to further economic relations in Central Asia, for example. In China's foreign policy since 9/11, the role of the military has been to support foreign policy through its military diplomacy and bilateral engagement, while striving to achieve concrete results in military modernization to provide a more credible military deterrent and to be prepared to fight, if diplomacy fails.

At an operational and tactical level, we can expect the Chinese military to adapt relevant methods and equipment from the Iraq War that the PLA deems applicable to its border and sovereignty challenges, particularly Taiwan, and that fit within the overall defense budget. For example, as recognized by many Chinese observers of the Iraq War, an essential component of Chinese military modernization is advanced communications, and the ability to command space (satellites). In military logistics, emulation and integration of best practices in asset visibility, accountability, precision resupply, surge capacity—all of which are based on advanced communications—also is essential to the modernization of the PLA.

We can expect, consequently, that the Chinese military will continue to emphasize the importance of communications, as well as advanced weaponry. China must buy more modern military assets to enhance its capability, where feasible, while continuing to tilt priority toward economic strength as the base of China's growing power.

Although it has not been discussed widely in the open literature, the Chinese should be both reassured and cautioned that Mao's People's War is still relevant to modern warfare. The Chinese military can rest assured that China retains a significant insurgency advantage if deterrence fails and China is invaded by a ground force, even of a superior military, such as the United States.

But they also may be sobered by how effectively an asymmetrical force can harass, tie down, and otherwise hamstring a superior force when they plan for possible operations against Taiwan, if China decided to resort to force to resolve this sovereignty issue. The Iraq insurgency has retaught the old lesson that a superior military force that is willing to endure casualties, may not be defeated militarily by an inferior force, but its strategic objectives may, nonetheless, be thwarted. At best, they may be achieved only after a much higher cost in troops, equipment, and treasure. Ultimately, the costs of prolonged low intensity war may undermine the strategic objectives of any "liberation," and in the case of a Taiwan liberation, there could be an even more effective native resistance than the United States has faced in Iraq.

While China, so far, faces small-scale and sporadic "insurgency" problems in Muslim areas in Xinjiang and elsewhere, this problem presently remains operationally manageable. China's assessment that it can better address these domestic insurgent (terrorist) problems through economic development, integration, Han migration, local control (through the good auspices of the police, PLA, and Party), as well as through cooperation with Muslim countries, may prove correct. China's ongoing collaboration with the U.S. global war on terror (GWOT) gives China's strategy to suppress Islamic extremism more legitimacy and urgency. Intelligence cooperation with the United States may even enhance the effectiveness of these efforts and may help China prevent this problem from growing over time.

**Lessons for China's National Security Calculus.**

> This model of occupying a country first and then forming a constitutional government . . . has become the United States' fixed way of thinking in the second half of the 20th century. From Haiti and Panama in Central America to Europe's Yugoslavia and Asia's Afghanistan, the United States was constantly reliving its fond dream [of] World War II.[46]

> The purpose of the United States in sending troops to Iraq is to realize U.S.-style democracy in Iraq. We believe that in the future, a U.S. democratic framework will emerge in Iraq. However, can the United States bring about the spirit of democracy? Absolutely not. Democracy realized with missiles is no democracy. It is the mockery of democracy.[47]

> In truth, the image of the United States was ruined entirely by the United States alone. As long as the United States does not change its biases against certain ethnic groups, certain countries and certain religions, there are more troubles to come for the power politics of the United States.[48]

> Solutions of major international issues need collective wisdom, enhanced international cooperation and the rule of the UN and the Security Council.[49]

China's international policy decisions since 2001, and especially since the war in Iraq in 2003, reflect an estimation that:

- A decline of U.S. power is not imminent, but its post-Cold War preeminence has eroded, and its domestic economy may be weakened by foreign debt-dependency and war expenditures. The United States is a wounded superpower, which makes it more dangerous and unpredictable, but one that is still critical to the stability of the world economy and China's economic development.

- Engagement, rather than confrontation, with the United States suits China's national interests for the foreseeable future. China must hedge its bets, however, by cooperating without getting too close, avoiding confrontation without sacrificing Chinese national interests.

- The present unpopularity of the United States throughout the world, especially in the oil rich Muslim areas, makes it prudent for China to balance its international policy with emphasis on cooperation that is dominated by diplomacy and economic development, while setting itself apart from the United States in basic principles.

- The relative decline of American prestige, particularly in the developing world, provides China with an opening to promote its own national interests throughout much of Asia and the world. Building on its long-term relationship with the developing world, China is well-positioned to enhance its position with the developing world through its emphasis on diplomacy, cooperation, multilateral fora, and economic development.

- Regardless of the risks of confrontation with the United States, China cannot allow the United States to intimidate it. It must rely on diplomacy as the first line of defense against the United States, but its national security depends upon its own military strength and its ability to use force, if necessary, even against the United States, in matters of national sovereignty, particularly Taiwan reunification.

- Anti-China forces within and outside the U.S. administration require China to remain on guard against U.S. movements that could damage China's national interests. China may be able to build a wider and deeper U.S. domestic coalition over time, but this always will be vulnerable to negative domestic trends. Anti-Chinese sentiment may even grow more hostile over time.

- The U.S. deemphasis, even dismissal, of multi-lateral mechanisms provides an opportunity for China to play a more active role internationally. Benefit may be accrued if China promotes regional and international initiatives and is seen to provide responsible leadership, all of which China has avoided in the past. China must continue to build wider coalitions to counter U.S. power and dominance. U.S. containment or constrainment of China can best be addressed through multilateral relations—a Chinese version of the coalition of the willing to counter American power.

- Resources: U.S. intervention into Central Asia and the Middle East has the long-term objective of ensuring U.S. (and its allies) access to oil. Given China's increasing dependence on foreign oil, China must proactively ensure access to multiple and dependable sources of oil and other key resources (water) in order to promote its own national security and foundation for future economic development.

- The U.S. mission to promote democracy is a cover for U.S. hegemony. It is an indirect threat to China, as the United States seeks regime change in China to eliminate the Chinese Communist Party's monopoly on power.

- Regardless of American intentions in the global war against terrorism, it provides an opportunity for China to address its domestic terrorism threat, while cooperating with the United States and the rest of the world. Within the context of antiterrorism, cooperation with Central Asia and Russia through the mechanism of the SCO can be strengthened. This strategy provides greater security to China's vulnerable west, enhances needed access to resources and trade, and helps check the limits of U.S. influence in Central Asia.

## CONCLUSIONS

Chinese leaders pragmatically engage the United States and the world to promote stability that provides a supportive environment for China's revival.[50] This national strategy reassures most regional and global powers that the outcome will be a "peaceful rise"[51] for China. Meanwhile, the Chinese military plays a supporting role to diplomatic and economic efforts, but continues on its long road to building a modern military that will be commensurate with China's great power status and provide more leverage with regional and global powers, such as Japan and the United States. Buying time for national development by avoiding confrontation with the United States tugs China's national policy toward cooperation with the United States for the near term. But the bilateral relationship still lacks solid stability and durability. Chinese leaders cannot hope for the best in this mercurial relationship with the United States. They must provide a credible military capability that can ensure China's national security. Looking into the future, a credible military capability also will be essential to China's global role, as it becomes increasingly dependent on imported resources, especially oil.

The lessons of America's wars in Iraq and Afghanistan, which displayed the latest and greatest of modern military might, lay bare China's historic vulnerability to powers with overwhelmingly superior military strength. Even though Chinese leaders have little choice today but to pursue cooperation and dialogue because the United States represents China's biggest potential threat, China also recognizes that the United States is its best hope for continued economic development and a chance to maintain peace and stability on China's doorstep through America's close ties to Japan and Taiwan, and America's legacy role on the Korea Peninsula. For both sides, there is still time to mature the relationship into a more lasting and stable arrangement to promote peace and stability, but the window is closing as China's comprehensive strength continues to grow.

China's need to sustain its national security strategy based on independence and greater multilateralism has been accentuated by the Afghanistan and Iraq Wars, and America's stark policy of preemptive and unilateral use of force. Following an initial setback, when the Chinese watched helplessly as Central Asia powers and Russia scurried to accommodate the United States with bilateral agreements that seemed to undercut the relevancy of the SCO, Russia and the Central Asia powers have since become even more receptive to promoting collective efforts with China under the SCO. The reinvigoration of the SCO sees China playing a key role, if not the leader, then certainly the coach, to keep the momentum going to deepen and mature the regional organization, an accomplishment that may radiate out, affecting China's role in the UN and ASEAN/

ARF, where China has become more proactive since 9/11. As China demonstrates its willingness to take a more visible role in hosting events and supporting initiatives, its "Five Principles of Peaceful Coexistence" mantra becomes more attractive, regionally and globally.

China's longstanding cooperation with the developing world, which arose out of mutual economic conditions and political necessity, has over time become a useful counterweight to the United States. China can develop these ties further as it increases its economic strength, leveraging its goods, services, and expertise for assured access to natural resources, and in return for access to China's long dreamed of market. This base of developing world support already has helped China fend off U.S.-sponsored human rights resolutions,[52] but these relations also may assist China in diversifying its oil supply.[53]

In a broader sense, the U.S. lack of interest, even hostility, toward collective bodies, such as the UN and international agreements, provides China an opportunity on the international stage to increase its multilateral cooperation and promote its influence through its ability to work with countries, large and small, on economic development and other concerns of interest throughout the world.[54]

For China's military modernization, the Iraq War, in particular, provides impetus and benchmarks for the next stage of its modernization. China can be expected to continue to combine domestic research and adaptation of advanced military methods and technologies. Its military contacts, which have deepened and widened in recent years, will continue to augment international relations, while providing the PLA exposure to diverse and specialized military capability throughout the world, where it can sample the variety of approaches to modernization among large and small powers with limited defense budgets. China's military will continue to adapt what is most relevant. But China's central military relationship likely will remain Russia for the foreseeable future. This military cooperation, which began largely as a marriage of convenience after the end of the Cold War, continues to mature in ways beyond arms sales of second-string Russian products and tentative cooperation. If the Peace Mission 2005 Exercise in August is any indication, China-Russia military ties in the wake of the Iraq War will continue to address a growing and mutual suspicion of the use and objectives of U.S. military power in the post-9/11 era.

Through a combination of imaginative and diversified foreign military cooperation, Chinese military modernization has in recent years moved beyond the "one step forward, two steps back" pace. This effort is now spiced up by a dogged persistence and eagerness that is especially reflected in a new generation of better educated military officers and buoyed by China's growing national wealth, confidence, and national expectations of revived greatness. Further, China's threat perception of Taiwan independence and U.S. intervention provide spark and urgency to China's military modernization. After feeling like watching paint dry for many years of observing China's military modernization, observers now express alarm and shock, as well as suspicion over China's motives for seeking a modern military capability. But the ease with which the U.S. military superpower defeated the Iraqi military and decapitated the regime in only 21 days should leave no doubt of the lesson for China. If China is to regain its great power status fully, it must further develop its military in all components of power — land, sea, and air. China cannot afford and likely does not want to achieve parity with the U.S. military because the cost to China's overall national development would be destabilizing. But China recognizes it must possess a credible military deterrent to protect China's national interests in the post-9/11, post-Iraq War era.

## ENDNOTES – CHAPTER 4

1. This chapter draws on material used during a panel discussion which the author participated in at the Wilson Center on January 13, 2005.

2. For an assessment of the EP-3 incident, see Shirley Kan, *et al.*, "China-U.S. Aircraft Collision Incident of April 2001: Assessments and Policy Implications," Congressional Research Service, Updated October 10, 2001; and John Keefe, "Anatomy of the EP-3 Incident, April 2001," The CNA Corporation, January 2002. For an account of the experiences of the EP-3 crew, see Lieutenant Shane Osborn with Malcolm McConnell, *Born to Fly: the Untold Story of the Downed American Reconnaissance Plane*, New York: Random House, 1991. U.S.-China relations under the new administration actually began on a rocky basis before April 2001. See "Summary of Statements and Events," 2001-05, attachment to this chapter. Also

see Michael Mann, *Rise of the Vulcans: The History of Bush's War Cabinet*, New York: Viking Books, 2004, pp. 281-286, for a discussion of the new administration's approach to relations with China and the handling of the EP3 incident. Mann, p. 281, writes that Condolezza Rice told a visitor that the Bush administration expected "some conflicts" with China and planned to get these out of the way early during 2001, so that they would not effect the 2002 16th Party Congress.

3. Within embassy circles in Beijing at the time, it was common knowledge that Jiang Zemin observed that he had called President Bush on his own initiative and without prior approval once he watched the events live on CNN.

4. In discussion with President Jiang in October 2001, President Bush said he thought military-to-military contacts were useful and should be resumed. DoD demurred for several months, while it reviewed all possible options for military-to-military contacts, and did not move toward a resumption of contacts with the Chinese military until well into 2002. The term military "engagement," which had been used since the late 1990s to characterize military contacts between the United States and China, was purged from the DOD vocabulary as sounding too weak or soft on China. Ironically, the Chinese had objected to the term "engagement" when the U.S. side first used it during the late 1990s, because the work in Chinese implies a military action and carried the implication of U.S. bullying and power politics. Nonetheless, the Chinese military came to accept "engagement" as appropriate and used it well into the Bush administration, while DoD used more general terms, such as "military contacts."

5. The anti-terrorism intelligence sharing between China and the U.S. intelligence frequently has been characterized as a one-way street — the United States gives and China takes. From China's perspective, however, this commitment, which followed the precedence of Cold War era intelligence cooperation, was, nonetheless, a significant step, particularly after the EP-3 incident. Although the PLA Second Department was involved on the Chinese side, this effort did not directly involve the U.S. military, which likely suited both sides.

6. Weng Ming, "Bushism is Emerging," July 10, 2002, *Xinhuanet.com*.

7. Jing-dong Yuan, "Making Sense of China's Iraq policy, Pacific Forum #40, October 3, 2002, available online at *www.csis.org*.

8. *Ibid*.

9. On September 5, 2003, former Secretary of State Colin Powell went so far as to say they were the "best" they had been since 1972, when President Richard Nixon visited China, reestablishing bilateral relations between the two countries. *Christian Science Monitor* Press Briefing Luncheon, St. Regis Hotel, Washington, DC, December 21, 2004, available online at *hongkong.usconsolate.gov/uscn/state/2004/1220101.htm*.

10. For a recent sampling of discussions of war with China, see Robert D. Kaplan, "How We Would Fight China," *Atlantic Monthly*, June 2005.

11. Professor Qiao Xinsheng, "Six Paradoxes of the Iraq War," *Renmin Ribao Wang*, April 4, 2003. Since scholars, technical experts, and layman alike can now

write for money in China, it has become increasingly difficult to determine how influential any writings are. The official press and publishing houses are still important in a political system where one party has a monopoly over power, however, the prevalence of articles throughout China also suggests that there was not only wide interest in the Iraq War, there also is a growing interest in military matters, in general, as well as a growing body of competent military observers throughout the country in both military and civilian positions. This growing interest and expertise may be the outcome of two additional factors beyond making extra money. First, the PLA has taken steps to inform the public about military matters. Of particular interest, are military books written for children. In 2000, for example, the PLA published a series of books on Chinese and Western military matters entitled, "Soldiers of the Future." Since that time, popular books and magazines that appeal to children and adults have mushroomed. Second, as a growing power with a history of military weakness and neglect, there may be a growing popular recognition that China cannot be a great power without a modern military as well. Third, the introduction of military training and affairs to new university students since 1989 is likely raising both the awareness and knowledge of military matters among China's intellectuals (thanks to Taylor Fravel for reminding me of this latter point).

12. John Keegan, in *The Iraq War*, New York: Knopf, 2004, marveled at how the Iraqi army failed to fight to protect its own homeland and key military objectives. He argues that the failure of the Iraqi military, and the general indifference of the Iraqi public, dispelled accepted military theory in the West that a military and its population will resist external invasion, and disputed the post-World War II paradigm of grateful populations greeting military liberators. He argues that this theory only applies to Western countries themselves and not to former colonies in the developing world, such as Iraq, where ethic unity and sense of nation are relatively weak.

13. Qiao.

14. *Ibid.*

15. *Ibid.*

16. *Ibid.*

17. Lin Bo, "Why the U.S. Military has Made Repeated Miscalculations," *Renmin Ribao*, March 27, 2003, in *Foreign Broadcast Information Service-China* (Hereafter FBIS-CHI)-2003-0324.

18. *Ibid.*

19. *Ibid.*

20. Yu Zi, "When Will U.S. Withdraw Troops from Iraq?" *Jiefang Junbao*, April 19, 2005, FBIS-CHI.

21. Li Xuejiang, "Viewing from the Sidelines — A Very Dramatic War," *Renmin Ribao Wang www*, April 15, 2003, FBIS-CHI-2003-0415.

22. *Ibid.*

23. *Ibid.*

24. Li also could have made the point that the lightly trained and protected logistics units lacked sufficient means to fend off attack when separated from combat forces as these barreled on to Baghdad.

25. Li.

26. *Ibid.*

27. *Ibid.*

28. *Ibid.*

29. Wu Liming and Liao Lei, "U.S. Military Strike Against Iraq Is a Suspense-Free Quick and Decisive War," *Beijing Xinhua Hong Kong Service,* January 31, 2003, *News Edge* Document No. 200303031477.1_68a3003a42d06f14.

30. See, for example, Tian Zhaoyun and Che Hui, "Talks on Iraq: Focus on [the] Second Battlefield—How the United States Wages Psychological War Against Iraq," *Xinhua Domestic Service,* March 24, 2003, FBIS-CHI-2003-0324.

31. During post-Cold War restructuring, many U.S. psychological operations assets were stripped out of the active force, but the Chinese do not appear to assess this as a shortcoming, either during the initial campaign or after the insurgency developed.

32. Tian and Che.

33. *Ibid.*

34. *Ibid.*

35. *Ibid.*

36. Cui Xuewu, "Psychological Warfare of U.S. Military Suffers Setback," *Renmin Ribao,* March 28, 2003, FBIS-CHI-2003-0328.

37. Tian and Che.

38. *Ibid.*

39. Wu and Liao.

40. For examples, see Han Mingguang, Guo Zhiming, and Zheng Jinzhang (Department of Logistics Information Engineering, Logistics Engineering University, Chongqing, China) "Observ[ing] Modern Military Logistics through [the] Iraq War," *Logistics Technology,* No. 1, 2005, pp. 83-86; Han Jin, "The Military Logistics Behind the War on Iraq," *China Water Transport,* No. 6, 2003, pp. 26-27; Wang Meng and He Liang (Military Economic Academy), "The Trends of Military Logistics in the Iraq War," *Logistics Management,* No. 1, 2004, pp. 63-64; Liu Weiguang, "Seeing Military Logistics Construction and Reform from the Iraq War," *Logistics Management,* No. 4, 2004, pp. 9-12; Bian Fengjie and Zheng Huaizhou, "Inspiration for Military Accurate Equipment Support Based on Modern Logistics Technology From [the] Iraq War," *Journal of the Academy of Equipment Command and Technology,* Vol. 15, No. 3, 2004, pp. 37-40; Yang Hongwei, Li Yong, and Li

Qingquan, "Primary Argument of Equipment Support of Iraq War," *Logistics Management*, Vol. 27, No. 104, April 2004, pp. 87-90; Chen Yao, Yang Xilong, Wan Jin and Jiang Honggang, "Intelligent Simulation of Military Logistics in Limited War," *Logistics Technology*, No. 1, 2005, pp. 83-86.

41. Wang Lianggang and Liang Dewen (Southwest Institute of Electronic Technology, Chengdu), "Foreign Army's Integrated Joint Battlefield Intelligence, Surveillance and Reconnaissance System: an Overview," *Telecommunications Technology*, No. 2, 2004, pp. 1-6.

42. Cheng Libin and Li Shanshan (PLA Engineering Institute, Hefei, China), "Analysis of GPS jamming and counter-jamming technique in Iraq War," *Electronic Optics and Control*, Vol. 11, No. 1, February 2004, pp.18-21.

43. Zhou Jianjun, *et. al.* (PLA Navy Information Engineering Techonology Research Institute), "Application of UAVs in the Iraq War and Its Enlightenment," *Aeronautical Science and Technology*, No. 1, 2004, pp. 30-33.

44. Zhang Zhengduo and Zhang Donghang, "The Motive Behind [Intelligence] 'Failure'" *Jiefang Junbao*, June 20, 2005, *News Edge* document No. 200506201477.1_ 5a08009fdcdzj341. A Xinhua article raised a similar question about U.S. reconstruction in Iraq, charging that it is "a cover for U.S. hegemony: They [neoconservatives in the Bush administration] stressed: To reform the work, it is not enough to cause "power changes." Consequently, "State rebuilding" must be pursued, sparing neither human resources nor financial resources. The fact that Bush talked voluminously about "disseminating liberty" in his [2005] inaugural speech indicates he has accepted [this] core idea." "When Will U.S. Troops Withdraw From Iraq?" *Xinua News Analysis*.

45. Local Uighurs whom the author talked with after 9/11, looked more to Saudi Arabia (Wahabism) and Pakistan for religious inspiration, and possibly some support, such as training and possibly economic support. The Taliban and al-Qa'ida did not appear to be a major source of influence within Xinjiang before 9/11.

46. Qiao Xin Sheng, "Six Paradoxes of the Iraq War," *Renmin Ribao*, April 14, 2003, FBIS-CHI-2003-0404.

47. *Ibid.*

48. Hai Lin, "Story Can Be Retracted Buts Facts Are More Difficult to 'Retract'," *Renmin Ribao*, May 21, 2005, available on *Dialog.com*.

49. "China: Iraq Resolution Is a Milestone," 09/06/04, *www.china-embassy.org*.

50. The author agrees with David Finkelstein's characterization of China's recent efforts to achieve comprehensive development and full integration into the international order as a "revival," from an historical perspective. See "China: Is it a threat, or an opportunity?" Transcript of a discussion posted on *People's Daily online* on August 23, 2005. In contrast to "China threat" or even the "rise of China" characterizations, which focus on potential disturbances to U.S. status and the post-World War II international system (which itself may be less relevant

to the United States since 9/11), "revival" more appropriately acknowledges that China is attempting to return the country to world greatness and power, a goal the Chinese have pursued since the collapse of the Qing Dynasty. "Revival" accords legitimacy to the Chinese endeavor, rather than simply comparing it to the destabilizing rise of Germany in the 1930s, as is frequently the case.

51. For discussion of the "peaceful rise" debate, see Evan S. Medeiros, "China Debates Its 'Peaceful Rise' Strategy," *YaleGlobal online*, June 22, 2004, *yaleglobal.yale. edu/display.article?:id=411b*.

52. The Tibetan Center for Human Rights and Democracy recently expressed outrage that another year will pass without a country sponsoring a resolution on China's human rights record at the UN Commission on Human Rights. The U.S. State Department announced on March 22, 2004, that the United States would sponsor a China human rights resolution, but backed off when it became apparent that a majority of countries would not support it.

53. Nico Colombant, "China's new African Oil Ties Create Concerns," *Energy Bulletin*, September 30, 2004, reported that Chinese trade to Africa overall had increased nearly 50 percent since 2003. According to the report, China sought to establish relations with newly emerging oil producing countries, such as Gabon, from the Gulf of New Guinea to Central Africa.

54. During President Bush's October 2003 visit to Asia, many foreign representatives expressed concern that America's focus on war and terror was out of sync with Asian countries' concern for economic development.

# CHAPTER 5

# WAR CONTROL:
# CHINESE CONCEPTS OF ESCALATION MANAGEMENT

## Lonnie D. Henley

War control is the deliberate actions of war leaders to limit or restrain the outbreak, development, scale, intensity, and aftermath of war. The objective of war control is to forestall the outbreak of war, or when war cannot be avoided, to control its vertical and horizontal escalation, to strive to minimize the consequences of war, or to strive to achieve the greatest victory for the smallest cost. War control includes arms control, crisis control, control of armed conflict, etc., and is a major component of contemporary strategic research and strategic guidance.[1]

Containing war is not only a task in peacetime; the issue exists in wartime as well. In wartime, it generally takes the form of containing enlargement of the scope of the war, restraining escalation of the war's intensity, and so forth. Sometimes it even finds expression in the war aim of "using war to restrain war," particularly by countries with a defensive strategy.[2]

This chapter examines Chinese military writings on how to prevent unwanted escalation of a crisis or conflict, and how to ensure that military operations are constrained and modulated so as to best serve broader political objectives. It relies primarily on the writings of scholars at the Academy of Military Science (AMS), National Defense University (NDU), Shijiazhuang Army Academy, and other leading military academic institutions. A central insight is that People's Liberation Army (PLA) military academics have only begun formal, methodical consideration of the issue since 1999, and that the concepts explored here will continue to evolve over the next decade. Notwithstanding the field's early stage of development, however, it draws on deeper springs of Chinese military and strategic thought to constitute a coherent strategic viewpoint significantly different from Western concepts of escalation control. It is likely that "war control" concepts will have a major influence on Chinese behavior in any future crisis, particularly a conflict with the United States over the Taiwan issue.

## GENERAL CONCEPT

Although preventing unwanted escalation is implicit in Chinese concepts of how to fight and win local wars under high-technology conditions, the term "escalation control" seldom appears in Chinese writings. Instead, preventing unintended escalation of a political crisis into a military conflict, or a small-scale conflict into a major war, is part of a broader Chinese concept known as "containment of war" (èzhì zhànzhēng) or "war control" (zhànzhēng kòngzhì). War control is a wide-ranging activity, uniting all elements of comprehensive national power to shape the international environment and reduce the risk of war; to manage crises and prevent unintended escalation; to put China in a favorable position if war does occur; to control the conflict once it is underway and ensure military operations serve larger political objectives; and above all to ensure China retains the political and military initiative and is not forced into a defensive or reactive position without control over the pace, scale, intensity, or conclusion of the war.

War control is not a prominent topic in Chinese military writings, but has attracted some serious examination in the past 5 years or so. It was not discussed in the 1987 edition of the landmark Academy of Military Science (AMS) volume Zhànlüè Xué (The Science of Strategy), or in the 1999 National Defense University book of the same name; by 2001, however, it merited a chapter in the second edition of the AMS volume.[3] Dan Xiufa, a researcher on Mao's military thought at AMS, noted in 2003 that "there has not been much deep research into Mao Zedong's thought on preventing and containing war," a sure sign it has not been central to Chinese military theories heretofore.[4] His is one of two recent articles that mine Mao's writings for insights on the issue, both reaching the unsurprising conclusion that Mao was a master of war control, despite his lack of any explicit reference to the concept.[5] The most in-depth treatment of the subject is a 2001 National Defense University (NDU) doctoral dissertation by Colonel Xiao Tianliang, an assistant professor in the Strategy Teaching and Research Institute at NDU.[6] This present study draws heavily on Xiao's dissertation, together with the 2001 Zhanlüe Xue and shorter articles by researchers from AMS, NDU, and other military academic institutions.

War control stresses the comprehensive employment of political, economic, diplomatic, and all other instruments of national power, but military means of course figure largely in the strategic equation.[7] War control includes many factors.

## Measures to Shape the International Security Environment, Peacefully Resolve Disputes, and Reduce the Threat of War.

These range from mediation and negotiation of economic and territorial disputes, through "military diplomacy" and confidence-building measures, to arms-control and arms-reduction treaties and formal international security mechanisms.[8]

## Measures to Manage Crises and Prevent or Postpone the Outbreak of War.

Crises should be contained both geographically and in terms of their subject matter and intensity. Allowing a crisis over one issue to expand and include other political, economic, or territorial issues is a sure way of losing control. Such horizontal escalation increases the risk of vertical escalation toward higher-intensity political or military confrontation. It also increases the risk of the crisis becoming internationalized, attracting unwelcome intervention by other concerned parties or, even worse, by great powers and international organizations. This could limit China's freedom of action and ability to control the crisis to its advantage. In some cases, however, deliberately enlarging the crisis may be a useful tactic to gain control and seize the initiative for China.[9]

Effective crisis management depends a great deal on whether the crisis has been foreseen and analyzed in advance, as well as the effectiveness of crisis management leadership structures. Anticipating crises, thinking through the causes and possible responses before they occur, and having appropriate resources at the ready are the key to gaining control and maintaining the initiative.[10] Leadership decisionmaking processes are at a premium in a fast-developing situation with too little information.[11]

Good crisis management does not preclude the use of military force. In fact, ostentatious force deployments may be a key part of the political and psychological pressure China uses to gain the initiative and win the contest of wills at the heart of any crisis. Xiao Tianliang notes that of four main approaches to a crisis, the war-mongering model (*hàozhàn xíng*) is too likely to provoke the other side to extreme action—besides being "unsuited to China's national character"—while a soft approach (*runruò xíng*) may overly embolden the opponent and lead him to do something rash. The recommended approaches are either military intimidation (*wēishè xíng*) or bargaining (*jiāoyì xíng*). Bargaining is often successful, but if one decides on intimidation, the intent is to use overweening military power to "cow the opponent into submission (*shèfú duìfāng*)."[12] (The meaning of *weishe* here is clearly "intimidation," not "deterrence.") In the extreme, as other authors note, the military approach may include "fighting a small war to prevent a large war."[13]

## Measures Taken During War to Control the Scale, Pace, Scope, or Intensity of the Conflict.

This includes efforts to prevent escalation, minimize destruction, and shape the course of the war to serve larger political and foreign policy objectives. The main principle underlying Chinese thought on war control is that military operations must be firmly subordinated to the larger national interest and broader political, diplomatic, and economic objectives. This may sometimes require halting military operations short of their intended objectives, or modulating the pace and intensity of operations to create the proper climate for pursuing political ends.

This does not always mean lowering the intensity; "sometimes political goals require decisive victory, sometimes creation of an advantageous situation, sometimes just a symbolic attack."[14] In particular, when issues of territorial sovereignty or national dignity are at stake, economic interests already are compromised, and firm military action is required. But in general, the prevailing international environment of peace and development, as well as China's long-term economic interests, are deemed to require preventing rather than inciting escalation, using closely coordinated political, economic, diplomatic, and military means, because "an excessive military attack can put us on the defensive politically."[15]

# THEORETICAL BASIS

Chinese military thinkers generally underpin their practical suggestions with an appeal to universal military theory, and those discussing war control are no exception. The central theoretical issues in war control are the evolution of warfare and human society on the one hand, and the changing international strategic situation on the other. Throughout most of human history, warfare necessarily was unlimited, because the political objectives were so out of proportion to the military means at hand as to provide no stopping point short of absolute victory or absolute defeat. From the stone age through the end of the Cold War, most conflicts involved existential threats to a country's political system or even the survival of its population. The material means of warfare, in the meanwhile, did not include sufficiently subtle or agile control mechanisms, or sufficiently detailed timely knowledge of the battlefield situation, to permit careful modulation of the pace and intensity of the conflict.

The current political and technological situation is seen to be fundamentally different as far as war control is concerned. The advent of "war under high-technology conditions," largely through the application of information technology to the mechanized warfare forces of the late industrial age, creates the novel possibility of grasping and directing large-scale far-flung military operations in real time.[16] At the same time, the advent of nuclear and other weapons of enormous destructive power make unlimited war far too dangerous to contemplate.[17]

The global strategic situation has also changed, such that no major power faces a fundamental threat to its existence or its most vital national interests. Crises are inevitable, maybe even more likely than in the past, and may well escalate into open war. But much less is at stake in such a conflict than in past eras. In China's view, the prevailing international trend is toward peace and development, driven by the strategic trifecta of multi-polarity, globalization, and "informationization." Furthermore, conflict is more "transparent" than in the past and much more subject to scrutiny by the international community and the general public, again due to the ubiquitous spread of information technology. Finally, of course, nuclear weapons make uncontrolled escalation far too dangerous. As a result, they feel, the era of unlimited warfare is over. The material ability to contain war exists, as does the political imperative to do so, a major reversal of the situation that prevailed throughout much of human history.[18]

## MILITARY MEASURES TO CONTAIN WAR

> What we call "shaping the situation" refers to making full use of the strategic commander's subjective initiative, on the basis of our own military power, through the rational concentration and employment of forces, to create a powerful posture and strong offensive capability that is irresistibly fierce and overpowers the enemy.[19]

As noted above, containing war requires comprehensive application of political, economic, diplomatic, and military capabilities. The military part of this effort encompasses a wide range of actions to shape the overall situation (*zàoshì*).

### Military Intimidation and Deterrence.

One of the first contributions the military can make to controlling a fast-developing crisis is the existence of a highly visible and capable military force obviously ready to take action. "Preparedness for war and containment of war are a dialectical unity."[20] Overt shows of force and vigorous deployments toward a crisis zone put pressure on the opponent, helping China gain the initiative and control development of the crisis. Depending on the situation, this may include moving strategic nuclear forces or elite conventional units. In other cases, it may be necessary to limit visible deployments so the opponent does not over-react and escalate more than China wants. Even then, however, clandestine deployments usually are necessary in case the crisis does escalate, because in modern high-technology local war, the first battle is often decisive.[21] One way or another, the proper posture (and posturing) of China's forces is seen as a central aspect of early crisis management.

In an age of local wars, Chinese strategists believe, the primary deterrent factor is no longer nuclear weapons, important though they remain. The ability to deter encroachment on China's territory or vital interests lies mainly in the nation's overall economic, political, diplomatic, and military strength, its comprehensive national power (*zōnghé guólì*). In addition to nuclear missile forces, the major military components of China's strategic deterrent include its large and increasingly capable conventional forces. PLA strategists also see the nation's perceived willingness to fight over issues of vital interest — Taiwan, for example — as an important deterrent factor that reduces the likelihood they will need to do so. Finally, the ability to mobilize and organize huge quantities of manpower, technology, and resources from society at large, under the rubric of People's War Under Modern Conditions, "is still the magic weapon for deterring and preventing a large-scale invasion by the enemy."[22]

### Control of Overall War Objectives.

Unless fundamental national interests are at stake, military objectives in the conflict should be constrained to stay in consonance with political objectives. The history of warfare reveals many instances where military war aims outstripped the guiding political objectives, resulting in uncontrolled escalation and complete loss of the political initiative.[23]

### Control of Military Targets.

A limited war requires careful balance in the selection of military targets. On the one hand, one must attack vital targets that have a decisive effect on the enemy's military capability and will to fight. On the other, the targets must be such that the opponent can endure the loss without being driven to an implacable quest for vengeance and that the international community can tolerate without being moved to large-scale political or military intervention. Failure to strike the right balance can cause unwanted escalation, or put China on the political defensive and cause it to lose control of the overall situation.[24]

### Control of Military Operational Parameters.

Having decided on overall war aims and the general nature of the target set, there is still a decision of what "form of warfare" (*zhànzhēng xíngshì*) the military operation should embody. Chinese theory groups these into the two broad categories of offensive and defensive warfare, each expressed in various "forms of operations" (*zuòzhàn xíngshì*) — mobile, positional, or guerrilla warfare; protracted war versus wars of quick decision; wars of annihilation versus wars of attrition or modern effects-based operations; whether the conflict should be high- or low-intensity, symmetric or asymmetric. A critical step in Chinese military planning is the "commander's determination" of the situation (*zhhuīyuán de juédìng*), which includes a decision on the overall military requirements and objectives, designation of the primary and secondary operational directions (*zuòzhàn fāngxiàng*), and selection of the size and type of forces to employ. A correct decision on these operational parameters at the outset has a significant effect on the ability to maintain control of the conflict.[25]

**Control of Warfighting Techniques (Zhànzhēng Shuduàn).**

The increased killing power of modern weapons, and the increased "transparency" of the battlefield due to modern news and information media, require strict control on the selection of weapons and tactics. Inflicting excessive damage on the enemy, especially on the civilian population or vital infrastructure, will stir up intense resentment and bring into play political factors that make it much more difficult to control the situation. This is not to say extreme measures are not sometimes necessary, of course; merely that they are inherently difficult to control, and should be carefully considered. The military commander must not succumb to the temptation to use whatever means is available to achieve the military objective. As always, the warfighting techniques should serve the overall political objectives of the war.[26]

**Control of the Pace, Rhythm, and Intensity of the Conflict.**

AMS specialists studying U.S.-British operations in Iraq in 2003 concluded that they represented the epitome of "highly-contained warfare." Allied forces tightly controlled the degree to which military operations interacted with political, economic, and psychological aspects of the situation, in addition to the more visible and unprecedented control over military targets and the overall pace and rhythm of the conflict.[27] Careful modulation of the pace and intensity of the fight can create favorable conditions for the political and diplomatic struggle. The side that holds the initiative can press the offensive and bring the conflict to a resolution while its advantage still holds; the side that lacks the initiative can slow and drag out the conflict while it seeks an opportunity to reverse the situation.[28]

## Control the End of the War.

Purely military considerations must not be allowed to determine when and how the conflict comes to an end. Throughout most of human history, wars were for national or societal survival, and political war aims could not be achieved without the complete achievement of military objectives. In an era of limited war, on the other hand, it is quite possible that political objectives may come within reach before the military operation has played out to its intended end. In such a case, continued conflict could harm rather than serve the national interest, and the wise leader will either terminate or prolong the conflict if it is politically advantageous to do so. PLA analysts assess that China has done this well in every conflict since 1949, and that it represents a particular strength of the Chinese strategic perspective.[29]

Properly ending the conflict is not only a matter of timing, but also of close coordination between military operations and political maneuvering in the final stages of the conflict. It may be necessary to pause the fighting to create space for negotiations, or intensify the fighting in order to force the opponent to the negotiating table; to spring unexpected "assassin's mace" weapons and throw the opponent off balance at a critical point; or to accelerate seizure of key objectives before the situation stabilizes. This is a particularly critical juncture in the struggle to "influence the situation" (zàoshi) and seize the initiative. It requires military superiority on the battlefield, which may entail rapid commitment of additional elite forces in the final stages of the war. But it also requires flexibility and precise control of military operations. If the war has gone badly for China, it may require great political agility to gain the best from a bad situation.[30]

## Control the Post-Conflict Situation.

The military's role in war control does not end when the shooting stops. Continued military pressure may be needed to make the enemy abide by terms of the settlement, potentially including a resumption of military conflict to make the enemy return to the agreement.[31]

## THE IMPORTANCE OF THE INITIATIVE

Mao Zedong incisively pointed out: "War is a competition of subjective capabilities between two military commanders competing for superiority and for the initiative, based on the material foundations of military and financial strength."[32]

Throughout Chinese discussion of war control, the emphasis is on seizing the political and military initiative (*zhēngq zhdòng*) and avoiding situations that would put China in a reactive, passive, defensive posture (*bèidòng*). Holding the initiative creates leeway and freedom of action, letting China set the agenda. A reactive position limits China's options, making it impossible to maintain control of the situation.

Seizing and holding the initiative requires rapid reaction to an incipient crisis, including immediate deployment of sizeable forces as early as possible. It requires clear, quick, and correct decisionmaking. It requires strong standing forces, as well as thorough contingency planning and rapid mobilization of societal resources. It requires a resolute and principled political stance, firmly asserted at the outset and throughout the confrontation. It requires a rapid transition to war when events reach that level, and employment of formidable military power at every stage, particularly when settlement talks seem near. And it requires avoiding internationalization of the problem or outside political and military intervention, especially by hegemonic powers.[33]

It is difficult to overstate how prominent the concept of the initiative is in Chinese writings. To an outside observer, there seems a clear risk that such strong emphasis on gaining the initiative may lead China to over-react to a developing crisis, creating a cycle of reaction and escalation. There certainly is some discussion about the need to avoid provoking the enemy beyond the point of tolerance, as discussed above, driving him to a quest for vengeance that renders the conflict beyond control. But Chinese war control theorists give little thought to the possibility that what China considers a resolute response that maintains the initiative, the opponent might misconstrue as alarming preparations for aggressive military action. Chinese military authors seem to be unable to get outside their own subjective view of China's innocent intentions, unable to view China as others might view it. The Chinese are certainly not alone in this weakness; our own society is not particularly good at seeing ourselves as others see us. But it is possible this strong belief in seizing the initiative as the key to crisis management and war control could itself contribute to unwanted escalation.

## RELEVANCE TO A TAIWAN STRAIT CRISIS

From America's perspective, and certainly from Taiwan's, the central question is how these concepts would affect a crisis involving China, Taiwan, and possibly the United States. Available Chinese writings do not provide direct answers to that question, but a bit of informed speculation is possible.

Before we can proceed, however, a few assumptions are necessary. First, we cannot be sure these publicly available writings accurately reflect the real state of Chinese thought on this subject. It is possible, indeed probable, that there are classified documents containing more explicit discussion of how to manage an emerging crisis and prevent undesired escalation. PLA contingency plans and war plans must address these issues, at least implicitly, and it is likely there is more systematic discussion in other classified venues. It seems reasonable to assume, however, that the public writings reflect the general tenor of any more detailed classified discussion, both in the general concepts involved and the level of interest in the subject.

Second, we cannot be certain that the theoretical and doctrinal discussion we observe among mid-level PLA academics reflects the thought processes and perspectives of the national-level political and military leadership. In fact, some differences are inevitable, given the different background, outlook, and professional experience of the two groups, in China or any other country. But given the nature of the Chinese political system, it is likely that the public writings of PLA academics do not diverge sharply from the general outlook of the top leadership, though with large caveats about the role of individual personalities within the leadership collective.

With those assumptions as a foundation, we can draw a few tentative conclusions about the relevance of Chinese war control concepts to a Taiwan conflict or crisis. First, these concepts have only recently become a factor in Chinese planning for a Taiwan contingency. From the available evidence, it appears serious theoretical consideration of war control among PLA academics began around 1999. Yu Shifu and Yin Xinjian's "Initial Exploration of Mao Zedong's Thoughts on Containing War" was among the first articles on the subject, published in early 2000. Other Western authors assert this is roughly the same time Jiang Zemin and the Central Military Commission (CMC) ordered the PLA to begin serious efforts to prepare for a Taiwan conflict, with a target readiness date variously cited as 2005, 2007, or 2010. (Some go further and portray this as an intention to attack on a certain date, but most interpret it as a target to achieve a specified military capability, separate from any political decision to go to war.)

It seems reasonable to view the interest in escalation control as part of the broader consideration of what a conflict with Taiwan really would require. If we are right that the PLA is currently working on its first serious, fully-developed operations plans for a Taiwan contingency, we can expect all aspects of those plans to improve as they are refined and updated in coming years. Like other aspects of serious operational thought and planning in China, Chinese concepts of war control are still evolving and will show increasing levels of sophistication and practicality over the coming 5 to 10 years.

As an aside, the PLA has shown a keen awareness of the need for more competent staff officers as an essential prerequisite for better planning. There have been several professional military education texts published in recent years on "military operations research" (jūnshì yùnchóuxué) — embodying an explicitly American approach to detailed military planning — as well as many studies on how to develop and train competent staff officers and guides to staff officer duties and functions in peacetime and wartime.[34]

A second conclusion we might draw is that large troop movements, mobilization of strategic nuclear forces, and other apparently threatening actions are likely in any serious crisis, whether or not Beijing intends to attack. The importance of maintaining the initiative, the value of troop movements for creating political leverage, and simple military prudence may all impel PRC leaders to order large deployments early in a crisis, whatever their ultimate objectives. Significantly, such movements are among the few visible indicators American and Taiwan intelligence can use for warning of attack, but the war control literature suggests they may provide little insight into China's real intentions.

Third, it is no great revelation to say the Chinese will take a rigid stance on issues of principle at the start of a crisis, but the war control and crisis management literature reinforces this expectation. Vigorous assertion of China's (invariably) correct and principled stance is seen not just as a political/moral imperative, but also as an effective tactic for gaining and maintaining control of the situation. It is less clear whether this means ultimate compromise on matters of principle is impossible, or merely unlikely.

Fourth, it is likely any attack on Taiwan will be designed carefully to achieve political rather than purely military objectives. Again, this is not an earth-shaking revelation, but war control literature provides another source of insight into Chinese thinking on the issue. In particular, war control theorists emphasize the careful selection of targets to undermine the enemy's will to fight, without arousing such resentment and hatred that it produces the opposite effect. That said, there is little indication in other Chinese writings of any concern over strong resistance from the Taiwan military or populace, and the war control writings do not mention Taiwan by name in this context, so perhaps we should be cautious in stretching to that conclusion. But even so, it is clear that war control thought advises careful attention to the negative as well as positive political effects of striking any particular target.

Fifth, in the immortal words of Yogi Berra, "it ain't over till it's over." Even in what seem to be the final stages of the conflict and negotiations for its termination, Beijing will struggle vigorously to hold or regain the initiative, particularly if the war has gone badly for China. Rather than putting the best face on defeat, war control theorists would advocate bold and unexpected actions to create a more favorable environment for the final political struggle. And as noted above, a political settlement may not end the fighting if China feels that "post-conflict" military strikes are necessary to keep the enemy within the terms of the settlement as China sees them.

## THE EFFICACY OF "WAR CONTROL" IN PREVENTING ESCALATION

Escalation control certainly does not occupy a central place in PLA strategic theory as it did in U.S. thought during the Cold War. War control is a new and still secondary part of Chinese strategic military thought, and escalation control is only one aspect of war control. But as discussed above, social and technological developments in recent decades are seen as making it easier to manage crises and prevent unintended escalation of a conflict. Chinese writers almost seem to think this makes the world safe for war once more, or perhaps safe for the first time. There is a danger that this belief in controllable war, together with the extreme emphasis on maintaining the initiative, could combine to increase rather than decrease the likelihood of escalation.

## FUTURE CONTINUED DEVELOPMENT OF WAR CONTROL DOCTRINE

It seems to this observer that since the early 1990s, the PLA has developed a fairly standard pattern for developing new operational concepts, best illustrated in the development of joint operations doctrine in the Eighth through Tenth Five-Year Plans (FYP).[35] The Eighth FYP (1990-95) was a period of discussion and experimentation, defining operational requirements and conducting small-scale, decentralized experimentation on various warfighting techniques at a number of units around China. The Ninth FYP (1996-2000) was a period of consolidation and codification, combining the new techniques into a comprehensive concept of operations and developing a body of written doctrinal regulations, teaching materials, and training standards published since January 1999. The

Tenth FYP was the period of implementation, focused on education in military academies and schools and training in military units to inculcate the new approach to warfare.

The flood of new doctrinal publications, teaching materials, and training standards since 1999 is likely to represent only the first generation of modern Chinese operational doctrine.[36] We can expect the PLA to continue refining and developing its doctrine to incorporate lessons learned from field training and foreign (primarily U.S.) developments, as well as new thinking on topics such as war control. The development, codification, and implementation of operational doctrine is a seminal event in PLA history, a new level of maturity and competence in the complex business of developing modern military capabilities.

Considering the concept of war control against this backdrop, its state of development seems to parallel that of joint operations in the early 1990s. Serious discussion began around 1999-2000, and it now appears as a major topic in works such as the 2001 *Science of Military Strategy*. It is being debated among the same genre of military academics who were central to the development and codification of joint operations doctrine in the 1990s. But it is not yet the topic of major authoritative monographs bearing the official imprimatur of the AMS or General Staff Department, as many other strategic and operational issues have been. In short, we can expect further development of war control concepts in the PLA over the coming decade.

## DOCTRINAL REFORM IN THE CONTEXT OF PLA MODERNIZATION

This codification of operational and managerial processes is only one reflection of a fundamental transformation of the Chinese officer corps. At the end of the Cultural Revolution, in 1975, Deng Xiaoping berated the PLA for being bloated, undisciplined, disorganized, lazy, and combat ineffective.[37] When Deng gained full power in 1979, and with the PLA's dismal performance in Vietnam to vindicate his criticisms, the PLA launched on a reform program that is now in its 25th year.[38] In the early stages of reform, the most serious obstacle to progress was the extremely low educational level and military competence of the PLA officer corps. For nearly 2 decades prior, since the end of the PLA's first reform period in the 1950s, the armed forces had focused on political education, intense factional strife, and public order amidst the chaos of the Cultural Revolution, even taking control of local and provincial government after party and government structures were destroyed in the political struggle. The generation of officers who led the PLA in 1979 largely were uneducated peasants recruited in the Civil War and anti-Japanese war era (1930s and 1940s), and had spent the previous 2 decades doing everything except develop competence in modern combat operations.

Twenty-five years later, a major improvement in the quality of the officer corps represents the most profound change in the PLA's military capabilities. For the first time in Chinese history, the PLA has reasonably well-educated officers chosen and promoted primarily on the basis of military competence. Even more important, the entire cadre of officers up to senior colonel (brigadier general equivalent), the core of military planning staffs at every level, have spent their whole career in a PLA dedicated to reform and modernization, where realistic training and complex combined arms operations are the norm. The previous period of professionalization, in the 1950s, lasted only 8 to 10 years by the most generous estimate. In contrast, the current reform period has lasted 25 years so far, and looks set to remain on course for decades to come. The PLA is achieving a critical mass of competent officers able to tackle the challenges of modern warfare in a way their predecessors never could. The same phenomenon is visible in every other aspect of Chinese government and society, from fiscal management to infrastructure development to international relations.

Chinese forces were starting from an extremely low base when today's colonels were lieutenants, and the program has suffered fits and starts along the way. Only 10 percent of PLA line officers, and 30 percent of all cadres (line officers, technical officers, and PLA civilian personnel) now hold a full university degree, for instance, compared to nearly 100 percent in the U.S. forces.[39] The PLA still has a long way to go before it is a fully competent, modern armed force. There is no question, however, that in every field, the PLA will achieve greater progress in the coming decade than it did in the last.

# CREDIBILITY OF DOCUMENTARY SOURCES

As discussed above, it seems likely the kind of sources consulted for this chapter—writings by faculty members and doctoral candidates at the AMS, NDU, Shijiazhuang Army Command Academy, etc.—accurately reflect the thinking of those charged with developing and implementing PLA doctrine. These sources are not authoritative, meaning they are not regulatory documents issued under authority of the Central Military Commission or General Departments. Such documents, with titles such as Outlines (*gāngyào*) and Regulations (*tiáolìng, tiáolì*), are the official promulgation of PLA operational doctrine and managerial procedures. Academic writings of the kind cited here occupy a lower but important place in the hierarchy of PLA doctrinal materials.

The official regulations provide only very general guidance. Responsibility for fleshing out these guidelines falls to military academic institutions, especially NDU, AMS, and the Command Academies, which produce materials to translate that guidance into detailed operational concepts and promulgate them throughout the officer corps. For example, the 2000 *Science of Campaigns* and 2002 *Guide to the Study of Campaign Theory* seem to implement the classified 1999 *PLA Outline on Joint Campaigns*.[40] There has been a flood of teaching materials published in the past few years, as the PLA implements and popularizes the new generation of doctrine developed and codified in the 1990s.[41]

The articles cited in this chapter rest on the third rung of the ladder of authoritativeness. They are neither official orders and regulations, nor the direct implementing materials used to train officers in the new concepts those orders dictate. Rather, they are the professional conversation ongoing among those who write such materials, intended for one another as well as for the more general military audience. They do not represent official doctrine, but they probably embody the general state of understanding of an issue among those who write doctrine. This is particularly true, in my view, of military science doctoral dissertations from NDU and AMS, like Xiao Tianliang's work cited here. The dissertations published in NDU's *Military Science Doctoral Dissertation Archive* series all seem to spend the first three-quarters of the work demonstrating mastery of the current state of the field, then add the student's thoughts and suggestions in the few chapters. The strong similarity between Xiao's dissertation and the shorter discussion of war control in the 2001 *Zhanlue Xue* reinforces this interpretation. In my view, this makes such dissertations particularly valuable for gauging the PLA's current thinking on a given issue.

**Limitations Imposed by the Sources.**

On a topic like war control, however, the PLA's is not the only perspective that matters, and perhaps not even the most important. It is indeed important for the PLA to be conscious that military operations must support broader political objectives. But it is the political leaders who determine those objectives, and determine what military posture best furthers them. Whether political leaders think in terms similar to those outlined here for the PLA remains an open question.

It is possible that a similar body of writings exists, perhaps from the Central Party School, to instruct rising political leaders on escalation control and crisis management in the same way these writings educate rising military leaders. If such writings do exist, however, we do not seem to have any window into their content or concepts. And of course, anything used to train today's rising mid-level cadres may have only limited relevance to how senior leaders would behave in a crisis. We can speculate that rising political leaders are being trained in concepts similar to what military officers are hearing, and that the training given mid-level political and military leaders reflects the perspectives of senior leaders who order such training. But without direct evidence on the issue, we can only draw tentative conclusions.

## CONCLUSION

The field of PLA studies has changed enormously in the past 10 years with the sudden flood of valuable Chinese-language materials readily available in PRC bookstores, mail-order catalogs, and online. We have long castigated the Chinese for insufficient "transparency" on military issues, and there remain important areas where Beijing continues to conceal information other countries believe a major power should make public in the interests of mutual understanding and stability. The transparency charge is beginning to wear thin, however, in light of the enormous and growing volume of public information on PLA issues that has not been examined in the English-speaking world. We should make a vigorous effort to better use these Chinese-language sources and incorporate them into our understanding of PLA modernization efforts.

In the field of war control and escalation control, we need to find more information about Chinese concepts of nuclear escalation, and to compare it to both U.S. nuclear escalation thought and Chinese war control thought. The writings discussed here make occasional reference to nuclear issues, such as the deployment of strategic nuclear forces for purposes of political signaling, but do not directly address nuclear escalation.

We also need to look for reflections of war control thinking in the statements and writings of the national political and military leadership. We may conclude tentatively that PLA writings on war control probably parallel the top leadership's views, but we need more direct evidence before we can be confident in that conclusion.

The discussion of crisis management, containment, escalation, and war control in Chinese military writings seems to represent a blend of modern and traditional Chinese strategic thought, practical considerations common to all modern militaries, sophisticated assessment of the political and military challenges the PLA would face in a crisis, and optimism about China's ability to mold the situation and control the course of events. Taken together, war control constitutes a distinctively Chinese perspective that may have a significant influence on Beijing's behavior in a crisis, to include a potential conflict in the Taiwan Strait. As in other aspects of Chinese military development, we can expect to see increasing sophistication and realism as PLA theorists continue to explore and develop this relatively new field of strategic thought.

# ENDNOTES – CHAPTER 5

1. Peng Guangqian and You Youzhi, chief editors, *Zhanlüe Xue (The Science of Military Strategy)*, Beijing: Military Science Press, 2001, p. 213. Cited hereafter as *Zhanlüe Xue 2001*. All translations by the author unless otherwise noted.

2. Yao Youzhi and Zhao Dexi, "'Zhanlue' de fanhua, shouheng yu fazhan" ("The Generalization, Conservation, and Development of Strategy"), *Zhongguo Junshi Kexue (China's Military Science)* September 30, 2001, pp. 120-127, *Foreign Broadcast Information Service* (FBIS)-CPP20011126000199.

3. Gao Rui, chief editor, *Zhanlüe Xue (The Science of Strategy)*, Beijing: Military Science Press, 1987; Wang Wenrong, chief editor, *Zhanlüe Xue (The Science of Strategy)*, Beijing: National Defense University Press, 1999; *Zhanlüe Xue 2001*, Chapter 8.

4. Dan Xiufa, "Shenhua Mao Zedong junshi sixiang yanjiu de xin shiye" ("A New Perspective on Deepening Study of Mao Zedong's Military Thought), at *www.pladaily.com.cn/item/mzd/jn/048.htm*. There is no date on the article, but it commemorates the 110th anniversary of Mao's birth, putting it in 2003. The author's affiliation is not mentioned in this article, but he is identified elsewhere as a researcher in the Mao Zedong Military Thought Research Institute of the Chinese Academy of Military Science; see, for example, *biz.sinobook.com.cn/press/newsdetail.cfm?iCntno=674*. All Internet materials last accessed in September 2004. All translations are by this author unless otherwise noted.

5. Yu Shifu and Yin Xinjian, "Mao Zedong ezhi zhanzheng sixiang chu tao" ("An Initial Exploration of Mao Zedong's Thought on Containing War"), *Junshi Lishi (Military History)*, Beijing, 2000, No. 1, at *www.cass.net.cn/zhuanti/y_kmyc/zhuanjia/a00130.htm*. Yu Shifu is a professor at the Shijiazhuang Army Command Academy; see "Jun xiao qunying shao cui; jiaotan jiang xing shenghui" ("Stars of the Military Academic World"), *Jiefangjun Bao*, September 8, 2000, at *www.pladaily.com.cn/pladaily/20000908/big5/20000908001013_Army.html*.

6. Xiao Tianliang, *Zhanzheng Kongzhi Wenti Yanjiu (On War Control)*, Beijing: National Defense University Press, 2002.

7. Yuan Zhengling, "An Active Defense Strategy to Protect National Interests — Understanding the 'National Defense of China 2002'," *Zhongguo Guofang Bao*, Beijing, December 24, 2002, p. 4, FBIS-CPP20021224000044. Excerpt here retranslated by the author.

8. *Zhanlüe Xue 2001*, Chapter 8; Ma Ping, "Shuli kexue de zhanlüe guan" ("Foster a Scientific Strategic Outlook"), *Jiefangjun Bao*, Beijing, May 1, 2001, p. 3, translated in FBIS-CPP20010501000034, original text at *www.pladaily.com.cn/gb/pladaily/2001/05/01/20010501001038_gdyl.html*; Xiao Tianliang, Ch. 4, pp. 96-133.

9. Xiao Tianliang, pp. 140-143.

10. Han Jiahe and Xiong Chunbao, "Qiantan junshi weiji kongzhi" ("A Brief Discussion of Military Crisis Control"), *Guofang Bao*, Beijing, October 22, 2001, p.

3, at *www.pladaily.com.cn/gb/defence/2001/10/22/20011022017053_zhxw.html*. Senior Colonel Han Jiahe is identified elsewhere as a professor at the Nanjing Army Command Academy; see FBIS-CPP20040218000058. One notes this was published not long after the April 2001 EP-3 crisis.

11. Xiao Tianliang, p. 147.

12. *Ibid.*, 148-149.

13. Yu Shifu; Dan Xiufa.

14. Xiao Tianliang, pp. 167, 170.

15. Yuan Zhengling.

16. Yu Jiang, "Zhanzheng kongzhi: zouchu suobujide weigu" ("War Control: Getting Out of an Exhausting Difficult Situation"), *Guofang Bao*, Beijing, March 25, 2004, at *www.pladaily.com.cn/gb/defence/2004/03/25/20040325017054.html*. The author is identified in the article as a researcher at the PLA Academy of Military Science.

17. "20 shiji zhanzheng liugei women de sikao yu qishi" ("Reflections and insights on 20th Century Warfare"), *Jiefangjun Bao*, Beijing, December 25, 2000, FBIS-CPP20001225000027. This article summarizes a round-table discussion among several PLA strategists; the thought cited was expressed by Professor Xu Yuan of the NDU Strategy Research Office.

18. Han Jiahe and Xiong Chunbao; Xiao, p. 164.

19. Xiao Tianliang, p. 171.

20. Feng Changsong, "Tigao daying zhanzheng he ezhi zhanzheng de nengli" ("Raise Abilities to Win and Contain Wars"), *Jiefangjun Bao*, Beijing, August 27, 2003, FBIS-CPP20030827000124.

21. Xiao Tianliang, p. 176.

22. Feng Changsong.

23. Yu Jiang.

24. Xiao Tianliang, p. 166.

25. *Ibid.*, p. 184.

26. Yu Jiang; Xiao, pp. 180-185.

27. "Zhongguo junshi zhuanye tichu xiandai zhanzheng mouqiu 'gao zhengzhi'" ("Chinese military specialists address the quest for 'high control' in modern warfare"), *Guangming Ribao*, April 28, 2004, at *news.xinhuanet.com/mil/2004-04/28/content_1444426.htm*.

28. Xiao Tianliang, p. 191; Yu Jiang.

29. Xiao Tianliang, p. 192; Dan Xiufa; Yu Shifu and Yin Xinjian.

30. Xiao Tianliang, pp. 193-198.

31. *Ibid.*, p. 199.

32. Yu and Yin, "An Initial Exploration of Mao Zedong's Thought on Containing War."

33. Xiao Tianliang, pp. 138, 145, 175; Xu Wen, "Xiandai jubu zhanzheng dui woguo wuqi zhuangbei dongyuan zhunbei de qishi" ("Insights from modern local war for China's weapons and equipment mobilization preparation"), *Zhongguo Hangtian (Aerospace China)*, No. 3, Beijing, 2004, at *www.space.cetin.net. cn/docs/ht0403/ht0403htzc03.htm*; Wang Congbiao, "Shishi keji qiang jun zhanlue: tigao wojun xiandaihua fangwei zuozhan nengli—Xuexi Jiang Zemin 'Lun Kexue Jishu'" ("Implement the Strategy of Strengthening the Military Through Science and Technology to Improve the Defensive Combat Capabilities of China's Military—Studying Jiang Zemin's 'On Science and Technology'"), *Jiefangjun Bao*, February 13, 2001, FBIS-CPP20010213000086.

34. For example, Li Zhangcheng and Jiang Jingzhuo, *Junshi yunchou xin fangfa yanjiu yu yingyong (Research and Application of New Methods in Military Operations Researc)*, Beijing: Military Science Press, 2002; Dai Feng, ed., *Junshi yunchouxue daolun (Introduction to Military Operations Research)*, part of the "Military School Students Mandatory Military Reading List Collection," Beijing: Jushi Yiwen Press, 2002; He Li, ed., *Canmouzhang lun canmou xiuyang (Chiefs of Staff On Cultivating Staff Officers)*, Beijing: Military Science Press, 2003; and Liu Leibo, ed., *Xinxihua zhanzheng yu gaosuzhi canmou rencai (Informationized Warfare and Highly Qualified Staff Personnel)*, Beijing: NDU Press, 2004, among many others.

35. For a longer discussion of this pattern, see Lonnie Henley, "PLA Logistics and Doctrine Reform, 1999-2009," in Susan M. Puska, ed., *People's Liberation Army After Next*, Carlisle, PA: Strategic Studies Institute, U.S. Army War College, 2000, pp. 55-77.

36. The current wave of publications is technically the second generation of Chinese written doctrine, but all involved concede that the doctrinal writings published in the 1950s were a cursory effort of little operational value.

37. Deng Xiaoping, "Zai Junwei Zuotanhui shang de Jianghua" (Speech to the Discussion Meeting of the Central Military Commission), in *Deng Xiaoping Wenxuan, 1975-82 (Collected Works of Deng Xiaoping, 1975-82)*, Beijing: Renmin Chubanshe, Hong Kong: San Lian Publishers, 1983, pp. 363-67.

38. For a detailed examination of the 1979 China-Vietnam conflict and the PLA's very low level of operational competence, see Edward C. O'Dowd, "The Last Maoist War: Chinese Cadres and Conscripts in the Third Indochina War (1978-91)", dissertation in candidacy for Doctor of Philosophy, Department of History, Princeton University, October 2004.

39. Zhang Yu, *Lun Zhongguo Tese de Junshi Rencai Chengzhang zhi Lu (On the Road for the Development of the Military Personnel with Chinese Characteristics)*, Military Science Doctoral Dissertation Collection, Beijing: National Defense University Press, 2001, p. 147.

40. *Zhanyi Xue (The Science of Campaigns)*, Beijing: NDU Press, 2000; *Zhanyi Lilun Xuexi Zhinan (Guide to the Study of Campaign Theory)*, Beijing: NDU Press, 2002;

*Zhongguo Renmin Jiefangjun Lianhe Zhanyi Gangyao* (*PLA Outline on Joint Campaigns*), Beijing: Central Military Commission, 1999. The text of the *Outline* has not been published, but its existence is discussed in *Guide to the Study of Campaign Theory* and many other places. Its issuance was announced in "Zhongyang Junwei zhuxi Jiang Xemin qianshu mingling wojun xinyidai zuozhan tiaoling banfa" ("CMC Chairman Jiang Zemin Signs Order Implementing Our Army's New Generation of Operational Regulations"), *Renmin Ribao*, January 25, 1999, at *www.people.com.cn/item/ldhd/Jiangzm/1999/mingling/ml0003.html*.

41. For discussion of the development of the new generation of doctrine, see Lonnie Henley, *loc. cit.*, and David Finkelstein, "Thinking about the PLA Revolution in Doctrinal Affairs," draft paper, November 2002, cited by permission of the author.

# CHAPTER 6

## CHINA AS A MAJOR ASIAN POWER:
## THE IMPLICATIONS OF ITS MILITARY MODERNIZATION
## (A VIEW FROM THE UNITED STATES)

### Paul H. B. Godwin

## INTRODUCTION

There is a seeming contradiction between China's increasing influence in global and regional politics and the apprehension seen in Beijing's perception of its security environment. Without a doubt, China today is more influential in world politics and the Asia-Pacific region than at any time in the modern era. Yet, Beijing's official national defense policy suggests China is extremely uncertain about its national security environment. So apprehensive is Beijing that it believes military power is becoming increasingly important in preserving China's security. This public anxiety comes after 15 years of double-digit percentage defense budget increases and what appears to be an acceleration of China's military modernization programs.

Over the 25 years since their initiation, China's current defense modernization programs have reached the point where they suggest that Beijing's objective is to build Asia's dominant defense establishment. In the United States, the improving capabilities of the Chinese People's Liberation Army (PLA—as the services and branches are collectively named) increasingly are perceived as a potential threat to U.S. strategic interests in the West Pacific. The purpose of this chapter is to assess China's military modernization programs by addressing seven issue areas. First, how does Beijing's enunciated defense policy fit into the overall objectives of China's security policy? Second, how does Beijing define the threats to China's security? Third, to what extent do China's acquisitions and indigenous development programs reflect Beijing's defense policy and the military strategy it suggests? Fourth, China's military capabilities will be assessed in light of Beijing's threat assessment and the strategy it has evidently developed in response to this perceived threat. Fifth, the issue of the PLA's conventional force projection capabilities will be addressed. Sixth, a brief assessment will be made of the progress in China's intent to develop a self-sustaining military industrial complex. Finally, an assessment will be made of possible events that could change the direction of China's defense policies.

In addressing these issues, the chapter's primary focus will be on the trends seen in China's military modernization programs rather than present capabilities. Given the broad scope of China's programs that range from modernizing the strategic nuclear deterrent to developing capabilities in information warfare, trends are a stronger indicator of possible intent than current capabilities. The chapter's conclusion will assess the policy implication these trends suggest for the region and the United States.

## CHINA'S PERSPECTIVE ON ITS NATIONAL DEFENSE POLICY

Beijing's defense policy is formulated in an era where China is more secure from imminent external military threat than at any time in the past 150 years. Moreover, although Beijing does not view China as a "great power" because it lacks the technological sophistication of the world's most advanced economies, Beijing has become a major player in the international system seeking great power status. Beijing is conducting an active diplomacy implementing a foreign policy strategy with multiple objectives collectively designed to transform China into a major world power.[1] This diplomacy is intended in large part to uphold an international environment conducive to sustaining and expanding the global trade and commerce necessary to build the economy and technological sophistication China needs to be a great power. This trade does more than enrich China and contribute to its domestic economic development. It also provides access to many of the technologies and manufacturing skills required to achieve Beijing's most critical long-term defense modernization objective: a self-sustaining defense research and development (R&D) infrastructure and military industrial complex (MIC).

This same foreign policy strategy now pursues positive relations with the world beyond its initial concentration on China's Asian neighbors. Beijing seeks to work closely with the European Union (EU) and to extend its diplomatic influence into Latin America, the Middle East, and Africa. While much of this diplomacy is intended to ensure China's access to the energy supplies demanded by a rapidly expanding economy, it also is designed to reinforce Beijing's status as an influential player on the world scene. Within Asia, this diplomacy has established Beijing as a primary player in regional security forums while simultaneously easing, but not eliminating, apprehension over China's increasing military capabilities. In brief, the strategy executed by Beijing has made China richer and more influential in the world than at any time since the mid-18th century. Nonetheless, Beijing's defense policy does not reflect the confidence one might anticipate from China's diplomatic achievements. What it does reflect is a fundamental apprehension of U.S. power and military presence both globally and in the Asia-Pacific region.

**National Defense Policy.**

The authoritative statements of Beijing's perception of its security environment and the defense policy and strategy it requires are found in China's defense white papers.[2] Whereas the most recent white paper, published in December 2004, sees the international system as stable, "factors of uncertainty, instability, and insecurity" are viewed as increasing. In an only thinly veiled reference to the United States, the white paper states that "tendencies of hegemonism and unilateralism have gained new ground, as struggles for strategic points, strategic resources, and strategic dominance crop up from time to time." This statement and the white paper's reference to the U.S. invasion of Iraq as exerting a "far reaching influence on the international and regional security situations"[3] demonstrates Beijing's apprehension over the power and influence of the United States. These judgments also explain the white paper's conclusion that "(t)he military factor plays a greater role in international configuration and national security."[4] The United States is unquestionably at the center of Beijing's military security concerns. The reason for this is found in the white paper's logic explaining why Beijing sees military power assuming greater importance in protecting China's national security.

First, the metric employed in describing the developments in military capabilities changing the conduct of war is clearly drawn from the technological advances and doctrinal changes found in the U.S. armed forces. The white paper focuses on the consequences for military operations of the transition from mechanization to "informationalization" —referred to as the "World Wide Revolution in Military Affairs (RMA)." In Beijing's view, as the world's major militaries undergo this transformation and battlefield technologies change the conduct of war to "[a]symmetrical, noncontiguous and nonlinear operations," the global military imbalance is widening. Because American armed forces are the leaders in this transformation and have applied advanced technologies to military operations in war, the imbalance of most concern to Beijing is between China and the United States. Second, as Chapter III of the white paper details,[5] the PLA's modernization is now dedicated to "building an informationalized force and winning an informationalized war...." The only military adversaries the PLA potentially will confront with the capabilities it fears most are the U.S. armed forces. Currently, should that confrontation occur, it could be over Taiwan. Preventing Taiwan's independence is declared the PLA's "sacred responsibility."[6] In preparing China's armed forces for this contingency, the white paper is explicit in its attachment of foremost priority to modernizing the PLA's naval, air, and strategic missile forces. This priority is necessary "in order to strengthen the capabilities for winning both command of the sea and command of the air, and conducting strategic counterstrikes."[7] A military confrontation with the United States over Taiwan is the only probable scenario requiring this combination of military capabilities.

This apprehension over U.S. capabilities is stated clearly in the white paper's assessment of the Asia-Pacific security environment. Although viewed as essentially stable, responsibility for any potential instability is placed on U.S. policies and strategy. Whereas the Six-Party Talks seeking to end North Korea's nuclear programs are described as weak and terrorism and transnational crimes are recognized as major problems, the United States and Japan are seen as the principal sources of potential regional instability. The white paper states:

The United States is realigning and reinforcing its military presence in this region by buttressing military alliances and accelerating missile defense systems. Japan is stepping up its constitutional overhaul, adjusting its military and security policies and developing the missile defense system for early deployment. It also has markedly increased military activities abroad.[8]

As expected, the United States is criticized for increasing the quantity and quality of its arms sales to Taiwan. The Taiwan issue, however, was to become even more salient following the February 2005 meeting of the U.S.-Japan Security Consultative Committee (SCC).

The SCC's joint statement issued on February 19 included a carefully worded reference to Taiwan as being among their agreed "common strategic objectives." Specifically, the United States and Japan agreed they would "[e]ncourage the peaceful resolution of issues concerning the Taiwan Strait through dialogue."[9] China's Foreign Minister, Li Zhaoxing, was inflexible in his response during a press conference. He declared that "[a]ny move to include Taiwan directly or indirectly in the scope of U.S.-Japan security cooperation constitutes an encroachment on China's sovereignty and an interference in China's internal affairs."[10]

This focus on the U.S. military presence in the region, the alliance with Japan, and the centrality of Taiwan in Beijing's perception of its Asian security environment contrasts sharply with Beijing's assessment of the role played by the Association of Southeast Asian Nations (ASEAN) and the ASEAN Regional Forum (ARF). The white paper declares:

China has established a strategic partnership with the ASEAN dedicated to peace and prosperity in the region, and engaged in comprehensive cooperation that has seen rapid expansion. Cooperation in East Asia, with the ASEAN and China, Japan, and the ROK [Republic of Korea] as the main players, keeps expanding, leading to greater economic development and political and security trust in the region. The ARF as the most important official channel for multilateral security dialogue in the Asia-Pacific region, plays a positive role in promoting security cooperation in the region.[11]

Even with the tensions so evident in Sino-Japanese relations, the contrast between China's apprehension over U.S. capabilities and strategy and the contributions ASEAN and ARF make to regional security could not be more starkly stated.

Nor are Beijing's concerns necessarily misplaced. Certainly, the degree of cooperation achieved between China and the United States in the years following the tragic terrorist attack of September 11, 2001 (9/11), on the World Trade Center and the Pentagon has increased significantly. Nonetheless, despite this enhanced cooperation, U.S. mistrust of China's long-term strategic intentions toward the Asian region has been stated in official documents laying out American national security and defense strategies. One year after the 9/11 tragedy, *The National Security Strategy of the United States* warned that "In pursuing advanced military capabilities that can threaten its neighbors in the Asia-Pacific region, China is pursuing an outdated path that, in the end, will hamper its pursuit of national greatness."[12] On September 30, 2001, the U.S. Department of Defense (DoD) *Quadrennial Defense Review's* (QDR) reference to a possible "military competitor with a formidable resource base emerging in Asia"[13] could only be read as referring to China. Secretary of Defense Donald Rumsfeld's statement at the recent Asian security conference held in Singapore would confirm to Beijing that U.S. concerns over China remain high among the Defense Department's priorities. In his prepared remarks, Secretary Rumsfeld asserted that because no country threatened China, Beijing's investments in its military modernization programs were questionable.[14]

Beijing's concentration on defeating or offsetting U.S. military capabilities can be seen in the trends found in China's acquisitions from foreign sources, especially Russia, and indigenous programs and R&D projects. Nonetheless, although the primary driver for China's current military modernization programs is preparing the PLA for a possible military conflict with the United States over Taiwan, the weapons, equipment, operational doctrine, and training being developed are fungible. The capabilities being developed can be applied to military contingencies other than a Taiwan scenario, and these are not minor capabilities. Simply listing them, some of which have their origins in the 1950s, attests to the level of military capabilities sought by Beijing.[15]

- R&D in space systems to provide wide area intelligence, surveillance, and reconnaissance (ISR) capabilities.

- R&D in anti-satellite systems.

- Cruise missile acquisitions and programs dedicated to improving the range, speed, and accuracy of land, air, and ship-launched weapons.

- Ballistic missile programs improving the range, survivability (mobile systems), reliability, accuracy, and response times of tactical, regional, and intercontinental-range weapons to augment or replace current systems.

- Construction of new classes of nuclear-powered attack and ballistic missile submarines (SSN/SSBN) to augment or replace those now in service.

- Acquisition and development of advanced diesel-electric submarines armed with sub-surface launched cruise missiles and guided torpedoes to augment or replace older vessels now in service.

- Development and acquisition of more capable surface combatants armed with advanced antiship cruise missiles, antisubmarine warfare, and air defense systems.

- Air power programs developing and acquiring technologically advanced multiple-role combat aircraft, together with airborne early warning and control system aircraft (AWACS) and aerial refueling to increase their effectiveness and combat radius, and unmanned aerial vehicles (UAV) designed to attack an adversary's air defense radars.

- Air defense programs developing and acquiring surface-to-air missiles (SAM) and aircraft capable of providing an integrated air defense of China's territory.

- Ground force programs modernizing armor and artillery weapons, deploying increasing numbers of helicopter aviation units, improving airlift for airborne units, deploying increasing numbers of special operations forces units, and increasing amphibious warfare capabilities.

- R&D in offensive and defensive information warfare operations.

- R&D and deployment of improved command, control, communications, and computer systems (C4).

- Increasing the tempo and complexity of exercises to make the PLA capable in the joint service operations essential for contemporary warfare, including amphibious operations.

Although undoubtedly now primarily intended for a possible military conflict with the United States over Taiwan, as they mature these trends will provide military capabilities China can apply to its maritime claims and defense of its land borders. Beijing's defense requirements should not be underestimated. China's land border stretches some 13,728 miles, extending from Russia and North Korea in the north and northeast to Southeast Asia and South and Central Asia, touching on no less than 14 countries. China's coastline extends some 9,000 miles from Russia in the north to Vietnam in the south. China's current threat environment, however, is low, and Beijing's regional diplomacy is dedicated to sustaining a cooperative relationship with all neighboring states, including resolving border disputes. Moreover, even now, no single Asian power can match China's military power on continental Asia. With the possible exception of Japan, it is likely that within a decade or so no Asian country will be capable of challenging China's naval and air power in maritime East Asia. Only India conceivably will be able to countervail a Chinese naval presence in the Bay of Bengal and the Indian Ocean, should Beijing choose to patrol that distance from its home waters.

The question arising from this unfolding range of military capabilities is what future security environments are China's defense modernization programs designed to prepare for? It is difficult to assume they are intended primarily to enhance China's prestige by presenting Asia and the world with technologically advanced highly trained armed forces. It is reasonable to conclude that China's defense programs, especially the intent to develop an indigenous capability to design and manufacture any defense items Beijing believes it requires, are calculated to make China Asia's dominant military power. If this should be the objective, then what are Beijing's strategic intentions when this goal is achieved over the coming two decades? Currently, the United States is the Asia-Pacific region's predominant power with every intention of remaining so.

**The Sino-American Paradox.**

Despite the undeniable focus of Beijing's defense modernization on potential military confrontation with the United States, Washington and Beijing recognize that their national interests are served best by avoiding direct confrontation. Both are expanding cooperation in all realms serving their mutual interests. That is, China and the United States are pursuing parallel polices of pragmatic mutual engagement. More recently, when the two leaders met on the sidelines of the November 2004 Asia-Pacific Economic Cooperation (APEC) meeting in Chile, President Hu Jintao asked President George W. Bush to engage in what he referred to as a "strategic dialogue." President Bush agreed, but because the term "strategic dialogue" is reserved for close allies, Washington chose to term the meetings a "global dialogue." Nonetheless, the United States and China agreed to hold regular high-level talks on political and security issues.[16] The first of these was held in Beijing on August 1, 2005, by Vice Foreign Minister Dai Bingguo and Deputy Secretary of State Robert Zoellick.[17] These meetings can be seen as paralleling the Sino-American Defense Consultative Talks (DCT) between the two defense establishments. This mutual engagement is a positive consequence both of reciprocal concerns over the potential costs of open confrontation, as well as the reality that Beijing and Washington have much to gain through cooperation. Nonetheless, the strong opposition the United States and Japan presented to the EU's potential lifting of its post-Tiananmen arms embargo on China is indicative of the tensions that mark this engagement. The central argument presented by the United States and Japan was that lifting the embargo threatened the regional balance of military power by potentially assisting China in its already accelerating military modernization programs.[18] Similar arguments were raised by the United States with Israel in the dispute over Israeli arms and technology sales to China.[19]

This reciprocal pattern of apprehension and cooperation reflects the utility China and the United States see in a pragmatic relationship.

Perhaps contradicting China's defense white paper, China's Ministry of Foreign Affairs (MOFA) has expressed the view that it welcomes a continuing strong U.S. regional presence because it contributes to regional security and stability.[20] A sustained American political, economic, and military presence provides those Asian states apprehensive over Beijing's growing influence the ability to hedge against any potential attempt by China to dominate the region. In this sense, the United States assists in providing the regional stability that allows Beijing to pursue its primary external strategic objective of sustaining an international environment conducive to enhancing China's economic development and modernization.

There is a paradox underlying this policy of mutual engagement. Even as this pragmatic cooperation forms the core of their relationship, China and the United States are simultaneously preparing for war with each other over Taiwan. Both will have contingency plans on the shelf containing operational designs to defeat the other.[21]

## ASSESSING CHINA'S MILITARY CAPABILITIES

Whereas Beijing's aspirations for its military modernizations programs seemingly are evident, PLA capabilities are far less so. As a matter of policy and despite improvements over the years, Beijing's lack of transparency in its military capabilities and programs makes a confident assessment impossible. For example, for some years now the PLA has focused on developing the capability to conduct joint warfare, but what can be known from reports on military exercises or the occasional visits of observers is too limited for reliable judgment. Nor can any estimate be confident that it properly assesses PLA logistic capabilities for joint operations. The effectiveness of PLA Navy (PLAN) anti-submarine warfare (ASW) and anti-air warfare (AAW) cannot be determined for the same reasons. The quality of training, maintenance, and all the other factors that contribute to effective ASW and AAW simply cannot be determined from the information available. Similar problems affect assessments of essentially all other realms of warfighting. Any evaluation therefore is left with trying to make informed guesses from the platforms, weapons, and supporting systems in the PLA's inventory joined with what is known about

PLA operational doctrine and the exercises conducted to train for this doctrine. This is not firm ground for assessing capabilities.

The second dilemma an assessment has to confront is the difficulty of determining the PLA's capabilities against a specific adversary or adversaries in a particular scenario. An example of this difficulty is found in the debate between Michael O'Hanlon of the Brookings Institution and Lyle Goldstein and William Murray of the U.S. Naval War College. The central issue they debated was the potential cost in U.S. Navy (USN) ships required to defeat a PLAN submarine blockade of Taiwan.[22] One could assume, given the overall ASW superiority and numbers of USN SSN, destroyers, aircraft carriers, and land-based P-3 aircraft that any Chinese attempt to enforce a submarine blockade of Taiwan would be defeated quickly. However, continuing improvements in China's submarine force joined with the complexities of ASW operations in the Taiwan area and the post-Cold War withering of U.S. ASW assets led Goldstein and Murray (an experienced retired USN submarine officer) to argue to the contrary.[23] In doing so, they criticized an earlier essay by Michael O'Hanlon, who had argued that in the most severe case while assisting the Taiwan navy, the USN could possibly lose two ships.[24] Goldstein and Murray conclude that in the best case, U.S. losses would be three ships, and in the worst case 14 ships could be lost in a single tactical exchange.[25]

In part, these problems are the result of basing analyses on open sources. It is possible that the U.S. intelligence community (IC), drawing on its multiple sources, can assess the PLA's capabilities with more confidence. Nonetheless, even the IC has to grapple with the secrecy enveloping China's modernization programs. The recent DoD report on China's military power states that because of this secrecy, the report's "findings and conclusions are based on incomplete data."[26] Furthermore, as China's armed forces modernize across the board and the MIC becomes more capable in the R&D and production of sophisticated platforms, weapons suites, and supporting systems, estimating the PLA's future capabilities is becoming even more difficult. Equally uncertain is the PLA's capability to command, control, coordinate, and provide timely intelligence to its modernized forces. The PLA could be moving faster or slower toward its aspirations than an external observer, especially one using only open sources, will know with any confidence.

## U.S. AND CHINA: MILITARY STRATEGIES

In terms of military strategy, the U.S. position in Asia serves as the maritime balancer to China.[27] In essence, the military strategies of China and the United States consist of a continental power countered by a maritime power. American forces deploy throughout the Asia-Pacific region from U.S. and foreign-hosted bases and facilities. These bases and facilities extend from the West Coast of the United States to Hawaii and Guam, and from the Republic of Korea and Japan in the north through Southeast Asia down to Australia and Diego Garcia in the Indian Ocean. Possibly, U.S. access to bases in Central Asia (Uzbekistan, which is ending, and Kyrgyzstan) could be included in this listing. Their purpose, however, is to support coalition operations in Afghanistan rather than serve as facilities for possible operations against China.

Given this continental-maritime structure, Beijing's basic military strategy for defense against the United States is to maintain strategic deterrence through a credible second-strike capability and to defend China's territory and littoral seas. Because of its location some 100 miles from the mainland, Taiwan is encompassed by this strategy. The trends in China's defense modernization programs listed earlier are designed in large part to make this strategy increasingly robust.

Strategic deterrence will be bolstered by the new class (094) of SSBNs armed with 12 JL-2 submarine-launched ballistic missiles (SLBM). These ships will grant China a survivable sea-based strategic force. It safely can be assumed they will be quieter and more reliable than the troublesome single-ship *Xia*-class that represents China's first generation SSBN. The new SSBN force will complement the solid-fueled, mobile land-based DF-31 and DF-31A intercontinental ballistic missiles (ICBMs) now under development for deployment in the near future. These new weapons will be quicker in responding, more accurate, and survivable than the 20 slow responding, liquid-fueled silo-based DF-5A ICBMs that form the core of China's current deterrent. Equally important, even if only two 094 SSBN are deployed in the coming decade, they would add 24 ICBM to the 20 land-based weapons now in place. When the DF-31/31A are deployed, the number of ICBMs capable of striking the United States will increase even more. There are many unknowns about China's nuclear force planning. Among them is how Beijing conceptualizes its future strategic force structure as it confronts the U.S. national missile defense (NMD) program and is capable of deploying increasing numbers of weapons at sea and on land. Possibly, rather than relying on a just a few weapons—a minimal deterrent—as it has in the past, Beijing will conclude that, with NMD on the horizon, a significantly larger force is necessary.

Strengthening littoral defense is sought by improving the PLA's naval and air power capabilities to conduct operations several hundred miles from China's coast. When employed in a joint service campaign, these capabilities will provide the basis for a "local sea denial" or "anti-access" defense potentially extending 200 miles or possibly much more from China's territorial waters. The military objective is to present a threat to U.S. aircraft carrier strike groups that will slow their advance into the Taiwan area of operations (TAO). Once in the TAO, the objective is to make U.S. Navy operations extremely hazardous and costly.

Although China is exploring the use of ballistic missiles to strike ships, the greatest imminent threat to U.S. naval forces is the deployment of modern Russian and indigenously developed quiet, diesel-electric submarines (SS) and a new class (093) of SSNs. The 093 SSN, Russian *Kilo*, the latest *Song*, and the *Yuan* SS are armed with submerged-launch long-range anti-ship cruise missiles (ASCM) and wake-homing and/or wire-guided torpedoes. This deployment is complemented by the acquisition and development of more modern and lethal surface combatants, including the *Sovremenny*-class guided-missile destroyers (DDG) from Russia and the indigenous development of DDGs and guided missile frigates (FFG). The ASCMs arming these ships are increasing in range, speed, and lethality.

Air power improvements focus on the acquisition from Russia and indigenous development of fourth-generation multiple-role combat aircraft. The new air-launched cruise missiles (ALCM) arming these aircraft have greater range, supersonic speed, and the ability to take evasive maneuvers to defeat the target ships' defenses. The combat potential of these aircraft will be enhanced by the deployment of AWACS and aerial refueling aircraft. When these two capabilities mature, they will grant PLAN aviation and PLA Air Force (PLAAF) aircraft greater range and effectiveness.

In response to U.S. "deep strike" operations, point defense of essential military, industrial, and political installations is being replaced by an integrated air defense system (IAD) that includes SAMs, air defense artillery, and offensive counter air operations. The "high-tech" contribution of advanced SAMs and air defense aircraft to IAD is joined by a 21st century version of "people's war." "People's Air Defense" units formed out of China's urban militia now are assigned the task of repairing bombing and missile damage, restoration of electricity and water supplies, reestablishing communications, and responding to all other consequences of enemy air and missile attacks.[28]

Although our ability to determine what progress has been made is minimal, the PLA's interest in offensive and defensive information operations must not be overlooked. The PLA views these operations as "Integrated Network Electronic Warfare" and as a capability essential to seizing battlespace initiative through "electromagnetic dominance in the early stages of a conflict."[29]

Looking further ahead, China's space programs are to provide two capabilities critical to a littoral defense strategy. Wide-area ISR capabilities will serve to locate and track U.S. aircraft carrier strike groups and permit over-the-horizon (OTH) targeting for China's air and ship-borne cruise missiles. Should China's anti-satellite program be successful, it would be used to damage the ISR and command and control satellites so important to U.S. military operations. Finally, as mentioned earlier, the 2005 DOD annual report states that China is exploring the possibility of using ballistic missiles to attack USN task forces.[30] Clearly, using ballistic missiles to target American aircraft carriers will require both maneuvering warheads and space-based ISR to locate, track, and target the strike force.

The actual number of modern platforms currently in the PLA's inventory is relatively small, therefore the current capacity to implement this antiaccess strategy is quite limited. The majority of China's air, naval, and strategic missile forces consists of older types incorporating updated 1960s technologies. For example, of some 2,600 combat aircraft in the PLAAF and PLAN aviation units, only about 300 are third and fourth generation types armed with sophisticated munitions.[31] Nor have the capabilities of AWACS aircraft and aerial refueling yet been developed sufficiently by training to be considered operational. The PLAN suffers from a similar imbalance in both its surface combatants and submarines. Most are older, although often updated, ships. More important is the direction the acquisition and development trends demonstrate.

It seems evident that in the foreseeable future, and even with the anticipated improvements in U.S. platforms, weapons, and supporting systems, China's littoral defense is going to become even more difficult to penetrate. Indeed, it would be prudent to anticipate that future Chinese SS will incorporate air independent propulsion (AIP). Extending the number of days PLAN diesel-electric submarines can stay submerged operating on their batteries would make them even more difficult to locate and kill than they are today. The same level of improvement also should be anticipated for China's new SSN over the noisy first generation *Han*-class. Similarly, the well-known deficiencies in the air defense capabilities of the PLA surface combatants evidently are being overcome by the introduction of two indigenously developed *Aegis*-type DDGs referred to as Project 052C.[32] None of this progress suggests that China's armed forces are intended to match overall U.S. capabilities. What PLA modernization programs do demonstrate is that China systematically is overcoming the deficiencies found in the existing legacy platforms and weapons systems as it brings its armed forces into the 21st century. Although China's naval and air forces clearly are not as numerous or well-equipped and trained as their U.S. counterparts, they are reaching for capabilities that will make a military confrontation with them more hazardous and costly.

As Thomas Christensen so concisely stated the problem several years ago, China can cause problems for U.S. security policy without matching American military capabilities.[33] The distribution of the U.S. Pacific Fleet's large inventory of sophisticated and extremely competent combatants serves as an example of the problem.[34] The submarine force contains 26 SSN, 7 SSBN, and 3 nuclear-powered guided missile submarines (SSGN-converted *Ohio*-class SSBN capable of being armed with 154 *Tomahawk* land-attack cruise missiles). Sea-based air power consists of five aircraft carrier air wings. A sixth aircraft carrier, the *Ronald Reagan* (CVN 76), does not have an assigned air wing. Each air wing contains 60-85 aircraft. A typical air wing's missions include strike, airborne early warning, electronic attack, ASW, and logistic support. The Pacific Fleet's surface combatants consist of 11 guided missile cruisers (CG), 22 DDG, 2 destroyers (DD), and 13 frigates (FFG). This inventory is divided among the Third and Seventh Fleets, Task Force 12, and Task Force 14. Only the Seventh Fleet, headquartered in Yokosuka, Japan, is forward-based in the West Pacific. The Seventh Fleet's combat power centers on the *Kitty Hawk* (CV 63) Strike Group composed of the aircraft carrier's air wing,[35] 2 CG, 3 DDG, 2 FFG, and 2 SSN.[36]

Thus, although the U.S. Pacific Fleet's aggregate capabilities are far superior to anything China can put to sea, few ships are forward-based in the West Pacific. Any major confrontation with China would require the redeployment of ships to the West Pacific, requiring considerable transit time.[37] U.S. naval vessels steaming at 14 knots would take 18 days to reach the East China Sea from the U.S. West Coast. From Pearl Harbor, the steaming time is 14 days; and from Yokosuka, 5 days. Ships in the Persian Gulf would steam for 15 days to reach the East China Sea. More rapid advance, say 20 knots, would result in ships arriving in the operating area with engineering problems and most likely with weapon systems and sensors needing maintenance. This speed of advance also would restrict crew training and readiness for combat operations, especially for the air wing embarked on aircraft carriers. Furthermore, the increased speed would require either additional refueling stops or additional replenishment ships for underway refueling. Therefore, a moderate advance of 14 knots would result in greater combat effectiveness in the area of operations despite the longer transit times. Nuclear-powered submarines have shorter transit times, because their speed is not affected by the sea state; therefore their machinery and weapons suites are not susceptible to the vibrations and other consequences of high-speed surface transit.

Recent U.S. responses to China's improving military capabilities are difficult to separate from what could also be preparation for a potential North Korea crisis. Nonetheless, changes being made to U.S.

air and naval forces in preparation for a Taiwan or North Korea crisis can be applied to either contingency.[38] The Pacific Fleet has moved three SSN to Guam, placing them closer to China. Consideration is being given to moving an aircraft carrier and its air wing from the Atlantic Fleet to be based in Pearl Harbor. In May 2005, the 13th Air Force moved from Guam to Hawaii. According to General Paul V. Hester, commander of U.S. Pacific Air Forces (PACAF), the new 13th Air Force headquarters will provide an air operations and warfighting center to cover the entire Pacific region. General Hester plans to establish a strike force at Andersen Air Force Base (AFB) on Guam composed of 6 strategic bombers and 48 fighters rotated from U.S. bases. These combat aircraft will be joined by 12 aerial refueling aircraft to provide a long-range force projection capability. In November 2004, Major General David Deptula, PACAF's Director of Air and Space Operations, anticipated the strategic bombers being employed for maritime control. Available technologies now provide strategic bombers with all-weather, day/night precision anti-ship capability.[39] In addition, three *Global Hawk* unmanned reconnaissance aircraft will be based on Guam. With 28 hours endurance and a range of more than 11,780 miles at altitudes up to 65,000 feet, a *Global Hawk* will be capable of missions covering 62,000 square miles a day, from Bangkok to Beijing. Adding to these developments, Lieutenant General Henry Obering, USAF, Director of the Missile Defense Agency, has stated that China would be treated as a potential missile threat in the development program for national missile defense. This decision was made, he said, because it was "prudent" to do so.[40]

As these contingency preparations were being made, the paradox of Sino-American relations continued. In April 2005, the DCT were held as scheduled in Washington. General Xiong Guangkai of the PLA General Staff Department met with his counterpart, Under Secretary of Defense for Policy Douglas Feith, and other senior officials, including National Security Adviser Stephen Hadley. China's news agency *Xinhua* reported that General Xiong discussed China's December 2004 defense white paper, and that both sides had agreed they should strengthen their military dialogue and exchanges "in order to enhance mutual understanding and trust."[41] Other patterns of normal military ties between the two countries also were sustained. U.S. and Chinese centers of professional military education (PME) continued their exchange of visits, and on July 16, General Liu Zhenwu, commander of the Guangzhou Military Region, departed China for a visit to U.S. PACOM at the invitation of its commander, Admiral William J. Fallon, USN. In a press interview before General Liu's arrival, Admiral Fallon stressed that he sought to strengthen military ties between his command and the PLA. Admiral Fallon is reported as saying "I don't see a threat, I don't want to be perceived as the military commander here to be offering or proposing a threat to China."[42]

Moreover, in October Secretary of Defense Rumsfeld made his first visit to China, and in July 2006 General Guo Boxiong, Vice Chairman of the Central Military Commission, visited the United States. Symbolically, these two official visits restored military relations to the point they were prior to the 2001 collision between a PLA Navy fighter and a U.S. Navy reconnaissance aircraft.

## CHINA'S FORCE PROJECTION CAPABILITIES

Although in principal the emerging capabilities of the PLA are applicable to scenarios other than Taiwan, the current DoD report judges that "China's ability to project conventional military power beyond its periphery remains limited."[43] The question arising from this statement is how limited are these capabilities? With the PLAN conducting exercises in the South China Sea and its nuclear submarines patrolling further east, on one occasion circling Guam,[44] this question requires more detailed assessment.

Assessments of PLA conventional force projection capabilities have to address how far from China's borders and against what adversary? Beijing is working diligently to resolve its remaining land border disputes, and no state in Asia is contemplating an invasion of China. Consequently, beyond possible border incidents that China must prepare for, a ground war is so unlikely that it does not warrant discussion. Should a border incident flare up, PLA ground forces are capable of responding effectively. These forces have been undergoing modernization, including PLAAF initial training in close air support. Furthermore, and despite the uncertain results of Beijing's 1979 incursion into Vietnam, ground warfare is the PLA's forte.

In China's maritime realm, tensions in Northeast Asia involve primarily territorial disputes with Japan. With Japan an ally of the United States, a major military confrontation over these disputes is improbable. Moreover, Japan's Maritime and Air Self-Defense Forces (MSDF/ASDF) are themselves extremely capable. Indeed, the only potential but still unlikely use of China's force projection capabilities other than in a Taiwan crisis is over the continuing territorial disputes in the South China Sea.

In a South China Sea scenario, as in all other uses of military force, one has to ask the purpose of the force projection. Is it to establish a "presence" or to conduct sustained combat operations? If it is the former, perhaps as an act of coercive diplomacy, the PLAN can carry out the mission with ease. A surface action group (SAG) flotilla composed of four or five DDGs and FFGs accompanied by one or two submarines and an underway replenishment ship would make China's intent clear. If, however, a PLAN SAG has to prepare for possible sustained combat operations, then two deficiencies come into play.

Despite the PLAN's introduction of *Aegis*-type DDGs, the fact remains that almost all PLAN surface combatants only have limited AAW capabilities. This means that if the PLAN is conducting sustained combat operations in the South China Sea, its surface combatants are exposed to land-based air attack from several regional air forces. Some protection for the SAG could be provided by China's land-based aircraft using aerial refueling, but this technique has not been operationalized thus far. Moreover, the defending aircraft would require frequent refueling to ensure sustained loiter time over the area of operations. This is far beyond the PLA's capabilities. An aircraft carrier with fixed-wing aircraft would be needed for sustained air operations in an area as distant as the South China Sea. Such a ship remains only a distant dream for the PLAN.

A second deficiency is the limited wide-area surveillance capability available to the PLAN.[45] In the 1990s, China equipped Y-8 turbo-prop transports with British *Skymaster* surveillance and early warning radars capable of identifying surface and air targets and vectoring ships and aircraft. With a flight endurance of 10.5 hours and a cruising speed of 340 mph, the Y-8 could partially compensate for this deficiency. A potential third PLAN deficiency is ASW. The PLAN is acquiring improved ASW helicopters for its surface combatants and the new submarines will have an improved ASW capability, but how competently these capabilities can be employed simply is not known. Nonetheless, a PLAN flotilla would not be defenseless. Assuming one or two submarines are part of the SAG, surface ships attacking with ASCM confront a daunting task. In addition to facing the SAG's submarines, the PLAN's newest DDGs, especially the *Sovremenny*, are armed with lethal, supersonic long-range ASCM.

This discussion of the strengths and weaknesses of a PLAN SAG operating in the South China Sea, however, begs a basic question. Should Beijing employ military coercion to enforce China's sovereignty claims, would any state in Southeast Asia choose to challenge the kind of SAG the PLAN can dispatch today? Would any regional navy and air force choose to challenge a SAG escorting an amphibious group planning to seize one of the many of the disputed Spratly islets? Looking ahead a decade, does any Southeast Asian nation's military modernization programs contemplate developing the capabilities to challenge China's future naval and air power? Even without an aircraft carrier, China's drive for a major regional navy is marked clearly by current acquisitions and indigenous programs. Thus far, the only regional navies that will sustain the capabilities to meet or exceed the PLAN are those of Japan and India. Indeed, today the capabilities of Japan's air and naval forces exceed those of the PLAN and the PLAAF.

## CHINA'S MILITARY INDUSTRIAL COMPLEX[46]

As it has been since the first defense modernization programs began in the mid-1950s, Beijing's long-term strategic objective is to build a self-sustaining defense R&D and military industrial complex. Extensive industrial reforms undertaken in the late 1990s have made a substantial improvement in China's defense production. R&D procedures and production methods have all improved, with consequent progress in the quality of the output. Nonetheless, even in the sector that has demonstrated the most progress other than the missile industry, shipbuilding, reliance on imported components and technologies continues. Whereas significant headway has been made in the production of platforms, China's most advanced ship types contain critical imported components and technologies. The PLAN's newest diesel-electric submarine, the *Yuan*-class, likely draws upon some Russian submarine technology. The most recent *Song*-class submarines rely on German diesel engines and copies of the French DUUX-5 digital sonar system and other copies or imports of European, Russian, or Israeli components.[47] The PLAN's newest destroyers use Ukrainian gas turbine engines and Russian antiaircraft missile systems and search radars.[48]

The aviation industry has demonstrated the least progress. Despite China's development of the *Kunlun* turbo-jet engine and the anticipated WS-10 advanced turbo-fan power plant, the engine for China's first indigenous fourth generation combat aircraft, the F-10 designed with Israel's assistance, is supplied by Russia — the A1-31FN built by Salyut. That China continues to rely on importing Russian aircraft for the PLAAF and PLAN aviation demonstrates the aviation industries' continuing deficiencies. Naval aviation, for example, is being enhanced by the purchase of Russia's Su-30Mk2 armed with the supersonic Kh-31 ASCM.[49]

Even China's missile industry, which has had pride of place among the defense industries since the mid-1950s, has its own weaknesses. The industry's successes can be seen in the development and production of solid-fueled ballistic missiles and new classes of cruise missiles. China's cruise missiles are increasing in range and accuracy and a land-attack cruise missile (LACM) is under development as is a long-range surface-to-air missile perhaps comparable to the U.S. *Patriot* or Russian S-300. These successes must be tempered with the recognition that the United States has had solid-fueled ICBMs since the 1960s. Moreover, whereas LACMs, beyond-visual-range air-to-air missiles, and anti-radiation missiles have long been in the inventories of Western and Russian militaries, they are new to China. This observation is not made to denigrate all the industry has accomplished in the last few years, but to provide a perspective that does not exaggerate these achievements.

While not a defense industry, the information technology (IT) sector has established a close working relationship with the PLA.

IT corporations provide command, control, communications and intelligence ($C^4I$) equipment to the armed forces, thereby providing an important modernizing component. This has allowed the PLA to incorporate major improvements in its communications abilities and operational security. Presumably, these same technologies have assisted the PLA in developing capabilities in offensive and defensive information operations often now referred to as "computer network operations" (CNO).[50]

Although Chinese rightly feel pride in the success of their manned space program, China's space industries and R&D have had a military purpose since their origins in the mid-1950s. China's military space and counterspace programs[51] are focused primarily on countering U.S. capabilities. Beijing's primary interests are space-based command, control, communications, computers, intelligence, surveillance, and reconnaissance ($C^4ISR$), targeting for a variety of weapons, including cruise and ballistic missiles and anti-satellite (ASAT) systems. China's progress in these realms is difficult to estimate. Nevertheless, as in other areas of advanced technologies, in addition to its indigenous programs Beijing works in cooperation in other countries, including Brazil and the EU and in a joint university program between Qinghua University and the United Kingdom's (UK) University of Surrey. Four state-owned space industries are supervising China's R&D as part of Beijing's participation in the EU's *Galileo* satellite navigation system.[52] Additionally, China is developing its own *Beidou* satellite navigation system[53] and has access to Russia's Global Navigation System (*GLONASS*). How close China is to disrupting U.S. space systems while employing its own systems for $C^4ISR$ and targeting cannot be determined from unclassified sources, and perhaps not by the intelligence community. What is important, nonetheless, is the concentrated and expensive priority Beijing has placed on developing these capabilities.

The effort Beijing has directed at improving China's defense industries and R&D over the past 25 years, and particularly in the past 5 years, demonstrates China's commitment to a self-sustaining MIC. Beyond extensive reorganization and reform, Beijing has increased its R&D investments and raised expenditures on the importation of foreign manufacturing technologies. These policies have generated an expanding cohort of technicians, engineers, and scientists. With all its deficiencies, especially in view of the heavy baggage the MIC carried over from the 1960s and 1970s, the improvements made are remarkable. Whether these improvements signify a take-off stage for the MIC is not knowable. It is clear that the groundwork has been prepared for the time when further progress in military technologies will depend on China's indigenous R&D and production capabilities.

## RESOURCES, POTENTIAL POLITICAL CHANGE, AND CHINA'S FUTURE COURSE

What could cause China to change its current course? Will economic expansion stagnate, limiting the resources Beijing can allocate to military modernization? Will China's political system undergo such change that Beijing will alter its strategic objectives? There are no firm answers to these and similar questions, but exploring them could shine some light on Beijing's determination to pursue China's current defense policies.

**Resources.**

Can Beijing sustain the level of defense expenditures it has accepted since 1989? With an average annual increase of 14.5 percent, the official defense budget has doubled in real terms about every 5 years. Even with these increases, the official defense budget over this period consumed a modest 1.6 percent of gross domestic product (GDP). When the recent RAND study[54] adjusted the official budget to reflect probable total military expenditures, the defense burden in 2003 was 2.3 to 2.8 percent of GDP. This is not an unusual defense burden. It is reasonable to assume that China's future economy will slow from its current high rate of expansion and grow at an average annual rate of 5 percent. This rate of growth will triple the size of China's economy by 2025. Maintaining defense expenditures at some 2 percent of GDP as China's economy expands at 5 percent a year will provide the defense establishment with sufficient funding to sustain its modernization programs. Nevertheless, it is questionable whether the *rates* of increase seen in recent years can be sustained if the economy grows at 5 percent per annum. To maintain such a high rate of annual increase, estimated by the RAND study to average 9.8 percent a year in real terms, would require Beijing to accept defense expenditures ranging from 6.2 to 7.6 percent of GDP by 2025. This level of spending is excessive; China's military expenditures would exceed those of any NATO or Asian country. [55]

Moreover, the central government confronts demands for more societal spending. China's economic expansion will be accompanied by an older, more urbanized population that, although wealthier, also will be making more demands on government expenditures. Currently neglected areas such as pensions, health care, education, public infrastructure, and the environment will compete with military spending. These demands joined the bad debts created by nonperforming loans granted by government banks to state-owned enterprises, placing an increasing burden on government expenditures. Even with these competing demands, sustaining military expenditures that require only around 2 percent of GDP is acceptable.

Nonetheless, defense spending at 2 percent of GDP could be viewed as inadequate, should Beijing perceive its security environment deteriorating to the point it believes a major war is probable. Under this condition, Beijing could consider it necessary to increase its defense expenditures to the range of 3 to 5 percent. Such a decision would create a serious friction with the increasing societal demands on central government expenditures.

Although the probability of economic collapse is slim, defense expenditures would be threatened by economic stagnation. If stagnation did set in, societal demands for spending on pensions, health care, and other societal needs would increase with the growth in unemployment and other consequences of prolonged economic decline. Unless China confronted a severe and immediate external military threat to its security, fear of internal unrest could well result in priority placed on domestic spending to ease societal tensions with the cost paid by decreased expenditures on military modernization. It also is possible that, even without economic stagnation, China's political leadership could conclude that mounting national debt and increasing societal demands required diminishing military expenditures.

# Political Change.

The swelling demands on future government spending are accompanied by tensions afflicting China's polity stemming from uneven economic expansion, unemployment, corruption, and the malfeasance of many government and party officials. It would be imprudent to assume, however, that the Chinese Communist Party (CCP) is about to lose control and China disintegrate. Certainly, popular protests are increasing in number rapidly, growing larger and better organized. This pattern of protests is strong especially in China's northeast "rustbelt" and in rural areas. In urban areas, the organization of protests is being aided by the wide use of cell phones, e-mail, and the Internet. China's police, however, are becoming more sophisticated in their responses. The police now admit that the protesters often have legitimate complaints against such problems as avaricious managers and corrupt local officials. Moreover, police techniques for controlling these protests have begun to change from blunt suppression to containing and placating the protestors.[56]

China's political elite is worried about the implications of increasing unrest for the CCP's continued monopoly of political power, but the response across China's polity has been mixed.[57] At the top of the political system, the CCP has indeed sought to increase its control over the political process and over the mass media and internet. At lower levels, however, experiments first seen in village elections have been repeated in urban areas. Moreover, experiments in "e-government" are underway in some provinces and municipal governments, including electronic bulletin boards that seek feedback and public opinion on government policies. There are even the early signs of an emerging civil society, especially in the rich, Internet, and cell phone-linked urban areas. In short, changes underway in China suggest continued CCP rule in a still controlled but more open political climate. Collapse of CCP rule and the disintegration of China seem far less probable than an incremental easing of authoritarian controls beginning at the level of local governance.

More importantly, from the PLA's point of view, maintaining an authoritarian but slowly liberalizing political system that eases societal tensions minimizes the possibility that it will be used to bring mass protests under control as it was in the Tiananmen debacle. Unless public protests get completely out of control, they are the responsibility of the civilian Ministry of Public Security police and the People's Armed Police (PAP). The PLA can be used for domestic security purposes only when requested by local authorities and approved by the central government.[58]

## POLICY IMPLICATIONS AND SPECULATIONS

For the United States, the major unresolved question hovering over China's military modernization programs is whether Beijing's intent is ultimately to challenge U.S. military supremacy in maritime Asia. From an American perspective, the trends potentially are ominous. China's programs embracing strategic nuclear force enhancements, space exploitation for the conduct of military operations, information warfare, naval and air power modernization, and homeland defense against air and missile attack are all designed in large part to counter U.S. capabilities. From a Chinese perspective, beyond a possible confrontation over Taiwan, these programs are a necessary hedge against an uncertain future security environment that has at its center a potential U.S. shift to a more confrontational policy as China's power and influence increases. Beijing's defense white papers consistently signal such apprehension. Consequently, in Beijing's eyes there is no contradiction between China's expanding regional and global political influence and the aspirations of its military modernization programs. China's most dangerous potential adversary wields the world's most powerful military.

For the coming decade, China's national interests drive Beijing toward maintaining its policy of fostering a pragmatic mutual engagement with the United States. Similarly, although Chinese military capabilities developed in response to U.S. military power are applicable to scenarios other than a Sino-American confrontation, Beijing will continue to rely on expanding trade, commerce, foreign direct investment, and technology transfers to build China's economy. This will constrain China's use of force. Aggressive military action in Asia would undermine the international environment Beijing correctly believes China needs to achieve its long-term strategic objectives. For this reason, even as China prepares for a possible war with the United States over Taiwan, Beijing does not seek such a war. It is more probable that Beijing believes the PLA's overt war preparations serve as a deterrent to Taiwan and stimulate the United States to keep pressure on Taipei to avoid unnecessarily provocative actions and statements.

Beyond this decade, the strategic landscape is uncertain. Because each is suspicious of the other's strategic intent, neither China nor the United States accept the legitimacy of each other's defense policies and strategies. At the root of the problem is what former Deputy Assistant Secretary of State Randall Schriver recently has defined as "strategic distrust." Schriver suggests the gravest political danger underlying Sino-American relations is a "steady drift toward great power global rivalry, if not outright adversarial relations."[59] Such mutual suspicion does not serve the interests of the United States, China, or Asia. East Asia long has looked to the United States as the region's security guarantor, with U.S. allies and friends contributing the bases and access to facilities that make America's military strategy possible. Despite the stability the U.S. military presence brings to the region, thereby serving China's near-term interests, the role of East Asia's security guarantor is an aspect of U.S. policy and strategy that feeds Beijing's suspicions of Washington's strategic intent.

Nonetheless, the opportunity to ease this reciprocal mistrust exists. Although senior defense and military officials from China and the United States can play an important role in this task, the objective cannot be accomplished at this level of authority. Because it is a matter of strategic intent, easing mutual apprehension can be achieved only by the most senior political leadership in both capitals. This requires Beijing and Washington to face the reality of their reciprocal suspicion. The best avenue for approaching this sensitive area today is the "strategic dialogue" suggested by President Hu Jintao and initiated this summer in Beijing by Vice Foreign Minister Dai Bingguo and Deputy Secretary of State Robert Zoellick. Ultimately, however, mutually acceptable visions of the roles the United States and China will fulfill in Asia have to be agreed upon by the two countries' political leaders. Beijing and Washington undoubtedly would anticipate political and economic competition.

The difficult task will be to find reciprocal acceptance of their military security policies. No such agreement is now in sight, but the perilous consequences of a sustained military rivalry should spur initial steps toward easing their mutual apprehension.

## ENDNOTES – CHAPTER 6

1. For detailed assessments of Beijing's foreign policy over the past decade, see Evan Medeiros and M. Taylor Fravel, "China's New Diplomacy," *Foreign Affairs,* Vol. 82, No. 6, November-December 2003, pp. 22-35; David Hale and Lyric Hughes Hale, "China Takes Off," *Foreign Affairs*, Vol. 82, No. 6, November-December 2003, pp. 26-53; and David Shambaugh, "China Engages Asia: Reshaping the Regional Order," *International Security*, Vol. 29, No. 3, Winter 2004/05, pp. 64-99.

2. China has published defense white papers since in 1995. The 1995 white paper was entitled *China: Arms Control and Disarmament* but was functionally a defense white paper. Beginning in 1998, defense white papers have been published in alternate years. The following discussion is drawn from *China's National Defense in 2004*, Beijing: State Council Information Office, December 27, 2004, pp. 2-4.

3. *Ibid.*, p. 2.

4. *Ibid.*

5. Chapter III is entitled "Revolution in Military Affairs with Chinese Characteristics," pp. 5-12.

6. *Ibid.*, p. 4.

7. *Ibid.*, p. 6.

8. *Ibid.*, p. 3.

9. "Joint Statement of the U.S.-Japan Security Consultative Committee" issued by the U.S. Department of State, Washington, DC, February 19, 2005.

10. Hu Xiao, "Japan and U.S. Told: Hands Off Taiwan," *China Daily*, March 7, 2005.

11. *China's National Defense in 2004*, p. 3.

12. *The National Security of the United States of America*, Washington, DC: The White House, September 17, 2002, p. 27.

13. *Quadrennial Defense Review Report*, Washington, DC: Department of Defense, September 30, 2001, p. 4.

14. *Remarks Delivered by Secretary of Defense Donald H. Rumsfeld, Shangri-La Hotel, Singapore, Saturday, June 4, 2005*, U.S. Department of Defense, Office of the Assistant Secretary of Defense, Public Affairs.

15. This listing is drawn primarily from *Annual Report to Congress: The Military Power of the People's Republic of China 2005: A Report to Congress Pursuant to the National Defense Authorization Act Fiscal Year 2000*, Washington, DC, Office of

the Secretary of Defense, July 2005 (hereafter *DOD Report 05*), Chapter 5, "Force Modernization Goals and Trends" pp. 26-36.

16. Glenn Kessler, "Senior Level Meetings to Focus on Politics, Security, and Possibly Economics," *The Washington Post*, April 8, 2005.

17. Yuan Peng, "China-U.S. Strategic Dialogue, a Trust Building One," *People's Daily*, August 2, 2005.

18. Steven R. Weisman, "European Union Said to Keep Embargo on Arms to China," *The New York Times*, March 22, 2005.

19. Sharon Weinberger, "New Technology Transfers to China on Hold, Pentagon Official Confirms," *Defense Daily*, June 16, 2005.

20. See Shambaugh, "China Engages Asia: Reshaping the Regional Order," p. 91, where Professor Shambaugh cites both then-Foreign Minister Tang Jiaxuan in 2001 and more recently Ministry of Foreign Affairs Director General for Asian Affairs Cui Tiankai as taking this position.

21. See Michael A. McDevitt, "The China Factor in Future U.S. Defense Planning," in Jonathan D. Pollack, *Strategic Surprise: U.S.-China Relations in the Early Twenty-first Century*, Newport, RI: Naval War College Press, 2003, pp.149-157, for a valuable discussion of U.S. DoD planning and the paradox raised on p. 154.

22. Michael O'Hanlon, Lyle Goldstein, and William Murray, "Damn the Torpedoes: Debating Possible U.S. Navy Losses in a Taiwan Scenario," *International Security*, Vol. 29, No. 2, Fall 2004, pp. 202-206.

23. Lyle Goldstein and William Murray, "Undersea Dragons: China's Maturing Submarine Force," *International Security*, Vol. 28, No. 4, Spring 2004, pp. 161-196.

24. Michael O'Hanlon, "Why China Cannot Conquer Taiwan," *International Security*, Vol. 25, No 2, Fall 2000, pp. 51-86, esp. pp. 75-79.

25. Michael O'Hanlon, *et. al.*, "Damn the Torpedoes," p. 205.

26. *DOD Report 05*, "Executive Summary."

27. The logic of this strategy is best described by Robert S. Ross, "The Geography of Peace: East Asia in the 21st Century," *International Security*, Vol. 23 No. 4, Spring 1999, pp. 81-118.

28. Dennis J. Blasko, "People's War in the 21st Century: The Militia and the Reserves," presented at the conference *Swimming in a New Sea: Civil-Military Issues in Today's China*, convened by the CNA Corporation, Alexandria, Virginia, March 21-23, 2004.

29. *DOD Report 05*, p. 25.

30. *Ibid.* p. 4.

31. "Country Briefing: China," *Jane's Defense Weekly*, April 13, 2005, reports the number of PLAAF combat aircraft as 3000. The *DOD 05* report in Figure 11, p. 44, credits the PLAAF and PLAN aviation with some 2600 combat aircraft.

32. James C. Bussert, "China Debuts Aegis Destroyers," *Signal*, July 2005.

33. Thomas J. Christensen, "Causing Problems Without Catching Up: China's Rise and Challenges for U.S. Security Policy," *International Security*, Vol. 25, No. 4, Spring 2001, pp. 5-40.

34. Pacific Fleet submarine force can be found at *www.csp.navy.mil*. Surface combatants can be found at *www.surfpac.navy.mil*. Amphibious warfare ships are not included in this listing.

35. USS *Kittyhawk*'s Air Wing composition can be found at *www.kittyhawk.navy.mil*.

36. Seventh Fleet ships can be found at *www.c7f.navy.mil*. Amphibious warfare ships, the command ship, mine countermeasures ships, and salvage ship and submarine tender are not included in this listing.

37. This discussion is taken from Bernard D. Cole, "The Modernization of the PLAN and Taiwan's Security," in Martin Edmonds and Michael M. Tsai, eds., *Taiwan's Maritime Security*, London and New York: Routledge Curzon, 2003, pp. 72-73.

38. This discussion is taken from Richard Halloran, "Checking the Threat That Could Be China," *Japan Times*, June 12, 2005.

39. "The Air Force's Emergent Strategy for the Pacific," *Jane's Defense Weekly*, November 17, 2004.

40. Ann Scott Tyson, "U.S. Missile Defense Being Expanded, General Says," *Washington Post*, July 22, 2005."

41. "China, U.S. to Enhance Military Exchanges," *Xinhuanet*, April 29, 2005.

42. Audrey McAvoy, "Fallon Hopes to Boost Defense Ties with China," Associated Press, July 7, 2005.

43. *DOD Report 05*, "Executive Summary."

44. "Chinese Sub Near Guam Before Breaking into Japan Waters, Possibly in Training to Constrain U.S. Military Moves," *Asahi*, December 7, 2004.

45. Lyle Goldstein and William Murray, "China Emerges As A Maritime Power," *Jane's Intelligence Review*, October 2004.

46. The following discussion draws primarily from Keith Crane, Roger Cliff, Evan Medeiros, James Mulvenon, and William Overholt, *Modernizing China's Military: Opportunities and Constraints*, Santa Monica, CA: The Rand Corporation, 2005, pp. 135-190 (Chapter 5, "China's Defense Industry"); and Evan S. Medeiros, "Analyzing China's Defense Industries and the Implications for Chinese Military Modernization," RAND Corporation, Testimony presented to the U.S.-China Economic and Security Review Commission on February 6, 2004.

47. Goldstein and Murray, "China Emerges As A Maritime Power."

48. Richard D. Fisher, Jr., "China accelerates Navy Building," Jamestown Foundation, *China Brief*, Vol. 3, Issue 15, July 29, 2003.

49. Goldstein and Murray, "China Emerges as a Maritime Power."

50. *DOD Report 05*, p. 25.

51. This discussion draws upon *Ibid.* pp. 35-36.

52. David Lague, "EU Satellite Project Could Improve Accuracy," *International Herald Tribune*, April 19, 2005.

53. Geoffrey Forden, "Strategic Uses for China's Bei Dou Satellite System," *Jane's Intelligence Review*, October 2003.

54. The following discussion is taken from Crane, *et. al.*, Chapter 7, "Future Expenditures on the Military," *Modernizing China's Military*, pp. 205-237.

55. *Ibid.*, pp. 224-227.

56. Murray Scot Tanner, "Protests Now Flourish in China," *International Herald Tribune*, June 2, 2004.

57. The following discussion is taken from Dr. Richard Baum, "China's State Control Mechanisms and Methods," Testimony before the U.S.-China Economic and Security Review Commission, April 14, 2005.

58. I am grateful to Dennis Blasko for bringing this point to my attention. See Article 22, *Law of the People's Republic of China on National Defense*, adopted at the Fifth Session of the Eighth National People's Congress (NPC) on March 14, 1997, Beijing, Xinhua Domestic Service, March 18, 1997.

59. Randall G. Schriver, "Addressing the Rise of China and Rise of Strategic Distrust in U.S.-China Relations," *CSIS Freeman Report*, September 2005, pp. 1-2. Schriver served as Deputy Assistant Secretary of State for East Asia and Pacific Affairs from 2003 to 2005.

# PART III

# NORTHEAST ASIA

# CHAPTER 7

## HOW THE PLA SEES NORTH KOREA

### John J. Tkacik, Jr.

## Introduction: Was North Korea Worth Fighting For?

A half-century ago, Chinese military commanders did not necessarily believe North Korea was worth a war. Consider Chinese People's Liberation Army (PLA) General Peng Dehuai's first direct encounter with the Korean problem at an expanded Politburo meeting in the afternoon of Tuesday, October 4, 1950.[1] He had left his Field Army headquarters in the western Chinese city of Xi'an that morning—suddenly, and under urgent orders to present himself at the Politburo conclave. The Party Center in Beijing had even sent a "silvery" *Illyushin* passenger plane out to the ancient capital of Xi'an to retrieve the General who was, at least that day, the top Communist official charged with the pacification and reconstruction of the nascent People's Republic of China's (PRC) Northwest Bureau.

When General Peng arrived at the old imperial Zhongnanhai compound abutting central Beijing's Forbidden City, he was completely unaware that he would be asked to command China's secret invasion of Korea set to commence in less than 2 weeks.

It was 4:00 pm, and the meeting was already in progress as the General entered the conference room within the ancient Yi Nian Hall. Chairman Mao himself greeted the General and beckoned him to enter. "Old Peng-ah," the Chairman called out in apparent relief that he might now have an ally, "you're just in time . . . sorry we had to call you so suddenly, but the American Imperialists don't let us rest."

The General commented that he had not been in Xi'an but a short time; his family was just settling-in—or "lighting the fire" as they say in Chinese—when he received his orders to Beijing.

"I don't care if your family's lighting a fire," Mao retorted in mock impatience, "our Korean neighbors have just 'lit a fire', and when our neighbors are on fire, we can't sit around crying about it, can we?"

And, (now that he was on the subject) Mao continued that "Korea" was exactly what this Politburo meeting was about — sending troops to Korea, to be precise.

"In a while," the Chairman addressed the General in a courteous third-person syntax, "Old Peng should also be prepared to make a statement."

Peng was caught by surprise. What statement did anyone need of him? Out in northwest China's deserts, he had not really thought much about Korea — nothing at all, really. He knew that the Chairman had deployed 300,000 troops from General Lin Biao's Fourth Field Army, now in Southern China, back to its old Manchurian haunts in August when the North Korean army's invasion stalled under American bombing and strafing runs at the Naktong River. But that was someone else's problem.

He quietly took a chair and ruminated to himself that he had enough problems coping with the post-liberation economic crises in the Northwest Bureau. Moreover, it did not seem that they really needed him here at this meeting — virtually all the attendees were top PLA generals. One more general was not going to be much use.

He was jarred from his reverie by a tug at his sleeve. Next to him on his right was Gao Gang, senior Politburo member and Chairman of the Northeast People's Government that ran Manchuria as a virtual independent country since 1946 and had not yet been brought administratively under the Center's jurisdiction.

"Get ready, Old Peng," Gao muttered. The General gave Gao a puzzled look but got nothing but a knowing smile in return. *Sotto voce*, the General asked Gao when he had arrived in Beijing. "A few days earlier," was the reply. "So, has the Center decided to send troops to Korea?" Gao nodded, then slurped at his tea mug, "on October second" and added "we've already sent a report to Stalin."

"Then why are we still debating it?" "There are still differing opinions . . ." He paused, "let's put it this way, this is a big deal, if it's screwed up, we'll be in a real mess, so let's be prudent about this. . . ." Gao's whisper trailed off.

"You say there're differing views? Whose?" In a low voice, Gao asserted that "an absolute majority is very concerned . . . Mao Zedong is no exception." "And you?" "I'm in the 'against-faction',"

Gao admitted. "Who decided to send in the troops?" "Mao Zedong," said Gao flatly, not bothering to use the title "Chairman" or even the honorific "comrade."

At which point there came a high-pitched Hunanese voice from the head of the conference table. "I say, Gao Gang," Chairman Mao interjected (also dispensing with the "comrade" formalities), "you can't hold your own side meetings here . . . we all want to hear your views, you, with your 'lofty' mountain 'outpost' [a play on Gao Gang's name]. The higher you are, the farther you can see!" At the sound of the Chairman's voice, the room suddenly fell silent. Mao's intervention focused all attention on Gao.

Gao, who obviously was not the Chairman's favorite in the Politburo, screwed up his courage. "I still feel the same way, we should be cautious. Our land has been through over 20 years of war, we've only just been united, a sense of peace has yet to be restored. If we fight again, I'm afraid our economy won't be able to bear the strain. We've only just gained power, we should be thrifty. Fighting a war isn't all fists, it's money . . ."

Looking around the room, Gao continued, "Then there are Lin Biao's views, I think we ought to take them very seriously. Our army has backward weapons, most of them are junk [sanba dagai] from the Japanese. Each American corps has 1,500 artillery pieces, one of ours only has 200, even fewer tanks . . ."

General Lin Biao had evidently made these same arguments when Mao asked him to command the Korean campaign many days earlier. Of all the Chinese generals, Lin had the most operational military experience on the Korean border as chief of the PLA's Fourth Field Army during the Manchurian campaigns. And the brave General Lin was adamant against sending Chinese troops into Korea.

("Who could have imagined that Lin Biao believed this?" was the way the Communist Party's Party History Research Office put it, by way of explaining Lin's suspicious absence from the October 4 meeting.) Lin warned, "rushing headlong into Korea against the Americans can only mean we will all be consumed in flames [yinhuo shao shen]."[2]

Puzzled by Lin's reaction, General Nie Rongzhen recalled "Lin Biao said he was ill, blinding headaches, hot flashes, insomnia; and on that pretext, he obstinately refused to go" to Korea. "This was very strange, for we used to work together, and I had never seen him so frightened of anything."[3]

Korea wasn't important either to General Lin Biao or Chairman Gao Gang. Even if the Americans were to occupy the entire peninsula, in their view, the threat to China was minimal. And most historians agree that the general consensus among the Chinese Politburo in September and October 1950 was against Chinese participation in the war. The logistical strains alone would overwhelm China's fragile economy which was just emerging from the Chinese Civil War, the military risk of confronting a United States armed with atomic weapons was grave, and much of Southwestern China had still not been pacified despite the defeat of Chiang Kai-shek's main force armies.[4]

Yet, when it dawned on him that he was going to lead the battle in Korea, General Peng Dehuai gave an ironic rebuttal to those in the October 4, 1950, Politburo meeting who said China's entry into the Korean War would severely damage China's economy. He asked them, "what are the ramifications of *not* entering the war?" He warned that "in the past, Japan has used Korea as a springboard for aggression into China."[5] As passionate as Peng's words seemed to be, it is unlikely that this argument actually swayed anyone — Peng also cheerily pointed out, ". . . if we are devastated, it would just mean that our victory in the War of Liberation would be several years late [*dalanle, dengyu Jiefang Zhanzheng wan shengli ji nian*]."[6] This deadpan observation, no doubt, was intended as cold water on Chairman Mao's enthusiasm. Instead, Chairman Mao played it as support. The Chairman, himself, favored entering the war, and as long as he had at least one other sane individual backing him up — tongue in cheek or otherwise — the rest of the Politburo apparently was willing to follow suit.

But with 50 years of hindsight, it is now clear that Mao was in a distinct minority if he truly considered Korea to be of dramatic strategic importance to China. Apparently in an effort to prod the Politburo into supporting him, the Chairman told an expanded Politburo meeting on October 2, 1950, that he had, that very day, sent a telegram to the Soviet leader, Marshal Stalin, confirming that China would move 12 divisions of Chinese troops into North Korea, beginning October 15.

In all probability, Chairman Mao, recent archival revelations now indicate, was testing the waters. In fact, Mao had sent an entirely different telegram to Marshal Stalin on October 2, indicating that perhaps North Korea was not all that important to China's security. Mao explained that China would *not* immediately send troops to Korea after all.

> However, having thought this over thoroughly, we now consider that such actions may entail extremely serious consequences. In the first place, it is very difficult to resolve the Korean question with a few divisions (our troops are extremely poorly equipped, there is no confidence in the success of military operations against American troops), the enemy can force us to retreat.

> In the second place, this will provoke an open conflict between the USA and China, and as a consequence of which the Soviet Union also can be dragged into war, and the question thus would become extremely large.

> Many comrades in the CC/CPC [Central Committee of the Communist Party of China] judge that it is necessary to show caution here.[7]

There are several explanations for Mao's duplicity. Perhaps Mao wanted to give himself room to back down if his Politburo rebelled. Perhaps he wanted to pressure Stalin for vastly more military aid than Stalin theretofore had been willing to provide.

In any case, Mao's *real* telegram to Stalin (as opposed to the one in the Chinese archives which apparently was never sent[8]) reflects a realization that North Korea was not as strategically important as the "lips and teeth" metaphor might suggest. The idea that the United States had any intention whatsoever of invading Chinese territory simply was not credible in the Chinese Politburo. In retrospect, one is led to believe that Mao made the ultimate decision to enter the Korean War primarily to demonstrate that China, under his leadership, was ready to lead the Socialist Revolution in the East.

This is not to say that the Chinese leadership lacked a sense of responsibility or loyalty to their North Korean socialist comrades. North Korean archives seized when the U.S. Army occupied Pyongyang in October 1950 show that the Communists' People's Liberation Army (PLA) had several divisions of ethnic-Koreans fighting in Manchuria during the first part of the 1945-49 Chinese Civil

War.[9] Korean War scholar Bruce Cumings cites estimates that assert 15-20 percent of PLA troops in Manchuria in 1947—"fully seventy thousand"—were ethnic Koreans, and a Joint PLA-North Korean-Soviet Military Council controlled the movements of all troops and materiel across the Sino-Korean border in support of the Communist side during the Civil War in Manchuria.[10] The PLA began detaching ethnic Korean infantry divisions back to North Korea as early as 1948, and by the beginning of the Korean War, 80 percent of Korean People's Army (KPA) officers had served in China. By the autumn of 1950, at least 100,000 ethnic Korean troops were veterans of the Chinese Civil War, some of whom had fought "all the way down to the 'last battle' for Hainan Island in May 1950."[11]

### The PRC-DPRK Alliance.

This was a relationship "sealed in blood" in the Chinese Civil War and the Korean War that followed immediately after. But North Korea's leader Kim Il Sung (himself a creation of Stalin) remained deeply suspicious of China's potential influence within his own military.[12] No doubt the Beijing purges of pro-Soviets in the Chinese Communist Party (CCP) leadership in 1954 following Stalin's death sharpened Kim's worries. And no doubt, the CCP leadership was sensitive to Kim's suspicions. In the early 1960s, the pressures of the Sino-Soviet ideological dispute impelled China to conclude a rather broad treaty of alliance with North Korea, an alliance unlike any others in its utter lack of hedging. Article II of the Treaty signed in 1961 requires China, in the event of an armed attack against North Korea, to "immediately render military and other assistance by all means at its disposal."[13] China also is required "to adopt *all* measures to prevent aggression" against the North. There are no provisions for head-scratching or shilly-shallying should the *casus belli* for "aggression" against the North be unclear. Indeed, China's commitment to defend the North Koreans is articulated far more directly and categorically than the Soviet-North Korean alliance, signed just 5 days before.[14]

To China's credit, it made sure that Article IV of the Treaty also obliged North Korea to "continue to consult . . . on *all important international questions* of common interests." In return, North Korea persuaded China to "render . . . every possible economic and technical aid in the cause of socialist construction" including "scientific and technical cooperation." Moreover, Article VII deprives China of any possible legal way to unilaterally revise or terminate the alliance should relations with North Korea become strained. In fact, one Chinese scholar recommended a renegotiation of the alliance to gain leverage with both Pyongyang and Washington, a suggestion that was ignored—though not removed from the Chinese internet site that published it.[15] Thus far, the PLA appears completely committed to the precise terms and spirit of the treaty.

Despite this relationship "sealed in blood," Chinese military strategists are no doubt asking themselves, "*Is* North Korea Still Worth Fighting For?"

**The PLA's Strategic Concerns in Korea.**

China has had a peculiarly possessive relationship with North Korea for millennia. In 2003, Chinese archeologists and linguists resurrected an ancient controversy by claiming that most of the Korean peninsula, running down as far as the 38th Parallel, had been governed for 700 years by a Chinese king and essentially had been a Chinese Kingdom—and before that, it was part of China.[16]

Koreans in general view the kingdom in question, known in Korean history as "Koguryo" (and in Chinese as "Gaogouli"), as one of their most glorious dynasties. Nonetheless, the claim made its way onto the website of the Chinese Foreign Ministry and throughout 2004, horrified South Korean scholars and diplomats demanded a retraction, an explanation, and promises that Chinese academics would never allude to it again. In August, Jia Qinglin, the fourth ranking member of the CCP Politburo, visited Seoul and supposedly reached an unpublicized "oral agreement" on the controversy. But just days later, the CCP propaganda department blocked Chinese domestic access to the Chinese pages of Seoul's *Chosun Ilbo*, pages which reported the Jia Qinglin compromise, and completely shut down an ethnic-Korean website in China that also reported the Jia visit.[17]

But North Korea was oddly circumspect—"Some Great Power-minded historians in other countries are scheming to erase *Koguryo* history and our nation-state's traditions and position" was about as direct as the Democratic People's Republic of Korea (DPRK) media got. Pyongyang's reticence puzzled South Korean observers who commented that "North Korea draws its legitimacy from *Koguryo*, so it would be difficult for it to continue to remain silent . . ."[18] Since then, Pyongyang has remained silent—except to say that *Koguryo* was indeed a "Korean" nation, a "model kingdom," and worthy of Korean emulation.[19]

Pyongyang's equanimity toward Chinese assertions of historical sovereignty over a good part of North Korean territory was odd— like Sherlock Holmes's "dog that didn't bark." But like so much of the Chinese-North Korean relationship, a relationship that is husbanded by deeply secretive bureaucrats and ideologues on both sides of the Yalu River, the reasons for Pyongyang's complaisance are hidden from view. Few Chinese scholars—if any—are willing or able to comment on it or any other aspect of Beijing-Pyongyang ties with any authority. And even fewer from the Chinese PLA.

Yet both Chinese and North Korean military commanders certainly have very sophisticated strategies to manage their relationship. And these strategies often are reflected indirectly in open sources, and in unguarded comments to foreign diplomats and scholars.

Historians of Sino-North Korean relations understand that links between China's PLA and the KPA predate both the founding of the People's Republic and the Democratic People's Republic—and their friendship is "sealed in blood," as both Chinese and DPRK military leaders insist every time they meet. That friendship undoubtedly underwent a metamorphosis during the Sino-Soviet ideological schism from the late 1950s through the collapse of the Soviet Union in 1991, as the North Korean leadership skillfully played off Beijing and Moscow (mostly in Moscow's favor). And when the Union of Soviet Socialist Republic's (USSR) demise left North Korea without a generous great-power patron, China was quick to step in to prevent a similar collapse of its little Korean socialist brother. It is apparent that Chinese strategists no longer see North Korea as strategic real estate essential to an outside aggressor—like the hegemonic United States—which may want to invade Manchuria. Rather, North Korea's survival has now become essential to China, which does not want to see a unified Korea emerge on its borders as a large, advanced industrial state with a modern military and nuclear weapons.

Pyongyang is one of Beijing's last remaining revolutionary allies (although it is no longer even "communist" in name), yet it has become a major liability. It is an economic disaster held together only by outside aid. It is a ruthlessly "feudal" dictatorship that most Chinese have a hard time stomaching. It is a reckless nuclear brinkman. And it is a major source of social instability and violent lawlessness in China's Yalu-Tumen border areas.

How the PLA (as opposed to the rest of the Chinese foreign policy establishment) intends to postpone Korean unification while mitigating the liabilities of the Pyongyang regime is a question that appears to be at the heart of its 21st century strategy for Northeast Asia. Understanding the PLA's dilemma requires an historic perspective, a strategic examination, and a look at the available evidence of military-to-military contacts over the past few years.

For over 2,100 years, Chinese strategists considered the Korean Peninsula either a part of China or a vassal state. Since the end of the 19th century, however, the Chinese have seen Korea as a potential corridor of invasion; first by Tsarist Russia, then Japan, and now by the United States. As one Chinese strategic writer, Senior Colonel Shen Weilie of China's National Defense University, writes:

> The Northeast Asia region has been the locus of several instances of Imperial Russian and Militarist Japanese aggression; and now it has again become an area where the strategic interests of the United States, Russia, Japan, and China clash. Although the United States is far removed on the shores of the Eastern Pacific, nonetheless, as a superpower, it has established a so-called U.S. defensive front line on the island chain abutting our nation in the Western Pacific and Northeast Asia from Japan to Korea. Moreover, it has set up many military bases and deployed troops, signed treaties of military alliance with Japan and Korea, whose strategic target is China, and has thereby become a main adversary that threatens the security of China's northeast.[20]

Colonel Shen's thesis is that U.S. aggression in the Korean War directly threatened the security of Northeast China, and that after the war, Japan experienced a metamorphosis, turning from a "major economic state" into a "major political-military state" which aims to become the "central player" (*fahui 'zhongxin zuoyong'*) in the Western Pacific, and particularly in Northeast Asia. Colonel Shen believed that Japan refuses to acknowledge its historical criminal behavior in its aggression against China and, in this failure, Japan is witness to the resurgence of militarism. As such, Japan also is a potential adversary that threatens the security of China's northeast. On the other hand, China and Russia have reached a strategic understanding and are now partners in Asia. And, with the final demarcation of the Sino-Russian border in the Far East, "Russia will not again become a threat to China's security." The situation on the Korean Peninsula, says Shen, always has been unstable, and "is a potential flashpoint in Asia." As soon as military conflict erupts, it will pose a grave threat to China's security.[21]

In short, says Colonel Shen,

> in any future anti-aggression war to defend the national security of China's northeast, the U.S. and Japanese military alliance and the U.S.-ROK [Republic of Korea] alliance under U.S. hegemonism and Japanese militarism, the seaborne aggression may come from the Yellow Sea area of the Liaodong Peninsula, while the land invasion still may come from the area of the Korean Peninsula, and the air attacks will come mainly from bases in Japan and South Korea.[22]

Following the terrorist attacks against the United States on September 11, 2001, one would think Chinese strategists would either be relieved that America's attention would be distracted from China (which is indeed a sentiment I heard during a closed conference October 6-8, 2001, in Shanghai between The Heritage Foundation and the Shanghai Institute for Strategic Studies), or at the very least would worry that the United States would suddenly achieve a strategic presence in Central Asia. It is surprising that the Chinese also argued that "under the pretext of the opportunity offered by anti-terrorism, the United States expanded and strengthened their military presence in Northeast Asia." This situation was complicated when the United States intercepted intelligence that North Korea had a "nuclear program" and was "exporting guided missiles." According to the China Institute of Contemporary International Relations [CICIR], North Korea was still the "biggest problem in the Asia-Pacific region left over from the Cold War" and the two sides

(United States and DPRK) were plagued by mistrust. Both sides were "playing the nuclear card." The United States used it to "impede the over-rapid progress of DPRK relations with Japan and the ROK," while the DPRK used the nuclear card to "drag" the United States into a dialogue "in an effort to improve relations with the United States."[23]

Obviously, this view of the overland vulnerability of China's Northeast provinces (Manchuria) to an attack from Korea has been influenced by the PLA's experience in the Korean War. Still, it is very difficult to believe that the Chinese military has any fear that the United States (or anyone else) will ever again plan to invade Manchuria via North Korea. Nonetheless, that is the published story, and the PLA is sticking to it for the time being.

It is clear that the opposite is the case, that the PLA sees North Korea as a strategic problem—not as a corridor for invasion of China's northeast—but in its own right.

## China's Interests in Korea.

The late Nobel laureate Francois Mauriac would have understood China's current Korean dilemma. In 1952, the French writer explained that he "loved Germany so much," he was "glad there are two of them."

China likewise loves Korea very much. The collapse of the Pyongyang regime would result quickly in a unified peninsula of 70 million Koreans with a world-class heavy industrial base, advanced technology, wealth, a massive modern military machine (with who-knows-how-many nuclear devices) and—last, not least—an irredentist claim on nearly 18,000 square miles of China's Changbai Mountain (Korean: "Paektu-san") region, which is regarded as the birthplace of the Korean race.[24]

In private discussions with U.S. academics, senior PLA strategists have commented that "Korea is a victim of East-West confrontation . . . reunification should not jeopardize another country's security."[25] No doubt, the other country is China. The last thing China wants, therefore, is another powerful, assertive and sullen neighbor on its borders.

In March 1994, a group of U.S. intelligence community Asia specialists gathered near Washington with colleagues in academia and think tanks for a round-table discussion of North Korea. Their unclassified views no doubt were informed by a broad spectrum of information sources, as well as their own professional intuition.[26]

The consensus of the conferees was that China's primary strategic objective on the Korean Peninsula was to impede (if not delay indefinitely) North-South unification. In the aftermath of the disintegration of the USSR, North Korea's preeminent patron had ceased the provision of significant amounts of aid. North Korea was in the midst of an industrial and agricultural catastrophe and in total economic collapse; unless China—or someone—intervened, the crisis would eventually precipitate unification under Seoul's ROK government. Faced with this, China was not overly concerned about North Korea's withdrawal from the Nuclear Nonproliferation Treaty (NPT) and its repudiation of safeguards under the International Atomic Energy Agency (IAEA) in January of that year. While China might prefer a non-nuclear North Korea, the conferees believed, "it is willing to live with ambiguity." But Korean unification was something China would work hard to avoid.

China's objectives, therefore, were to prevent economic and social chaos in North Korea by infusions of massive amounts of food and energy aid—preferably *not* paid for by the Chinese government. At the time, China was accepting North Korean currency in payment for all exports to the DPRK. One Chinese expert explained in July 1993 that

> we have not reduced economic aid. We are still supplying the same level of oil exports, only now we no longer accept barter, but insist on trade in dollars. In fact, however, we have not demanded any hard currency. The change is only a written policy, but has not been implemented. In the past, we had barter trade and North Korea had nothing to provide us, so it built up debt—now it has no hard currency, so it is still building up debt. They owe China a lot . . . We don't force them to pay.[27]

The massive amounts of food and fuel aid that North Korea needed to avoid a meltdown would have to come from the developed world—and with the approval of the United States.

## The PLA Role in the 1993-1994 Nuclear Crisis.

Accordingly, China saw the 1993-94 nuclear crisis as an opportunity to bring about some form of Washington-Pyongyang *rapprochement* and to "begin the process of integrating North Korea into the world community."[28] This objective was very much in Beijing's mind when it normalized relations with Seoul in 1992.

China nevertheless was concerned that the United States would use the nuclear crisis to play a dominant role in Northeast Asia under cover of multilateralism. Instead, Beijing wanted to assure itself of the primary role in determining the fate of the Peninsula. *In extremis*, the conferees judged, Beijing could abandon its stance of nonintervention on the Peninsula, using direct and assertive diplomatic pressure on Pyongyang or "even intervene militarily" if it perceived the North Korean situation to be dangerous to its national security.

But a nuclear-armed North Korea was not viewed in 1993 as a major problem by Chinese scholars closely associated with the PLA. One was asked, "Could China live with a North Korea having the bomb?" The response was "Yes, I can live with it. I wouldn't like North Korea having nuclear weapons, but it is inevitable for more and more countries to have nuclear weapons."[29] In July 1993, then-CCP Politburo Standing Committeeman Hu Jintao visited Pyongyang with an entourage of PLA generals to celebrate jointly the 40th anniversary of the "victory of the Korean Liberation War [sic]." In his speech at the festivities, Comrade Hu "welcomed the positive progress achieved in the Korean-U.S. dialogue and hoped that the involved parties would solve existing problems through continued dialogue and consultation based on equality."[30] Since North Korea, just 10 days before, had managed to get U.S. negotiators in Geneva to "support the introduction of LWRs [light water reactors] and . . . explore with the DPRK ways in which LWRs could be obtained," Hu's sentiments were understandable.[31] Evidently, the CCP and the PRC government were of the opinion that North Korea's nuclear policies made "positive contributions to maintaining peace and stability in Asia and throughout the world."[32] Significantly, this last phrase, which once presaged optimism for a peaceful settlement of the North Korean nuclear issue, was to return again a decade later.

In 1994, as North Korea's economy went into a free fall and whole provinces sank into starvation, Beijing was terrified that North Korea would implode. Chinese leaders feared hundreds of thousands of refugees would stream into Manchuria, and that eventually China would have an assertive unified Korean nation poised on its northeast border like the unified Germany that appeared in Europe after the collapse of communism there. A "soft landing" for North Korea became China's strategic imperative.

Imperative to China, maybe, but not to whomever was in charge in Pyongyang. By March 1994, it was clear to all that the DPRK was dragging its collective feet on the nuclear issue. At one point, a DPRK negotiator at Panmunjom, apropos of nothing, declared "Seoul is not far from here. If a war breaks out, it will be a sea of fire." The war crisis that followed is well-chronicled in Don Oberdorfer's 1997 book, *The Two Koreas*. Suffice it to say, by mid-June, all sides in the Korean crisis had itchy fingers on their triggers. When the Chief of the KPA General Staff, General Choe Kwang, arrived in Beijing on June 7 for long-planned meetings, there were reports that Chinese President Jiang Zemin was to warn North Korea to accept negotiations on the nuclear crisis. According to reliable reports, however, "it has been learned this is not true."[33]

Apparently, what was true was that General Choe was consulting in depth with the PLA on preparations for a war. A North Korean military delegation was in China in February 1994; KPA Major General Kim Hak-san, director of the Foreign Affairs Bureau of the North Korean Army, met PLA Chief of General Staff General Zhang Wannian in March. And educated speculation was that General Choe Kwang's trip was in preparation "for 'an emergency on the Korean peninsula' since he is the one who controls the general command of 'military operations' under the Supreme Commander and Chairman of the National Defense Committee, Kim [Jong]-il."[34]

For their part, the PLA leaders were saying all the right things. General Zhang Wannian warmly welcomed his KPA counterpart and gushed that "the Armies of the two countries of China and the DPRK have a long tradition of friendly relations" and emphasized "the friendship concluded between the people and Armies of the two countries through blood ties is invincible." The next day,

Chinese Defense Minister Chi Haotian repeated to General Choe that the "Armies of the two countries fought shoulder to shoulder . . . opposing the Japanese imperialist aggressors, and that during the fatherland liberation war, they shed blood and fought together in one dugout against the U.S. imperialist aggressors." And, as if he hadn't mentioned "blood" enough, Minister Chi again "emphasized that the friendship between the two countries was truly bonded by blood."[35]

In Chinese President Jiang Zemin's meeting with General Choe, Jiang apparently did not even broach the nuclear issue. He did, however, repeat that Beijing-Pyongyang ties were "interdependent, like teeth and lips." Jiang insisted to Choe that "we are satisfied with the current development of relations between the two parties and countries. Strengthening and developing Sino-Korean friendship is a firm policy of our party and government, and it also is the wish of our entire party and the people throughout the country. We will make an effort for this on our part."[36] These were hardly the words of one ally trying to walk a reckless partner back from the brink.

One foreign interlocutor, hopeful that China's message to the North Korean militarist was at least tough in private, confidentially queried a Chinese strategist about Chairman Jiang's words, asking "maybe [Jiang] said very different things in private [to Choe] than he said in public." The Chinese counterpart explained the facts of life to the American. "I don't know what was said privately, but what Jiang said publicly means something. I think that if Jiang had said different words in private, then he would not have said such positive things in public."[37]

Given that the possibility of economic sanctions against the DPRK was, at that precise time, under serious review in both the United Nations (UN) Security Council and the International Atomic Energy Agency (IAEA), and that Pyongyang had preemptively declared that sanctions would be regarded as "a declaration of war," it would have been unthinkable for either the PLA or the KPA *not* to prepare for the unthinkable.

How far the "unthinkable" might go was anyone's guess. But a respected South Korean journalist wrote from Hong Kong on June 11 what he considered to be a reliable report that "China promised to send a ground army of approximately 85,000 troops to North Korea if a war breaks out." KPA General Choe had, according to the report, reviewed the entire panoply of military assistance and operations with his PLA brethren in Beijing, including credit assistance for Chinese food and fuel if UN economic sanctions were imposed. Another source told the journalist in some detail that under the PRC-DPRK alliance treaty, three divisions of the 39th Mechanized Group Army (about 50,000 to 75,000 men) from the Shenyang Military Region (MR) and 10,000 Rapid Deployment Troops from the Jinan MR would be ready for deployment to Korea in the event of hostilities.[38]

The sources, some of which were described as "Western diplomats," said the PLA movements would only be ordered if North Korea was invaded by the United States, but that if North Korea invaded South Korea, "China will not directly provide military support to North Korea, except for spare parts or ammunition for the Chinese-made weapons North Korea currently possesses."[39]

Another reputable Hong Kong journalist, Jen Hui-wen, political commentator at Hong Kong's respected *Hsin Pao* newspaper, filled in the outlines of this message in a later article. China, he said, believed an effective strategy to deal with the pressures on the DPRK required that: 1) the DPRK should never initiate any shooting; 2) the DPRK's reaction to international sanctions should be commensurate with the sanctions, but should not be an overreaction; 3) in order to avoid friction, the KPA should be removed a distance from the demilitarized zone; and, finally, 4) that "a political solution is the best strategy, stalling is the second best strategy, conflict is a bad strategy, and taking the initiative to launch an attack is the worst strategy. It should not emphasize the word 'fighting,' it should emphasize the word 'talking'."[40]

These, apparently, were not trial balloons from a Chinese source to the South Korean, but rather a signal that had already been received by "Western diplomatic sources" in Hong Kong, that the PLA and the KPA were well along in the combat planning aspect of the nuclear crisis. The PLA was involved in the diplomacy of the nuclear crisis as well. *Hsin Pao* reported that Jiang Zemin, as Chairman of the Central Military Commission (CMC), addressed a PLA forum on June 9, 1994, where he posited a "denuclearized Korean peninsula" and "peace and stability on the Korean peninsula" as China's two strategic goals in the nuclear crisis. Jiang reported that a CCP delegation led by Politburo propaganda chief Ding Guangen, accompanied by Wen Jiabao (then an alternate Politburo member), General Wang Ruilin (Deng Xiaoping's military confidant), and veteran Manchurian MR commander Li Desheng had been sent to the DPRK to sensitize Pyongyang to China's concerns.

The fine print of this politico-military delegation's presentation is instructive. The Ding delegation told its North Korean counterparts that 1) China would "do what it could" to support economic reforms in the DPRK; 2) if the DPRK developed nuclear weapons, China would be opposed; and, 3) if the DPRK was attacked, China would fulfill its obligations under the PRC-DPRK alliance treaty. [41]

### The PLA's Role in the 2002-Present Nuclear Crisis.

There is considerable circumstantial evidence indicating that the PLA leadership has coordinated with its KPA counterparts to the same extent that it did prior to the July 1994 negotiations that ultimately led to the Agreed Framework. On April 19, 2003, just 6 days before the first session of U.S.-PRC-DPRK "Three Party Talks" on North Korea's nuclear weapons program, Pyongyang suddenly announced that the KPA's top commander, General Jo Myong Rok, would visit Beijing from April 21-23. The terse one-line press release was not posted in English until the following day. [42] While the purpose of General Jo's visit was never announced, Seoul's *Yonhap* news agency quoted Chinese sources as saying "his trip was seen as aimed at fine-tuning its talks stance with China." [43] A DPRK press report issued after Jo's departure reported that "Jo Myong Rok and General Pak Jae Gyong and Colonel General Pak Sung Won of the KPA" had met with Chinese CMC Vice Chairman Guo Boxiong and CMC members General Xu Caihou and General Xiong Guangkai. "Jo also met and had a friendly talk with" PRC Defense Minister (and state councilor and CMC vice chairman) General Cao Gangchuan. [44] The following day (April 22), General Jo's party also conferred with Chinese President (and CMC Chairman) Jiang Zemin in a meeting again attended by Generals Guo, Xu, and Xiong, as well as vice foreign minister Wang Yi. [45]

The level of General Jo's meetings, and the comprehensive array of Chinese military leaders with whom he met, was firm evidence that the General's visit was intended to coordinate a bilateral position on the talks with the American negotiators who arrived in Beijing the same day that General Jo's party departed. But the "Three Party Talks" abruptly ended 2 days later after only a few hours of meetings, when the North Korean representative reportedly "pulled aside Assistant Secretary of State James A. Kelly and in effect told him: 'We've got nukes. We can't dismantle them. It's up to you whether we do a physical demonstration or transfer them.'"[46]

Chinese negotiators evidently painted this shocking behavior on the part of the North Koreans as unexpected. Chinese Foreign Minister Li Zhaoxing, said *The New York Times*, "did not seek to disguise the fact that the talks had broken down," and the *Times* headline speculated that "North Korea May Be Angering Its Only Ally."[47] But this was hardly the case. While Chinese diplomats may have been hinting at some distress at the DPRK's shenanigans, at no time did the foreign ministry ever utter a cross word about Pyongyang's stance.

Four months later, in August 2003, on the eve of the first round of "Six Party Talks" in Beijing—this time including representatives from South Korea, Japan and Russia, supposedly to act as witnesses to North Korea's antics and thereby to moderate them—the same routine played out. On August 17, China announced that General Xu Caihou, would make a quick visit to Pyongyang—no date mentioned.

The following day, the delegation arrived—and met with the same cast of characters who had visited Beijing in April. The Chinese delegation left Pyongyang on August 23 "after winding up its 5-day visit."[48]

On August 27, the first session of "Six Party Talks" began in Beijing. In that session, the North Koreans continued to vituperate their threats and insults, saving the most pointed jibes for the hapless Russian deputy foreign minister to whom the North Korean delegate referred by name as a "liar" and a "lap dog" of the Americans.[49] Moreover, the North Koreans refused to budge from their insistence on the right to develop and maintain a nuclear arsenal. Even Russia's normally sympathetic Deputy Foreign Minister Alexander Losyukov was said to have shaken his head in dismay and mutter, "there go 55 years of history."[50] The Russian remained noncommittal in public and would only "suggest" in private "that the North Koreans had not been listening to Mr. Kelly's presentation."[51] The session ended acrimoniously but was nonetheless painted as "a good beginning" by the State Department.[52]

China, however, remained firmly in North Korea's corner. The weekend after the talks, Chinese Vice Foreign Minister Wang Yi declared that "the main problem we are facing" was not North Korean histrionics, but "the American policy towards [the] DPRK." This, after the vice minister was described by all present at the six-party talks (in an unmistakable incidence of mass hallucination) as "visibly angered" by the North Korean delegates' outbursts.[53]

Again, the PLA and its North Korean counterparts had engaged in lengthy talks immediately prior to multiparty nuclear talks in Beijing—talks that were marred by North Korean bombast and insults. Meanwhile, as Chinese diplomats evinced frustration with the North Koreans during the closed negotiation session, in public they blamed the United States for the impasse.

There were no press reports of similar PLA-KPA coordination in anticipation of subsequent rounds of "Six Party Talks" in February or June 2004, or in July, September, or November 2005, but it is likely that they occurred. At the end of October 2005, Chinese CMC Chairman Hu Jintao visited North Korea and met DPRK Leader Kim Jong Il. Ten days later, the "first session of the fifth round of the Six Party Talks" began in Beijing and, again, ended with no progress.[54] It is apparent that Chinese leaders, especially its military commanders, were in close contact with their North Korean counterparts immediately prior to each round of nuclear negotiations, and it is therefore highly unlikely that the Chinese were surprised by anything that the North Koreans did at those sessions.

### Fortifying the Sino-Korean Border.

Close coordination of diplomatic negotiating positions, however, was probably the least concern of the PLA's Korea strategists. When the North Korean nuclear crisis erupted again in October 2002, China was left as the only world power with any sway over North Korea.

Over 88 percent of all North Korean oil comes from China (the rest comes in aid from the West) as does more than 90 percent of North Korea's non-aid food imports.[55]

In the 8 years since 1994, North Korea's economic condition had not improved, and pressures along the Sino-Korean border had steadily increased. By August 2003, economic and social tensions in Manchuria from the flood of North Korean migrants (and lawless KPA soldiers) had grown so bad that the imminent deployment of 150,000 regular PLA soldiers had become common knowledge in Hong Kong. Hong Kong press reports said the PLA was replacing People's Armed Police (PAP) border troops in an effort to bring under control a Korean crime wave on the border. The deployments were confirmed indirectly by the Chinese foreign ministry, which said the new troop dispositions were meant to streamline administration of the border and was "a normal adjustment carried out after many years of preparation by the relevant parties."[56]

Mysteriously, for 2 weeks in July 2004, the PLA conducted river-crossing maneuvers complete with floating bridges on the Yalu River near the major Korean border city of Sinuiju. Reportedly, the drills involved placing 10 floating bridges out to the middle of the Yalu, but not beyond. One observer told a Japanese newspaper that "we witnessed a few hundred of soldiers, but considering the fact that there were about 100 tents that can accommodate up to 10 soldiers each pitched near the river; I guess there were a total of 1,000 soldiers participating in the training."[57]

While the PLA was conducting precautionary maneuvers along the Yalu River border, the CCP was still trying to assuage North Korea's political sensitivities. In July 2004, when a Chinese scholar published a rather intemperate policy blast at North Korea—charging "Dear Leader" Kim with starving his people, and commenting favorably on President Bush's antipathy toward the DPRK regime, the CCP propaganda department not only expunged the offending work from the Internet, but also recalled all print issues of the offending publication, *Strategy & Management*, and shut down the publication altogether.[58]

One Hong Kong magazine reported that one of the first things Communist Party General Secretary Hu Jintao did upon ascending to the Chairmanship of the CMC was to issue a document declaring that "although North Korea has suffered temporary economic difficulties, in politics it has been consistently correct."[59]

The CCP Politburo Standing Committee's propaganda czar, Li Changchun, then visited Pyongyang on September 24, and repeated the encomium of a decade earlier:

> [Li Changchun] said all nations and all peoples, benefit from this nation's [the DPRK's] practical choices and determination of its own road to development, and this is advantageous to the formation of all manner of characteristic theories and policy lines of social development, and advantageous to the realization of the people's wealth and happiness, to the embodiment of the multi-polar world, and also is fundamentally beneficial to the protection of regional stability and world peace. He expressed that China will continue to support North Korea's party and people in their insistence on the socialist road to development, and support the North Korean comrades in their exploration for development models that are suitable to this nation's [DPRK's] actual situation, and support the Korean side's calls for Juche and peaceful unification, and *support the positive force that North Korea has put forth in improving the international environment.* (Emphasis added)[60]

Sympathetic as the CCP party-hacks may have been to North Korea's "development model," the PLA was keeping its powder dry. In October 2004, the PLA deployed an additional 10,000 regular soldiers to reinforce another 20,000 troops in China's Tumen River border area in a move that reportedly startled Western intelligence agencies. A Japanese newspaper said the move was intended to prevent North Korean soldiers from crossing the border. The troops apparently needed extra assistance from police dogs because the following week, there was a report that every police dog unit in North Korea had been deployed away from the Demilitarized Zone and transferred up to the Sino-Korean border to stem the flow of Korean migrants—and the PLA committed to providing the necessary supplies of dog food.[61] The Chinese foreign ministry confirmed the troop movements but insisted the troops were sent to the border to help with a "communication engineering project."[62]

For a change, the foreign ministry spokesman was stating the simple truth. According to a Shenyang MR logistics department officer, "the communications infrastructure along the Chinese-Korean border is very advanced." The system includes electronic monitoring technology to assist border patrols. Said the Shenyang MR officer, "every single road that is monitored by a surveillance camera can be viewed by the CMC back in Beijing."[63] Another Chinese periodical confirmed the deployments in 2005, noting that then-Chinese CMC Chairman Jiang Zemin personally approved funds for the construction and renovation of over 100 military base camps along the Korean border.[64]

The PLA then discovered that elaborate electronic surveillance systems are no substitute for manpower. Five armed North Korean bandits crossed the Yalu river at Guangping in Yanbian Korean Autonomous Prefecture on October 16, 2005, an area within the responsibility of the Jilin Provincial Military District, and killed a 19-year-old PLA soldier in a nighttime gunbattle. The doomed soldier, four other troopers, and a PLA officer had gotten the Chinese equivalent of a "911" call and had hustled out to a remote vacation villa in the border town of Guangping to rescue several tourists and hotel workers who were being held hostage by the bandits. The bandits escaped into nearby woods and presumably slipped back across the border into North Korea.[65]

The inescapable impression is that the PLA views the PRC-DPRK border region as porous and lawless. It is not unexpected, then, that the PLA gives every appearance of planning to do something about it.

**Peace Mission 2005: The Korea Scenario.**

On the surface, any joint China-Russia military exercise that begins in Vladivostok with a "strategic planning" exercise, and then continues on with separate joint amphibious landing and airborne demonstrations on China's Shandong peninsula has to raise suspicions that the two nations are practicing for a North Korea contingency. China actually billed *Peace Mission 2005* (PM2005), which was held between August 18-25, 2005, as a simulated mission "to aid a third state where law and order has broken down because of terrorist violence" according to *The Washington Post*.[66] The Associated Press described "a fictional scenario" where Russia and China "have been given a UN mandate to stabilize a country plunged into violence by ethnic strife."[67]

Indeed, terrorism is a major consideration for China, Russia and their "Shanghai Cooperation Organization" (SCO) allies, all of whom were invited to send military intelligence officials to the drills—as were SCO observer nations India, Pakistan, and Iran. The *Peace Mission 2005* operation plan centered on a coordinated Russian seaborne and airborne landing near a coastal town, "in advance of an inland offensive coordinated with the Chinese military."

Preliminary reporting from Western media set the China-Russia PM2005 military drill in the context of "mutual unease at U.S. power and a fear of Islamic extremism in Central Asia," and Russia's particular concerns about "the United States' expanding military presence in oil-rich Central Asia." The Chinese Ministry of National Defense statement of August 1, 2005, declared that the exercises were meant to "strengthen the capability of the two armed forces in jointly striking international terrorism, extremism and separatism." But it was clear from the beginning that Moscow did not want anything to do with China's designs on "separatist Taiwan" and insisted against Chinese pressure that the plans take place in Central Asia—or some place far away from Taiwan.

According to one Japanese magazine, PM2005 was entirely China's idea[68]—and was entirely paid for by Beijing.[69] Beijing was paying for the show, so a compromise was reached—Vladivostok and Shandong. While China no doubt hoped that the exercise would send a signal to the United States that China was determined to take Taiwan whatever the cost, there was little in *Peace Mission 2005* that had "Taiwan" written on it. The naval staging was unopposed, the beach landings met minimal opposition—"62 minutes of pitched battle in the pouring rain" according to *Xinhua*. The Russian paratroop drops were to link up with an "inland offensive"—apparently by Chinese troops coming in force from another direction.

And there was certainly nothing in it relevant at all to "Central Asia." Indeed, the Russians were reported to have asked to hold the maneuvers in China's western deserts, bordering on potential Central Asian havens for real terrorists and extremists. PM2005's centerpiece, however, was PRC-Russian naval coordination of a beach landing and a near-shore airdrop. There are, after all, no beaches and no shorelines in Central Asia.

On the contrary, the more one looks at *PM2005*, the more it looks like it was a very serious effort to plan for the collapse of North Korea. On August 19, the PRC-controlled *Wen Wei Po* newspaper in Hong Kong speculated that the Shandong site indicated that China and Russia were preparing for problems with North Korea — as well as Taiwan.[70] From its Korean War experiences, the Chinese PLA is all too aware of the problems of penetrating the mountainous border areas between China and the DPRK in an effort to occupy the political centers in and around Pyongyang. It makes far more sense to stage beach landings on North Korea's western shores somewhere on the 50 miles of flat shorelines north of Nampo port and move smartly inland 20 miles to Pyongyang.

China's military planners easily can imagine North Korea's economy in full collapse, and Chinese border troops can estimate that the existing stream of North Korean refugees would turn into a full-fledged human-tsunami. But in a state of collapse, the Chinese army cannot assume that the DPRK leadership or the army will simply disappear. Nor can the PLA assume that the South Koreans will not want a piece of the action — and this concern may have inspired the PLA Navy to establish a "military hot line" with South Korea in April 2005.[71]

They understand all too well that the sole function of the DPRK's military leadership is "the preservation of the memory of the leader" (i.e., Kim Il Sung) at the absolute core of the "Kim il sung Constitution."[72] This duty will be carried on "generation after generation." As such, the DPRK's guiding ideology of "Army First" (*Songun*) — which replaced "Self Reliance" (*Juche*) as the supreme light of North Korean wisdom — places the "Army above the workers and peasants"; and the Army is the "supreme organ of state power" (not the Korean Workers' Party, much less the DPRK government). Any Chinese military planners who contemplate offensive operations inside the DPRK will have to deal with the KPA one way or another. It will likely be a tad tricky to persuade North Korea's leader Kim Jong Il and his army "whose sole mission is to defend the headquarters of the revolution headed by Kim Jong Il at the cost of their lives,"[73] to quietly lay down their arms.

PM2005 is a plausible indicator that the Chinese military is planning for a possible invasion and occupation of North Korea —

perhaps even under the auspices of the UN and at least in nominal partnership with the Russian Federation. And China would, of course, impose a pro-China civil government in Pyongyang that will be committed wholeheartedly to the eventual "unification" of the Korean Peninsula at some point in the coming millennium, or shortly thereafter. After all, North Korea (or *Gaogouli*) has been Chinese territory more often than not in the past two millennia, so what real difference would another century or two make?

The operational aspects of PM2005 seem also designed to keep the United States at an arms-length when such an occupation takes place.[74] Chinese and Russian naval operations included, said *The Washington Post*, "strategic long-range bombers capable of carrying nuclear weapons, which will fire cruise missiles at targets on the surface of the sea." There was also a test firing from the Russian destroyer *Burny* of a Russian-made *Moskit* supersonic anti-ship cruise missile that is designed to keep U.S. carriers and other surface combatants away, but there was only one reported anti-submarine drill and no shipboard air defense drills.

**Mystery Boats, Mystery Planes.**

Although the very peculiar relationship between the Chinese and North Korean militaries rarely comes out into view, a few anecdotes will give a flavor of how close they are. For example, during the evening of December 22, 2001, three suspicious maritime vessels — which looked for all the world like Chinese fishing boats — were challenged by a Japanese Coast Guard cutter in the East China Sea some 390 km west of the island of Amami-Oshima in Kagoshima Prefecture. As the Japanese cutter approached the flotilla, it came under automatic weapons and anti-tank missile fire from one of the ships. When one of the "fishing boats" launched a missile in its direction, the Japanese cutter responded with a withering volley which apparently disabled the ship. But rather than let the Japanese authorities board the boat, its crew scuttled the vessel and it quickly sank — with all hands. The other two ships fled the scene under very high speed.

The Japanese Coast Guard had challenged the boats because their peculiar behavior led the Japanese to suspect they were North

Korean spycraft. Their suspicions were confirmed when underwater cameras revealed that the craft's fishing bridge, which had separated from the hull and lay in the seabed several meters away, was a dummy structure. Video of the remains of the sunken ship's crew in 90 meters of water also indicated that at least some of the crew had committed suicide, and the rest had been shot with small arms.

Despite considerable diplomatic pressure from China (which insisted that the sunken ship was in Chinese waters), Japanese salvage ships eventually brought the spyvessel to the surface, and put it on display at the Museum of Maritime Science in Tokyo. The mystery boat may have looked like a fishing vessel, but it had 4,000 horsepower engines and a top speed of 30 knots. It also had wide doors in the stern, which could permit smaller vessels to launch secretly, no doubt in order to conduct clandestine operations. And the vessel carried a hefty arsenal of weaponry including rocket launchers, an 82mm bazooka, an antiaircraft machine gun, and two surface-to-air missiles.

But the most curious aspect of the incident was a report in Tokyo's respected *Asahi Shimbun* newspaper that quoted several government officials as saying that Tokyo has obtained U.S. satellite photos showing a vessel looking identical to the alleged spy ship calling at a Chinese military port some 100 km south of Shanghai and 130 km northwest of the spot where it sank on December 22. Japanese officials cited by *Asahi* believed the ship at the Chinese naval berth was either the one that was sunk or a very similar one that left North Korea around the same time. Japanese Defense Agency Director General Gen Nakatani told a separate news conference, "I cannot comment on details of information we receive from the U.S. military. I cannot say whether such information has been provided to us."[75] In contemplating this incident, American and Japanese policymakers must have been left scratching their respective heads, "Why on earth is the Chinese navy providing basing for North Korean special operations vessels?"

Consider another example. In July 2002, U.S. intelligence-collectors had happened upon a Pakistani military C-130 transport plane that had flown through Chinese airspace carrying a cargo from Pakistan's top-secret nuclear weapons base, the Khan Research

Laboratory. The C-130's cargo was probably $75 million worth of equipment relating to a uranium enrichment centrifuge. It landed at a Chinese military base to refuel, and proceeded on to North Korea. The aircraft returned to Pakistan carrying a North Korean *Nodong* ballistic missile, again, via a refueling stop at a Chinese military base.[76] The flights were only the latest in a series of secret Pakistani C-130 missions to North Korea that dated back at least to 1998.[77]

While the North Korean military seems to have a special relationship with its counterparts in Chinese military intelligence, there is certainly much skepticism about the value of keeping company with the North Koreans among China's nonintelligence military analysts.

Just what exactly the PLA thinks about North Korea is a mystery to outside observers. This is partially due to the secretive nature of PLA strategic thought, partially to the less-than-monolithic composition of PLA strategists, but mostly due to conflicting evidence in the meager historic record. Senior Colonel Shen Weilie's theories about the Korean Peninsula as a corridor for aggression against China notwithstanding, the way the PLA acts on the Korean border reflects a PLA consensus that North Korea is a strategic conundrum all its own — and, when the time comes, the PLA will be fully prepared to deal with it by force.

## ENDNOTES – CHAPTER 7

1. The dialogue that follows is based on Ye Yumeng, *Hei Xue, Chubing Chaoxian Jishi* [*Black Snow, A True Account of Entry Into the Korean War*], Beijing: Zuozhe Chubanshe [Authors' Publishers], 1988, pp. 46-47. Whether Mr. Ye based this on a transcript of the meeting that somehow picked up the side conversation, or reviewed Gao Gang's confession file (following his purge and death in 1954) or embellished existing files with fictional dialogue is unclear. I suspect that the meeting was recorded via several microphones around the conference table in order to catch incriminating comments.

2. Zhang Xi, "Peng Dehuai Shou Ming Shuai Shi, Kang Mei Yuan Chaode Qianwian Houhou" ["Peng Dehuai Appointed to Lead the Troops, Background for the Korean War"], in *Zhonggong Dangshi Ziliao* [*CCP Party History Materials*] Issue 31, Beijing: Zhonggong Dangshi Ziliao Chubanshe, 1989, p. 126.

3. Nie Rongzhen, *Inside the Red Star, the Memoirs of Marshal Nie Rongzhen*, Beijing: New World Press, 1988, p. 636. This is a fairly accurate English translation of *Nie Rongzhen Huiyi Lu*, published in 1986.

4. See, for example, Shen Zonghong, ed., *Zhongguo Renmin Zhiyuanjun Kang Mei Yuan Chao Zhanshi* [*The Chinese People's Volunteer Army's Military History of the War against the United States and in aid of North Korea*], Beijing: Junshi Kexue Chubanshe [Military Science Publishers], 2nd ed., December 1990; pp. 3-9. Hong Xuezhi, *Kang Mei Yuan Chao Zhanzheng Huiyi* [*A Memoir of the Korean War*], Beijing: Jiefangjun Wenyi Chubanshe [People's Liberation Army Literary Publishers], November 1990, p. 10.

5. Zhang Xi, pp. 133-134.

6. Peng Dehuai, *Peng Dehuai Zishu* [*Peng Dehuai's Confession*], Beijing: Renmin Chubanshe, December 1981, p. 258. Also see Nie Rongzhen, p. 636.

7. *Cold War International History Project [CIHP] Bulletin*, Issues 6-7, Winter 1995/1996, pp. 114-115 (with photocopy of the original telegram in Russian).

8. See Shen Zhihua, "The Discrepancy between the Russian and Chinese versions of Mao's 2 October 1950 message to Stalin on Chinese entry into the Korean War: A Chinese Scholar's reply" in *CIHP Bulletin* Issues 8-9, 1996/1997, pp. 237-242.

9. The entire State Department volume entitled *North Korea: A Case Study in the Techniques of Takeover*, Publication 7118, Far Eastern Series 103, released in January 1961 by the Superintendent of Documents, U.S. Government Printing Office, Washington, DC, was based on these archives and on debriefs of captured Korean People's Army officers.

10. Bruce Cumings, *The Origins of the Korean War, Vol. II, The Roaring of the Cataract 1947-1950*, Princeton, NJ: Princeton University Press, 1990, pp. 351-376. See also Chen Jian, *China's Road to the Korean War, The Making of the Sino-American Confrontation*, New York: Columbia University Press, 1994, pp. 109-111.

11. *Ibid.*

12. Cumings, p. 365.

13. A text of the *Treaty of Friendship, Co-operation and Mutual Assistance between the People's Republic of China and the Democratic People's Republic of Korea* is found in Sukhee Han, "Alliance Fatigue amid Asymmetrical Interdependence: Sino-North Korean relations in Flux," *The Korean Journal of Defense Analysis*, Vol. XVI, No. 1, Spring 2004, pp. 177-179.

14. *Ibid.*

15. As recently as September 2003, some Chinese scholars had published recommendations that China unilaterally declare Article VII void and renegotiate the terms of the alliance. See Shen Jiru, "Weihu Dongbeiya Anquande Dangwushiji — Zhizhi Chaohe Wentishangde Weixianboyi" ["An Urgent Mission to Maintain Security in Northeast Asia — Control Risk from North Korean Brinkmanship"], in *Shijie Jinji yu Zhengzhi* [*World Economy and Politics*], No. 9, 2003, pp.53-58, at *www. iwep.org.cn/wep/World%20Volume/2003/2003,9/shenjiru.pdf.*

16. See Tan Qixiang, ed., *Zhongguo Lishi Ditu Ji* [*Cartographic Compendium of Chinese History*], Beijing: Cartographic Publishing House, 1985-89, Vols 2-10. Tan Qixiang's work is considered the authoritative Chinese historical work on China's boundaries with its Asian neighbors. See Vol. 2, pp. 27-28; Western Han Dynasty (from 221 BCE to about 8 CE). *Youzhou* is shown as China Proper stretching from near present-day Beijing in the west across the *Liaodong* Peninsula to cover over half the Korean Peninsula in the east. Vol 2, pp. 61-62, shows Eastern Han China (to 220 CE) as comprising *Yuelang Jun* which covered the Western half of the North Korea, the Eastern half occupied by a suzerain state, *Gaogouli*. Vol. 3, pp. 13-14, shows the Chinese Kingdom of *Wei* (one of the Three Kingdoms) retaking the northern half of the Korean peninsula. Vol 3, pp. 41-42, shows the Western *Jin* dynastic borders encompassing the same territory. Vol. 4, pp. 3-4, depicts *Gaogouli* as a Chinese kingdom during the Eastern *Jin* and the 16 Kingdoms period, co-equal with the Former *Qin*, eastern *Jin*, and several other smaller principalities. By the Northern Dynasty period (ending 464 CE), *Gaogouli* is delineated as a kingdom separate from China. Vol. 5, pp. 32-33; at the beginning of the Tang Dynasty (606 CE), *Gaogouli* is once again incorporated into metropolitan China's "Marches North of the River," *Hebeidao*. Vol. 5, pp. 36-37, show the post-An Lushan rebellion (741 CE) Tang Dynasty Korean Peninsula south of present-day Pyongyang as a non-Chinese realm of *Xinluo*, while Korea from Pyongyang north is divided between Metropolitan China's Qidan, and a suzerain Chinese kingdom of *Bohai*. This demarcation persists in the Five Dynasties and Ten Kingdoms period (the Tenth Century CE), Vol. 5, pp. 78-79. The non-Chinese kingdom of *Gaoli* then pushes north to the mouth of the Yalu River by Liao-Northern Song Dynasties, with the rest of Korea north and east of the Yalu's mouth subsumed into the *Nyuzhi* principality (Vol. 6, pp. 8-9). This swath of Korea becomes part of the "East Capital Route (*Dongjinglu*) in China's Jin Dynasty (according to a Chinese map of 1134 CE). After that period, Korea was occupied by the Mongolian armies of Chinggiz Khan, and reoccupied by Chinese at the end of the Mongols' Yuan Dynasty. For a description of the controversy see James Brooke, "China Fears Once and Future Kingdom," *The New York Times*, August 25, 2004, at *www.nytimes.com/2004/08/25/international/asia/25korea.html*.

17. (No author cited), "Bi Tan Gaogouli, Liang Hanguo Wangzhan Guanbi" [Prevent Discussion of Koguryo, Two Korean Websites Shut Down], *China Times*, Taipei, August 30, 2004. For Jia's visit to Seoul see *Agence France Presse* report, "China Drops Claims to Ancient Korean Kingdom" carried in the *Taipei Times*, August 25, 2004, p. 5, at *www.taipeitimes.com/News/world/archives/2004/08/25/2003200148*.

18. (No author cited), "Why Is North Korea Silent on Koguryo?" *The Chosun Ilbo*, Seoul, August 8, 2004, at *english.chosun.com/w21data/html/news/200408/200408080018. html*.

19. (No author cited), "Pyongyang Says Koguryo Kingdom is Model for Unified Korea," *Yonhap* News Agency, Seoul, September 23, 2004, at *english.yna. co.kr/Engnews/20040923/300200000020040923113422E9.html*. This article appeared during the visit of CCP Politburo member Li Changchun to Pyongyang.

20. Shen Weilie and Lu Junyuan, eds., *Zhongguo Guojia Anquan Dili* [*China's National Security Geography*], Beijing: Shishi Chubanshe [Contemporary Affairs Publishers], September 2001, page 386. (Hereafter ZGAD). Although labeled "INTERNAL PUBLICATION" [Neibu Faxing], the author purchased his copy at the main Shanghai *Xinhua* Bookstore in October 2001.

21. *Ibid.*

22. *Ibid*, p. 402.

23. Lu Zhongwei, ed., *Guoji Zhanlue yu Anquan Xingshi Pinggu* 2002/2003 [*International Strategic and Security Review 2002/2003*], Zhongguo Xiandai Guoji Guanxi Yanjiusuo [CICIR], pp. 160-162.

24. Tsinghua University international studies professor Chu Shulong says out loud that the Chinese government is not in a hurry to see a unified Korea, "it brings up the question of our Korean minority and how they will react if Korea is one again." See Jehangir S. Pocha, "Separated by River and Reform — One Country Busy Catching Fish, Another Enjoys the View," Calcutta, *The Telegraph*, November 29, 2005, at *www.telegraphindia.com/1051129/asp/frontpage/story_5536195.asp*. My personal notes say Chu Shulong, unlike many other Chinese foreign affairs exports, served in the military and continues to have very close ties with a wide range of military personnel. He joined the PLA Air Force when he was still in his teens and came up through the ranks to become a teacher at an air force academic institute. The PLA air force sent him to graduate school in China, but he did not return to the military after getting a degree. Rather, he went to the China Institute for Contemporary International Affairs (CICIR).

25. Memorandum dated June 25, 1993, in author's personal files.

26. Personal notes of a meeting on "Korean Outcomes and Major Power Interests: Implications for the United States" held under the auspices of the Office of the Secretary of Defense OSD/RSA/EAPR and the Defense Nuclear Agency on March 17, 1994.

27. Memorandum dated July 2, 1993, in the author's personal files.

28. Personal notes of March 17, 1994.

29. Memorandum dated June 13, 1993, in author's personal files.

30. "Hu Jintao's Activities in DPRK Reported; Addresses Pyongyang Banquet," *Xinhua* Domestic Service in Chinese 1408 GMT, July 28, 1993, in *Foreign Broadcast Information Service-China* (henceforth FBIS-CHI)-93-144.

31. Donald Oberdorfer, *The Two Koreas: A Contemporary History*, Reading, MA: Addison-Wesley, 1997, p. 291.

32. See "Greeting the 45th Founding Anniversary of the Democratic People's Republic of Korea" an editorial in *Renmin Ribao* [*People's Daily*], September 9, 1993, p. 1; at FBIS-CHI-93-175.

33. Sin Yong-su, Envoy Denies PRC Warned DPRK on Negotiations, *Kyonghyang Sinmun*, Seoul, June 9, 1994, p. 1; at FBIS-EAS-94-111.

34. Yu Yong-ku, "Significance of Choe Kwang Visit to PRC Viewed," transcribed from *Chungang Ilbo*, Seoul, June 7, 1997, at FBIS-EAS-94-109.

35. "DPRK Military Delegates' PRC Visit Reported," Pyongyang Korean Central Broadcasting Network, June 8, 1994, at FBIS-EAS-94-111.

36. Zhang Rongdian, "Jiang Zemin Meets DPRK Military Delegation," transcribed from *Xinhua*, Beijing, June 7, 1994, at FBIS-CHI-94-110. "*Xinhua* Cited on PRC, DPRK High-Level Meeting," transcribed from Yonhap, Seoul, June 8, 1994, at FBIS-CHI-94-110.

37. Memorandum dated June 21, 1994, in author's personal files.

38. Kim Song-yong, "Daily Reports PRC To Send 85,000 Troops If War Breaks Out," Transcribed from *Choson Ilbo*, Seoul, June 12, 1994, p. 1, at FBIS-CHI-94-113.

39. *Ibid*.

40. Jen Hui-wen "Beijing Political Situation: Inside Story About China Briefing DPRK on How To Act," transcribed from *Hsin Pao*, Hong Kong, June 24, 1994, p. 25, at FBIS-CHI-94-122.

41. *Ibid*.

42. (No author cited), "First vice-chairman of DPRK NDC to visit China," KCNA, April 19, 2003, at *www.kcna.co.jp/item/2003/200304/news04/21.htm#13*.

43. (No author cited), "North Korea Says It's Ready For Talks," *The Taipei Times*, April 20, 2003, p. 1 (citing Reuters News Agency), at *www.taipeitimes.com/News/front/archives/2003/04/20/202750*.

44. "Jo Myong Rok's sojourn in Beijing," KCNA, April 23, 2003, at *www.kcna.co.jp/item/2003/200304/news04/23.htm#10*.

45. "Chinese President meets Jo Myong Rok," KCNA, April 24, 2003, at *www.kcna.co.jp/item/2003/200304/news04/24.htm#8*.

46. Glenn Kessler, "N. Korea Claims to Have Nuclear Weapons, US Officials Say," *The Washington Post*, April 25, 2003, p. A-01.

47. Joseph Kahn, "North Korea May Be Angering Its Only Ally," *The New York Times*, April 26, 2003, p. A-01, at *www.nytimes.com/2003/04/26/international/asia/26KORE.html*.

48. "High-level Military Delegation of China to Visit DPRK," KCNA at *www.kcna.co.jp/item/2003/200308/news08/18.htm#14*; "High-level Military Delegation of China Arrives," KCNA, at *www.kcna.co.jp/item/2003/200308/news08/19.htm#9*; "Jo Myong Rok Meets Chinese Military Delegation," KCNA, at *www.kcna.co.jp/item/2003/200308/news08/19.htm#10*; "Chinese Military Delegation Winds Up Its Visit to DPRK," KCNA at *www.kcna.co.jp/item/2003/200308/news08/23.htm#13*.

49. Private conversation with U.S. government officials. See the Author's Heritage Foundation Backgrounder #1717, "Time for Washington to Take a Realistic Look at China Policy" at *www.heritage.org/Research/AsiaandthePacific/bg1717.cfm#pgfld-1071493*.

50. *Ibid.*

51. David E. Sanger, "U.S. Said to Shift Approach in Talks with North Korea," *The New York Times*, September 5, 2003; p. A-03.

52. See "State Department Background Briefing Attributable To A Senior State Department Official Re: Six-Party Talks On North Korea" at the State Department Briefing Room, Washington, DC, September 4, 2003, transcript provided by Federal News Service, Inc.

53. Joseph Kahn, "Chinese Aide Says U.S. Is Obstacle in Korean Talks," *The New York Times*, September 2, 2003, at *www.nytimes.com/2003/09/02/international/asia/02KORE.html*.

54. The July-August "fourth round" of talks was continued for a "second session" ending September 19, 2005. The "Statement of Principles" that emerged on September 19 was, at best, a restatement of the "Agreed Framework" of 1994, and could hardly be called "progress." See John Tkacik, "Agreed Framework, Part Deux," Hong Kong, *Far Eastern Economic Review*, September 2005 (published September 23, 2005), pp. 21-24, at *www.feer.com/articles1/2005/0509/p021.html*.

55. Statistics on North Korean trade are spotty at best, nonexistent at worst. Assistant Secretary of State for East Asia and Pacific Affairs James Kelly told a U.S. Senate hearing on September 11, 2003, that "China is the supplier of last resort to North Korea of fuel, and I would say food as well. Numbers of perhaps some $500 million a year turn up with some regularity. It's not clear how much of that is paid for by the North Koreans." See "U.S. Senator Richard G. Lugar (R-IN) Holds Hearing on Relations with China," September 11, 2003, Verbatim Transcript by Federal Document Clearing House. The Food and Agriculture Organization estimates that North Korea agricultural imports in 2003 were about U.S.$284 million (see FAO webpage at *www.fao.org/es/ess/toptrade/trade.asp?lang=EN&country=116*). See also Nicholas Eberstadt, "Statistical Blackouts in North Korea: Trade Figures Uncovered," *Beyond Transition*, World Bank, Washington, DC, March-April 1998, at *www.worldbank.org/transitionnewsletter/marapr98/pgs21-23.htm*.

56. Philip P. Pan, "China Deploys Troops on N. Korea Border," *The Washington Post*, September 16, 2003; p. A13. See also Christopher Bodeen, "China Assigns Army to Guard Korean Border," The Associated Press, September 15, 2003.

57. Won-Jae Park, "People's Liberation Army Trains River Crossing at Aprok River," Seoul *Donga Ilbo* in English, August 8, 2004, at *english.donga.com/srv/service.php3?bicode=060000&biid=2004080953828*.

58. The article apparently appeared in July, but was not noticed until mid-August. See Wang Zhongwen, "Yi Xin Shijiao Shenshi Chaoxian Wenti yu Dongbeiya Xingshi" ["Examining the DPRK Issue and Northeast Asian Situation from a New Viewpoint"], Beijing *Zhanlue Yu Guanli* [*Strategy and Management*], No. 4, July/August, pp. 92-94, transcribed by FBIS at CPP20040825000196. For a full description of the incident, see John J Tkacik, Jr., "China's 'S&M' journal Goes Too Far on Korea," *The Asia Times*, Bangkok, September 2, 2004, at *www.atimes.com/atimes/China/FI02Ad06.html*.

59. Yu Senxue, "Hu Jintao Jiuzhi Jianghua Shaqi Tengteng" ["Hu Jintao's Inauguration Speech Filled With Sound and Fury"], Hong Kong *Kaifang*, No. 216, December 2004, p. 13.

60. Luo Hui, "Jin Richeng hui Li Changchun: Chaozhong Renmin Chuantong Youyi Bu Ke Po" ["Kim Jong Il Sees Li Changchun: The Traditional Friendship Between the Peoples of the DPRK and China Is Unbreakable"], *Xinhua*, September 12, 2004, at *www.people.com.cn/GB/shizheng/1024/2778612.html*.

61. (No author) "Zhong-Chao Bianjing Zhujunquan, Fang Jumin Tiaotou" ["PRC-North Korea Border Police Dogs Intended to Stem Flow of Migrants], Taipei *China Times*, October 18, 2004. (Cites Seoul *Chosun Ilbo*.)

62. Kang Chan-ho, Ser Myo-ja, "Chinese Reinforce Border Near North," Seoul *Joongang Daily*, October 13, 2004, at *joongangdaily.joins.com/200410/13/20041013222 0434579900090209021.html*.

63. (No author), "Han, Mian Liang Bianjing Gai you Junfang Zhushou, Jieti Wujing chengdan Fangwu, Bianjing Tuxiang ke zhijie da Beijing" ["Borders with Korea, Myanmar Will Now Be Guarded By Military, Replacing Armed Police and Assuming Defense Duties, Border Images Can Be Viewed Directly From Beijing"], New York, *World Journal*, November 22, 2005. Report cites "the latest issue of *Liaowang Eastern Weekly*, a subsidiary of Xinhua."

64. *Ibid.*

65. "Zhong-Han Bianjing Bao Qiangzhan, Ren Xunxhi" ["Gunfight at the China-North Korea Border, Chinese PLA Soldier Killed In Action"], New York *World Journal*, December 13, 2005, p. A-08. Cites *Changsha Wanbao*.

66. Peter Finn, "Chinese, Russian Militaries to Hold First Joint Drills; Alliance May Extend to Arms Sales," *The Washington Post*, August 15, 2005; p. A10, at *www. washingtonpost.com/wp-dyn/content/article/2005/08/14/AR2005081400927.html*.

67. Burt Herman, "Chinese-Russian Military Exercises Begin," *The Associated Press*, August 19, 2005.

68. (No author cited), "Assault Landing Requested by China; Display of its Capability in Dealing With Taiwan?" Transcribed by FBIS, Tokyo *Kyodo Clue II* (Internet Version) August 18, 2005, at FBIS JPP20050818000018.

69. (No author cited) "E Bao: Ejun Yanxi, Zhongguo Maidan" ["Russian Paper: China Foots Bill for Russian Military Exercise"], Taipei *China Times* Internet Edition, August 19, 2005.

70. cited in FBIS Analysis: PRC Media On Sino-Russian Military Exercise FEA20050831007588 — FBIS Feature — 1304 GMT August 31, 2005.

71. (No author), "Huwei Huang Hai, Zhong Han She Junshi Rexian, 'Chaoxian Ribao' beilou, Nanhan yu Dalu jiu haijun hezuo da gongshi, you zhu Hainan Zhengqiu, fangfan tufaxing chongtu" [Protect the Yellow Sea, PRC-ROK Establish Military Hot Line; *Chosun Ilbo* Reveals South Korea and Mainland Reach Consensus on Naval Cooperation, To Aid in Sea Emergencies and Rescue, Guard Against Sudden Confrontations"], *New York World Journal*, April 17, 2005, p. A-08.

72. North Korea is not governed by a "Korean Constitution" but a "Kimilsung Constitution." See "Kim Il Sung Constitution," Korean Central News Agency (KCNA), Pyongyang, December 26, 2005, at *www.kcna.co.jp/item/2005/200512/news12/27.htm#8*. This document officially is praised as follows: "The world history of constitution has not known such constitution as one of the DPRK which is run through with the revolutionary outlook on the leader to perpetuate the memory of the leader."

73. "National Meeting Marks 14th Anniversary of Kim Jong Il's Assumption of Office as KPA Supreme Commander," KCNA in English, December 23, 2005, Pyongyang, at *www.kcna.co.jp/item/2005/200512/news12/24.htm#11*.

74. In addition to pacifying an occupied North Korea, China, at least, may also want to know where North Korea's government archives are. Who knows what secrets may fall into the wrong hands if North Korea is suddenly absorbed by South Korea after an economic collapse? See "DPRK, China Cooperate in Documentary Field," Korean Central News Agency, August 13, 2005, at *www.kcna.co.jp/item/2005/200508/news08/15.htm#1*.

75. David Ibison, "Pyongyang's spy ship reveals a dark secret," *Financial Times*, May 28, 2003, p. 3. See also (No author), "U.S. Photos Show Mystery Ship Look-Alike," *Japan Times*, March 2, 2002, sourcing *Asahi Shimbun*, p. 1; "Japan Ends Ship Probe," *Japan Times*, March 2, 2002 (sourcing Kyodo News Agency).

76. David E. Sanger, "In North Korea and Pakistan, Deep Roots of Nuclear Barter," *The New York Times*, November 24, 2002, p. A-01. Danny Gittings, "Battling the Bribers," *Asian Wall Street Journal*, October 29, 2002, p. 18. William C. Triplett II, "Road to Pyongyang through Beijing?" *The Washington Times*, February 21, 2003, p. A18. On September 11, 2003, Senator Feingold asked Assistant Secretary of State James Kelly "about North Korean planes flying through Chinese airspace or even making refueling stops in China when these planes may well be involved in proliferation activities. . . . have we raised this issue with the Chinese?" Kelly responded "Yes, sir, we have raised that issue with the Chinese. It would probably be best to brief you more completely on that particular topic in a closed hearing, sir." See U.S. Senate Committee On Foreign Relations "Hearing On U.S.-China Relations, September 11, 2003."

77. Paul Watson and Mubashir Zaidi, "Death of N. Korean Woman Offers Clues to Pakistani Nuclear Deals," *The Los Angeles Times*, March 1, 2004.

# CHAPTER 8

## THE PLA, JAPAN'S DEFENSE POSTURE, AND THE OUTLOOK FOR CHINA-JAPAN RELATIONS[1]

### Robert G. Sutter

## INTRODUCTION

The Chinese People's Liberation Army (PLA) is broadly influenced by the many nationalistic and other political issues that have served to bring about the most serious deterioration in Sino-Japanese relations since the establishment of diplomatic relations over 30 years ago. More concretely, PLA priorities evident notably in recent Chinese National Defense White Papers reflect a number of key national security issues with Japan that on the whole are worsening in recent years.

The outlook for China-Japan relations is uncertain and subject to debate among U.S. and other specialists. Regarding the PLA, it remains unclear exactly what role in Chinese leadership deliberations over policy toward Japan is played by PLA priorities regarding Taiwan and securing territorial integrity and strategic resources such as oil and gas. On the whole, the PLA priorities clearly emphasize the negative and support those who argue that Sino-Japanese relations are bound to deteriorate further. Moreover, this year, more than in the recent past, PLA naval forces have been deployed in ways that exacerbate tensions with Japan, worsening relations.

On the other hand, however, this paper demonstrates that there also are powerful reasons why Chinese leaders, as well as Japanese leaders, will seek to avoid further deterioration and restore more businesslike relations. Among them is China's drive to project an image of leadership in Asia as a benign good neighbor, showing flexibility and accommodation to regional partners.

Deepening disputes, rivalry, and conflicts with Japan contradict important Chinese goals at home and abroad. While PLA leaders no doubt share such broad policy goals to some degree, PLA emphasis on national security issues and their obvious negative implications for Sino-Japanese relations means that the PLA will serve as a drag on broader Chinese efforts to establish a position as a trusted partner in Asia with a benign agenda in the broad interest of regional peace and stability.

The debate among U.S. specialists over the outlook for China-Japan relations tends to drive differences among them over the implications of the tense relations for U.S. interests. On the one hand are U.S. specialists who argue that the Sino-Japanese friction is against U.S. interests and the United States should take concrete measures to reduce tensions. Such measures include U.S. efforts to get the Japanese prime minister to stop visiting the controversial Yasukuni war memorial and for Japanese government officials to be more rigorously forthright in accepting responsibility for Japanese aggression in the Pacific War; and U.S. efforts for Chinese officials to curb nationalistic excesses, avoid the widespread perception that Beijing manipulates history and other issues to weaken Japan, and manage territorial and other disputes without popular violence and in accordance with accepted international norms. On the other hand are U.S. specialists who see Sino-Japanese relations as unlikely to deteriorate substantially, as incentives on both sides offset sources of recent tensions. They see U.S. actions in this context as unwise and unwarranted.

## DETERIORATING SINO-JAPANESE RELATIONS

The future stability of East Asia will depend heavily on the relationship between the main regional powers, China and Japan. Relations between the two swung markedly in the post-Cold War period. At first, both powers adjusted their bilateral relations amicably following the demise of the Soviet Union and its strategic influence in East Asia. The rise of China's power and influence in Asian affairs in the 1990s, combined with Chinese military assertiveness over Taiwan and the South China Sea in the mid 1990s, coincided with a protracted period of lackluster Japanese economic performance and weak political leadership. This called into question the past disparity of the economic relationship between the two powers, added to ongoing differences over territorial, strategic, historical, and economic issues, and strengthened the wariness and occasional antipathy between the two countries.[2]

More recently, Chinese relations with Japan have worsened. Chinese government, and specifically PLA concerns with Japan's defense posture, including its notably strengthened alliance relationship with the United States, have added to this trend in worsening relations. The result has seen Chinese and U.S. relations with Japan move in markedly different directions. This has undermined Chinese influence in Japan, while enhancing that of the United States. It also has seriously complicated China's broader strategy in Asia, which is based on a good neighbor policy seeking to enhance China's influence by dealing with Asian countries in an accommodating way, putting aside differences and seeking greater areas of common ground. China's uncompromising approach to and deteriorating relationship with Japan, its most important neighbor, belies Chinese broader declarations of goodwill, accommodation and "win/win" solutions. It prompts Japan, a country with half of Asia's wealth and its most modern military force, to prepare for protracted difficulties and rivalry with China in Asia, while adding to broader regional wariness over Chinese intentions.[3]

The Bush administration has worked assiduously to strengthen the alliance with Japan and has found a willing partner in the Japanese administration of Prime Minister Koizumi. Both sides have played down persisting trade and other disputes as the bilateral relationship has reached new heights of strategic and political cooperation. While Japan also pursues alternative paths to support its national security and other interests, its reliance on the alliance with the United States has deepened to an unprecedented degree. In response, Japan is prepared to take new and more expansive military actions in support of allied interests in Asian and world affairs.[4]

By contrast, China has seen political and security relations with Japan deteriorate markedly despite burgeoning economic trade and large Japanese investment in China. Disputes range widely and involve competing and highly nationalistic views of Japan's military expansion in Asia prior to 1945; territorial and resource conflicts in the East China Sea; rising Japanese concerns over China's military buildup focused on Taiwan and Chinese concerns about Japan's closer cooperation with the United States regarding Taiwan; Chinese concerns over Japan's closer military cooperation with the United States over ballistic missile defense and in regard to international deployments of Japanese forces; Sino-Japanese competition for Russian and other energy resources; and Chinese opposition to Japan's strenuous efforts seeking a permanent seat in the United Nations (UN) Security Council.[5] Several of these issues are of specific concern to the PLA, as was highlighted notably in the Chinese Defense White Paper of December 2004, discussed below.

Popular Chinese anger at Japan saw Chinese demonstrators attack Japanese diplomatic and business installations in China in 2005. The Chinese government allowed the violence to take place for several days before cracking down, suggesting to some in Japan that the Chinese authorities were using the popular outbursts to intimidate Japan. The crisis alarmed many other governments in Asia, fearful that China might follow such forceful policies toward them in the event they differed with China over sensitive issues.[6]

Underlying the crisis was a continuing change in regional power relationships. China's rising power and influence in Asian affairs since the 1990s combined with Chinese military buildup and assertiveness focused on Taiwan and coincided with Japan entering a second decade of poor economic performance. As China loomed larger as Asia's leader in economic growth, Japan responded with deepening concern over its place in Asian and world affairs. This added to ongoing differences over territorial, strategic, historical, and economic issues, and strengthened the suspicion between the two countries. Meanwhile, stronger nationalism in both countries put them at odds over a variety of sensitive issues related to history and territorial claims.[7] Notable in this regard was Chinese concern over a U.S.-Japan declaration on February 19, 2005, where the Japanese government joined the United States in expressing a joint position on Taiwan.[8]

## DEBATE OVER SALIENT TRENDS AND KEY DETERMINANTS IN SINO-JAPANESE RELATIONS

There is an active debate among specialists about the determinants and direction of Sino-Japanese relations. Some experts have predicted an increasingly intense competition, including likely confrontation and possible conflict in future China-Japan relations.[9] They highlight changes in attitudes of Japanese and Chinese decisionmakers, opinion leaders, and popular opinion about the status and outlook of their mutual relations. They tend to see initiatives reflecting strong Sino-Japanese friction and rivalry.[10] Signs of Sino-Japanese competition and rivalry in Asia include:[11]

- Separate and seemingly competing proposals by China and Japan in 2001-02 to establish free trade arrangements with the ten Southeast Asian nations in ASEAN.

- Strong Japanese competition with China to gain improved access to Russian oil in the Far East.

- Greater Japanese support for Taiwan and for stronger U.S. backing of Taiwan during the Bush administration.[12]

- The first significant cutbacks in Japanese aid to China since the normalization of relations in the 1970s.

- Increased Japanese willingness to deploy military forces in Asia in support of U.S. and UN initiatives.

- Stepped up Japanese efforts to improve security, aid, and other relations with India and other nations on China's southern and western flanks, including strong Japanese aid efforts for Pakistan, Afghanistan, and Central Asian countries.[13]

- In the face of China's steadily increasing economic ties and political influence in South Korea, on-again, off-again Japanese efforts to improve ties with Seoul, attempting to ease differences over historical, trade and other issues.[14]

Underlying changes in Japan said to foreshadow greater Japanese-Chinese rivalry involve:

- With the collapse of the Soviet Union and the end of the Cold War, strategic thinkers in the Japanese government and elsewhere in Japan have focused more on China's rising power as the major long-term regional security concern for Japan.

- China's continued remarkable economic growth, along with its rising political and military standing, has prompted more Japanese to view China as a rival for regional influence.

- Previous Japanese sensitivity and responsiveness to Chinese demands for special consideration on account of Japan's negative war record in China over 50 years ago have lessened with the passage of time, the change in Japanese leadership generations, and Beijing's loss of moral standing in Japan on account of its crackdown after the Tiananmen incident, its nuclear testing, and its intimidating military actions against Taiwan and in the South China Sea.[15]

- Undergirding Japan's more critical approach to China is a strong sense of national pride and determination among Japanese leaders and public opinion to preserve Japanese interests in the face of perceived efforts by PRC officials to use charges from the past and recent economic, political, and strategic issues to prompt Tokyo to give way to Chinese interests.

Meanwhile, changes in China said to be leading to greater friction with Japan include:

- Chinese strategists' long-standing concerns about Japan's impressive military capabilities have increased as a result of U.S.-Japanese agreements from 1996 onwards, which, to Chinese observers, appear to broaden Japan's strategic role in East Asia and to provide U.S. strategic support for Japanese politicians wishing to strike a military posture in the region less deferential to China than in the past.[16] U.S. support for Prime Minister Koizumi's strong military actions and deployments to the Indian Ocean in support of the U.S. war against terrorism in Afghanistan during 2001-02 and the Japanese leader's strong stance in support of the U.S.-led attack on Iraq in 2003 and deployment of Japanese forces to Iraq in 2004 represented new developments in this perceived trend.

- Chinese government specialists have acknowledged changes in Japanese attitudes toward China and judged that Beijing appeared likely to meet even more opposition and gain less support from Japan as it sought to expand China's influence in Asian and world affairs. The Japanese decisions to cut aid to China seem consistent with this trend.

- Chinese nationalism has been a focal point of government-sponsored media and other publicity in recent years especially following the Tiananmen Incident and the collapse of communism in Europe and the Soviet Union at the end of the Cold War. Appealing to the sense of China as having been victimized by foreign aggressors in the past, the publicity focused heavily on Japan, by far the most important foreign aggressor in modern Chinese history. The government-sponsored publicity has elicited widespread positive response in China and soured the overall atmosphere of China's relations with Japan.[17]

A contrasting perspective gives greater weight to the common interests and forces that continue to bind Sino-Japanese relations and to limit the chances of serious confrontation or conflict. Mutual interests center on strong, growing economic and strategic interdependence between Japan and China, and the influence of the United States and other third parties, including other national powers in Asia—all of whom favor and could be expected to work to preserve Sino-Japanese stability. Specific elements of the argument against the development of serious Sino-Japanese rivalry involve:

- Both the Japanese and Chinese governments remain domestically focused, and continue to give top priority to the economic development of their countries, which they believe require a prolonged, peaceful, and cooperative relationship with their Asian neighbors, notably one another.

- China depends heavily on Japan for economic relations, for technology and investment, and as a market for Chinese goods; Japan increasingly depends on China as a market, source of imports, and offshore manufacturing base.

- Personnel exchanges between Japan and China have grown markedly. Tens of thousands of Japanese students visit or study in China each year. Government sponsored exchange programs abound, and even if they do not always promote positive feelings, they probably do promote more realistic mutual perceptions.

- Few, if any, governments active in Asian affairs would benefit from or seek to promote greater Sino-Japanese friction. This includes the Bush administration, which is careful to balance its strong pro-Japanese slant with reaffirmation of continued interest in closer mutually beneficial relations with China designed in part to sustain regional peace and stability. Such cooperation is especially important to the United States, and to China and Japan, in regard to efforts to deal diplomatically with the North Korean nuclear issue and related provocations coming from Pyongyang in 2002-05.

- Because the United States remains such a dominant military and economic power in the region, the U.S.-Japan alliance results in a marked asymmetry in Japanese and Chinese perceptions of competition and rivalry. While Japanese elite and popular opinion are more focused on China as a future concern, Chinese elite and popular opinion are more preoccupied with the United States as a possible concern; Japan's role is seen as secondary, the junior partner in one of the U.S. alliances and security arrangements that affect Chinese interests. Given the Chinese focus on dealing with the primary concern posed by the United States, one result that works against Sino-Japanese rivalry is that Chinese officials at times have sought to avoid disputes with Japan and rather have tried to woo Japan away from close alignment with the United States and toward positions more favorable to China.[18]

## THE RECENT TURN FOR THE WORSE

The Asian Economic crisis of 1997-98 added to the already strong preoccupations of leaders in Tokyo and Beijing with their respective domestic problems, especially economic problems. At least for the time being, neither government sought to exacerbate tensions over the array of issues that continued to divide them. Thus, they went ahead with senior leaders' meetings in Tokyo and Beijing, capped by President Jiang Zemin's November 1998 visit to Japan. That visit saw Japanese officials stand firm in the face of Chinese pressure on issues related to Taiwan and the history of China-Japan relations.

Chinese leaders adjusted their approach, as leaders in both capitals endeavored to emphasize the positive and give less public attention to important and often deeply-rooted differences. Lower level commentary in China and Japan made clear such differences over history, the U.S.-Japan alliance, Taiwan, theater missile defense, and competing visions of regional leadership had not been forgotten.[19]

While he emphasized Sino-Japanese economic and other compatible interests, Japanese Prime Minister Koizumi tested Chinese tolerance on the sensitive history issue with his repeated visits to the Yasukuni Shrine — a Japanese war memorial that included commemoration of the Japanese leaders during the Pacific War who were later convicted as war criminals. After his third visit despite Chinese admonitions, Chinese officials made it known in 2003 that the Japanese Prime Minister would not be welcome in Beijing; but they were flexible in arranging a meeting between the Japanese Prime Minister and China's recently installed President at the sidelines of an international summit in Europe in mid 2003. (There were several subsequent meetings between Koizumi and top Chinese government leaders, but none in Beijing.)

At that time, the burgeoning crisis over North Korea's nuclear weapons program and the danger that tensions on the Korean peninsula might escalate and result in military confrontation and war saw Chinese leaders take unprecedented measures to work cooperatively and pragmatically with the United States and others in order to deal with the crisis through diplomatic means. For their part, Japanese officials were anxious to work closely with South Korea, China, and Russia, while Japan relied strongly on close collaboration with the Bush administration in seeking a political solution to the crisis. At bottom, dealing with the North Korean nuclear challenge posed an added preoccupation for Chinese and Japanese leaders that, at least over the short term, reduced the likelihood that they would adopt more assertive and potentially disruptive policies. They presumably were loath to appear to worsen an already delicate situation in ways that could affect their interests adversely in stability, development and security.[20]

The sharp turn for the worse in China-Japan relations seen during the violent anti-Japanese demonstrations in China during April 2005 was marked by concurrent deterioration of relations regarding political and security issues on several fronts, even as economic relations prospered. Prime Minister Koizumi remained unapologetic about visiting the Yasukuni shrine.[21] Another textbook seen to white-wash Japanese aggression prior to 1945 was approved for publication by Japanese government officials. First China, then Japan, engaged in exploitation of gas in disputed waters in the East China Sea. Russia vacillated between strong incentives from Japan and China in determining whether to favor one or the other in building a pipeline to East Asia for Siberian oil. Repeated intrusions into Japanese claimed waters by Chinese "research" and other ships presaged the intrusion of a Chinese nuclear powered submarine that was found and tracked by Japanese forces in Japanese territorial waters near Okinawa. Growing Japanese concern about the implications for Japanese interests posed by the rapid Chinese military buildup focused on Taiwan elicited more explicit Japanese government expressions of concern and a variety of countermeasures, many involving strengthening Japan's alliance relationship with the United States. In this context, Japan engaged in bilateral consultations with the United States over the Taiwan situation; worked in a trilateral forum with Australia and the United States that dealt with Taiwan and other Asian issues; was explicit in noting Japanese government concerns over the Taiwan situation; and backed the United States in seeking curbs on European and Israeli arms sales to China.[22] A large Chinese-Russian military exercise involving naval and air forces in the East China Sea in August 2005 was followed by Japan's detection in September of a flotilla of Chinese warships sailing near a Chinese gas rig exploiting resources in the East China Sea that are claimed by Japan.[23]

Japanese leaders used the marked increase in Japan's international profile seen at the time of Japan's impressive aid and relief efforts after the Tsunami disaster in South Asia in December 2004 to launch a series of high-level international visits and associated economic and other gestures in an effort to garner support for a permanent seat for Japan on the UN Security Council. Despite strenuous government efforts, China remained in the second echelon among tsunami relief donors. The Chinese government opposed Japan's UN bid. As noted earlier, public opinion in China was fed by a long-standing Chinese government media and education campaign to build nationalism by emphasizing the evils done to China by past imperial powers, notably Japan. In these circumstances, whether by design or happenstance, tens of thousands of Chinese responded to an Internet campaign against Japan's UN bid by taking to the streets, with many attacking Japanese businesses and diplomatic properties in April 2005. For several days, the Chinese police attempted to regulate but did not attempt to stop the violent anti-Japanese acts, bringing bilateral relations to the lowest point since the normalization of relations in 1972.[24]

Subsequently, government officials on both sides endeavored to restore order and maintain mutually advantageous business ties. However, neither side gave ground on the various political and security disputes that gave rise to the recent deterioration of relations.[25] Fresh from his success in leading his party to a decisive victory in the Diet election of September 2005, Prime Minister Koizumi again visited the Yasukuni Shrine in October, prompting shrill Chinese protests and cancellation of foreign minister talks to improve relations.[26]

## PLA PRIORITIES AND JAPANESE POLICY AND PRACTICE—ADDING TO THE NEGATIVES IN CHINA-JAPAN RELATIONS

Forces of nationalism, anger over Japanese leaders visiting the Yasukuni Shrine, and outrage over Japanese textbooks white washing aggression in China prior to 1945 almost certainly have an important impact on the feelings of Chinese military leaders and policy inclinations of the PLA. However, the impact of these powerful but often poorly defined sentiments or movements is hard to measure.

This chapter endeavors to focus on the more clear-cut enumeration of PLA concerns and priorities seen in the Chinese National Defense White Paper issued in December 2004.[27] That document in some respects marked an advance in criticizing Japan over a previous White Paper in 2002.[28]

Both the 2002 and 2004 documents gave top priority to the Taiwan issue. Clearly, any perceived effort by Japan supporting

Taiwan separation from China would be viewed as a major concern. Also highlighted in both documents is the PLA determination to protect Chinese territory and territorial claims and to secure strategic resources such as oil and gas. As Chinese-Japanese territorial conflicts grow in scope and intensity, they intrude ever more directly on these PLA priorities.

Discussing the Asian-Pacific regional situation, the 2002 document was vague in noting the sources of such adverse developments as strengthening military alliances and enlarging operations of armed forces. Not so the 2004 White Paper. It first explicitly criticized the United States for "realigning and reinforcing its military presence in this region by buttressing military alliances and accelerating deployment of missile defense systems." It then explicitly criticized Japan for "stepping up its constitutional overhaul, adjusting its military and security policies, and developing the missile defense system for future deployment." The White Paper added further criticism of Japan, that the Japanese government "also has increased markedly military activities abroad."

The evidence of Japanese policy and practice in these key areas of PLA concern and Chinese responses criticizing such Japanese policy and practice (noted below) show that on balance the PLA priorities add to friction in Japan-China relations. They offset continued efforts by military leaders on both sides who continue to engage in some business-like contacts seeking to maintain communications and avoid conflict. They also offset efforts by military and other Chinese officials to cooperate with Japan on such key issues as the Six Party Talks regarding North Korea's nuclear weapons program and the global war on terrorism.[29]

Based on the authoritative White Paper, it also appears that PLA priorities give less attention than other Chinese official commentary regarding China's priority, emphasized repeatedly by top level Chinese leaders, to be seen as accommodating and flexible in dealings with neighbors, seeking wherever possible "win-win" solutions to problems involving China and neighboring states.[30] Some Chinese officials continue to stress China's determination not to be seen as adverse to the United States or its security and other interests in Asia, including its relations with key allies, emphasizing China's determination to develop and rise in influence in a manner that does not disturb Asia's prevailing powers, which are led by the United States and include notably Japan. These themes are central to China's recent foreign policy in Asia, resting on mutually advantageous trade ties, adroit and flexible bilateral and multilateral diplomacy, and "soft power" highlighting the attraction of China to its neighbors.[31]

Unfortunately for Chinese priorities concerning what some Chinese officials have called China's "peaceful rise" in Asia,[32] PLA priorities vis-à-vis Japan add to factors that lead to Chinese policies and actions that widen the gap between China and Japan, solidify China's broadly acknowledged unattractive image in Japan, and complicate China's efforts to reassure Asian neighbors. It remains hard to discern exactly what role in Chinese leadership deliberations over policy toward Japan is played by PLA priorities regarding Taiwan and securing territorial integrity and strategic resources such as oil and gas. On the whole, however, the PLA priorities clearly emphasize the negative and support those who argue that Sino-Japanese relations are bound to deteriorate further. Moreover, this year, more than in the recent past, PLA naval forces have been deployed in ways that exacerbate tensions with Japan, worsening relations.

A review of the successes and failures in China's recent policies with its neighbors in Asia[33] shows that China's greatest failure is in relations with Japan. Given that Japan has half the wealth of Asia and other major attributes and influence, the inability of China to establish a stable and constructive relationship with Japan is a major source of weakness in any Chinese strategy to seek a more prominent role as an accommodating and attractive leader in Asian affairs.

## Taiwan.

Evidence of Japan's growing involvement with Taiwan in ways that are adverse to Chinese interests includes repeated reports of Japanese consultations with the United States, and other U.S. allies, regarding deterring China's use of force against Taiwan, and preparation for actions in the event of such a use of force.[34] The Japanese foreign minister now publicly says that Taiwan is covered under terms of the U.S.-Japan security treaty, which the Japanese government is endeavoring to strengthen.[35] Recent reports in mainstream media say that Japan is redeploying forces to protect southern Japan from Chinese attack, that Japanese officials acknowledge that U.S. marines in Okinawa will play a rapid response role under some Taiwan conflict contingencies, and that retired Japanese military officers are assisting Taiwan in preparing for mine warfare.[36] Official Japanese statements increasingly are explicit about their concerns over the Chinese military buildup targeted against Taiwan, and have joined with the United States in urging a peaceful resolution of the issue. The Japanese prime minister criticized China's March 2005 so-called antisecession law directed at Taiwan.[37] Japan's strong recent commitment to missile defense cooperation with the United States has direct implications for Taiwan, which are discussed below. Japanese politicians travel often to Taiwan and controversial Taiwan leaders like Lee Teng-hui are permitted to visit Japan.[38]

**Territorial Issues.**

The disputed Senkaku/Diaoyu Islands controlled by Japan are at the center of the many active territorial issues between China and Japan. The two governments dispute ownership and the resources (e.g., gas, oil, fish) that are related to the economic zone that comes with the territorial claim.[39] The issue is related to the U.S.-Japan security treaty, which the 2002 and 2004 White Papers seem to criticize. Bush administration officials have claimed that the United States is bound under the treaty to help Japan in the event Japanese forces come under attack protecting the disputed islands.[40] Meanwhile, disputes over how and where to divide competing territorial claims in the East China Sea have become more prominent recently than at any time since the normalization of relations between the two governments in 1972.[41]

**Missile Defense.**

A review of Japanese missile defense efforts and Chinese comments about them show that China views the recently beefed up Japanese efforts as decreasing China's ability to hold Japan at risk, increasing the strength of the U.S.-Japan alliance to compete with China in the region and complicating China's ability to use force against Japan, U.S. forces in Japan, and Taiwan in the event of the conflict over Taiwan.[42] The missile defense efforts planned by Japan in conjunction with the United States clearly diminish the effectiveness of one of the few classes of weapons in which China is superior to Japan: ballistic missiles.[43] China has hundreds of ballistic missiles that can hit Japanese territory. Beijing presumably has the ability to saturate any Japanese missile defense system, but Chinese ballistic missiles have a number of missions, and Beijing presumably would prefer not to be forced to focus them on Japan. Meanwhile, if the Japanese missile defense system, developed in conjunction with the United States, seems successful, it might encourage others to join with the United States and Japan in pursuing a closer missile defense cooperation. Reasons why a successful U.S.-Japan missile defense would affect PLA interests regarding Taiwan include:

(1) Japan would have some more assurance that it could offer assistance to aid American forces and deal with possible Chinese response. This would especially be the case if the U.S. and Japan combined missile defense efforts to protect Japan.

(2) Also, if Japanese ships substitute for U.S. ships guarding against missile attack from North Korea, U.S. ships would be free to help with missile defense for Taiwan.

**Expanded Scope of Japanese Military Activities.**

The recent trend of the Japanese government to break with past precedent and undertake a variety of military actions in support of U.S., UN, or other objectives continues to develop in ways that are of concern to China.[44] Japanese military forces are the most modern in Asia. The Japanese government has now reached a point where Japanese officials discuss preemptive actions against North Korea and push for revision of article nine in the Japanese constitution and other constraints on "normal" use of Japanese military forces. Feeding back to Chinese concern over the strengthened U.S.-Japan alliance, the Japanese efforts to undertake more security responsibilities and revise the constitution in ways that allow even greater scope for Japanese military activities abroad are welcomed and encouraged by senior U.S. officials.

## "Shaping" China's Role in Asia.

The Bush administration has been explicit that U.S. policy in Asia remains unsure whether a rising China will be a friend or foe, a force for stability and development, or a source for disruption. They point to what they see as positive elements in China's growing influence and negative aspects. They prudently prepare for both. In this regard, they work closely with Japan, seeing the U.S.-Japanese alliance as the key foundation for U.S.-led efforts to "guide" China onto the right paths and to deter China from taking the paths opposed by the United States.[45] The latter involves U.S.-Japan discussions on dealing with Chinese military expansion, threats to Taiwan, and related questions. These U.S.-led efforts are a direct challenge to the goals of Chinese independence and opposition to infringement on Chinese rights set forth in the Chinese National Defense White Paper. Nonetheless, the Japanese government joins with the United States in this effort. Notable in the past year were Japanese efforts to persuade European and Israeli governments to follow U.S. advice and refrain from military sales that would increase Chinese capabilities in Asia.[46] Meanwhile, Japanese official statements and documents support U.S. public concerns about the purpose and scope of China's rapid military buildup.[47]

## Short-Term Outlook and U.S. Policy Implications.[48]

The wide range of recent Sino-Japanese differences, reinforced by PLA priorities highlighting worsening security related issues between the two countries, makes it hard to be optimistic about future Sino-Japanese relations. Nonetheless, forces working against further deterioration of relations and encouraging more businesslike Sino-Japanese relations remain strong and appear powerful enough in this author's view to keep tensions within bounds and avoid strident rivalry or military conflict. As noted above, both the Chinese and Japanese leaderships are likely to remain focused for some time to come primarily on domestic issues involving economic development amid favorable surroundings. In these circumstances, they can ill afford the dangers and negative fallout that would come from an escalating conflict with an important neighbor.

Both countries will continue to rely on advancing China-Japan economic relations as key measures in their domestic agendas focused on tasks of development and nation-building. Meanwhile, the United States and other powers in Asia will continue to seek moderation in Sino-Japanese tension. Whenever China or Japan take steps that escalate tensions, they will risk jeopardizing their influence among their regional colleagues and undermining this goal held important by leaders in both China and Japan.

The national security priorities of the PLA suggest that PLA leaders will remain less attentive to the economic and diplomatic consequences of escalating disputes in Sino-Japanese relations. In effect, PLA concerns will serve as a drag on efforts by Chinese leaders to manage relations with Japan in a businesslike and nonconfrontational way. They will add to the serious impediments burdening China's ongoing effort to create a favorable and moderate image in Asia and to build an Asian order of regional cooperation that will help buffer China from suspected efforts by the United States to contain Chinese rising influence.

So long as Sino-Japanese tension persists amid conflicting assessment among U.S. specialists as to the causes and seriousness of the tensions, there will continue to be debate on what role the United States should take in regards to China-Japan differences. On the one hand are U.S. specialists who argue that the Sino-Japanese friction is against U.S. interests and the United States should take concrete measures to reduce tensions. Such measures include U.S. efforts to get the Japanese prime minister to stop visiting the controversial Yasukuni war memorial; to persuade Japanese government officials to be more rigorously forthright in accepting responsibility for Japanese aggression in the Pacific War; and to press Chinese officials to curb nationalistic excesses to avoid the widespread perception that Beijing manipulates history and other issues to weaken Japan, and manage territorial and other disputes without popular violence and in accordance with accepted international norms. On the other, are U.S. specialists, including this author, who see Sino-Japanese relations as unlikely to deteriorate substantially, as incentives on both sides offset sources of recent tensions. They see U.S. intervention in Sino-Japanese disputes in this context as unwise and unwarranted.

# ENDNOTES - CHAPTER 8

1. This is a revision of a paper presented at the 2005 PLA Conference sponsored by the Heritage Foundation and the Army War College, September 23-25, 2005. Thanks are due to panel commentator Thomas Christensen and to the many participants at the conference who offered constructive comments on the conference paper.

2. See among others, Greg Austin and Stuart Harris, *Japan and Greater China*, Honolulu: University of Hawaii, 2001; Caroline Rose, *Sino-Japanese Relations: Facing the Past, Looking to the Future*, New York: RoutledgeCurzon, 2005; Christopher Howe, *China and Japan: History, Trends, Prospects*, Oxford: Oxford University Press, 1996; Ming Zhang and Ronald A. Montaperto, *A Triad of a different Kind: The United States, China, and Japan*, London: Macmillan Press, 1999; *Asia's Global Powers: China-Japan*, Canberra: East Asian Analytical Unit, Government of Australia, 1996.

3. See "New Thinking on Japan," in Peter Hays Gries, "China Eyes the hegemon," *Orbis*, available online May 23, 2005.

4. Mike Mochizuki, "Japan: Between Alliance and Autonomy," in Ashley Tellis and Michael Wills, eds., *Strategic Asia 2004-2005*, Seattle WA: National Bureau of Asian Research, 2004, pp.103-138; Ralph Cossa and Brad Glosserman, "U.S.-Japan Defense Cooperation: Has Japan become the Great Britain of Asia?" Pacific Forum CSIS, *Issues and Insights*, Vol. 5, No. 3, March 2005. See quarterly reviews of U.S.-Japan relations by Brad Glosserman in *Comparative Connections, www.csis.org/pacfor*.

5. Mike Mochizuki, "Terms of Engagement: The U.S.-Japan Alliance and the Rise of China," in Ellis Krauss and T. J. Pempel, eds., *Beyond Bilateralism: U.S.-Japan Relations in the New Asia-Pacific*, Stanford: Stanford University Press, 2004, p. 87-114; Thomas Christensen, "Have Old Problems Trumped New Thinking? China's Relations with Taiwan, Japan, and North Korea," *China Leadership Monitor*, No. 14, June 2005; "China and Japan: In the pipeline," *Economist*, April 29, 2004, at *taiwansecurity.org*, May 3, 2004. See quarterly reviews of China-Japan relations by James Przystup in *Comparative Connections, www.csis.org/pacfor*.

6. Robert Marquand, "Anti-Japan Protests Jar an Uneasy Asia: Demonstrations Spread from Beijing to Several Southern Cities Sunday," *Christian Science Monitor*, April 11, 2005. "Lee Kuan Yew: China Must Teach Youngsters Not to Let its Might Threaten Neighbors," *The Star* (Malaysia), May 17, 2005 (Internet version); Eric Teo Chu Cheow, "Feuding Risks for East Asia," *The Japan Times*, April 22, 2005, at *taiwansecurity.org*, April 25, 2005.

7. See, among others, Mike Mochizuki, "Terms of Engagement," p. 87-114; and Robert Sutter, *China's Rise in Asia: Promises and Perils*, Lanham MD: Rowman and Littlefield, 2005, p. 125-150.

8. This statement and other U.S.-Japan steps to strengthen the alliance, and their possible implications for China and Taiwan are reviewed in Dan Blumenthal, *The Revival of the U.S.-Japanese Alliance*, Washington, DC: American Enterprise

190

Institute, Asian Outlook, February-March 2005; "China and Japan: So Hard to be Friends," *Economist*, March 23, 2005, at *Taiwansecurity.org*, March 28, 2005. The Taiwan Foreign Minister welcomed the U.S.-Japan declaration of February 19, 2005. "Taiwan's MOFA Welcomes U.S.-Japan Security Statement," *Central News Agency*, February 20, 2005 (Internet version). The Taiwan government seeks closer cooperation with Japan as well as the United States in their common concern about China's military buildup. Interviews, Taiwan, June 2005.

9. Michael Green, "Managing Chinese Power: The View from Japan," in Alastair Iain Johnston and Robert Ross, eds., *Engaging China*, London: Routledge, 1999; Michael Green and Benjamin Self, "Japan's Changing China policy: From Commercial Liberalism to Reluctant Realism," *Survival*, Vol. 38, No. 2, Summer 1996; Benjamin Self, "China and Japan: A Façade of Friendship," *Washington Quarterly*, Vol. 26, No. 1, Winter 2002-03, pp. 77-88.

10. Yoichi Funabashi, "New Geopolitics Rages over Various Parts of Asia," *Asahi Shimbun*, January 15, 2002.

11. See, among others, Hisane Masaki, "Fresh Irritants May Still Derail Sino-Japan Ties," *The Japan Times* (Internet versions), March 29, 2002.

12. "Tokyo-Taipei Links 'Good' Despite Damning Reports," *Asia Times* (internet version), March 29, 2002; Dan Blumenthal, *The Revival of the U.S.-Japanese Alliance*, Washington DC: American Enterprise Institute, Asian Outlook, February-March 2005.

13. See, for instance, S. Frederick Starr, "A strong Japanese initiative in Central Asia," *Central Asia-Caucasus Institute Analyst*, October 20, 2004.

14. "China and Japan: So Hard to be Friends," *Economist*, March 23, 2005, at *Taiwansecurity.org*, March 28, 2005. For a review and chronology of developments in China-Japan relations and Japan-Korea relations over the past 5 years, see the quarterly assessments of these respective topics in *Comparative Connections*, Honolulu: CSIS, Pacific Forum, *www.csis.org/pacfor*.

15. See as a particularly articulate example of this line of thinking, Yoshihisa Komori, "Rethinking Japan-China Relations: Beyond the History Issue," A Paper presented at the Sigur Center for Asian Affairs, George Washington University, Washington DC, December 5, 2001.

16. For example, see Tian Peiliang, "Nationalism: China and Japan," *Foreign Affairs Journal*, Beijing, Chinese People's Institute of Foreign Affairs, No 63, March 2002, pp. 63-83.

17. Benjamin Self and Michael Green are among the specialists associated with the view of seeing hardening, especially in Japanese policy and behavior toward China. See also David Fouse, "Japan's China Debate," *Asia's China Debate*, Honolulu: Asia Pacific Center for Security Studies, December 2003; Yong Deng, "Chinese Relations with Japan," *Pacific Affairs*, Vol. 70, No. 3, Autumn 1997, p. 379; Michael Armacost and Kenneth Pyle, "Japan and the Engagement of China" (Seattle), *NBR Analysis*, Vol. 12, No. 5, 2001; Joseph Y. S. Cheng, "Sino-Japanese

Relations in the 21st Century," *Journal of Contemporary Asia*, Vol. 33, No. 2, 2003, p. 268; Wu Xinbo, "The Security Dimension of Sino-Japanese Relations," *Asian Survey*, Vol. 40, No. 2, March-April 2000, p. 301; Denny Roy, *Stirring Samurai, Disapproving Dragon*, Honolulu: Asia Pacific Center for Security Studies, September 2003; "Noted Scholar Discusses 'New Thinking' in Sino-Japanese Relations" (Beijing), *Renmin Wang*, January 1, 2004 (Internet version); Liu Xiaobiao, "Where are Sino-Japanese Relations Heading?" (Beijing) *Renmin Wang*, August 13, 2003 (Internet version); Shi Yinhong, "On Crisis Formation, Control in Sino-Japanese Relations," (Hong Kong) *Wen Hui Po*, June 1, 2005 (Internet version). For an assessment based on extensive interviews with Chinese and Japanese officials, see Robert Sutter, *China's Rise in Asia: Promises and Perils*, Lanham, MD: Rowman and Littlefield, 2005, pp. 125-150.

18. David Pilling, "China and Japan Look to Restore Relations," *Financial Times* (Internet version), April 3, 2002; Kwan Weng Kim, "China-Japan Ties Lack Spontaneity," *Straits Times* (Internet version); April 5, 2002; Robert Sutter, "China-Japan: Trouble ahead?" *The Washington Quarterly*, Vol. 25, No. 4, pp. 37-49; Mike Mochizuki, "Terms of Engagement," pp. 96-100; Ma Licheng, "New Thoughts for China-Japan Relations" (Beijing), *Zhanlue yu guanli*, December 1, 2002, pp. 41-47.

19. James Przystup, "Progressing But Still Facing History," *Comparative Connections*, October 1999, *www.csis.org/pacfor*.

20. James Przystup, "Political Breakthrough and the SARs Outbreak," *Comparative Connections*, July 2003; James Przystup, "Cross Currents," *Comparative Connections*, April 2003; James Przystup, "Congratulations, Concern, Competition, and Cooperation," *Comparative Connections*, January 2003.

21. "Japan's PM Koizumi Continues High-Profile Diplomacy Challenged by China," *Agence France Presse*, May 8, 2005, at *taiwansecurity.org*.

22. Thomas Christensen, "Have Old Problems Trumped New Thinking? China's Relations with Taiwan, Japan, and North Korea," *China Leadership Monitor*, No. 14, June 2005; James Przystup, "China-Japan: No End to History," *Comparative Connections*, July 2005.

23. James Przystup, "Japan-China: Summer Calm," *Comparative Connections*, October 2005.

24. "Japan's PM Koizumi Continues High-Profile Diplomacy Challenged by China," *Agence France Presse*, May 8, 2005, at *taiwansecurity.org*.

25. "Hu's Points Show Way for Sino-Japan Ties," *China Daily*, June 21, 2005, at *taiwansecurity.org*.

26. Norimitsu Onishi, "Koizumi Provokes Anger Around Asia," *New York Times*, October 17, 2005 (Internet version).

27. *China's National Defense in 2004* published by the PRC State Council's Information Office and released on December 27, 2004 is available at *www.fas.org/nuke/guide/china/doctrine/natdef2004.html*.

28. *China's National Defense in 2002* published by the PRC State Council's Information Office and released on December 9, 2002 is available at *english1.people. com.cn/features/ndpaper2002/nd.html.*

29. Chinese and Japanese Foreign Ministry officials meet at the vice ministerial level to deal with various issues in relations. Some military contacts also continue, though at a level lower than Chinese military contacts with other neighbors.

30. David Shambaugh, "China Engages Asia: Reshaping the Regional Order," *International Security*, Vol. 29, No. 3, Winter 2004-05, pp. 64-99.

31. The concept of soft power, as distinct from hard power involving military, economic, or political pressure and persuasion, refers to nations getting what they want in international affairs through attraction rather than coercion, especially the attractiveness of a country's culture and ideas. Joseph Nye, *Soft Power: The Means to Success in World Politics*, New York: Public Affairs, 2004; Yoichi Funabashi, "China's 'Peaceful Ascendancy,'" *Yaleglobal*, December 19, 2003, at *www.taiwansecurity.org*; Willy Wo-Lap Lam, "China aiming for 'peaceful rise,'" *CNN.com*, February 3, 2004; Speech by Premier Wen Jiabao in New York City, December 9, 2003, *www. fmprc.gov.cn* (accessed December 20, 2003); Fu Mengzi, "China's Development and Security Concept," *Beijing Review*, June 9, 2005, p. 18-19; "No Anti-U.S. Plan in Asia: China," *Reuters*, June 18, 2005 (report of speech at Brookings Institution of Zheng Bijian, at *Taiwansecurity.org*); David Sands, "Military Strategy 'Defensive,' Envoy Insists," *Washington Times*, June 29, 2005 (at *taiwansecurity.org*, July 9, 2005).

32. Zheng Bijian, "China's 'Peaceful Rise' to Great-Power Status," *Foreign Affairs*, Vol. 84, No. 5, September/October 2005, pp. 18-24.

33. Sutter, *China's Rise in Asia.*

34. "U.S. Proposes Talks with Japan Over Taiwan Strait Contingencies," *Kyodo*, December 14, 2004 (Internet version); Dan Blumenthal, *The Revival of the U.S.-Japanese Alliance*, Washington, DC: American Enterprise Institute, Asian Outlook, February-March 2005, pp. 3-5.

35. "China Shocked by Japanese Foreign Minister's Comment on Taiwan, Says Spokesman," *Xinhua*, May 4, 2005; "Taiwan Covered in Japan-U.S. Security Pact: Machimura," *Asahi Shimbun*, April 30, 2005, p. 3.

36. "Retired Japanese Officers Advised Taiwan Navy on Mine Warfare," AFP, April 26, 2005 (Internet version); "Troop Relocation Difficult; U.S. Says Okinawa Marines Serve to Deter China-Taiwan Crisis," *Yomiuri Shimbun*, June 30, 2005.

37. "Japanese PM: [Anti-Secession Law] Will Bring Negative Influence on Cross-Strait Ties," *United Daily News*, March 15, 2005 (Internet version).

38. Reviewed in James Przystup's quarterly assessments of Sino-Japanese relations in *Comparative Connections*. See also Dan Blumenthal, *The Revival of the U.S.-Japanese Alliance* Washington DC: American Enterprise Institute, Asian Outlook, February-March 2005, pp. 3-5.

39. "China Lodges Solemn Representations to Japan's Approval of Oil, Gas Drilling," *People's Daily* online, July 15, 2005.

40. Yoichi Funabashi, "Maintain the Armitage Doctrine Quietly," *Asahi Shimbun*, February 10, 2004.

41. "Japan and China Dispute a Pacific Islet," *New York Times*, July 11, 2005.

42. "Why Does U.S. Preach 'China Military Threat'?" *People's Daily*, June 20, 2005, at *taiwansecurity.org*; "Sino-Japanese Relations Under the 'New U.S.-Japan Security Alliance'," *People's Daily* online, March 1, 2005; Blumenthal, *Revival*, p. 4.

43. Ann Scott Tyson, "U.S. Missile Defense Being Expanded, General Says," *Washington Post*, July 22, 2005, p. A10. "Japan Faces $545 Million Tab for Interceptor," *Yomiuri Shimbun*, June 20, 2005.

44. "China Criticizes Japan's New Defense Guidelines," Associated Press, December 12, 2004, at *taiwansecurity.org*.

45. "Secretary Condoleezza Rice En Route to Tokyo, Japan," On-the-record Briefing, March 17, 2005, at *www.state.gov/secretary/*; "Interview with Former U.S. Deputy Secretary of State Richard Armitage," *Toyko Chuo Koron*, May 2005, pp. 194-203.

46. "Japanese Request that Israel Suspend Arms Sales to East Asia, *www.haaretz.com*, January 17, 2005; "Japanese Prime Minister Urges EU to Keep Arms Embargo on China," *Agence France Presse*, May 2, 2005.

47. "China Urged to be More Open on Defense," Associated Press, June 4, 2005, at *taiwansecurity.org*, June 12, 2005; "White Paper Focuses on Chinese Navy," *Yomiuri Shimbun*, July 4, 2005; "Japan's White Paper Adds Chill to China Ties," *China Daily*, July 5, 2005.

48. This section benefited from the lively discussion among specialists at the September conference where this paper was presented, as well as subsequent conferences dealing with China and Japan, notably "U.S.-China Relations: Key Issues and Prospects," sponsored by the DACOR Bacon House Foundation and the China Policy Program at the Elliott School, George Washington University, October 28, 2005.

# PART IV

# SOUTH AND SOUTHEAST ASIA

# CHAPTER 9

## THE CHINESE MILITARY EYES SOUTH ASIA

Srikanth Kondapalli[1]

## Introduction.

> The South Asian region—bordering on Central Asia in the north, adjoining the Middle East in the west, and controlling the Indian Ocean to the south—is in a very important strategic position, while India is deservedly South Asia's top power—whether in terms of territorial area, human resources, scientific and technological capabilities, military strength, or economic strength.[2]

South Asia has not been the principal focus of China's attention over the last 5 decades. This is not to say that it has been overlooked: China fought a war with India in 1962, assisted Bangladesh and Pakistan in their sovereignty efforts, and has been a major military and foreign assistance supplier to both of the latter countries. The People's Liberation Army (PLA) was a major actor in all of these matters. However, the PLA's attention in the recent period generally has been on the eastern seaboard of the country, specifically towards Taiwan, Japan, Korea, and the South China Sea. The Soviet Union and its successor states, including Russia, also have drawn strong attention from China.

In interpreting the PLA's perspectives on South Asia, Chinese scholarship has reflected on the major problems between the two countries, such as the Tibet issue, the 1962 war, and relative configurations of power in Asia. Scholars in China also have explored the three major problems in India-China relations: the border dispute, the Tibetan issue, and China-Pakistan relations.[3] Yang Pingxue believes that the root of many of the India-China border problems, including Pakistan and Bangladesh, are a consequence of India's inheriting British colonial security policies.[4]

## Reviewing the Literature on India-China Relations.

Many Indian Army officers assess China's basic approach as one with an objective of the "marginalization" of India. For instance, Sahgal argued that the PLA is "creating a ring of anti-India influences aimed at the strategic marginalization of India" and "leveraging the strategic configuration of power to its advantage, in South Asia."[5] Pravin Sawhney has argued that Chinese military deployments and preparations pose a threat to India.[6] Other scholars outside the region view the PLA's perspectives on India as a part of its strategic encirclement.[7] For Mohan Mallik, continuing Chinese strategic weapons proliferation to Pakistan is intended against India.[8] For Valerie Niquet,

> Even though tactically Beijing acknowledges the demographic importance and the cultural prestige of India, it is not ready to share its supremacy, strategic and economic, with its Asian neighbour. Like the Sino-Japanese relations, the Sino-Indian equation hinges on the scope of China's ambitions, the nature of the Beijing regime, and the overall issue of leadership in Asia.[9]

John W. Garver, a prominent American scholar on Sino-Indian relations, has argued that China systematically has downplayed perceptions of a threat from India in its media coverage in the recent period.[10] Mark W. Frazier viewed Chinese and Indian military and security establishments at a crucial juncture in the post-1998 period. In contrast to the civilian leaderships' broad agenda of joining globalization and reform process, according to Frazier, the military constituents are protectionist "statist" in their agenda.[11]

Andrew Scobell has argued that the subject must be understood in terms of Chinese strategic culture, influenced, as it were, by the Confucian tradition and the thinking of the military scholar, Sun Zi. The resulting strategic culture combines traditions of pacifism and realpolitik in its notions of security. A negative image was portrayed by the Chinese military leaders about India, given the overall threat perceptions of the Chinese leadership about its neighbouring countries. Tracing Tibet as a crucial issue in this milieu, Scobell argued that China and India are likely to witness "simmering tensions" in their relations.[12]

Michael Pillsbury looks at China's assessment of its own "comprehensive national power" and the strategic outlook vis-à-vis India and Japan. While India's comprehensive national power is not yet a match to China's, Pillsbury identifies and analyses several Chinese military and civilian perceptions of a rising India that could challenge China in military and economic terms. The greatest concern in the Chinese publications reviewed by Pillsbury was in the sphere of maritime power.[13]

From China's perspective, India's actions on Tibet are seen as critical issues affecting China's sovereignty and territorial integrity, while India's 1998 nuclear tests were only a threat to its national security.[14] China is sensitive to its sovereign claims in Tibet and hence waged war against India in 1962.[15] For Xia Liping, 1962 was "not a purely military action, but a complicated political, diplomatic, and military war." The main objective of the Chinese government was "not to recover the territory, but to wipe out more Indian effective strength so as to give more serious lessons to Indian Army." The purpose here was "to shatter the attack by Indian troops, hit their arrogance, and give serious lesson to Indian Government."[16] The hostilities between China and India also drove China to change its nuclear nonproliferation policies and help Pakistan develop a nuclear capability. According to John Garver, helping Pakistan against Indian domination is a way to enhance Chinese security. While China's response to Indian nuclear tests in 1974 was low key, its response to the 1998 tests was "strident."[17]

Chinese military action in the 1962 events were termed by Larry M. Wortzel as reflective of the PLA's "good strategy and strong initiative in campaign art," and he attributed its success to "a combination of audacious action on the battlefield, good leadership, taking advantage of the terrain, good logistics, and strong ideological preparation."[18] Several of these themes of the recent period shall be analysed below.

## Determinants.

The major determinants in the PLA's considerations on South Asia are the structural and dynamic aspects of the security environment in the region and how this regional environment fits into the international security situation. PLA scholars and analysts recognize that the domain of policy perspectives on South Asian countries is principally that of the foreign ministry. The Ministry of Foreign Affairs (MFA), Asian Affairs Department is tasked to manage China's relations with South Asia. On strategic matters, the MFA Arms Control and Disarmament Department has the principal role in formulating policy. Its actions became more focused after the 1998 Indian and Pakistani nuclear tests. China's foreign policy goals were to "cap, roll back, and eliminate nuclear weapons" in South Asia (United Nations (UN) Security Council Resolution #1172).

Notwithstanding the MFA's lead on policy, the Chinese military also has a major say in deciding about China's equations with this region. The PLA's participation in the foreign affairs of the country is done through a structured process in the Chinese Communist Party's (CCP) Foreign Affairs Small Leadership Group. This is headed by Hu Jintao, who is also the chairman of the Central Military Commission (CMC). In addition to Hu, the PLA is represented in this body by the Minister of National Defense, also a CMC member.[19] The CMC receives feedback from various defense personnel stationed abroad and from strategic think tanks, associated with the Academy of Military Science (AMS), National Defense University (NDU), and other PLA bodies; PLA newspaper articles; and security analysts' views. This input goes to all of the CMC leaders. The PLA General Staff Department Overseas Foreign Intelligence Gathering and Assessment and Foreign Affairs Section also provides input to the military leadership through its branch devoted to South Asian affairs.[20]

Another major factor in security relations between China and the countries in South Asia is the PLA presence in contiguous provinces in China. Chinese troops are present in Tibet Military District, frontier guards and other policing units, Chengdu Military Region (MR), and Lanzhou MR certainly are considered in the decisionmaking process on issues related to India, Pakistan, Bangladesh, and Nepal. However, it is difficult to know the extent to which the views of PLA leaders in contiguous areas are solicited formally.

There are divergent views between the foreign ministry and the PLA on several issues relating to South Asia, especially on border dispute resolution, nuclear issues, and Indo-Pakistan balancing strategy. Charged with national defense, the PLA often has been less willing to compromise on Chinese territorial claims with the neighbouring countries. It has been overtly sensitive on issues related to sovereignty aspects.

A major difference between PLA and the civilian leadership perspectives on the region is that, while China's civilian leaders are critical of U.S. hegemony, they have been relatively silent on how India should fit into a multipolar world. In contrast, in the past 4 decades, the PLA has been critical of "Indian hegemony" in South Asia. Even while willing to enhance confidence-building measures (CBMs), PLA assessments constituents still express concern about Indian hegemony in South Asia.

While the PLA may focus on security threats in the region, China's civilian leadership works toward economic development and trade, seeking a relatively peaceful environment. Hence the civilian leadership is more willing than PLA leaders to explore cooperation with India in the World Trade Organization and develop more nuanced strategic relations with Russia and India. These divergent views blended together in the agenda of the 16th Communist Party Congress with its focus on creating a peaceful environment for the next 2 decades even as the country explores the need to resolve the Taiwan issue.

Beijing's "Western Development Strategy" also affects how China handles security and economic relations with South Asia. The success of the "Western Development" campaign is crucial to China's balanced geographical development as well as domestic security. It affects the level of Beijing's control over west and southwest China.[21] The 10th five-year plan (2001-05) envisages about 70 major projects for Xinjiang involving an expenditure of several billion. A stable environment across its western and southwestern borders would not only lead to security in Xinjiang and other regions, but also focus on economic development. In the post-September 11, 2001, counterterror environment and given the festering of the Xinjiang Uighur "separatist" movement, China is poised to take more than a cursory interest in this region.[22] This factor is significant because a crucial actor in implementing the western development campaign is the PLA, or paramilitary units, or those PLA units now integrated into the civilian sectors like the engineering corps or construction corps.

## PLA Deployments and Relative Capabilities.

The PLA pays close attention to the relative force levels in South Asia. The naval visits Beijing conducted to Bangladesh, Sri Lanka, and Pakistan in late 1985 and early 1986 are examples of how China manages security relations in the region. Indian military operations in controlling Siachen Glacier in the early 1980s were viewed with concern by the Chinese military for their possible impact on military operations in Tibet and Xinjiang. The Indian joint military exercise, Operation CHECKERBOARD, conducted in the late 1980s, appears to have raised Chinese concerns. The PLA paid particular attention to the kill ratio in the exercise, which showed a strong Indian military response.[23] By the 1990s, the PLA had strengthened its presence in the region, and the recent 2004 White Paper of the PLA discusses the enhancement in the revolution in military affairs potential of surrounding countries, probably including India. These have again led to a reevaluation on the part of the PLA to support other South Asian countries militarily.

Overall, China has about 400,000 troops from four corps (group armies) and eight to ten independent divisions and brigades in the Chengdu and Lanzhou MRs.[24] India has deployed four army corps in areas contiguous to China or as their operational focus, a total of about 235,000 troops. These include the 14th Corps at Tezpur in Assam, the 3rd Corps at Rangapahar (Dimapur) in Nagaland, and the 33rd Corps at Siliguri in West Bengal. There are also 10 mountain infantry divisions and engineering and medical units.[25]

The Chinese Air Force has about 300 J-7 II, J-6, and Q-5 aircraft in the South Asia region.[26] In addition, the Su-27s, Su-30s, and J-8IIs may be pressed for air support duties. The Indian Air force (IAF) has a total of about 1,400 aircraft in its active inventory deployed in five air commands, three of which have a direct operational focus on China. India probably has the qualitative advantage in the air.

The entry of Su-30 fighters in the Indian inventory was seen as threatening the security of China's south-western region. One Chinese writer identified three main problems with the Su-30MKI: the need to achieve air domination [*duoquan zhikongquan*]; an increase in the threat of air warfare in the southwest; and the difficulty in supporting ground troops.[27] About 15 airfields in and around Tibet are in the western sector: Kashgar, Yarkhand, and Khotan; the central sector: Hoping, Gonga Dzong, Donshoon, and Nagchuka; and the eastern sector: Gormo, Jeykundo, Chengdu, Kantzu, Bangda, Kunming, Paoshan, and Mangshi.[28] These airfields can accommodate up to a maximum of 15 fighter squadrons and 12 bomber squadrons.

China's strategic weapons capabilities surpass those of India.[29] According to Vijai K. Nair, citing U.S. Air Force National Intelligence Center's declassified documents and Russian reports, China has been upgrading its nuclear and ballistic missiles to target India. Not only are the numbers of CSS-2 missiles at the 53rd Army at Jianshui, with a range of 3,100 km, not changed, but the crew training program at Kunming training area is being enhanced, in addition to the probable replacement of CSS-2 by CSS-5 Mod#1. Large-scale training activities were reported from Datong field garrison, Haiyan training facility in the 56th Army (with missile bases at Da Qaidam, Delingha, and Xiao Qaidam). The interconnecting communications among the missile bases from Jianshui-Kunming-Yunan-Chengdu-Lhasa-Haiyan-Datong are being upgraded for faster mobility.[30] Additionally, the U.S. Department of Defense (DoD) estimates that China has been producing about 60 missiles a year for operations against Taiwan for which it reportedly has deployed about 400 short and medium range missiles. If the Taiwan issue is resolved, it is likely that at least some of these could be shifted to the Indian front.

F China, with its railway line construction activity, road-building and airfield expansion, also has been improving its logistical capabilities. Nonetheless, in 1988, for instance, it was estimated that the Indian armed forces had an edge over China in Tibet in terms of logistics. India also has better road and rail communications to the border areas.[31]

In terms of military capabilities, several outcomes are possible. Depending on the "resolution of the Taiwan issue," Chinese military deployments could be altered in the southwest portions of China. While the PLA may not be adept in simultaneously waging two-theater warfare—say on Taiwan and India—it has shown flexibility and agility in coping with challenges at multitheater levels. For instance, in 1962, soon after operations on the Taiwan front, the PLA shifted troops to the India front. However, it would be difficult for the PLA to deploy more than half of its field divisions on the Indian front in the current scenario, even though it has improved military logistics in the India-China border areas.

Donald Goel estimated that in terms of tanks; air force; command, control, communications, computers, intelligence, surveillance, and reconnaissance (C⁴ISR); and troop transportation, India leads, while China has an edge in the areas of ground-to-ground missiles and heavy caliber artillery. The Indian lead in ground force air defense systems is traced to 50 SA-11s, while China has 8 SA-10 launch systems. The Chinese disadvantage in this field may be overcome with their acquisition of HQ-7, FM-90, FT-2000, and LY-60 in the short to medium term. Goel estimated that the IAF can employ 80 percent of its fighter bombers (about 280 planes, with a maximum of 500) capable of dropping 1,500 tons of bombs in the first air attack. This is estimated to be double the Chinese air force capability. The air war may include about 300 Indian fighters pitched against about 200 that China can deploy. Indian frontline airfield availability may prove to be advantageous in terms of weapon/troop load capability.[32]

Andrei Pinkov's assessment of the Chinese military view of future campaigns against India is as follows:

- The enemy (a synonym for India) that has hi-tech weapons and equipment will conduct a large-scale invasion of some Chinese territory;

- An operational force with certain hi-tech weapons and equipment will be organized and put into operation for the purpose of counterattacks;

- The campaign actions will include the defense, commitment of reserves, and initiation of the counterattack. Most of the time for this action is spent outside of the boundary line;

- Hi-tech weapons and equipment will be brought into full play, especially tactical missile troops (ground-to-ground missiles); and,

- The firepower should be combined organically. As to the form of combat, all the firepower should be combined, including short-range fires, light cannon fire, air attack, tactical missiles (ground-to-ground missiles), and surprise attack by non-line-of-sight long-range artillery.[33]

Chinese security concerns in the naval and nuclear fields are related to the Indian Ocean Zone of Peace of the 1970s after the U.S. bases in Diego Garcia came into being, and the 1974 South Asian Nuclear Free Zone proposals.[34] Indian naval modernization and ballistic missile deployments evoked concern among the PLA, specifically as these have potential implications for China's energy security in the Indian Ocean. These will be elaborated on below.

**India.**

Despite the general opinion that the PLA has not focused much on India, an elaborate list below indicates its major appraisals and reappraisals. These are concerned with the PLA's views on Indian defense policies, defense budgetary allocations, troop deployments, intentions, the emerging cooperation between the United States and India and the like. The three main basic goals of Indian defense policy, according to *World Military Yearbook of 2001*, are:
dominate South Asia [*chengba nanya*],

- control the Indian Ocean [*kongzhi yindu yang*],
- strive to be a world class military power [*zheng dang shijie yiliu junshi qiangguo*].

The *Yearbook* further noted that, in order to pursue "great power diplomacy," India has:

- actively competed with regional militaries, and actively developed its strength to influence security aspects of the world and the Asia-Pacific region.
- carried out "minimum credible nuclear deterrence" to contend with China and deter Pakistan, intended to extend India's second-strike capability in the Indian Ocean so as to check U.S. influence.
- insisted that its defense buildup is linked to economic growth but has enhanced its defense budget, dual-use technologies, information technology (IT), nuclear energy, and aerospace capabilities.
- took the policy of hi-tech weaponry as the core principle in building technology intensive armed forces.

- ensured overwhelming military superiority along its borders with Pakistan for the security of Kashmir.

- enlarged its influence in the Indian Ocean, made preparations to enter the South China Sea, and made efforts to conduct exercises with the Japanese, Vietnamese, and South Korean navies.

Further, the *Yearbook* mentioned Indian:

- defense strategy as "regional deterrence" [*diqu weishe*];

- strategic objectives as dominating South Asia, containing [*ezhi*] China, controlling the Indian Ocean, and becoming a great military power;

- strategic policy of waging limited hi-tech war under nuclear deterrence conditions and preparing for changes from one theater to multiple theaters;

- strategic objectives: consider Pakistan and China as two adversaries [*duishou*]; possess overwhelming superiority over Pakistan and force it to vacate occupied territory; regard China as a potential threat; do not give up on China's "vested interest"; seek an opportunity to expand; control South Asia through diplomatic, military, economic, and nuclear deterrence; control the areas from the Arabian Sea to the South China Sea; and develop military cooperation arrangements with Southeast Asian countries.

- Current Indian military operational concepts are: the basic purpose of war is to eliminate the enemy's war fighting ability, attack must be combined with defense, limited war is to be waged under hi-tech conditions, with dozens of nuclear strikes. The basic themes of these ideas are: emphatic offensive battles; first strikes; crossing the boundary; extending damage into enemy territory; fully implementing three-dimensional war through attack in depth and defense; placing the emphasis on flexible battles, combined operations, and the role of the air force; focus on coordinated air-land battle; emphasis on the concentration of absolute military strength in one major direction; seeking quick resolution; paying attention to the role of electronic war, deception, electronic countermeasures, and concealment of operational intentions; and the efficient conduct of operational command.[35]

The above long citation is a dominant theme of the PLA and is reflected and reproduced in several forms. These have not only influenced the subsequent PLA discourse but also the views of Chinese scholars studying the region. Despite the launching of a "constructive cooperative partnership" (*xing he zuo huo ban guanxi*) during Jiang Zemin's visit to New Delhi in 1996 and the gradual normalization of relations between the two countries, the PLA continues to sport such views. For instance, according to the PLA paper:

> Since the 80s, India started pursuing a policy of "regional deterrence" and a military strategy aimed at seeking a strong military . . . consolidating [its] gains, containing China and deterring Pakistan, controlling weak and small neighbors, and intercepting big power penetration outside the region, thereby clearing hurdles in its path towards becoming a world power. Indian armed forces development took a path of attaining regional military superiority, importing and incorporating advanced weapons technology, spending on indigenous production, and speeding up weapons modernization.[36]

The Indian Defense Ministry's annual report mentioning that there is a huge imbalance in Chinese and Indian nuclear power and that several Indian cities are within Chinese nuclear range was termed the "spread of sheer fallacy." China's strategic weapons transfers to Pakistan were dismissed as "fabricating rumors out of thin air." The citing of a "China threat" by Indians to further their defense modernization, specifically their strategic weapons program, was termed as holding a "shield." A commentator, writing in the *PLA Daily*, wondered:

> How could one win the trust of others if he seeks to benefit himself at others' expense? The Chinese people wish those people in India who are eager to advertise the "theory of China threat" could really proceed from the interests of the Chinese and Indian people to say more things favorable to their interests and do more things beneficial to the two countries so as to promote a sound and steady development of the relations between China and India.[37]

Yan Liwei argued that India playing a greater role from the Persian Gulf to the Strait of Malacca "is bound to further push India and Pakistan to the brink of war." Commenting that Indian political leaders are whipping up a war frenzy against Pakistan after the Kaluchak attack by terrorists in Jammu and Kashmir, Yan argued that:

> . . . Pakistan reiterated to the international community through various ways that it has always upheld the stance of cracking down on terrorism, and the activities of the Muslim militia in Kashmir are "freedom and democracy" activities and should be distinguished from terrorist organizations. In order to prevent India from profiting, after weighing up the pros and cons the Pakistani Government did not shrink from deciding to cooperate with the United States in the face of strong domestic pressure, thus easing the pressure from the United States. [38]

India's entry into the Central Asian arena was viewed with caution by a military journal. Four main factors were mentioned as to why India has embarked on linking with the Central Asian region: contain [*ezhi*] Pakistan; protect energy security; combat terrorism; and pin down China's development [*qianzhi Zhongguo fazhan*].[39]

**Nuclear Tests and China's Response.**

The Indian nuclear tests of 1998 evoked a sharp response from China. This is natural, given the strategic importance of this event to the Asian balance of power, with China as the sole declared nuclear power in Asia. Indeed, the shrill Chinese tone against India peaked, with reports that then CMC Chairman Jiang Zemin hardly slept during the night India tested its nuclear weapons.[40] Several comments in this regard are set forth below.

According to Cheng Ruisheng, speaking to the *Liberation Army Daily*, which started a special column on experts' opinions on Indian nuclear tests,

> . . . the main reason for this is that the Indian authorities, foreseeing that India's nuclear tests would evoke strong condemnation in the international community, had to find an excuse that could confuse world opinion to reduce the pressure from the international community. The "China threat theory," which still enjoys some support in the international

community, came in handy as a "shield." Viewed at a deeper level, this incident shows that a handful of people in India still harbor hostile sentiment toward China, despite the fact that the constant improvement of Sino-Indian relations over the years is moving gradually to eliminate the shadow of the 1962 Sino-Indian border conflict.[41]

A May 20, 1998, an article in the *PLA Daily* criticized the Indian nuclear tests, commenting that:

> Since independence, India has pursued a military expansionist line. After 50 years of development, it now has a strong military that is the world's fourth largest. While other countries have capitalized on the opportunity arising from the end of the Cold War to develop their economies, India has intensified its efforts to build up its military and make war preparations. Since the beginning of the nineties, its military spending has grown continuously and has remained fairly high. . . . India has always viewed China and Pakistan as its biggest threat, thinking that it could rival China and Pakistan and consolidate its hegemonic status in South Asia only if it developed nuclear weapons.[42]

Another article in the *PLA Daily* published on the same day stated:

> The Indian authorities have engaged in double-dealing, calling loudly for nuclear disarmament while quietly implementing a nuclear weapons plan. They also have intentionally orchestrated a clumsy show of recrimination, with key Indian Government officials openly dishing up "the China threat theory" with the aim of finding an excuse for its nuclear weapons development and diverting attention. . . . History has proved and will continue to prove that any country that vainly hopes to dominate the world or a region will end up lifting a rock only to drop it on its own toes.[43]

The *PLA Daily* articles criticized the Indian nuclear tests for going against the "current international trend" and destabilising regional and world peace. While it was silent on the Chinese and French nuclear tests of 1996, the article criticized the Indian leaders' quest since independence to become a global power and charged that all successive leaderships have taken active steps in developing nuclear and ballistic missile capabilities.[44] Yet another writer viewed the 1998 nuclear tests as India seeking hegemony over South Asia.[45] According to a Chinese radio bulletin, acquisition of nuclear weapons in 1998 was a part of India's desire "to establish its regional supremacy status in sub-continental South Asia."[46] Cao Yongshang and Xu Yong, after mentioning that India is developing a nuclear deterrent policy, conducted successive long-range ballistic missile tests in April 1999 and January 2001, enhanced its conventional military capabilities, and established a joint command facility in the Andaman and Nicobar Islands, opined that "Through an active and flexible diplomatic policy, India has won relatively widespread strategic room and interests, and is stepping closer to the goal of being a military and political superpower in the 21st century.[47]

Recent Chinese assessments note a growth in the Indian national defensive power in the last few decades. Hu Angang and Liu Taoxing, for instance, argued that Indian military power has increased, especially between 1980 and 2000.[48] While reflecting on the growing interactions between India and major powers, especially with the United States and Russia, and acquisitions from Israel, Liu Siyuan argued that, while India acquired more than 70 percent of its inventory from Russia in the fields of ground, air, and naval fields, it also is, in the recent period, acquiring several weapons/weapon systems from Israel, with the U.S. blessing to become a great military power.[49]

**Other Strategic Issues.**

It is not only on the nuclear issue that the PLA's views on India have hardened. There are other issues as well that exhibited an inveterate animosity between the two countries. According to Zhang Wenmu, ". . . the concept of the 'big power' of India should imply the historical concept that brings Pakistan, Bangladesh, Chinese Tibet, and all countries along the coast of the Indian Ocean into the India-controlled 'federation'." Zhang equated Nehru's political agenda with that of the Bharatiya Janata Party's (BJP) views about "greater India." Identifying two regions as the security focus of India, the northern (Pakistan-Tibet-Bangladesh regions) and southern (Indian Ocean) regions, Zhang argued that India has a program to make Tibet an independent region in order to eliminate the threat emanating from China, which is viewed purely as a geographic threat. He further stated that the "deeper meaning of that statement [by George Fernandes in 1998] is that China is the "biggest" obstacle to India's pursuit of hegemony in South Asia and that China's capability to resist Indian hegemonism in South Asia is greater than that of Pakistan."[50]

According to Jian Hua, India is not satisfied with being a South Asian power but has been:

> . . . ambitiously preparing to dash out of the Indian Ocean and march toward the whole world. In addition to its nuclear deterrent, India has formulated a military strategy of "guarding against China in the north, attaching Pakistan in the West, occupying the Indian Ocean in the south, and expanding the scope of its influence in the East." In this extremely ambitious strategy, the "eastward expansion" is a very important link. Its nucleus is to expand the scope of its influence and activities to the South China Sea and part of the Pacific Region.[51]

Wang Tao, reflecting on the Indian defense allocations to several top of the line weapon systems from Russia, France, Israel and the United States, stated "India's continuous engagement in arms expansion under the present high-tension situation of the southern Asian regions is a very risky move, because the 'erroneous message that such a move has helped to relay' will definitely give rise to an increasingly fierce arms race in these regions."[52]

Wang Ming argued that in order to control the Indian Ocean and compete to become a big power in the world, India has embarked on a military modernization program. Wang pointed to Indian plans to become a "futuristic military" by increasing the technical arms of the services; transforming the Army into a "strategic strike service"; raising its three-dimensional operational ability; acquiring 400 T-90 tanks from Russia; acquiring 24 attack submarines, 200 extra warships, and 3 aircraft carriers, long-range air lift capabilities, air refuelling, and airborne warning and control systems (AWACS); increasing its air fighting detachments from 39 to 55; procuring 190 Su-30 aircraft from Russia and 126 F-16 or F-18 aircraft from the United States; enhancing its strategic bomber, strategic reconnaissance, and strategic transport aircraft; and ensuring its ability to conduct reliable and effective strategic nuclear strikes.[53] Wang and Yan identified four commando units as the special operation forces in the Indian military. Numbering a total of 20,000, these forces are variously tasked for para-dropping, assault operations, amphibious operations, and counterterrorism.[54]

Nie Yun has mentioned that the Indian Army plans to increase its special operation forces from the current level of 5,000 to about 20,000 to gear up for the higher responsibilities that would be bestowed on India after it becomes a permanent member of the UN Security Council. Nie stated that the Indian Army has been training several such forces at a secret base and has plans to acquire digital battlefield equipment, global positioning systems (GPS), night vision equipment, etc.[55] Li Lin has argued that the Indian ground forces have embarked on a hi-tech modernization program for its tanks; armored personnel carriers; self-propelled artillery; and *Prithvi*, *Agni*, and *Surya* series of missiles and have allocated several billion dollars for the period 2001-15 in order to "seek hegemony" [*changba*] in South Asia.[56]

On the Indian Navy, PLA writers mention its impact on the Indian Ocean. While former PLA General Logistics Department (GLD) director Zhao Nanqi observed in the early 1990s that the Indian Ocean is not India's ocean, others have pointed out its impact on the energy security of China in the event of a war between the two countries. The key here is the power projection capability of the Indian Navy. An Binggong reported that India launched an indigenous aircraft carrier program in May 2005 at Cochin Shipyard, making it the fifth country in the world having this technological ability. The ship, to enter service in 2012, is 252 meters wide, has about a 37,500 ton displacement, can carry 30 aircraft, and is to cost about $1 billion.[57] According to Jiang Nan, in the last 50 years of naval ship-building and operational activity, India has achieved several landmarks.[58] Li Jie focused on Indian efforts in acquiring nuclear submarines.[59] Another writer underlined the growth of the Indian Navy, especially its modern destroyer program, and termed it as a "specter" [*youling*] for the Indian Ocean.[60] While the IAF reportedly has pressed into service Israeli-made *Heron* and *Searcher* -2 unmanned aerial vehicles (UAV) on the Pakistan and China borders for surveillance and reconnaissance purposes, the Indian Navy reportedly is preparing to form a UAV base in the eastern Andaman and Nicobar Islands to counter Chinese installations on the Myanmar-held Great Coco Islands.[61] Citing Indian naval plans to acquire warships, submarines, aircraft, and UAVs, a PLA writer argued that this reflects the Indian desire to control the Indian Ocean region. He said:

> For a long period of time, India has regarded the Indian Ocean as an "ocean of destiny" and an "ocean of the future" and strived to turn it into an "ocean of India." With the guidance of the strategic idea of "looking east, going out from the west, and going south," India has had an ever increasing desire to become a maritime military power. Since the 1990s, India has stepped up implementing the "Indian Ocean control strategy" and the "blue water project" to enhance its Navy's maritime attack capability.[62]

Su Ping, in a general introduction on the Indian military in *PLA Daily*, after explaining in detail the services, force structures, weapon systems, deployments, training, etc, observed that the IAF is one of the highly modern and professional services.[63] Cui Jianchuang and Bi Shuqin argued that IAF is increasing its precision strike capabilities by acquiring and conducting test flights of low altitude missiles and strengthening its air defense network.[64] A writer noted the IAF acquisition of nine new type *Jaguar* fighters with precision navigational aids, laser-range finders, and operational systems on July 15, 2005. While India has acquired nearly 130 *Jaguar* aircraft from the British firm BAE since 1979 and has assembled 100 more, this type of aircraft has become one of the mainstays of the IAF in its long-range precision strike missions. Song Dazhao has argued that these fighters, in addition to the other military aircraft, high modernization levels, and operational expertise, have provided the Indian military the ability to project force. Along with long-range precision strikes, Song identified strategic deterrence preparation as the other major objective of the IAF modernization.[65] As peace and tranquillity prevails on the line of actual control areas with China, the IAF reportedly is increasingly conducting "mercy missions" of air drops and logistic support in the remote border areas of Arunachal Pradesh in the recent past. No hostile air intrusions by China were reported.[66] Another report, however, indicated that the IAF has not lowered its guard in the eastern sector and indeed has maintained nearly 10,000 sorties of flying time for its pilots at Tejpur, a forward airbase near China.[67] Reflecting on the IAF plans to send a team to Alaska for exercises (which used to be reserved for Asian countries like Japan, South Korea, Singapore, or Thailand); a Chinese writer indicated that the United States and India are evolving a common "understanding" regarding China. The Indian effort, according to this report, is to fit into the U.S. "strategic orbit" and carry forward U.S. policy and its global strategic needs.[68]

Another PLA concern is the growing Indian missile capability. This is of serious concern to the PLA as any enhanced reach of the missile capability of India could neutralize the nuclear deterrent capacity of China. Chun Xiao identified the recent series of Indian missile tests in the category of *Akash* [sky] as a part of the Indian plan to achieve the capabilities of that of the *Patriot II* series of missiles.[69] An unidentified writer underlined the large missile capability of India in the Asian region in terms of quantity and quality. This writer has traced the origins of the Indian missile program to Britain, France, and the former Soviet Union/Russia. *Prithvi, Agni,* and *Surya* series missiles and their parameters are identified, and he argues that it is not the technological barriers but political signals from the Indian establishment that are crucial in launching the latter intercontinental ballistic missile (ICBM) programs.[70] These will be augmented by the acquisition of a second strike nuclear capability. India also plans to buy two nuclear submarines from Russia.[71] Fang Hua predicted that India is on the threshold of launching several long-range ballistic missiles with solid propellant fuel in a short period of time. Fang mentioned that India has accelerated the missile program with an array of new series of missiles, including the enhanced versions of *Agni II* IRBM (2,000-2,500 km range), *Agni III* IRBM (3,500 km range from May 2001), *Surya* ICBM (5,000 km range), and *Surya III* ICBM (12,000-20,000 km range) to "be out by 2003."[72] Indian attempts to build an anti-missile defense system are traced to the 1990s. Developments in this regard include acquisitions from Russia of S-300 PMU batteries, acquisition of the *Barak* system from Israel, support in 2001 of President George W. Bush's missile defense proposals, etc.[73] Dong Guozhong argued that Indian missile tests of the *Agni* in January 2002 [of a range of about 700 km) "made the people of the world become nervous" and warned of an arms race in the region.[74]

On a related issue of strategic significance, Dai Wenming mentioned that India is on the verge of acquiring strategic intelligence through satellite imageries in the South Asian region and beyond to serve its security interests in the changed conditions after both India and Pakistan acquired missile capabilities. Specifically tracing such programs to 2001, Dai stated that India has a plan to launch a series of satellites that can observe the region more accurately, with picture resolutions reduced from 2.5 meters to 1 meter to 500 millimetres. With the help of Israel in January 2004, India is now in a position to acquire "absolute advantage" over Pakistan in information collection. These systems can be used for the proposed missile defense systems' early warning.[75] Yi Fan has summarized the recent Indian space program and argued that India has ambitions to become one of the great countries in the world in the 21st century, and estimated that by 2020, India would be a space power in the fields of military surveillance, telecommunications, and meteorological aspects and will acquire the ability to launch mini-satellites for military purposes.[76] A PLA writer, after tracing the Indian space program from the 1980s (implying that these have dual use applications), argued that ". . . the development trend of India's missile technology has been vigorous, and that India is constantly accelerating the steps to realize its intention to dominate South Asian affairs and to enter into competition with the world's great powers." More intriguing is the comment that the defensive and offensive space and missile programs "might upset the existing strategic balance in the South Asia region. What the influence this series of changes will have on the Kashmir region in South Asia, people will just have to wait and see.[!]"[77]

To overcome the challenges posed by the Indian military capabilities, the PLA adopted a policy of supplying arms to other South Asian countries, expanding military-to-military ties, in the belief that it can thereby exert pressure on India and check its rise (see the two appendices). Besides, in 1999 China reportedly set up a special task force to engage in information warfare activities against not only Taiwan, Japan, the United Staates, and South Korea, but also India. Reportedly the program included the following four methods, as reported by Prasad. These remind one of the methods proposed by senior PLA colonels in their work on *Unrestricted Warfare*.

1. China would not attack military or political targets in these countries but would target their financial, banking, electrical supply, water, sewage, and telecommunications networks.

2. Chinese companies would establish business links with private companies in these countries. After carrying on legitimate business for some time, they would insert malicious computer codes and viruses over commercial e-mail services.

3. The viruses and malicious codes would be sent through computers in universities in third countries so that they could not be traced back to China, but would be thought to be the handiwork of adolescent pranksters.

4. The attacks would be launched when the political leadership of the target countries was preoccupied with election campaigns.[78]

**The U.S. Factor.**

Several Chinese military experts have reflected on the possible impact of growing U.S.-India relations on Chinese security. Most of them have expressed concern that such relations are detrimental to Chinese security interests. Moreover, a realignment of the global strategic equation—that shifted in 1971 into U.S.-China-Pakistan axis and Soviet Union-India treaty and then to the gradual post-Cold War U.S.-India rapprochement—may not augur well for China, as the latter increasingly came under the U.S. scanner. On the other hand, the earlier shrillness against the United States in the Chinese security outlook of the 1950s and 1960s is giving way to a more accommodative "peaceful coexistence" approach in the recent period. In this context, with then U.S. Secretary of State Colin Powell's announcement in March 2004 designating Pakistan as a major non-North Atlantic Treaty Organization (NATO) ally, the region is poised to emerge once again in the Chinese security calculus as it did after a similar agreement was arrived at by the United States and Pakistan 50 years ago. Though the contexts are different, China has shown remarkable flexibility in the recent period to the presence of U.S. forces in Pakistan, if not in other parts of Asia. On the other hand, the physical presence of U.S. troops in Pakistan, with its implications for any possible "control" of Chinese supplied strategic weapons, may be causing the PLA to think of opening up another front in Bangladesh against India.

Despite U.S. opposition to Indian nuclear tests in May 1998, Chinese security analysts viewed President Bill Clinton's visit to India in March 2000 and President Bush's policies as anti-China in orientation and pro-India in content. Liberal democratic political systems, similar perspectives on ballistic missile defense systems, closer defense relations as exhibited in reinstatement of defense policy group consultations, joint military exercises, a common perspective on free navigation on the high seas, lenient sanctions regimes, and alleged similarities in strategic agendas of countering China and separating Tibet were all cited as contributing to the improvement in recent U.S.-India relations.[79] These are, according to Liu Ying, in accordance with the Indian interests in becoming a great power and U.S. interests in sustaining and expanding global and regional strategies.[80] Another reporter criticized the alleged Indian drive for achieving "one-sided nuclear superiority" and linked Indian nuclear and ballistic missile build up—which he estimated at about 30-70 nuclear weapons with the prospect of developing 100 weapons by 2005 and 200 missiles—to the U.S. strategy of engaging with South Asia.[81] Nie Hongyu has drawn attention to the Indian military commanders' conference in October that is intended to take steps to deploy nuclear weapons.[82] The People's Daily, 3 days before the September 11, 2001 (9/11), events, drew linkages to the U.S. ballistic missile defense plans and the Indian nuclear program thus:

> Currently, India is one of the few countries in support of the NMD [National Missile Defense] program of the United States, so the Americans naturally do not want to offend India, therefore they actually give tacit consent to India's practice of expanding its nuclear arsenal and developing a "reliable and minimal nuclear deterrent force". . . . India's current acceleration of its pace of using nuclear power to equip its armed forces is inseparable from the profound background of U.S. change of its South Asian strategy.[83]

The January 2002 visit of Indian Defense Minister Fernandes to the United States was seen as ending the Cold War between the two countries but also as furthering military cooperation.[84] According to Ding Zengyi, the U.S. objectives in enhancing relations with India are to:

- raise U.S. troops' combat capabilities by conducting training in the Indian Ocean (thereby ensuring U.S. energy security in the Indian Ocean) and by joint exercises with Indian troops;

- check the spread of terrorism;

- ensure peace between the two nuclear states of India and Pakistan so that the nuclear factor does not affect its strategic plan in South Asia; and,

- contain India-Russia relations and wean away India into the U.S. camp.

In the case of India, the main reasons for improving relations with the United States are, according to Ding:

- The United States provides India with a "shortcut" to fulfil its dream of becoming a great power.

- India can acquire the latest military technologies from the United States and replace its aging inventory.

- India can receive prestige, security, and the possibility of playing an increasingly important role on the international stage.[85]

According to Zhang Guoping, U.S. interests in conducting joint military exercises and enhancing cooperation with India are due to its objective of linking up Central, West, and South Asia, while the Indian objective is to become a military and political power and force Pakistan into "submission."[86] Reports about a potential formation, dubbed the "Asian NATO," with U.S.-Israel-India forming the western wing in Asia, while U.S.-Japan-India make up the eastern wing, were viewed by the *PLA Daily* as reflecting the Cold War mentality of working towards strategic containment of a rising China. Nevertheless, Wang Yusheng argued that since India-China relations improved after the June 2003 joint statement between the two premiers and enhancement in confidence-building measures (CBMs) between the two militaries as reflected in the November 2003 joint naval operations and mutual military exchanges, these measures would usher in greater cooperation between the two countries.[87] Another writer viewed U.S. plans for restructuring West

Asian political contours as a part of its larger scheme for global supremacy, reduction of Russian and Chinese influence and control over energy resources, and measures to form an "iron triangle" over West Asia, Central Asia, and South Asia to include the United States, Israel, Turkey, and India.[88] According to an observer, the China-Pakistan joint naval operation off Shanghai was viewed as "resolutely breaking out of the circle of containment" strategy of India and the United States, who held a major naval exercise in October 2003 and formed a "military alliance."[89] The U.S. President's decision to send Defense Secretary Donald Rumsfeld and others to India was seen by a PLA writer as an attempt to mediate between the two countries.[90] Another commentator viewed such mediation efforts as part of a U.S. plan to not just curb potential South Asian conflict, but as a part of the U.S. grand strategy of facilitating oil and gas exports of Central Asian Republics to the Indian Ocean and beyond through Afghanistan and Pakistan.[91]

Some analysts in China have cautioned India against improving relations with the United States. Mentioning that Indian military exercises in May 2002 and joint exercises with the United States and France have revealed an Indian desire to dominate South Asia and expand its influence, Shi Chun-yu warned India that this would be detrimental to Indian interests. He suggested that,

> India should not forget that once the U.S. military strength grows in South Asia and the Indian Ocean region, India unavoidably would be the first to be suppressed. By that time when the wolf is brought into the house, it will be too late for India to repent![92]

## Kashmir.

While China has exhibited a flexible policy towards the Kashmir issue in the recent period compared to its "self-determination" policy of the 1960s and 1970s, the PLA appears to be still taking time to readjust to this policy. The Chinese PLA or other officials stationed in India appeared not to have visited Kashmir, Sikkim, or other areas near to the border or contentious areas. The PLA shows concern about the Indian control of Siachen Glacier for its potential impact on not only the Pakistani airfield at Skardu but also for operations in Tibet and Xinjiang. However, given the spurt in activity by Uighurs in Xinjiang, the PLA appears to be concerned more about its counterterrorism drive. Nevertheless, it needs to be pointed out that soon after the U.S. strikes on al-Qa'ida and the Taliban in Afghanistan, the PLA has not only blocked the China-Afghan border areas, but also has enhanced its troop presence and its chief of general staff visited these areas. On a related subject, maps published in China generally depict Kashmir as a separate territory. Certain think-tanks in China like the China Institute of International Strategic Studies (CIISS) have published maps which depict Kashmir as an independent territory. This used to be the case with Sikkim as well until about 2003. After the Indian prime minister's visit to China in June 2003, China has sent signals that it recognizes Sikkim as a part of India, a position that it had not accepted since Sikkim's integration with India in 1976. More concrete developments are visible, with some Chinese maps depicting Sikkim as a part of India. In a major departure from the past practice, in October 2003 the Chinese defence attaché to India joined his counterparts in the Indian Army organized trip to Sikkim.[93]

**Transgressions.**

An issue between China and India, specifically in the context of the unresolved border dispute is the growing number of transgressions of the line of actual control by both sides. While many such transgressions are unintentional in nature, given the high-altitudes and inhospitable weather conditions, intentional transgressions to enforce sovereignty claims also have increased in the last 7 to 8 years. This issue may be seen as one more difference in perspective between the civilian leadership's desire to evolve normalization and the PLA or the frontier guards' resolve to enforce sovereignty claims in the region.[94] It was estimated that nearly 1,000 transgressions a year were reported in the last 4 years, even though the May-July 1998 transgressions (coinciding with Indian nuclear tests) were considered to be more political in nature.[95] Then Indian Army Chief General Padmanabhan reportedly wrote a note to the government, drawing attention to the aggressive patrolling done by Chinese troops during the Kargil events, often five to ten kilometres deep inside the Indian territories.[96]

According to Arunachal Pradesh chief minister Mukul Mithi, Chinese troops, often in the guise of herdsmen, not only have transgressed the border areas, but have built infrastructure facilities in the region.[97] The following year, Chinese Deputy Director-General of the Asian Department of the Foreign Ministry Sun Guoxiang denied that Chinese troops violated the India-China boundary areas.[98] Chinese troops' intrusion in Ladakh was detected by local authorities at Sheshoon and Chemoon in 2003.[99]

A related issue is whether India can permit Chinese companies bidding for projects in border or security sensitive areas. India has concerns over Chinese bidding for projects in areas closer to the border region or in fields related to defense and strategic areas. Proposals by Hutchinson Port Holdings and Huawei Technologies and proposals to set up hydro-electric projects in Himachal Pradesh reportedly were denied by the Indian side.[100] In March 2001 the United States criticized the Huawei Company for allegedly laying down fiber optic lines in Baghdad. In December, the U.S. Federal Bureau of Investigation (FBI) reportedly alerted Indian agencies on possible supplies of telecommunication networks for the Taliban in Afghanistan. Huawei Technologies invested about $120 million, and 513 people work at its Bangalore branch.[101] The Indian Navy also reportedly cancelled a Chinese tender for dredging of the Mazagon Dockyard.

**Counterencirclement By India.**

If the PLA's policy is to exert pressure on India by supporting Pakistan, Bangladesh, and other countries, such "encirclement" also may be replicated by the Indians. While India had little strength or intention to enter into such escalation during the Cold War period, the rise of India and the reformulation of its security interests from the Persian Gulf to the Strait of Malaccas in 2001 could extend its reach. Indian naval exercises in 2001 and 2004 in and around the South China Sea were seen by the PLA as a part of this Indian design. In October and November 2000, the Indian Navy, following deliberations at its naval commanders conference, intends to conduct unilateral and bilateral exercises with its Vietnamese and South Korean counterparts. This decision is in line with Defense Minister

Fernandes' statement on April 14, 2000, that India's interests extend from the north of the Arabian Sea to the South China Sea. This is considered by an analyst as a direct challenge to China.[102] A Chinese analyst viewed this as "a daring attempt out of deepgoing and long-term strategic considerations."[103] Emerging contacts between India and Taiwan are another area of concern to the PLA.

A major concern for the PLA is the emerging relations between India and Taiwan. While both do not have diplomatic relations, any contacts between the two were viewed with suspicion by the PLA. The then Indian military chief's statement during the 1962 war that India and Taiwan should exert pressure on the People's Republic of China (PRC) could have opened two unmanageable war theaters for the PLA. This may result in the same situation that the PLA has adopted over the last 4 decades—that of putting pressure on India during the Indo-Pakistan conflict, as in the 1965, 1971, or in the 1999 Kargil events. In the recent period, India and Taiwan reportedly are developing military cooperation—to start with military intelligence sharing—according to a Chinese website report. Liu Weijun reported that IAF officials visited Taiwan and met Taiwanese air force chief Chen Chao-min. Tracing such contacts to Lee Teng-hui's administration, this report argued that "Taiwan wants to use India to diffuse military pressure from the mainland China, and India tries to play the Taiwan card to weaken China's tie with its long time enemy Pakistan."[104]

**PLA on CBMs and Normalization.**

Overall policies of building a "well-off society" in the next 2 decades by the 16th Party Congress meant emphasis on furthering CBMs and normalizing relations with the neighboring countries. The PLA and Indian armed forces have initiated several CBMs in the last 3 decades, with the 1996 agreement formalizing such measures.[105] The following points flowing across the lines of actual control (LAC) were observed by both militaries:

- Reducing/limiting combat tanks, infantry combat vehicles, guns with 75 mm or bigger caliber, mortars with 120mm or bigger caliber, surface-to-surface missiles, and surface-to-air missiles.

- Exchanging data on such military forces and armaments and ceilings.
- Avoiding large scale military exercises involving more than one division (15,000 troops).
- Prior notification of an exercise by more than a brigade (5,000 troops).
- Prevent air intrusions, with restrictions on flying combat aircraft within 10 km of the LAC.
- No fire/blasts, etc., within two km of the LAC.
- Self-restraint on the LAC and deescalation.
- Meetings between border personnel at designated places.
- Expanding telecommunication links between the border meeting points.
- Contacts between border authorities.
- Assistance to personnel and information on forced or inadvertent LAC crossings.
- Information on natural disasters, etc.

Certain concrete results in the CBMs are in the regular meetings between border personnel. In 1978 the first flag meeting between border personnel took place at Chushul in the western sector. Border security personnel met in the eastern and western sectors for a second time in July 1991.[106] Soon after the CBM agreements were signed, the number of such meetings has increased to nearly four to five. During these meetings, both sides raised issues related to the transgressions of the LAC. In addition, both sides also have instituted courtesy calls on each other on the Indian Independence Day on every August 15th and the Chinese National Day on October 1st. These have been furthered in the recent period, with plans for joint exercises between the two.

Two Chinese naval ships visits to Bombay on May 27, 2001, for a 3-day visit were termed as having political rather than military significance.[107] India and China conducted joint naval search and rescue operations in November 2003 at Shanghai a month after the Chinese navy conducted similar operations with the Pakistani navy.[108] Indian naval ships *INS Ranjit*, guided-missile corvette *INS Kulish* and *INS Jyothi* with about 900 personnel participated in drills with the Chinese navy off Shanghai in November 2003.[109] While viewing this joint operation more in terms of its political significance rather than having any major military significance, a writer vividly described the different scenarios involved in the operation:

> The first step is an exchange exercise; the second step, formation of ships; and the third step, a maritime search-and-rescue exercise. In the course of the search-and-rescue exercise, a crew member from the Indian side would board a Chinese ship and, in a scenario where some incidents have happened on the Chinese ship, a helicopter would be dispatched to "rescue" this crew member from the Chinese ship and bring him back to the Indian ship. Besides, the ships on both sides would conduct a joint exercise to put out a fire.[110]

According to Meng Xiangqing of the NDU, with the joint operations with Pakistan and Indian navies, China is sending signals that it is following a "balancing strategy" between these two South Asian countries, and that it is not playing favorites between the two in the region.[111]

On November 6, 2004, the Indian side invited for the first time a Chinese border guards' team to participate in a volleyball sports event at Chushul in the border areas.[112] The Indian military also has plans to invite Chinese military delegations to participate in counterterrorism maneuvers. In 2004, two such events took place between the two sides.[113]

Increasing CBMs between the PLA and Indian armed forces are not without their problems, though. The Indian Army chief's suggestion that India and China should conduct a joint military exercise to counter terrorism was viewed by the Pakistani side with concern. A Pakistani foreign ministry spokesman warned against "crossing red lines" — meaning these exercises should not be conducted in disputed areas.[114] On November 18, 2003, Indian Army Chief General N. C. Vij stated that, even as India-China relations are improving in the recent period, India should not be complacent about the growing Chinese military capabilities and rail and road infrastructure developments in Tibet and that India needs to match these capabilities.[115]

Nevertheless, with the Indian prime minister's visit, according to a PLA commentator, bilateral relations:

> . . . have entered a new stage of development, which has laid a solid foundation for good-neighborly relations and mutually beneficial cooperation . . . China's responsible behavior in handling international problems of various kinds and the role played by China in safeguarding world and regional peace over the past several years have been obvious to all countries. More and more Indian people are all the more willing to regard China as a friendly neighboring country and a trade partner, and the market for the "China Threat Theory" has been getting smaller and smaller in India."[116]

Another commentator in the *PLA Daily* hailed the improvement in bilateral relations because this belied the "Asian NATO" concept and the talk about improving relations between the United States, Israel, India, Australia, and Japan. With improvement in India-China relations after the Indian prime minister's visit and the joint naval operations in November, according to Wang Yusheng, certain views of the strategic experts of the United States and Japan were rejected.[117] Meng Xiangqing of the NDU viewed the Indian prime minister's visit to China in June 2003 as a second major effort towards normalization of relations between the two countries after such efforts were made in the 1950s.[118] These have set the pace for enhancing military exchanges between the two militaries. Chinese Defense Minister Cao Gangchuan visited India in 2004, followed by Chinese Chief of General Staff Liang Guanglie in 2005. Cao Gangchuan, before setting out from Beijing, mentioned that "China is willing to actively create a harmonious, stable, and peaceful regional political and security environment with all Asian countries, including Pakistan, India, and Thailand."[119]

While bilateral relations improved further, important differences still persist between the two countries on continuing Chinese assistance to Pakistan, its role in the Southern Asian region, and divergence between the Indian desire to discuss and participate in global issues of concern and the Chinese position of confining discussions to "regional" security issues only. From the Chinese point of view, despite eliciting a favorable response from the Indian government for its position on Tibet, as reflected in the Joint

Declaration of June 2003, it is still concerned about the economic and military rise of India.

## Rise of China and India.

The economic growth of India and enhancement of its military capabilities pose a challenge as well as an opportunity for China. The PLA responses to the rise of India, in light of the rise of China, are mixed in nature, with a dominant view arguing that this could pose a challenge to China. The overall perspective of the PLA during the rise of China may be gleaned from the following: For Jiang Lingfei, Professor at National Defense University, China's rise poses historical opportunities as well as challenges. Jiang viewed the 9/11 events as shaping China's rise but adds that it would be conditioned by socialist development and the enhanced role of the country in international relations. Luo Yuan, chairman of the Strategy Research Institute of the Academy of Military Science, argued that China's rise would result in national cohesion and would make it the most powerful country in the Asia-Pacific region. He proposed three stages in such a rise:

1. The construction [*yingzao*] stage, in which China should promote a peaceful environment on its periphery and safeguard national sovereignty and territorial integrity.

2. The molding [*suzao*] stage, in which China would pursue policies to shape events and regain lost territories.

3. The plan and control [*jinglue*] stage, in which by political [or military ?] means, the international community accepts China's efforts in building a new political economic international order that ensures strategic balance and stability.

Luo stated that China currently is at the first stage mentioned above. He contended that emphasis on peace does not mean that China should neglect the defense sector. Indeed, it should strengthen its defense forces. In his support, Luo cites an old proverb "*youguo wufang, guojiang buguo*" [a country without defense would not be a country]. On the other hand, even if China rises without any military backing, it will not be able to retain its influence long and will certainly decline. The experience of the Qing Dynasty clearly validates this assertion, according to Luo. Therefore, for a rising China, the military should have to provide "escort" functions. Indeed, the only existing powerful countries in the world are those with strong military strength. Luo advocates higher attention should be paid to the defense sector during the course of China's rise. This is conducive for China to achieve a higher strategic ability not only to wage a dozen local wars successfully but, more importantly, to restrain a war from breaking out. The second ability that China can possess, by emphasizing military modernization, is strategic autonomy that ensures independence from an adversary's control of strategic resources. The third quality that Luo bestows on China, on the path to rapid rise with defense preparation, is its strong international coordinative [xietiao] ability. Luo warns China that if it neglects/forgets war preparation, it would face disaster in its path to a peaceful rise [heping jueqi, wangzhan biwei]. [120]

According to Professor Gu Haibing of the People's University, China needs to adopt a great power strategy for the coming years as the international influence of China is set to grow phenomenally. Gu notes that China's rise faces stiff competition [qiangli jingzheng] from India and from the economically resourceful Japan. In order to overcome problems in China's rise, Gu argued that China should choose this as the "fulcrum" of all its strategies and enhance the military capabilities of the country to ensure the country's "independence." Emphasis is placed by Gu on the powerful nation [qiangguo] (with priority given to building military capabilities of the country), rather than on the other elements of enriching the people (fumin) and environment (huanqing meijing). [121]

Hu Xin, of the PLA International Relations Academy's International Research Institute, argued that the peaceful rise of China is all set to become the strategic guiding principle of the country in the 21st century. Hu identified the main challenges facing the country as relations with the United Staates, issues related to Taiwan, and the security of the country in its border regions. He introduced the concept of "multiple rises" as a part of China's interaction with the international system. While agreeing that the United States is able to maintain its dominant international position for several decades, he noted the simultaneous rise of several nations (like China, the European Union (EU), Russia, Japan, and India), with their consequent influence on adjusting the international power. However, it is possible that these rising powers may compete or even come to blows in the international power struggle. It is here that Hu suggests that China should have the ability to control events, restrain negative domestic or international hostile factors, enhance qualitative and quantitative aspects of its strategic resources, etc. As a rising power, China should, according to Hu, shoulder responsibility in the international arena and actively participate in resolving international problems. This calls for a change in its foreign policy. Interestingly, Hu suggests that, as in a long-distance race, China should acquire sustenance from its fellow competitors.[122] The above statement implies that the PLA needs to work along with India, at least in the short to medium term, to enhance its IT potential and expand military exchanges for probable benefits in more closely understanding Indian military intentions and capabilities and like.

The above discussion of China's rise and "multiple rise" of other countries, and the consequent influence on the strategic environment and policy options, poses fresh challenges to the inherited wisdom of the PLA. These factors are bound to influence the PLA's views on South Asia, although it is not clear at the moment how exactly the PLA will respond.

**Pakistan.**

China's relations with Pakistan have been beneficial to the former, given the latter's geographical proximity to the Islamic world in Southwestern and West Asia,[123] as a counter to the growing economic and military power of India,[124] as a source of western military technology, in light of Pakistan's support to China in securing its UN Security Council membership between 1961 and 1971,[125] and other factors. However, the Pakistani establishment reportedly collaborated with American agencies in covert operations in Tibet in the 1950s.[126] Nevertheless, from the 1962 war between India and China, both China and Pakistan have evolved an "all weather" [*quantianhou*] relationship, which remained relatively undisturbed despite the end of the Cold War and the spread of terrorism.

In general, Chinese security perceptions on Pakistan are related to efforts to build bridges with China's neighbors in the overall policy of "good-neighborliness" [*mulin zhengce*], overcome the U.S. trade embargoes, and nullify the influence of encirclement of China by the Western powers through the Southeast Asia Treaty Organization/Central Treaty Organization (SEATO/CENTO) security treaties that came up in the 1950s; secure Tibet and Xinjiang from outside influence and intervention; create conditions in the international arena for the reunification process of the PRC with Taiwan and other regions; provide assistance to the third world countries so as to maintain independence of these countries and keep at bay the "hegemonic" influences in the region, and the like. Building close relations with its neighbors will also contribute to forming allies and friends for China that may, in the short term, create cushions for the security of the country as well as contribute to the global rise of China in the long term. In the nonmilitary fields, given the restive Xinjiang Uighur movement, efforts by China in persuading the concerned [such as the then Taliban-led Afghanistan and Pakistan] would be conducive to its national security. Another dimension is that, since the four modernization programs were launched, energy requirements of China have increased, underlining the requirement for oil and gas supply routes security. Joint efforts with Pakistan in the Gwadhar naval port construction comes in handy, as it overlooks the Strait of Harmuz that accounts for about 47 percent of the Persian Gulf oil exports. Environmental considerations, drug and human trafficking, and illegal financial flows are other areas China also is concerned about.

Several scholars have viewed the enduring Sino-Pakistan relations from different prisms. Samina Yasmin, for instance, in her doctoral dissertation on the subject, contends that such relations should be viewed from a "dominant-bilateral equation," which is "characterised by differing strategic outlooks and responses . . ."[127] One aspect of the neo-realist perspective is the view that forming security alliances provides cushions against drastic and negative changes of the international relations. John W. Garver has argued that the fundamental rationale for such bilateral relations has not changed despite the changes in the international scenario, but that the "entente cordiale remained unchanged." According to him,

"China's overriding strategic interest in South Asia is to maintain a balance of power favorable to itself. Most fundamentally, this entails the perpetuation of Pakistan's existence as a strong center of power in South Asia, independent of Indian domination . . ."[128] However, while several elements of neo-realist perspective are visible in the Sino-Pakistan security relations, one crucial variable, i.e., an explicit security/defense alliance, is missing in such relations.

Sino-Pakistan relations withstood the vagaries of international relations in the Cold and post-Cold War eras alike. According to General Yu Yongbo, a member of the CMC, speaking in May 1997, "no matter what changes may take place in international situation and in each other's countries, the two peoples always support each other, sympathize with each other, and help each other."[129] Cai Bingkui, Vice Chairman of the PLA's think-tank (CIISS) and a member of the newly formed (in March 2003) Sino-Pakistani Friendship Forum, argued that such relations withstood the test of time because of the "mutual trust" evolved between the two countries based on "common understanding and common interests" and on a "broad consensus in understanding the international and *regional* issues." The Friendship Forum, composed of the two countries "celebrities" and specialists, met for the first time in September 2003. Its goal is "to promote and *enhance* the friendly ties between the two nations."[130] Meeting the Pakistan Chairman of the Joint Chiefs of Staff on January 16, 2002, at Beijing, Jiang Zemin, who worked in Pakistan in the 1970s,[131] stated that China would "coordinate positions" with Pakistan in order to "safeguard peace and stability in the region."[132]

Contrary to the general belief that the Sino-Pakistani military relations may have affected post-9/11 events, and in light of China's problems in Xinjiang, the Chinese foreign ministry declared in its 2003 assessment that such relations are "continuing and maintained" [*ZhongBa zai junshi lingyu jixu baochi youhao zhulai*].[133] However, given the Chinese problems related to the growth of Uighur separatism and the reported support the militants received from al-Qa'ida/Taliban or from some in Pakistan, Chinese leaders like Li Peng and others have emphasized measures to curb cross-border terrorism. As a part of this strategy, some interpreted Chinese responses to the Kargil crisis in 1999 as maintaining neutrality between India and Pakistan.[134]

The discussion above on the PLA's views on India mentioned Indian plans to emerge as a great power and impose its hegemony on the region. As a policy option to curtail such influence, the PLA followed a policy of supporting Pakistan to counter India. PLA statements in this regard are implicit in nature. A brief historical account may be useful in explaining this position. The Indo-Pakistan wars of 1965 and 1971, as several Chinese authors contend, led to a "common strategy" between the two countries, especially in the late 1970s, that was further strengthened after the Union of Soviet Socialist Republic's (USSR) Afghan occupation.[135] In the 1965 Indo-Pakistan war, soon after India attacked Lahore on September 6, Premier Zhou Enlai reportedly advised Pakistan to wage a people's war of withdrawing from the territories and luring the adversary deep inside the country to be drowned later. As India had superior strength numerically, Pakistani forward postures would be detrimental to the latter.[136]On the occasion, Zhou said:

> . . . the Indian reactionaries could not have engaged in such a serious military adventure without the consent and support of the United States. Everybody knows that for several months now, U.S. imperialism has used every means in an attempt to compel Pakistan to give up its independent policy. The Indian reactionaries' armed attack on Pakistan was an inevitable result of this policy of the United States.[137]

During President Liu Shaoqi's visit to Pakistan in March 1966, a commentator, Anjam, wrote in *Beijing Review*, acknowledging Chinese support. He said: "At the time of the Indian attack [in 1965], China boldly stood by Pakistan . . . This will be remembered by all posterity in our country." Another article, an editorial of Ta'Meer, in the same issue of the *Beijing Review* stated: "No intrigue, threat, or pressure can stand in the way of the ever-increasing mutual friendship and cooperation" between the two countries.[138] Liu Shaoqi himself outlined the Chinese security concerns during this visit. He stated, at the State Banquet on April 1, 1966:

> Last year, when Pakistan was subjected to India's armed attacks, its Government, people, and army put up a heroic resistance and dealt a heavy blow at the aggressors. The Chinese Government and people *firmly* supported Pakistan in its righteous fight against aggression . . . [Sino-Pakistan] relations are in the fundamental interests of our two peoples.

> . . . The Pakistan people can rest assured that, when Pakistan resolutely fights against foreign aggression in defense of its national independence, sovereignty, and territorial integrity, the 650 million Chinese people will stand *unswervingly* on their side and give them resolute support and assistance . . . We have always held that the Kashmir dispute should be settled in accordance with the wishes of the Kashmir people.[139]

In the joint communiqué issued during the 1966 visit, the "[Pakistan] President expressed the deep gratitude . . . for the support they received from the Government and people of China in resisting aggression . . ."[140] The period of the 1970s was described by the Chinese as a common struggle with Pakistan against "expansionism [*kuozhang zhuyi*] and hegemonism [*baquan zhuyi*]" in Southern Asia.[141] In the 1971 Indo-Pakistan war, the Chinese reportedly advised Pakistan to make a political settlement with the leaders of East Pakistan, but in vain. In the event of war, there was no concrete Chinese support to Pakistan's operations, even as some pressure was exerted by China on the India-China border areas. The Indo-Soviet Treaty and possible Soviet military buildup on the Chinese northeastern and western borders were too unnerving to the Chinese to get involved militarily in the war.[142] Nevertheless, Chinese civilian and military aid to Pakistan increased by leaps and bounds from this period onward.[143] For instance, Pakistan reportedly received nearly one-third of its arms from abroad from the PRC in the 1966-80 period that is worth about U.S. $1.5 billion. Subsequently, Pakistan signed several agreements for further import of weapons from China.

According to a Pakistani commentator, China has established military cooperation arrangements with Pakistan from the 1970s. The year 1989 witnessed a military cooperation agreement between China and Pakistan. The agreement envisaged "purchase of military goods, mutual research, and cooperation, along with the manufacturing of arms, the transfer of technology, and the sale of these arms to third countries with mutual understanding." This was followed by another supplementary agreement in 1993 that made China "the most important military seller" of weapons or systems to Pakistan. China also promised and fulfilled the pledge related to supply and cooperation in the manufacturing of fighter aircraft, tanks, and missiles. Thus China provided M-11 missiles to Pakistan.[144] On March 12, 2002, Deputy Chief of General Staff Xiong

Guangkai reportedly signed an agreement with Pakistan for further cooperation between the two militaries.[145]

Mutual high level military visits between China and Pakistan have increased over a period of time as Appendix I indicates. Indeed, such visits far outnumber India-China military visits. This is another indication of the importance attached by the PLA towards Pakistan. A few days before the 9/11 events, a high level military team from China reportedly visited Pakistan to enhance military cooperation. At the same time, it was reported that a joint high level commission would meet in Beijing to review and enhance military relations between the two countries.[146] However, after the 9/11 events and entry of the United States in the region, specifically with the Afghan war, China has mobilized its troops to block any al-Qa'ida/Taliban infiltration into Xinjiang through the 96-kilometer-long border with Afghanistan.

Pakistan continues to receive advanced weapons systems from China (see Appendix II). The Pakistan Navy has opened negotiations with China for the transfer of F-22P frigates in early 2003.[147] Pakistan reports indicated that the Super 7 aircraft is being developed indigenously, with the assistance of the China Aero Technology Import and Export Corporation and the Chengdu Aircraft Industry Corporation. The first flight test was reported in May 2003, and two more were conducted subsequently, and the aircraft was declared fit for development. About 300 are to be manufactured with Italian-made *Kreno* S-7 fire control radar system, 3,800 kg weight of weapon carriage, and 3,000 km range.[148] Pakistan also has plans to buy 50 F-7MG aircraft from China to replace its aging F-6 aircraft.[149]

Due to the nature of warfare conditions between India and Pakistan, China emphasized supplying armored equipment to Pakistan. It has supplied equipment in this regard.[150] The *Al-Khalid* Main Battle Tank is being manufactured in Taxila with Chinese technical cooperation. Under Project 711 that began in the 1980s, these tanks are considered to be modern. Pakistan is said to be graduating from mere assembly of such tanks to manufacturing them in the country with Chinese collaboration.[151] Post 9/11, China has not only beefed up its security in Xinjiang by redeploying to the region several ground-attack fighters but also reportedly has enhanced its military cooperation with Pakistan. According to a Hong Kong report, China supplied

Pakistan with a new type of missile system, the LY-60N ground-to-air missiles, for air defense purposes even before these were supplied to the PLA units. In addition, China reportedly supplied tanks and communication equipment.[152]

Several reports indicated Chinese cooperation with Pakistan in a strategic weapons program. These include not only supply of about 5,000 ring magnets, but also designs of nuclear weapons, missiles, and missile technologies. With Pakistani inveterate animosity towards India, these weapons of mass destruction (WMD) transfers of the PLA appear to be well thought out. Whereas the Indian ballistic missile program generally is termed by the PLA writers as part of the Indian designs to become a great power, similar plans by Pakistan were termed as only having a defensive impact. A PLA writer stated that the Pakistani missile tests of *Ghauri* (1,500 km range) IRBM, *Hatf*-2 (180 km range), and another missile of 290 km indicated that Pakistani:

> ... intention is as plain as daylight—showing its real strength to prevent war. After all, given the situation that its conventional military strength is inferior to that of India, Pakistan can only rely on the deterrent role of its nuclear strength to control the offensive that may be launched by India.[153]

### Counterterrorism and Joint Exercises.

China conducted naval operations with a foreign naval force for the first time in its contemporary history with Pakistan in October 2003 at Shanghai.[154] After agreeing to conduct exercises in July 2003, the Chinese navy (with *No. 521* vessel) had maritime operations with the Pakistan naval ships (*Babur* and *Nasr*) in October 2003, involving nearly 1,600 personnel and several surface vessels, submarines, and anti-submarine helicopters in search and rescue operations and damage control following attacks involving nuclear, biological, or chemical weapons.[155]

The 2004 PLA White Paper issued in December 2004 emphasized measures to strengthen nontraditional security issues such as countering terrorism, drug trafficking, and piracy, and enhancing maritime search and rescue operations. The paper specifically mentioned cooperation with Pakistan and India in this regard.[156]

Pakistan's counterterrorism campaign has been much appreciated by China.[157] The Chinese army conducted military exercises with the Pakistani army in the Taxkorgan Tajik autonomous county of Xinjiang from August 3-6, 2004. Code-named *Youyi* (Friendship)-2004, these are high-altitude operations performed by about 200 troops of both countries at about 4,000 meters on the Pamir Mountains bordering China, Pakistan occupied areas, Afghanistan, and Tajikistan. According to Major General Cheng Bing, the "exercise is aimed to further strengthen cooperation between the two countries and armies in nontraditional security fields and maintain security and stability in the region, and to improve the capacity of jointly combating terrorism, separatism, and extremism." This live-fire operation achieved "great success" and involved encirclement, assault, and mop-up practices.

These exercises came in the wake of a series of events that highlighted security concerns for China in the Xinjiang region, which declared itself independent in the early 20th century before the People's Republic was formed in 1949. While differences with the Soviet Union on the agreement to keep foreigners from a third country from entering into Xinjiang were kept under the carpet, these surfaced soon after the Sino-Soviet split in 1960, when nearly 60,000 Uighurs migrated to the Soviet Central Asian Republics. The pan-Turkic movements spread during the Soviet occupation of Afghanistan with the active support of the United States, Pakistan, and China from 1979-89. Chinese transfers of arms to the *mujahideen* against the Soviets during this period appear to have boomeranged in the recent period as *al-Qa'ida* trained separatists started entering into Xinjiang in the last few years. Most are suspected of having been trained in Pakistani camps. Chinese Deputy Chief of Staff General Xiong Guangkai estimated in his book published in late 2003 that nearly a thousand such armed separatists have entered Xinjiang.[158]

To counter these flows, in the 1990s China closed its Karakoram highway connecting with the Pakistan-occupied northern areas to stop the flow of "separatists" from Afghanistan into Xinjiang. Later, after the United States launched its strikes on Taliban-held Afghanistan following the 9/11 incidents, China closed its borders with Afghanistan and Pakistan due to fears that fleeing al-Qa'ida/ Taliban activists would sneak into Xinjiang. Nevertheless, the Uighur movement spread fast, with several incidents of attacks against state organizations like the military, police, and judiciary, and against infrastructural projects and administration.

In addition to the Pakistan link in the Uighur movement, a spate of incidents in which Chinese were killed in Pakistan and other places have led the Chinese to seek the active cooperation of the Pakistan government. A car bomb attack on May 3, 2003, at the Gwadar Port construction site killed three Chinese engineers and injured eleven, including nine Chinese and two Pakistanis. These engineers were employed by China Harbor Engineering Company, which was overseeing the port project. While Pakistan authorities saw a Baluchi hand in this incident, the Chinese authorities suspected Uighur "separatists" were responsible. A Pakistan air force plane carried the deceased to China, and the Pakistani government has paid U.S.$145,000 compensation to the Chinese victims. The matter of safety of Chinese was discussed in the first week of August 2004 when Pakistan Senate Chairman Soomro met Chinese Premier Wen Jiabao in Beijing. Wen also demanded the security of over 3,000 Chinese working in Pakistan on several military and civilian projects. Other incidents also underlined the plight of Chinese working in these areas. On April 11, 2004, for instance, seven Chinese construction workers were taken hostage briefly in the Iraqi town of Falluja, although they were freed in 36 hours. On June 10, 11 Chinese road workers were gunned down and five wounded at Kunduz, Afghanistan. In the last week of July, an explosion in a Chinese national-run restaurant in Islamabad injured several people. The Chinese suspect the involvement of Uighurs in these incidents and blame them for the general deterioration of the situation in Pakistan and Afghanistan.

These incidents have alerted the Chinese leadership to take concrete measures to counter "separatism" in Xinjiang, and seek the support of Pakistan in this regard. In a late 2001 visit to Xian, the capital of the Chinese western province of Shaanxi, Pakistan President Pervez Musharraf issued a statement at a famous mosque in the city that the Chinese Muslims should be patriotic and work for the good of China. In early November 2003, Hu Jintao, in his first meeting with President Musharraf since taking office as the President of China, said that both countries must tackle the Chinese version of the "Axis of Evil" — the "three evil forces," viz., extremism, separatism, and terrorism. He also urged Pakistan to step up its fight against transnational crime and drug trafficking. President Musharraf said that Pakistan stood resolutely against terrorism and did not allow anti-China forces, including Uighurs seeking independence for Xinjiang, to use Pakistan as a base. To facilitate this, both countries signed an extradition treaty in the same month

On December 15, 2003, the Chinese Ministry of Public Security publicized a list of terrorist organizations and 11 terrorists to include the East Turkistan Islamic Movement (ETIM), the East Turkistan Liberation Organization, the World Uighur Youth Congress, and the East Turkistan Information Center. The ministry requested other countries to ban these four organizations and their activities, their support base, and financial aspects and to deny protection to these organizations. When the head of ETIM, Hasan Mahsum, was killed by the Pakistani army on October 2, 2003, in a joint antiterrorism raid along the border of Pakistan and Afghanistan, China thanked Pakistan for this operation as Hasan was accused of plotting several incidents in Urumqi and Hotan in Xinjiang.

A joint working group was established in 2001 to discuss and suggest measures to counter narcotics trafficking, illegal border trade, and money-laundering, besides other trans-border crimes. The frequency of these meetings was increased after 1 year in view of the worsening situation on the border of these two countries. In July 2004 Pakistani Interior Minster Syed Faisal Saleh Hayat met Chinese Minister for Public Security Zhou Yongkang at Beijing to "neutralize" the threat posed by *al-Qa'ida*.

However, despite China seeking the Pakistan government's support in countering these nontraditional security challenges, there appears to have been no respite, given the popular support and discontent in Xinjiang and the short-sighted policies of these governments.

## Bangladesh.

The three key principles governing China's relations with Bangladesh are, according the Chinese Foreign Ministry yearbook, "treat each other with equality [and] mutual benefit, mutual trust [and] mutual help, concerted cooperation" [*pingdeng xiangdai, xianghu xinren, huzhu hubu, xietiao hezuo*].[159] The PLA's views appear to be not entirely at variance from the above civilian leadership's guidelines. Indeed, by supporting Bangladesh in military and economic infrastructure projects, China would not only enhance its influence in the region, but also exert pressure on India. The PLA has been active in building linkages with this country in terms of arms transfers, as Appendix II indicates, and through periodic interactions with the Bangladesh military for enhancing "mutual trust" and cooperation, as Appendix I indicates. Indeed, the number of China-Bangladesh mutual military visits almost surpasses that of the China-India military visits to each other. This indicates the relative importance given by the PLA and the civilian leadership to Bangladesh.

At the strategic level, Chinese cooperation with Bangladesh could enhance the latter's position in the region. In certain cases, such as in any joint cooperation in the control of vulnerable Siliguri corridor, the PLA may place enormous military pressure on Indian troop movements to the Indian northeast, specifically if it has any arrangement with Bangladesh forces. The late 2002 defense cooperation agreement between the two sides has been cited as an instance of elevation of bilateral relations between the two armed forces. While the document has not been published, this is intended to further "institutionalize" the military links between the two and enhance systematic training, arms exports promotion, etc.

The military interaction between the two armed forces highlights the security dynamic in Sino-Bangladesh relations. In general, statements issued during these meetings indicate common concern and understanding on the need to "maintain independence" of Bangladesh, strive for "stability" in South Asia and the like. Given the PLA's assessment that India is hegemonic and intends to be a big power, as noted above, the context of these statements between the Chinese and Bangladesh militaries make it amply clear that such interactions are not purely bilateral in nature.

Making Dhaka as his first overseas visit after taking over as the Air Force Commander, Cao Shuangming assured his hosts in 1993 that China would continue to extend defense cooperation with Bangladesh, especially in Air Force related issues.[160] Lieutenant General Tang Tianbiao, deputy director of the General Political

Department (GPD) told the Bangladeshi foreign minister on November 2, 1998 that,

> China and Bangladesh, as well as the Chinese and Bangladesh armed forces, have been maintaining a traditional friendship and friendly and cooperative ties. Further developing bilateral Bangladesh-Chinese friendly and cooperative ties will be beneficial to the basic interests of the people of the two countries and to peace and stability in South Asia and even in the whole of Asia. He commended Bangladesh for its unwavering efforts in developing its own economy, in enhancing regional cooperation, and safeguarding peace in south Asia.[161]

Then Chief of General Staff Fu Quanyou, meeting Bangladesh Army Chief Muhammad Mustafizur Rahman at Beijing on May 7, 1999, said that bilateral "ties between the armies of the two countries are becoming tighter, thanks to the great attention given by government and military leaders."[162]

While the visiting Rear Admiral Abu Taher, chief-of-staff of the Bangladesh navy, thanked China "for its selfless aid to Bangladesh," CMC vice chairman Zhang Wannian told the former in March 2000 that,

> Military relations between China and Bangladesh are the important component part of bilateral relations and have fully demonstrated good-neighborly relations between the two countries. The development of military relations between China and Bangladesh not only accords with the basic interests of the two countries but are also conducive to promoting peace and stability in the region.[163]

In December 2002, Bangladesh PM Khaleda Zia signed four pacts with China, including one on defense cooperation that reportedly called for "institutionalizing" current defense ties between the two.[164] This agreement is expected to plug loopholes in the existing defense ties and cooperation and further elevate such interactions in the future. The April 2005 nuclear agreement during Premier Wen Jiabao's visit to Dhaka was set to be in the civilian field, though the strategic significance of such a move is quite evident.

One of the concrete manifestations of cooperation between the two militaries, apart from the training activities and 2002 defense cooperation agreement, is in the growing arms transfers of China to Bangladesh, as Appendix II indicates. These include supplies of frigates, fast attack craft, ship-to-ship missiles and launchers, fighter aircraft, etc. A few examples include the Bangladesh-considered purchase of eight F-7MB fighter aircraft from China on "very easy financial terms," i.e., no payment for at least 2 years and a "spread out" payment schedule to be worked out through negotiations with the Chinese government.[165] The Bangladesh Air Force already had some of these aircraft in addition to the Chinese supplied A-III ground-attack aircraft. The letter "B" in the F-7MB stood for the Chinese export version of the aircraft for Bangladesh. The policy approval for procuring these aircraft came in 1997.[166]

## Nepal.

Major objectives of China in building relations with Nepal are protecting its interests in Tibet, curtailing the influence of India, expanding its influence in the region through infrastructure building projects, curtailing the spread of Maoists, etc. Several of these are appealing to the PLA. Relatively, the PLA's interactions with Nepal have not been as intensive as they are with other countries in the region (see Appendix I), although it has supplied small arms and other weapons and equipment to Nepal in the late 1980s and agreed in 2005 to train the Nepalese army to counter Maoists.

Chinese civilian and military leadership alike have shown interest in ties with Nepal. During the visits of President Jiang Zemin in 1996 and subsequently during other occasions, such as Li Peng's visits, it was reiterated that relations with Nepal are important, even in the security fields. Meeting the Nepalese Army Chief in December 1999, vice president and vice-chairman of CMC Hu Jintao said that China wanted to fulfil its strategic goal of building good neighborliness by enhancing relations with Nepal.[167] On a hastily arranged visit to Nepal as a part of his visit to southeast Asian countries, defense minister Chi Haotian began the first visit to Nepal in February 2001. This visit comes a few days after the Maoists injured a Chinese national at Sindhuphulchok in the first of such attacks on Chinese.[168]

China has emphasized extending cooperation with Nepal in infrastructure development programs connecting Tibet and Nepal. In the infrastructure projects, reports indicated plans to extend the

Golmud-Lhasa railway line to Kathmandu. If implemented, these could enhance further the logistics facilities of the PLA in the region. Apart from the economic benefits that such projects entail, especially for Tibet, the strategic and logistics importance of overcoming Himalayan barriers may not be out of place.[169]

China and Nepal had agreed in 1994 to start transport service along the 873 km highway linking Kathmandu and Lhasa. It took nearly a decade for this proposal to materialize. The Nepalese government-run transport organization, Sajha Yatayat, announced that in September 2004 such trips will be made.[170] However, this was delayed further until May 1, 2005, when in March 2005, both sides signed an agreement to start a two-way bus ride.[171]

A careful reading of the statements issued during the mutual visits from China and Nepal, especially by military personnel, indicates the need for both parties to arrive at an "understanding" on issues related to India. During the visit of Political Commissar of the General Armaments Department Li Jinai in June 1999, King Birendra said that emerging "new issues" like Kosovo and Kashmir should be resolved through consultation and dialogue. Li, on his part, emphasized the need for stability in South Asia.[172] While seeking "further support" from Nepal on issues like Tibet, Taiwan, and human rights, General Fu Quanyou, during his visit to Nepal in April 2000, emphasized closer relations between the two neighbors. King Birendra stated that "Although China is much larger than Nepal, China showed understanding and support to Nepal's struggle for independence and sovereignty and has extended much assistance to Nepal's economic development."[173] On September 4, 2001, the Commander of the Chengdu MR, Liu Baochen, told the Nepalese PM that the PLA will work with the Nepalese Army in "in maintaining peace and stability of the bordering areas." He stated:

> The goodwill visit of my delegation is in response to the consensus reached by the leaders of our two countries in 1996 to build a good-neighborly partnership that will be handed down from generation to generation. In particular, our visit is aimed at further strengthening the good relations between the armies of the two countries, especially promoting the relations between the Royal Nepal Army and China's Chengdu Military Region and Lanzhou Military Region.[174]

In reply to Royal Nepalese Army Chief Pyar Jung Thapa's remarks that the PLA has helped the Nepalese Army modernization program, Lieutenant General Zou Gengren, Commander of the Lanzhou MR, on a visit to Kathmandu in September 2002 said:

> The goodwill visit of my delegation is aimed at further strengthening the good relations between the armies of the two countries, especially promoting the relations between the Royal Nepal Army and China's Lanzhou Military Region. . . . [W]e will cooperate more closely with the Nepali army in maintaining peace and stability of the bordering areas.[175]

However, despite a relative enhancement in the interactions between the two militaries of Nepal and China, there exist underlying tensions between the two. For instance, the border interactions between Nepal and China are not without problems. Specifically, the Chinese border guards' role in the border trade and smuggling were highlighted by the Nepalese side. For instance, in March 3, 1997, at Friendship Bridge, the only border post for vehicles between the two countries, the Nepalese truck drivers and traders protested for 2 1/2 days against Chinese Armed Police brutality on Tashi Gyaltsen. In August 1994, two Tibetans were stabbed by the Chinese police at Zhangmu (Dram). In August 1996, Tibetans protested against the Chinese police for beating to death a Tibetan at Dram Public Security Office.[176] Another report indicated that Chinese police personnel maltreat common people and officials from the Nepalese side several ways at and across the border check post in Humla district.[177]

## Sri Lanka.

While the civilian leadership of the PRC has been making efforts to build relations with Sri Lanka for the last 5 decades, the PLA's role has been relatively less pronounced. Even though the Sri Lankan government recognized the PRC in 1950, full diplomatic relations started only from 1957. More important from the Chinese national security point of view, the Rubber and Rice Pact signed between the two countries in 1952 was to come in handy in the difficult years of U.S. trade embargoes against the PRC.[178] Also, the Sri Lankan position on Taiwan, and more importantly, given its predominantly Buddhist orientation, Tibet and human rights are crucial for consolidating the PRC's national interests.[179]

Other issues in which China has shown security concerns related to its support of Sri Lanka's policy of "independence, peace, neutrality, and nonalignment" and its backing for the Sri Lankan proposal for declaring the Indian Ocean as a Zone of Peace in the backdrop of the UN Resolution of 1971.[180] However, Sri Lankan support for the Indian nuclear tests in 1998 was unpalatable to China.

Nevertheless, one main area that directly affects security relations between the two countries is arms transfers. China has exported arms to Sri Lanka in the recent period to counter the Tamil rebels. During the tsunami events, the PLA logistics department exhibited interest in Sri Lanka.[181] The China North Industries Corporation (NORINCO) carried out most of the military transactions with Sri Lanka, although they are not without controversies related to corruption, etc.[182]

## Conclusions.

The PLA has an active interest in South Asia and regional security that forms a crucial element in China's policies toward the region. Although China's overall role in South Asia has been limited except in times of crisis, recent policy initiatives from Beijing have been proactive. The PLA has been one of the crucial players as it has pushed for a role to deal with India and build linkages with other South Asian states. Among the issues addressed by the PLA on South Asia are countering "splittism" in Tibet and "separatism" in Xinjiang; promoting the recently launched Western Development Campaign in Tibet, Xinjiang, Yunnan and Sichuan; having a maximalist position of no compromise on border dispute resolution with India and Bhutan; having nuclearization of the region; the growing international clout of India with its economic and military rise; growing concern over the U.S. role in the region; and evolving strategies to enhance energy security in the Indian Ocean.

The PLA's views on South Asia as an institutional actor at times have differed from those of the civilian leadership. While such views on India differed between the PLA and civilian leadership during normal or nonconflict times, there has been a surprising coincidence of views of both the PLA and civilian leadership on other South Asian countries. Of late, with CBMs increasing in content and scale in the military and nonmilitary fields between India and China, there also has been a division *within* the PLA constituents. While some in the PLA have argued for "encircling" India or helping other South Asian countries against India in order to curb its "regional hegemony" and drive to become a "great power," others saw in India the benefits of normalization in relations in the overall context of unipolarity and resolve to reunify with Taiwan. Given the "multiple rises" of China, Japan, and India in the recent period and renewed U.S. interest in the region, PLA responses are expected to be less confrontational but firm on India.

While the PLA's strategy of confronting India has become more nuanced in the recent period, earlier policy called for exerting pressure on India. In Indian military circles, China's actions were seen as an attempt by the PLA at the "strategic encirclement" or "marginalization" of India. This can be seen in the late 1985 PLA naval visits to Chittagong, Colombo, and Karachi, skipping Indian ports; continuing arms transfers to most of the South Asian countries, with Pakistan receiving the strategic weapons; and Bangladesh elevated in the Chinese security calculus with extensive military exchanges with these countries. The PLA military exchanges with the region indicate emphasis placed on Pakistan and Bangladesh, while ties with Indian armed forces remain sparse and defensive and conflict prevention in nature. Along with security considerations of both the countries, PLA's close relations with Pakistan and Bangladesh have not been conducive to the full normalization of relations between China and India.

Overall, the PLA has painted a negative picture of India as dominating South Asia through increased defense preparation. In this context, policy fallout to counter such domination by India has been the PLA efforts to prop up other countries like Pakistan and Bangladesh. To a large extent, the PLA has been successful in pushing through this policy of the PRC in the last 4 decades. However, with the civilian leadership's emphasis on building a "well-off society" by 2020 and the resolve to focus on solving the Taiwan issue, it appears the PLA has adopted a nuanced approach to its South Asia policy, even as it maintained its traditional relations with the concerned countries. While there has been no let down on military cooperation with Pakistan, Bangladesh, or Nepal and Myanmar, the PLA has been expanding its contacts with the Indian military forces in terms of preventive CBMs and exchanges. The PLA leadership continues to follow a policy of balancing India by supporting Pakistan, Bangladesh, or Nepal; supplying nuclear and missile systems or components; and supplying small arms to insurgents in northeast India through a third party as "commercial" transactions. The PLA displayed identical views with the civilian leadership on Pakistan, Bangladesh, and Nepal and supported them to balance India. While there has never been a military alliance between China and Pakistan or with Bangladesh, these states are being courted extensively for their value in countering India, besides being sources for raw materials and markets for low technology arms of China. However, the PLA's arms market and military cooperation with Pakistan, Bangladesh, and Myanmar are witnessing a rise in sophisticated arms transfers in the last few years.

# APPENDIX I

## CHINA'S MILITARY DIPLOMACY WITH SOUTH ASIA

### a. China-India Defense Personnel/Security Meetings.

| Period | Place | Remarks |
|---|---|---|
| 1956 | Different China | Indian Defense Services delegation of nine members from the places in three services led by Lieutenant General J. N. Chowdhury. |
| 1958 | Shanghai | *INS Mysore* headed by Admiral Srinivasan's port call. |
| April 1987 | Beijing | Defense Minister KC Pant's stop over visit *en route* to India from Pyongyang. |
| March 15-22, 1991 | New Delhi | Defense MFA bureau delegation visited. |
| May 15-31, 1991 | Beijing | Former Indian Army chief visited Beijing Strategic Studies Institute. |
| June 23-30, 1991 | Beijing | Indian Army Intelligence Bureau chief's visit. |
| November 14-22, 1991 | New Delhi | NDU vice-president visited. |
| March 26-April 6, 1992 | Beijing | IDSA Director visited Beijing International Strategic Studies Institute. |
| July 24-30, 1992 | Beijing | Defense Minister Sharad Pawar's visit. |
| August 30-September 5, 1992 | Beijing | National Defense College (NDC) delegation visited. |
| April 30-May 9, 1993 | New Delhi | GLD deputy chief of staff visited. |
| November 15-19, 1993 | Bombay | Visit by Chinese naval training ship *Zheng He*. |

| December 18-23, 1993 | New Delhi | Deputy Chief of General Staff Lieutenant General Xu Huizi's visit. |
|---|---|---|
| March 6-16, 1994 | New Delhi | Chinese Air Force deputy chief of staff delegation visit. |
| June 26-July 2, 1994 | Beijing | NDC delegation visited. |
| July 22-30, 1994 | Beijing | Chief of Army Staff General B.C. Joshi's visit. |
| September 7-12, 1994 | New Delhi | Minister for National Defense General Chi Haotian's visit. |
| November 9-15, 1994 | Beijing | IAF intelligence bureau chief's visit. |
| March 15-22, 1995 | Beijing | Indian Army delegation's visit. |
| September 8-11, 1995 | Shanghai | Indian naval vessels port call at Shanghai. |
| December 20-27, 1995 | New Delhi | PLA Air Force delegation headed by deputy commander Liu Shunyao's visit. |
| March 10-19, 1996 | New Delhi | Chief of Naval Staff Admiral V.S. Shekhawat's visit. |
| June 23-29, 1996 | Beijing | NDC Army department chairman visited. |
| July 3-10, 1996 | New Delhi | Jinan MR commander visited. |
| October 3-11, 1996 | New Delhi | PLA delegation visited. |
| May 26-31, 1997 | Beijing | Five-member delegation headed by Vice Chief of Army Staff General Vice-President Malik visited. |
| June 6-12, 1997 | New Delhi | Chengdu MR Commander Lieutenant General Liao Xilong visited. |
| April 12-17, 1998 | New Delhi | Chinese NDU delegation led by Lieutenant General Dong Lisheng's visit to NDC. |
| April 26-May 1, 1998 | New Delhi | Chief of General Staff Fu Quanyou's visit. The first ever visit by a Chinese chief of general staff. |

| | | |
|---|---|---|
| November 21, 1999 | Nathu La Pass | A telephone link was established in the Sikkim sector between Yatung garrison in Tibet and the 17th Mountain Division of the Indian Army to keep each other informed of activities along the border and "defuse border tensions." |
| March 6-7, 2000 | Beijing | As a result of E. A. M. Jaswant Singh's visit to Beijing in June 1999, the first ever security dialogue between the two countries held by MEA Joint Secretary (Disarmament) Rakesh Sood and Director-General of the Asian Department of the MFA, Zhang Jiuhuan. PRC told India to abide by the Chinese-backed UN Resolution 1172, calling for India to roll back its nuclear program. The meeting cames 2 weeks before U.S. President Clinton's visit to India. |
| April 1, 2000 | Nathu La Pass | Commemorative border meeting of the Nathu La Brigade of India and Yatung garrison of the Chinese army authorities on the occasion of the 50th anniversary of the establishment of diplomatic relations between the two countries. |
| May 22-26, 2000 | Beijing | NDC delegation visit. |
| August 18-23, 2000 | New Delhi | Chinese Academy of Military Science delegation's visit headed by General Tian Shuyan. |
| September 16-19, 2000 | Shanghai | Indian naval port calls at Shanghai with *INS Delhi* and a frigate. |
| April 1-7, 2001 | Beijing | Lieutenant General Kalkat, GOC-in-C, Eastern Command. |
| May 20-26, 2001 | Beijing | Air Chief Tipnis visited. |
| May 22-26, 2001 | New Delhi | NDU delegation headed by Zhang Xingye visited. |
| May 27-30, 2001 | Mumbai | Two Chinese naval ships from the North Sea Fleet made a port call. |

| September 7-12, 2001 | Mumbai | Deputy commander of the Chengdu MR, General Liu Baochen, with seven-member delegation, including those from the Lanzhou MR. |
|---|---|---|
| December 16-22, 2001 | Mumbai | Deputy Chief of Staff Lieutenant General Zhang Li. |
| November 23-December 1, 2002 | Chengdu and other places | Indian Central Command delegation's visit. |
| April 2003 | Beijing | Defense Minister George Fernandes visit with a 16-member delegation. |
| July 2003 | New Delhi and other places | Chinese Air Force delegation's visit. |
| November 10-14, 2003 | Shanghai | India-China naval drills near Shanghai with *INS Ranjit, INS Kulish,* and *INS Jyoti.* |
| November 2003 | Tibet | Indian military delegation's first visit to Tibet. |
| March 26, 2004 | New Delhi | MND Cao Gangchuan's visit to New Delhi as a part of his Pakistan, India, and Thailand visit. |
| December 2004 | Beijing | Indian Army Chief General N. C. Vij's visit. |
| January 24, 2005 | New Delhi | First "strategic dialogue" between the two countries with F. S. Shyam Saran and Wu Dawei delegations in talks on globalization and multipolarity, energy security, reform of the UN, border disputes, etc. |
| April 12, 2005 | Beijing | Yashwant Prasad, vice chief of the Indian naval staff, and his party met CGS Liang Guanglie. |
| May 2005 | New Delhi | CGS Liang Guanglie's visit with 11-member delegation. |

## b. China-Pakistan Defense Personnel/Security Meetings.

| Period | Place | Remarks |
|---|---|---|
| March 1988 | Islamabad | Chinese Air Force Chief Wang Hai visited. |
| March 1988 | Beijing | Pakistan naval chief of staff visited. |
| October 1988 | Islamabad | PLA deputy chief of staff visited. |
| December 1988 | Beijing | Pakistan Army chief of staff visited. |
| February 27-March 3, 1989 | Islamabad | Chief of Staff Chi Haotian visited. |
| March 20-26, 1989 | Islamabad | Xinjiang MR Commander visited. |
| September 9, 1989 | Beijing | Pakistan defense secretary's delegation visited. |
| October 8-13, 1989 | Beijing | Pakistan Army deputy chief of staff visited. |
| December 11-19, 1989 | Islamabad | Guangzhou MR Commander's visit. |
| December 24-26, 1989 | Beijing | Pakistan defense minister's visit. |
| February 19-27, 1990 | Islamabad | Minster for National Defense visited. |
| May 13-23, 1990 | Beijing | Pakistan naval chief of staff visited. |
| November 18-26, 1990 | Beijing | Pakistan Army delegation visited. |
| December 30, 1990-January 2, 1991 | Beijing | Pakistan Army chief of staff visited. |
| March 17-24, 1991 | Islamabad | PLA deputy chief of staff visited. |
| June 2-9, 1991 | Beijing | Pakistan Chairman of the Joint Chiefs of Staff visited. |
| October 24-30, 1991 | Beijing | Pakistan Army chief of staff visited. |

| | | |
|---|---|---|
| February 7-14, 1992 | Islamabad | Chinese naval commander's visit. |
| May 10-18, 1992 | Beijing | Pakistan Air Force chief of staff. |
| May 17-25, 1992 | Beijing | Pakistan Army head of Chief of Staff Bureau. |
| August 16-25, 1992 | Beijing | Pakistan's Chairman of Joint Chiefs of Staff visited. |
| September 27-October 2, 1992 | Beijing | Pakistan defense minister's visit. |
| November 15-23, 1992. | Beijing | Pakistan Army's air defense commander's visit. |
| March 11-15, 1993 | Beijing | Pakistan's newly appointed Army chief visited. |
| May 6-14, 1993 | Beijing | Pakistan's naval chief visited. |
| May 20-27, 1993 | Islamabad | Chinese Air Force commander's visit. |
| December 1-7, 1993 | Islamabad | Chief of General Staff Zhang Wannian's visit. |
| December 2-6, 1993 | Beijing | Pakistan defense minister's visit. |
| February 27-March 6, 1994 | Beijing | Pakistan Army chief's visit. |
| March 18-24, 1994 | Islamabad | Chinese Ordnance Factories delegation visited. |
| July 17-25, 1994 | Beijing | Pakistan's tri-services public relations bureau delegation visited. |
| July 17-21, 1994 | Islamabad | Defense Minister Chi Haotian's visit. |
| September 18-25, 1994 | Beijing | Pakistan Air Force chief's visit. |
| October 6-14, 1994 | Islamabad | Chinese Navy's East Sea Fleet's naval aviation commander and others visited. This is the first time a naval aviation delegation visited Pakistan. |

| | | |
|---|---|---|
| November 17-22, 1994 | Islamabad | NDU delegation headed by its vice-president. |
| November 20-24, 1994 | Beijing | Pakistan Army chief's visit. |
| November 20-27, 1994 | Islamabad | Lanzhou MR deputy commander's delegation. |
| January 6-12, 1995 | Islamabad | General Logistics Department Director Fu Quanyou's visit. |
| April 23, 1995 | Beijing | Pakistan National Defense College delegation. |
| April 27, 1995 | Beijing | Pakistan Air Force chief's visit. |
| May 28-June 4, 1995 | Beijing | Pakistan naval chief's visit. |
| September 29-October 8, 1995 | Islamabad | NDU delegation. |
| October 22, 1995 | Beijing | Chairman of Joint Chief's of Staff's visit. |
| November 16-20, 1995 | Islamabad | PLA's China North Industries delegation's visit. |
| December 7-13, 1995 | Islamabad | PLA naval deputy commander's visit. |
| December 8-17, 1995 | Islamabad | Lanzhou MR deputy commander's visit. |
| June 22-27, 1996 | Beijing | Pakistan chief of army staff visited. |
| June 28-July 2, 1996 | Islamabad | PLA Navy Commander Zhang Lianzhong's visit. |
| August 15-21, 1996 | Islamabad | PLA deputy chief of staff visited. |
| November 23-29, 1996 | Islamabad | PLA Air Force chief visited. |
| November 29, 1996 | Beijing | Pakistan Army delegation's visit. |
| December 29, 1996-January 4, 1997 | Islamabad | Chinese Air Force Commanders Academy's high-level unit's visit. |

| | | |
|---|---|---|
| February 23-28, 1997 | Beijing | Pakistan Defense College commandant's visit. |
| May 5-9, 1997 | Islamabad | Director of General Political Department Yu Yongbo visited. |
| August 21-27, 1997 | Islamabad | General Political Department's Cadre Department deputy director visited. |
| October 31-November 7, 1997 | Islamabad | PLA Naval Commander Shi Yunsheng visited. |
| November 10-15, 1997 | Islamabad | PLA Logistics Department's health department's deputy director visited. |
| December 7-12, 1997 | Islamabad | Chinese Air Force Command Academy's high level unit's visit. |
| December 22-28, 1997 | Islamabad | Academy of Military Science vice president's visit. |
| March 1-8, 1998 | Beijing | Pakistan naval chief's visit. |
| April 26-29, 1998 | Beijing | Pakistan's National Defense College delegation visited. |
| May 10-16, 1998 | Beijing | A delegation of 20 members of Pakistan Military Medicine visited the PLA Medical Institute, No. 304 Military Institute, and the Naval Hospital Institute. |
| August 23-28, 1998 | Beijing | Pakistan's Chairman of Joint Chiefs of Staff visited. |
| October 23-29, 1998 | Islamabad | Deputy director of the GDP visited. |
| February 19-23, 1999 | Islamabad | Chinese Defense Minister Chi Haotian's visit. |
| May 24-31, 1999 | Beijing | Pakistan Chief of Joint Staff Musharraf's visit. |
| June 7-13, 1999 | Islamabad | Chinese General Armaments Department Political Commissar Li Jinai's visit. |
| August 16-22, 1999 | Beijing | Pakistan's Air Force chief visited. |

| | | |
|---|---|---|
| February 26-March 2, 2000 | Islamabad | Chinese Air force Commander Liu Shunyao's delegation. |
| May 6-11, 2000 | Beijing | Pakistan Defense College delegation's visit. |
| May 22-28, 2000 | Beijing | Pakistan's naval chief of staff's visit. |
| June 14-18, 2000 | Islamabad | Chinese Armed Policy Department's deputy political commissar's visit. |
| August 7-14, 2000 | Islamabad | Deputy chairman of the Commission of Science and technology for National Defense visited. |
| November 14-16, 2000 | Islamabad | Chinese naval delegation headed by its political commissar participated in the Pakistani-organized "2000 Year International Defense Exhibition." |
| November 16-21, 2000 | Islamabad | Nanjing MR political commissar's visit. |
| February 16-23, 2001 | Beijing | Pakistan Air Force chief's visit. |
| April 19-21, 2001 | Islamabad | Chief of General Staff Fu Quanyou's visit. |
| April 23, 29, 2001 | Beijing | Pakistan Military Academy chief visited. |
| May 2-June14, 2001 | Pakistan | Chinese naval visit. |
| July 23-30, 2001 | Beijing | Pakistan's Army chief of staff's visit. |
| January 14-21, 2002 | Beijing | Pakistan's chief of Joint Staff's visit. |
| July 2003 | Beijing | General Mohammad Youaf, first deputy chief of general staff visited to attend the Second Round of China-Pakistan Defense and Security Consultation. |
| August 25, 2003 | Zhurihe in Inner Mongolia | A Pakistani delegate participated along with 14 other foreign military officers in observing a PLA armored brigade exercise. |
| September 2003 | Islamabad | Chief of the General Staff Liang Guanglie visited. |

| September 2003 | Islamabad | First round of disarmament consultations between the two sides. |
| October 21 2003 | Beijing | Pakistani Air Force Chief Marshal Kaleem Saadat visited. |
| October 2003 | Shanghai | Port call of Pakistan naval fleet. Conducted joint search and rescue exercises with the Chinese navy, the first of its kind between the Chinese and foreign navies. |
| November 5, 2003 | Beijing | General Musharraf met Defense Minister Cao Gangchuan. |
| March 23, 2004 | Islamabad | Defence Minister Cao Gangchuan visited. |
| April 27, 2004 | Beijing | Pakistani NDC delegation led by Rear Admiral Syed Afzal met Lieutenant General Fan Changlong, assistant chief of the general staff of the PLA. |

## c. China-Bangladesh Defense Personnel/Security Meetings.

| Period | Place | Remarks |
| --- | --- | --- |
| April 2-11, 1988 | Beijing | Bangladesh Army chief of staff visited. |
| March 7-13, 1989 | Dhaka | Chief of Staff Chi Haitian's visit. |
| March 1989 | Dhaka | National Defense University President Zhang Zhen visited. |
| September 1989 | Beijing | Bangladesh Air Force chief of staff visited. |
| September 1989 | Beijing | Bangladesh naval delegation visited. |
| December 1989 | Dhaka | Naval Commander Zhang Lianzhong's visit. |
| February 8-13, 1990 | Dhaka | Chinese Air Force Commander Wang Hai visited. |
| February 27- March 4, 1990 | Dhaka | Defense Minister's visit. |

| April 25-May 1, 1991 | Beijing | Bangladesh Army chief of staff visited. |
|---|---|---|
| June 11-14, 1991 | Dhaka | PLA General Staff Department's second department chief visited. |
| October 3-11 | Beijing | Bangladesh naval chief of staff visited. |
| November 22-25, 1991 | Dhaka | Deputy chief of staff visited. |
| May 1992 | Dhaka | PLA Armored Corps commander's visit. |
| May 1992 | Beijing | Bangladesh's Armaments Unit's National Command Staff Institute's head visited. |
| September 1992 | Beijing | Bangladesh's Army Commander of Unit 9 and head of the Capital District visited. |
| November 1992 | Beijing | Bangladesh Air Force chief of staff visited. |
| May 17-20, 1993 | Dhaka | Chinese Air Force Commander Cao Shuangming's visit. This was his first overseas visit. |
| June 6-13, 1993 | Beijing | Bangladesh army chief visited. |
| October 24-29, 1993 | Beijing | Chinese naval vessel *Zheng He* from Dalian visited. |
| November 28-December 1, 1993 | Dhaka | Chief of Staff Zhang Wannian visited. |
| January 12-16, 1995 | Dhaka | General Logistics Department Director Fu Quanyou's visit. |
| February 13-16, 1995 | Dhaka | PLA Navy deputy commander's visit. |
| June 5-12, 1995 | Beijing | Bangladesh Army chief's visit. |
| October 29-November 6, 1995 | Beijing | Bangladesh Army's delegation. |
| August 21-25, 1996 | Dhaka | PLA deputy chief of staff visited. |
| October 8-18, 1996 | Beijing | Bangladesh Navy chief of staff visited. |

| | | |
|---|---|---|
| October 26–November 3, 1996 | Beijing | Bangladesh Chief of Air Staff Vice Marshal Jamal Uddin Ahmed visited. |
| November 7-12, 1996 | Beijing | Bangladesh Army chief visited. |
| August 17-21, 1997 | Beijing | Bangladesh Defense Secretary's visit. |
| August 30–September 4, 1997 | Dhaka | Eight-member delegation headed by Major General Zhou Shaojun visited to attend the commissioning ceremony of a Landing Craft Tank at Postogola. |
| November 1-4, 1997 | Dhaka | Lanzhou MR Commander visited. |
| November 4-8, 1997 | Hong Kong | Bangladesh naval vessel *Madhumati* made port call. |
| October 28–November 2, 1998 | Dhaka | Deputy Director of GDP Lieutenant General Tang Tianbiao visited. |
| May 4-12, 1999 | Beijing | Bangladesh Army Chief Muhammad Mustafizur Rahman's visit. |
| June 13-16, 1999 | Dhaka | General Armaments Department Political Commissar Li Jinai's visit. |
| September 10-15, 1999 | Dhaka | Ministry of National Defense Foreign Affairs Office chairman's visit. |
| October 31–November 8, 1999 | Beijing | An officer of the Armaments Bureau of the Prime Minster's Office visited. |
| March 28-April 5, 2000 | Beijing | Rear Admiral Abu Taher, Chief-of-Staff of the Bangladesh Navy visited. |
| August 15-18, 2000 | Dhaka | Academy of Military Science Vice President General Tian Shuyan led a delegation of military research and training personnel. |
| November 12-16, 2000 | Dhaka | Nanjing MR's political commissar led a delegation. |
| July 8-14, 2001 | Beijing | Bangladesh's Chief of Army Staff Ahsan N. Amin's visit. |

| | | |
|---|---|---|
| December 22-25, 2001 | Dhaka | Chinese Deputy Chief of Staff Gen Zhang Li's visit. |
| April 2002 | Dhaka | National Defense University delegation's visit. |
| June 2-8, 2002 | Beijing | Bangladesh's Army chief visited. |
| August 19-26, 2002 | Beijing | Bangladesh's Air Force chief's visit. |
| December 23-29, 2002 | Beijing | Prime Minster Khaleda Zia's visit. Defense Cooperation agreement signed. |
| December 2003 | Dhaka | Deputy Chief of General Staff General Wu Quanxu visited. |
| September 22, 2004 | Beijing | Hasan Mashhud Chowdhury, Chief of Army Staff of Bangladesh Army met Cao Gangchuan. Cao said China attached "great importance" to ties with Bangladesh and continued to support the latter's efforts to "play a greater role in regional and world affairs." |
| April 12, 2005 | Beijing | Mahbubur Rahman, advisor to the prime minister on national defense and security and chairman of the standing committee on the Ministry of Sefense of the Bangladesh Parliament met Chief of the General Staff Liang Guanglie. |
| May 21-24, 2005 | Dhaka | CGS Liang Guanglie's visit with an 11-member delegation. |

## d. China-Nepal Defense Personnel/Security Meetings

| Period | Place | Remarks |
|---|---|---|
| November 29-December 5, 1993 | Beijing | Nepal's defense secretary's visit. This is the first such visit in 30 years. |
| November 19, 1996 | Beijing | Visit of Army Chief Lieutenant General Dharmapalbar Singh Thapa. |
| May 13-19, 1997 | Beijing | Nepal defense secretary's visit. |

| June 12-17, 1997 | Kathmandu | Chengdu MR commander visited with a seven-member delegation. |
|---|---|---|
| November 24-December 2, 1998 | Beijing | Nepal military delegation's visit. |
| June 16-20, 1999 | Kathmandu | General Armaments Department Political Commissar Li Jinai visited. |
| September 15-20, | Kathmandu | Ministry of National Defense Foreign Affairs Office chairman visited. |
| December 7-13, 1999 | Beijing | Nepal Army Chief Prajwal Shumshere Jung Bahadur Rana's visit. |
| April 6-11, 2000 | Kathmandu | Chief of General Staff, Fu Quanyou and others visited. |
| October 17-24, 2000 | Beijing | Deputy chief of Army Staff's visit. |
| February 21-24, 2001 | Kathmandu | Chinese defense minister Chi Haotian's visit. This is the first visit of a Chinese defense minister to Nepal. |
| August 22-30, 2001 | Beijing | Nepalese military delegation visited. |
| September 4-10, 2001 | Kathmandu | Lieutenant General Liu Baochen, Commander of Chengdu MR, visited with a seven-member delegation. |
| October 30-November 7, 2001 | Beijing | Defense Secretary of Nepal's visit. |
| March 26, 2002 | Beijing | Army Chief Lieutenant-General Pyar Jung Thapa and delegation visited. |
| September 15-21, 2002 | Kathmandu | Lanzhou MR Commander Lieutenant General Zou Gengren's seven member-delegation visit. |
| April 2003 | Beijing | Defense Secretary MP Aryal visited. |
| October 15, 2003 | Beijing | Lieutenant General Victory Renan, Chief of General Staff of the Royal Nepalese Army visited. |

### e. China-Sri Lanka Defense Personnel/Security Meetings.

| Period | Place | Remarks |
|---|---|---|
| February 28-March 4, 1993 | Colombo | Ordnance Factories deputy manager visited. |
| March 21-April 2, 1994 | Beijing | Sri Lankan naval chief's visit. |
| June 10-17, 2002 | Beijing | Sri Lankan defense minister's visit. |

### e. China-Maldives Defense Personnel/Security Meetings.

| Period | Place | Remarks |
|---|---|---|
| April 14-18, 2001 | Male | Chief of General Staff Fu Quanyou's visit. |
| November 10-15, 2001 | Beijing | Maldives national security bodyguard chief's visit. |

**Notes:** This list is not exhaustive but reported in the sources below.

**Sources**: *Zhongguo Waijiao* (various Yearbooks from 1996-2005); *Zhongguo Waijiao Gailan* (Various Yearbook from 1989-1995); Various Indian Parliament debates and newspaper reports; *PLA Daily* website at *www.chinamil.com.cn \ site1 \ wjdwjlsl \ wjdwjlsl.htm* and *www.chinamil.com.cn \ site1 \ wjdwjlsl \ 2002 \ 2002.htm*.

# Appendix II

## CHINA'S ARMS TRANSFERS TO SOUTH ASIAN COUNTRIES

**a. Pakistan**

| Type | Designation | No. | Year | Delivery | Remarks |
|---|---|---|---|---|---|
| Fighter | F-6 | 100 | 1971 | - | - |
| Fighter/ ground attack | A-5 *Fantan* A | 98 | (1991) | - | With Pakistan Air Force Squadrons Nos. 7, 16, and 26. |
| Fighter | F-7M *Airguard* | 40 | (1991) | 1993 | Included 20 trainer version. |
| Fighter | F-7MG | (55) | (2001) | 2001-03 | Included nine F-7PG. |
| Fighter | F7MG | 11 | (2002) | 2003 | - |
| Fighter | F-7P *Skybolt* | 40 | 1992 | - | - |
| Fighter | FC-1 | - | 1991 | 2005 | Joint venture between China and Pakistan. Israeli avionics reportedly incorporated. |
| Fighter | Super 7 | - | 1999 | - | To Pakistan. Deal struck during PM Nawaz Sharif's visit to China in June 1999 |
| Fighter | F-7 | 75 | 1983 | 1986-90 | - |
| Fighter | JF-17 | 150 | (1999) | 2006 | Six reportedly delivered. |
| Air-to-air missiles | PL-12 | - | (2004) | - | For JF-17 contract to be signed. |
| Fighter/ ground attack | Q-5 *Fantan-A* | 100 | 1984 | 1986 | For final assembly in Pakistan. |
| Fighter trainer | FT-7P | 15 | - | - | With PAF squadrons No. 2 at Masroor, Nos. 18 and 20 at Rafique, and No. 25 at Mianwali. |
| Trainer aircraft | K-8 | - | 1999 | - | PRC offered for export to Egypt the *Karakoram* K-8 jets. Previously 75 of these also were offered to Pakistan from 1991. |

| | | | | | |
|---|---|---|---|---|---|
| Trainer | K-8 | (6) | (2001) | 2003 | Six delivered. |
| Transport | Y-12 | - | - | - | - |
| ASW Helicopter | Z-9C | (4) | (2004) | - | Contract to be signed. |
| Portable SAM | *Hong Ying-5* | 300 | 1988 | - | Arming M-113 APCs. |
| Portable SAM | *Anza* | 450 | 1988 | - | - |
| Portable SAM | HN-5A | - | 1988 | - | License-production under way in Pakistan. |
| Portable SAM | QW-1 *Vanguard* | (750) | (1993) | 1994-2003 | Pakistan design *Anza-2* (License production). |
| MBT-2000 | *Al-Khalid* (P90) | - | 1999 | - | Original agreement date back to 1988. Chinese NORINCO and Pakistan Heavy Industries Taxila are partners. |
| MBT | T-59 | 975 | (1975) | 1978-90 | - |
| MBT | T-69 II | 450 | 1989 | 1991-93 | Deal worth $1.2 billion. |
| MBT | T-85 II | 12 | 1990 | 1993 | - |
| Anti-tank missile | *Red Arrow 8* | 200 | 1989 | 1990-2003 | 10,600 to be delivered. Pakistan design *Bhaktar Shikan* (Licence Produced). |
| Towed Gun 85mm | Type 56 | 190 | - | - | - |
| Submarine | *Romeo* | 2 | 1988 | - | For final assembly in Pakistan. |
| Frigate | *Jiangwei* | 4 | (2004) | - | Deal about $500-700 million. Contract to be signed. |
| Fast Attack Craft (FAC) Patrol | *Hainan* class | 3 | 1977 | - | - |
| Hydrofoil | *Huzhuan* | 3 | 1971 | - | - |
| FAC patrol | *Huangfen* | - | 1971 | - | - |
| FAC gun | *Shanghai* | 12 | - | - | - |

| | | | | | |
|---|---|---|---|---|---|
| FAC | *Hegu* | 4 | 1981 | - | - |
| FAC | *Huangfen* | 4 | 1984 | - | - |
| FAC patrol | *Hainan* | 4 | 1976-80 | - | - |
| FAC torpedo | *Huzhuan* | 4 | - | - | - |
| ShShM system | C-801/802 | 4 | 1996 | 1997 | For the four *Jalata* class FAC. Eight probably delivered in 2004. |
| ShShM system | C-802 | 32 | 1996 | 1997 | For the four *Jalatas*. |
| Fire Control Radar | Type 347G | 2 | (2003) | 2004 | One delivered in 2004. For *Jalata* class |

## b. Bangladesh

| | | | | | |
|---|---|---|---|---|---|
| Frigate | *Jianghu* I class | 2 | (1988) | 1989 | The first, *Xiangtan*, was delivered in November 1989. Status of the second is uncertain. |
| Frigate | *Jianghu* class | 4 | - | 1989 | - |
| FAC | *Huangfen* class | 2 | 1992 | - | - |
| FAC-gun | *Shanghai* class | 8 | - | 1980-82 | - |
| FAC | *Huangfen* class | 4 | - | 1988 | - |
| FAC | *Hegu* class | - | - | 1983 | - |
| FAC | *Hegu* class | - | - | 1992 | - |
| FAC Patrol | *Hainan* Class | 2 | - | 1982 | - |
| FAC Patrol | *Hainan* Class | 1 | - | 1985 | - |
| FAC Patrol | *Hainan* class | 2 | 1991 | - | - |
| FAC Patrol | *Hainan* class | 6 | 1991 | - | Four delivered in 1993; six by 1995-96. |
| Patrol boat | *Haizhui* class | - | - | 1996 | - |
| Mine-sweeper (Ocean) | T-43 class | 4 | (1993) | 1995-96 | Bangladeshi designation *Sagar* class. |

| | | | | | |
|---|---|---|---|---|---|
| Amphibious warfare | LCU/LCP-Yuchin | 8 | - | - | - |
| Tugs | *Hujiu* class | - | - | 1984 & 1995 | - |
| ShShM L | *Hai Ying* 2L | 2 | 1988 | 1989 | For two *Jianghus* |
| ShShM L | *Hai Ying* 2L | 2 | 1992 | - | For two *Huangfens* |
| ShShM | *Hai Ying* 2 | (24) | 1988 | 1989 | Arming two *Jianghus* |
| ShShM | *Hai Ying* 2 | (8) | 1992 | - | - |
| ShShM | *Fei Lung* | - | 1988 | 1989-90 | Arming two *Jianghus* |
| Fighter/ ground attack | A-5 *Fantan* | 20 | 1989 | 1990 | - |
| Fighter | F-6 | 40 | 1992 | 1992 | - |
| Fighter | F-7M *Airguard* | 44 | 1992 | 1992-94 | - |

### c. Sri Lanka

| | | | | | |
|---|---|---|---|---|---|
| FAC Patrol | *Shanghai* class | 5 | - | 1972 | - |
| FAC Patrol | *Shanghai* class | 3 | 1991 | 1994 | Sri Lankan designation *Rana* Class |
| FAC Patrol | *Shanghai* class | 3 | (1996) | 1998 | - |
| Patrol craft | *Haizhui* class | 9 | 1994 | 1995-98 | Three supplied in August 1995, three in May 1996, and another three in August 1998. |
| FAC Patrol | *Haiqing* class | 2 | (1995) | 1997 | - |
| Landing Ship | *Yuhai* class | 1 | (1996) | 1997 | - |
| Artillery systems | 122 mm and 130mm | - | 1991 | 1991 | Two systems of 122 mm artillery acquired in mid-1991. |
| Air Surveillance radar | CEIEC-408C | (3) | 2004 | - | Designation uncertain. |

**Sources:** Yearbooks of SIPRI; *Military Balance* (various); *Foreign Broadcast Information Service*-CHINA (various).

# ENDNOTES - CHAPTER 9

1. The author thanks Andrew Scobell, Larry Wortzel, Paul Godwin, Brantly Womack, Bernard Cole, Michael Swaine, June Teufel Dreyer, Harlan Jencks, Kenneth W. Allen, Gregory K. S. Man, Andrew Nathan, and Shirley Kan for their critique and suggestions in improving this revised manuscript submitted at The Heritage Foundation and the U.S. Army War College organized conference on September 24-25, 2005. Nevertheless, none of the above is responsible for the views or errors expressed in this article.

2. Ding Zengyi, "Indian-US Military Cooperation Raises Concern," *Liberation Army Daily*, February 24, 2002, in *Foreign Broadcasting Information Service-China Report*-2002-0226 (hereafter FBIS-CHI), March 1, 2002.

3. Sun Jinzhong, "*Toushi ZhongYin guanxi jiuge*" ["A Look at the Sino-Indian Disputes in Perspective"] *Nanya Yanjiu Qikan* [*South Asia Quarterly*] (Chengdu), Issue 1, Serial No. 108, 2002, pp. 49-53. See Mao Zhenfa (Chief Editor), *Bianfanglun* [*Border Defence Theory*], Beijing: Military Academy Publication, 1996, pp. 132-134. Ma's arguments here are well-known, although the volume is valuable in terms of the Chinese perspective on various aspects of border defense in general.

4. See Yang Pingxue, "A Trial Analysis of Factors Limiting Development of Sino-Indian Relations," *Nanya Yanjiu Qikan*, No. 1, Serial No. 108, March 2002, pp. 38-41. Besides these, Yang also mentioned the irreconcilable disputes between India and Pakistan as also leading to tensions in the India-China relations.

5. Arun Sahgal, "China's Search for Power and Its Impact on India," *The Korean Journal of Defence Analysis*, Vol. XV, No. 1, Spring 2003, pp. 155-182, especially pp. 155, 171.

6. Pravin Sawhney, *The Defence Makeover: 10 Myths that Shape India's Image*, New Delhi: Sage Publications, 2002, chapter 1, pp. 19-64.

7. This is based on interactions with Indian military officials.

8. Mohan Malik, "Nuclear Proliferation in Asia: The China Factor," *Australian Journal of International Affairs*, Vol. 53, No. 1, 1999, pp. 31-41.

9. Valerie Niquet, "China and the Indian Subcontinent" *China News Analysis*, Taipei, No. 1555, March 1, 1996, p. 5.

10. John W Garver, "Asymmetrical Indian and Chinese Threat Perceptions," Sumit Ganguly, ed., *India as an Emerging Power*, London: Frank Cass, 2003, pp. 109-134.

11. See Mark W. Frazier, "China-India Relations Since Pokhran II: Assessing Sources of Conflict and Cooperation," *National Bureau of Asian Research Journal Access Asia Review*, Vol. 3, No. 2, 1999, at *www.nbr.org*. Frazier cited Chinese premier Zhu Rongji's TV interview in July 1998 as voicing the security establishment's usual depiction of India as striving for "regional hegemony."

12. See Andrew Scobell, "'Cult of Defense' and 'Great Power Dreams': The Influence of Strategic Culture on China's Relationship with India," Michael R. Chambers ed., *South Asia in 2020: Future Strategic Balances and Alliances*, Carlisle Barracks, PA: Strategic Studies Institute, 2002, pp. 329-59, see especially p. 348.

13. See Michael Pillsbury, "China's Strategic Outlook: A Case Study of Japan and India," in his *China Debates the Future Security Environment*, Washington, DC: National Defense University, 2000.

14. Lei Guang, "From National Identity to National Security: China's Changing Responses Toward India in 1962 and 1998," *The Pacific Review*, Vol. 17, No. 3, 2004. On the 1998 nuclear tests, see also John W. Garver, "The Restoration of Sino-Indian Comity Following India's Nuclear Tests," *The China Quarterly*, No. 168, December 2001, pp. 865-889. Some suggested that, while the Indian nuclear tests do not pose any fresh challenge to the PRC, the Indian prime minister mentioned in his letter to the U.S. president that China as a threat was seen in negative terms. See Zhuang Shengfu, "China Has Never Constituted a Threat to India," *International Strategic Studies*, Beijing, No. 1, January 1999, pp. 49-54.

15. Cheng Feng and Larry M. Wortzel, "PLA Operational Principles and Limited War: The Sino-Indian War of 1962," Mark Ryan, *et. al.* eds., *Chinese Warfighting: The PLA Experience since 1949*, Armonk, NY: ME Sharpe, 2005, pp. 173-197. On the 1962 war, see also S. V. Thapliyal, "Battle of Eastern Ladakh: 1962 Sino-Indian conflict," *USI Journal*, New Delhi, April-June 2005, pp. 282-98; and Roderick MacFarquhar, "War in the Himalayas, Crisis in the Caribbean," in his *The Origins of the Cultural Revolution: The Coming of the Cataclysm*, Vol. 3, Oxford: Oxford University Press, 1997, pp. 297-323.

16. Xia Liping, "A Perfect Application of PLA Operation Principles to a Limited War: Sino-Indian War of 1962," Shanghai, unpublished manuscript.

17. John W. Garver, "Nuclear Weapons and the China-India Relationship," Paper presented at conference on "South Asia's Nuclear Dilemma," Weatherhead Center for International Affairs, Harvard University, February 18-19, 1999, at *meadev.nic.in/govt/johngarver-1.htm*.

18. Larry M. Wortzel, "Concentrating Forces and Audacious Action: PLA Lessons from the Sino-Indian War," in Laurie Burkitt, *et. al.*, eds., *The Lessons of History: The Chinese People's Liberation Army at 75*, Carlisle, PA: Strategic Studies Institute, 2003, pp. 327-352.

19. See David L. Shambaugh, "China's National Security Research Bureaucracy," *The China Quarterly*, No. 110, June 1987, pp. 276-304; Ellis Joffe, "How Much Does the PLA Make Foreign Policy?" David S. G. Goodman and Gerald Segal, eds., *China Rising: Nationalism and Interdependence*, London: Routledge, 1997, pp. 53-70, especially pp.58-59.

20. Michael D. Swaine, "The PLA in China's National Security Policy: Leaderships, Structures, and Processes," *The China Quarterly*, No. 146, June 1996.

21. See Yang Jirui and Sun Jin, eds., *Zhongguo Xibu da kai fa yu Nanya: Xianzhuang yu qianjing* [*China's Western Development and South Asia: Current Situation and Prospects*], Chengdu: Sichuan Publication Group, 2004.

22. For an account of the policy shifts of China towards this region and the factors behind them, see Han Hua, "China and South Asia," K.Santhanam and Srikanth Kondapalli, eds., *Asian Security and China 2000-2010*, New Delhi: Shipra Publications & IDSA, 2004, pp. 290-300. See also Cheng Ruisheng, "Sino-Indian Relations After India's Nuclear Tests" May 20-22, 1999, at *lxmi.mi.infn.it/~landnet/NSA/cheng.pdf*.

23. The adverse kill ratio for China was mentioned Georges Tan Eng Bok, "How Does the PLA Cope with 'Regional Conflict' and 'Local War'?" Richard H. Yang, Chief ed., *China's Military: The PLA 1990/1991, SCPS Yearbooks*, Boulder: Westview Press, 1991, chapter 11, pp. 150-151.

24. Dennis J. Blasko, *The Chinese Army Today: Tradition and Transformation for the 21st Century*, New York: Routledge, 2006, pp. 80-87.

25. This is based on International Institute of Strategic Studies, *Military Balance 2004-2005*, London: International Institute of Strategic Studies, 2004, p. 151, and *www.bharat-rakshak.com*.

26. This is based on Donald Goel, "A Comparison of the Military Forces in the China-Indian Border Area," *Kanwa Special Report*, No. 1, October 1, 1998, at *www.kanwa.com/english/981001d.html*, accessed on March 14, 2001.

27. Yuan Gangkun, "*Yindu Kongjun : Zai Zhongyin bianjiang diqu bushu Su-30 zhantouji*" ["Indian Air Force: Deployment of Su-30 Fighter Aircraft in the India-China Border Areas"], *Xiandai Bingqi*, Issue 306, June 2004, pp. 2-3.

28. R. V. Kumar, *Chinese Air Force Threat*, New Delhi: Manas Publications, 2003, p. 152. See chapter nine for the operational conditions of the Chinese Air Force in Tibet, pp. 145-64.

29. See Ashley J. Tellis, *India's Emerging Nuclear Posture: Between Recessed Deterrent and Ready Arsenal*, New Delhi: Oxford University Press, 2001, pp. 58-75.

30. Vijai K. Nair, "The Chinese Threat: An Indian Perspective," *China Brief*, Vol. 1, Issue 9, November 8, 2001, at *china.jamestown.org.html*.

31. See Ravi Rikhye, "Thedo-Tibetan Border Today: Some Military Implications," *China Report*, Vol. 24, No. 3, July-September 1988, pp. 289-98.

32. Donald Goel, "The Differences between China and India in the Military Capabilities," *Kanwa Special Report*, No. 2, October 1, 1998, at *www.kanwa.com/english/981001e.html*, accessed on March 14, 2001.

33. This is based on Andrei Pinkov, "China Adjusts Its Military Strategy Against India," *Kanwa Special Commentary*, October 26, 1998, at *www.kanwa.com/english/981026e.html*, accessed on March 14, 2001.

34. Sardar Aseff Ahmad Ali, "A New Nuclear Doctrine," *The Nation*, Islamabad, June 25, 1998, FBIS-TAC-98-176, June 26, 1998.

35. See the entry on "*Yindu*" ["India"], *Shijie Junshi Nianjian 2001* [*World Military Yearbook 2001*], at *mil.qianlong.com/5051/2002-5-26/145@240422.htm,* accessed on August 8, 2005.

36. See Li Yanan, "India Dreaming to be a Military Super Power," *Liberation Army Daily,* June 12, 1999.

37. Wang Jiaqing, "International Watch: A 'Shield' That Doesn't Hold Water and Can't Stand Refuting," *Liberation Army Daily,* June 14, 2001, FBIS-CHI-2001-0614, June 18, 2001.

38. Yan Liwei, "Will India and Pakistan Go to War on a Large Scale?" *Liberation Army Daily,* May 27, 2002, FBIS-CHI-2002-0528, May 29, 2002.

39. See signed Editorial, "*Yindu chazu Zhongya*" ["India Participates in Central Asia"] *Bingqi Zhishi,* Issue 197, No. 3, 2004, p. 6.

40. This is based on my interviews in China in May-July 1998.

41. Cheng, cited at "Jiefangjun Bao Interview With Former Envoy to India Cited," *Zhongguo Xinwen She,* May 27, 1998, FBIS-CHI-98-147, May 29, 1998.

42. "What Is the Intention in Wantonly Engaging in Military Ventures," excerpted at "Jiefangjun Bao Cited on India Nuclear Tests," *Zhongguo Xinwen She,* May 20, 1998, FBIS-CHI-98-140 May 23, 1998.

43. "The Ambition of Seeking Hegemony Is Completely Exposed," excerpted at "Jiefangjun Bao Cited on India Nuclear Tests," *Zhongguo Xinwen She,* May 20, 1998, FBIS-CHI-98-140, May 23, 1998.

44. *Liberation Army Daily,* "Why India Is Making Haste to Cross Over the Nuclear Threshold," *Xinhua,* May 14, 1998, FBIS-CHI-98-134, May 19, 1998.

45. Ding Zengyi, "India's Attempt To Seek Hegemony Has Been Long-Standing - Interview With Liu Wenguo, Member of China South Asia Society," *Liberation Army Daily,* May 26, 1998, FBIS-CHI-98-154, June 4, 1998.

46. "Commentary on Nuclear Tests," Central People's Radio May 19, 1998, FBIS-TAC-98-141, May 23, 1998.

47. Cao Yongsheng and Xu Yong, "India Seeks 21st Century Major Power Status," *Liberation Army Daily,* February 11, 2002, FBIS-CHI-2002-0211, February 14, 2002.

48. This study compares the national defensive power between the United States, Japan, China, and India from the 1960s. See Hu Angang and Liu Taoxing, "*Zhong Mei Ri Yin guofang shili bijiao,*" *Zhanlue yu Guanli,* Issue 61, June 2003, pp. 40-45, especially see p. 42.

49. See Liu Siyuan, "*Yindu junzhong de 'dawei zhixing',*" *Shijie Junshi,* Issue 131, November 2003, pp. 36-37. Similar views were expressed by Du Zhaoping, "*E Yin haijun yanbing yinduyang,*" *Xiandai Jianchuan,* Issue 212, July 2003, pp. 37-38; and Qu Baolin, "*Yindu: Xunsu fazhan de junshi daguo,*" *Junshi Shilin,* Issue 157, June 2003, pp. 23-25.

50. Zhang Wenmu, "Issue of South Asia in Major Power Politics," *Ta Kung Pao*, September 23, 1998, FBIS-CHI-98-293, October 20, 1998. He viewed developments this regard as a part of a "mega chessboard" of U.S. strategy of expanding NATO as far as South Asia and separating Tibet and the western regions of China. This is a far cry from the Cold War period when the then two super powers did not show much interest in South Asia, as India's limited national strength did not allow it to "stand on its own." See also Zhang Wenmu, "The South Asian Post-Nuclear Tests Situation and Trends," *Ta Kung Pao*, March 3, 1999, FBIS-CHI-1999-0310, March 11, 1999.

51. Jian Hua, "The United States, Japan Want To Rope in India Which Cherishes the Dream of Becoming a Major Country," *Ta Kung Pao*, June 6, 2001, FBIS-CHI-2001-0604, July 6, 2001.

52. Wang Tao, "India's Military Expenditure, Effects on Region," *Liberation Army Daily*, March 18, 2002, FBIS-CHI-2002-0318, March 25, 2002.

53. Wang Ming, "*Yindu sanjun: 2015 'weilai jundui' dingxing*" ["Indian Three Services: Finalising the Design for 2015 'Futuristic Military'"], *PLA Daily*, at *www.chinamil.com.cn\site1\jsslpdjs\2005-04\28\content_194033.htm*.

54. Wang Xudong and Yan Weijiang, "Explore the Secrets of India's Special Forces," *Liberation Army Daily*, October 31, 2001, FBIS-CHI-2001-1031, November 5, 2001.

55. Nie Yun, "*Yindu lujun chongqin dazao tezhong budui wei 'ruchang'*," *Guofangbao*, May 24, 2005, at *www.chinamil.com.cn\site1\jsslpdjs\2005-05\26\content_213938.htm*.

56. See Li Lin, "*Yindu lujun wuqi zhuangbei mian mianguan*," *Junshi Shilin*, Issue 154, March 2003, pp. 11-13. Another set of writers focused on the special operation forces that India is building up. See Han Qingli, *et.al.*, "*Nanya hu: Yindu tezhongbudui*," *Bingqi Zhishi*, Issue 184, February 2003, pp. 40-41.

57. An Binggong, "*Yindu kaishi jianzao xin hangmu*" ["India Starts Building a New Aircraft Carrier"], *PLA Daily*, May 25, 2005, at *www.chinamil.com.cn\site1\jsslpdjs\2005-05\26\content_213942.htm*. See also Ge Lide and Wang Jingguo, "*Yindu hangmu, ni neng gaosu women shenme*," *Shijie Junshi*, Issue 138, June 2004, pp. 25-30.

58. Jiang Nan, "*Yindu quhujian 50 nian*" ["India at 50 Years"], parts 1 and 2, *Xiandai Jianchuan*, Nos, 223 and 224, June-July 2004, pp. 8-13 and 10-14, respectively.

59. This is the subject of Li Jie, "*Yindu jiasu fazhan heqianting de zhanlue sikao*" ["India's Speedy Development of Strategic Thought on Nuclear Powewred Submarines"], *Xiandai Jianchuan*, No. 4, Issue 209, April 2003, pp. 15-16, on Indian efforts to acquire such capability from Russia.

60. See Liang Guihua, "*Yinduyang shang de 'youling'*" ["An Actor on the Indian Ocean"], *Xiandai Bingqi*, Issue 295, July 2003, pp. 12-15.

61. Gautam Datt, "Navy To Set Up Base for UAV's in Andaman," *The Asian Age*, November 10, 2003.

62. Zhu Zaiming, "India Speeds up Development of Oceangoing Fleets," *Liberation Army Daily*, June 5, 2002, FBIS-CHI-2002-0605 June 10, 2002.

63. Su Ping, "*Yindu junshi liliang jieshao*" ["Introduction to Indian Military Power"] *PLA Daily* at *www.chinamil.com.cn\site1\ztpd\2004-09\07\content_4803. htm.*

64. Cui Jianchuang and Bi Shuqin, "*Yinkongjun tigao jingque daji nengli*" ["Indian Air Force Enhances Precision Abilities"] *PLA Daily*, May 25, 2005, at *www.chinamil. com.cn\site1\jsslpdjs\2005-05\26\content_213943.htm.*

65. Song Dazhao, "*Yindu kongjun zhuangbei shuangzuo xing 'meizhouhu' kongjiqi*" ["Indian Air Force Equips Double-Seater 'Jaguar' Deep Strike Aircraft"] at *mil. qianlong.com/4919/2005/08/04/228@2751343.htm*, accessed on August 5, 2005.

66. Sujan Datta, "Peace Games with China," *The Telegraph*, Calcutta, May 31, 2003.

67. Pratap Chakravarty, "India Relies on Aging MiGs to Guard Frontier Posts Near China," AFP, May 31, 2003, FBIS-NES-2003-0531, June 2, 2003.

68. "*Mei Yin junshi guanxi fazhan xunsu ezhi Zhongguo zhengwei 'gongshi'*", June 12, 2003, at *news.sohu.com/58/17/news210041758.shtml*, accessed on March 28, 2003.

69. Chun Xiao, "*Yindu 'akasi' dikong daodan jiang zai jinnian dizhuang pei budui*" ["The Development of U.S.-India Military Relations . . ."], *PLA Daily*, May 10, 2005, at *www.chinamil.com.cn\site1\jsslpdjs\2005-05\13\content_202998.htm.* For a comparison between the Akash series of missiles with that of the Chinese, see Chen Guoying, "*Yindu daodan 'yanghuo' duo 'guohuo' yutu chongwei*" ["India's Missiles . . ."], *PLA Daily*, at *www.chinamil.com.cn\site1\jsslpdjs\2005-04\28\content_194064.htm.* Chen adds that India preferred to acquire its missile systems through indigenous methods rather than from the United States.

70. See "*Yindu jundui zhuangbei de dandaodaodan*" [Indian Military Equips with Ballistic Missiles], *www.qianlong.com*, August 12, 2002, at *database.cpst.net.cn/popul/ guard/zbdg/artic/20812091326.html*, accessed on August 5, 2005.

71. See "*Yindu xiang Eluosi goumai 2 sou he qianting*" ["India to Purchase 2 Nuclear Submarines From Russia"], *Xiandai Jianchuan*, Issue 229, December 2004, p. 2.

72. Fang Hua, "India's 'Agni' Increasingly Intense, ICBM to Be Launched Soon," *Liberation Army Daily*, June 11, 2001, FBIS-CHI-2001-0611, June 14, 2001.

73. Qian Feng, "India's Attempt To Build Antimissile Defense System," *People's Daily*, August 7, 2004, FBIS-CHI-2004-0807, October 14, 2004.

74. Dong Guozheng, "A Dangerous Signal," *Liberation Army Daily*, January 31, 2002, FBIS-CHI-2002-0131, February 1, 2002.

75. Dai Wenming, "*Yindu jiasu fazhan zhencha weixing yongyu huoqu zhanlue qingbao*" ["India Accelerates Development of Reconnaissance Satellites to Obtain Strategic Intelligence"], *PLA Daily*, May 17, 2005, at *www.chinamil.com.cn\site1\*

*jsslpdjs \ 2005-05 \ 26 \ content_213827.htm*. India launched a high resolution satellite April 2005 and planned to launch one more later the year. See also *www.chinamil. com.cn \ site1 \ jsslpdjs \ 2005-05 \ 13 \ content_202992.htm*.

76. Yi Fan, "*Yindu hangtian fazhan zongshu*," Hangkong Zhishi, Issue 387, July 2003, pp. 41, 22.

77. "India's Missile System Gradually Takes Shape." *Liberation Army Daily*, February 6, 2002. FBIS-CHI-2002-0206. February 11, 2002.

78. This is based on Ravi Visvesaraya Prasad, "Hack the Hackers," at *37.s5. com/*, accessed on March 20, 2004. Prasad mentioned here the Chinese task force as headed by Xie Guang with members such as Chief of General Staff Fu Quanyou; Yuan Banggen, Head of General Staff Directorate; Major General Wang Pufeng; Senior Colonel Wang Baocun; Shen Weiguang; Wang Xiaodong; Qi Jianguo; Liang Zhenxing; Yang Minqing; Dai Qingmin; Leng Bingling; Wang Yulin; and Zhao Wenxiang. While Qi and Dai have formulated the program, Leng Bingling, Wang Yulin, and Zhao Wenxiang reportedly are in charge of mobilizing students and businessmen to support their military's cyber attacks against civilian targets in these countries. He also mentioned several information warfare exercises with India as a potential target.

79. Shih Chun-yu, "Why Are the United States and India Getting Close?" *Ta Kung Pao*, August 14, 2001, FBIS-CHI-2001-0814, August 15, 2001; and Zhang Wenmu, "Issue of South Asia in Major Power Politics," *Ta Kung Pao*, September 23, 1998, FBIS-CHI-98-293, October 20, 1998. See also Wang Ruolai, "What Are the Intentions of the United States and India in Cozying Up with One Another?" *People's Daily*, August 29, 2001, FBIS-CHI-2001-0830, August 29, 2001; Shih Chun-yu, "Both the United States and India Have Own Intention in Making Friends," *Ta Kung Pao*, September 5, 2001, FBIS-NES-2001-0905, September 5, 2001. Gong Yaowen has argued that Powell's visit to South Asia in the aftermath of the 9/11 events was to mediate between India and Pakistan so that a united fight against terrorism is made. See "Colin Powell Will Go to South Asia as a Mediator," *Ta Kung Pao*, October 14, 2001, FBIS-NES-2001-1015, October 18, 2001.

80. Liu Ying, "Reasons Behind Warming of India-U.S. Military Relations," *Liberation Army Daily*, August 22, 2001, FBIS-CHI-2001-0822, August 24, 2001. See also Shih Chun-yu, "Why Are the United States and India Getting Close?" *Ta Kung Pao*, August 14, 2001, FBIS-CHI-2001-0814, August 15, 2001.

81. See "India Needs to Eliminate 'Anxiety About China'," *People's Daily*, September 6, 2001, FBIS-CHI-2001-0906, September 7, 2001.

82. Nie Hongyi, "India Prepares To Establish Nuclear Armored Troops," *Liberation Army Daily*, September 3, 2001, FBIS-CHI-2001-0904, September 7, 2001. Nie mentioned that India is about to acquire 3,700 km range *Agni III* missiles by 2002 and a *Surya* ICBM with a range of about 5,000 km by 2003, Tu-22M3 strategic bombers, six SSBNs, and other long-range weapon systems the near future.

83. See "US Consent to India's Nuclear Weapons Program to Gain Support for NMD-China," as cited by PNS, September 8, 2001, at *paknews.com/top. php?id=1&date1=2001-09-08*.

84. Shih Chun-yu, "India and USA Accelerate Military Cooperation," *Ta Kung Pao*, January 25, 2002, FBIS-CHI-2002-0125, January 28, 2002.

85. Ding Zengyi, "Indian-US Military Cooperation Raises Concern," *Liberation Army Daily*, February 24, 2002, FBIS-CHI-2002-0226, March 1, 2002.

86. Zhang Guoping, "United States and India Hold First Joint Military Exercise in 39 Years; Each Has Its Aims in Developing Military Ties," *Liberation Army Daily*, May 20, 2002, FBIS-CHI-2002-0521, May 22, 2002. Zhang mentioned about the "Balance Iroqois" exercises held in Agra and Alaska. On this subject, the civilian assessments are similar to the PLA assessment. See Zhao Yuhua, "India's Domineering Military Exercises," *People's Daily*, May 14, 2002, FBIS-CHI-2002-0514, May 15, 2002.

87. Wang Yusheng, "Cold War 'Experts' Disappointed Again," *Liberation Army Daily*, November 24, 2003, FBIS-CHI-2003-1124, November 28, 2003.

88. Shih Chun-yu, "United States Draws India, Israel, and Turkey to Its Side To Form Alliance," *Ta Kung Pao*, February 14, 2003, FBIS-CHI-2003-0214, February 19, 2003.

89. Chu Yun-kai, "China, Pakistan Joint Military Exercise Aims at Breaking Potential Circle of Containment," *Hong Kong Economic Journal*, October 30, 2003, FBIS-CHI-2003-1030, November 12, 2003.

90. Yan Feng, "Why Is United States So Ill At Ease?" *Liberation Army Daily*, June 3, 2002, FBIS-NES-2002-0603, June 6, 2002.

91. Kung Yao-wen, "The Situation in South Asia Viewed in Terms of Central Asia's Energy Resources," *Ta Kung Pao*, June 2, 2002, FBIS-NES-2002-0603, June 6, 2002.

92. Shih Chun-yu, "India's Military Exercises Aim at Dominating South Asia," *Ta Kung Pa*, May 16, 2002, FBIS-WEU-2002-0516, June 3, 2002.

93. "Chinese on Sikkim Tour," *The Telegraph*, October 16, 2003.

94. For instance, even as Indian Prime Minister A. B. Vajpayee was attempting normalization of relations with the PRC in June 2003, Chinese frontier guards ill-treated the Indian patrols in the Arunachal Pradesh areas during the same period.

95. This is based on in interviews with several officials at Delhi and other places.

96. See Rahul Datta, "Indian Army Gives Priority to Mapping India-China Border," *The Pioneer*, September 6, 2001, p. 5; and "High Level Chinese Military Team to Visit India," *The Asian Age*, September 6, 2001, p. 3.

97. See Luke Harding, "The Forgotten Flashpoint between Nuclear Powers," *The Guardian*, October 16, 2000.

98. See "China Refutes Reports About Border Incursions," *PTI* report cited in *Times of India*, December 30, 2001.

99. "After Pak, It Is Intrusion From China: Thupstan," *UNI* Report, *Jammu Daily Excelsior*, September 27, 2003, FBIS-NES-2003-0927, September 29, 2003.

100. Jairam Ramesh, "Growing ambivalence," *The Telegraph*, May 29, 2003; and "Is India China's Imaginative Rival?" *People's Daily*, February 24, 2004, at *service. china.org.cn/link/wcm/Show_Text?info_id=88256&p_qry=India*, accessed on February 25, 2004.

101. The Huawei company reportedly denied these allegations. See Anita Narayan, "Huawei's Indian Branch Cleared of Taliban Link," December 14, 2001, at *www.chinaonline.com/issues/foreign_relations/NewsArchive/cs-protected/2001/December/C01121403.asp*.

102. "India Challenges China in South China Sea," *Strafor.com* weekly analysis, April 26, 2000, at *www.atimes.com/ind-pak/BD27Df01.html*.

103. Jian Hua, "The United States, Japan Want To Rope in India Which Cherishes the Dream of Becoming a Major Country," *Ta Kung Pao*, June 6, 2001, FBIS-CHI-2001-0604, July 6, 2001. Jian also implies Indian deployment of UAVs on the India-China border areas, wiretapping of telephone lines in Tibet bordering India, close collaboration with the United States and Japan, etc., as other features of this counter-encirclement strategy and to target China.

104. See Liu Weijun, "Taiwan, India Developing Secret Military Ties," AFP, citing *United Daily News*, January 3, 2002, at *museums.cnd.org/Global/02/01/03/020103-0.html*.

105. This is based on Srikanth Kondapalli, "China: Mixed Signals to Confidence-building Measures," *India and Neighbours*, New Delhi: CNF Publications, 2005, pp. 35-52. See also Rosemary Foot, "Chinese-Indian Relations and the Process of Building Confidence: Implications for the Asia-Pacific," *Pacific Review*, Vol. 9, No. 1, 1996, pp. 62-65.

106. Indian Ministry of External Affairs, *Annual Report 1991-92*, p. 17.

107. "Sino-Indian Joint Exercise; Strong Hint of Feeling Out Strategies," *World Journal*, May 28, 2001, as cited at *www.ndu.edu/inss/China_Center/Chinaframe.htm*.

108. According to Zhang Jingyu, "Indian Defense Minister Announces that India-China Naval Exercise Will Begin Soon," *People's Daily*, October 31, 2003, at FBIS-CHI-2003-1101, November 5, 2003. These operations were to be reciprocated by both sides, although only Indian ships visited Shanghai in November. See Meng Yan, "Chinese and Indian Navies Take to the Water Together," *China Daily*, November 14, 2003.

109. Wen Haiyan and Wu Hanyue, "Chinese and Indian Navies Conduct a Joint Search and Rescue Exercise at Sea for the First Time," *Liberation Army Daily*, November 15, 2003, FBIS-CHI-2003-1115, November 17, 2003.

110. Ts'ai Chih-ch'eng, "Chinese and Indian Navies Conduct Joint Search-and-Rescue Exercise in East China Sea," *Ta Kung Pao*, November 15, 2003, FBIS-CHI-2003-1115, November 17, 2003.

111. Liao Yameng, "Expert Analyzes the 'Balancing' Strategies of China, India, and Pakistan," *Wen Wei Po*, November 7, 2003, FBIS-CHI-2003-1107, November 13, 2003. Meng mentioned that South Asia is crucial as it forms China's "backyard" and that the region constitutes a potential "dynamite depot" of the world.

112. "*ZhongYin bianfang jun shouban tiyu jiaoliu shuangfang bing deng chang xianyi*" ["China-India from Her Defense . . ."], at *news.xinhuanet.com/newscenter/2004-11/07/content_2188597.htm*, accessed on March 11, 2005.

113. Zhang Tian and Ya Long, "*Yindu Junfang-Yi yaoqing Zhongguo jundui rujing canjia fangong yanxi*" ["Indian Military: Invitation to the Chinese Military to Participate in Counterterrorism Maneuvers"], *news.xinhuanet.com/world/2005-01/04/content_2413838.htm*, accessed on March 11, 2005.

114. See Qudssia Akhlaque, "Red lines Won't Be Crossed, Hopes Pakistan: Indo-China Joint Military Exercises," *The Dawn*, December 30, 2004, at *www.dawn.com/2004/text/top8.htm*, accessed on March 9, 2005.

115. "China's Development Cause of Concern: Vij," *PTI* Report, *Jammu Daily Excelsior*, November 19, 2003, FBIS-CHI-2003-1119, November 20, 2003.

116. Ding Zengyi, "China and India Jointly Write the New Chapter of Good Neighborliness and Friendship," *Liberation Army Daily*, June 30, 2003, FBIS-CHI-2003-0630, July 7, 2003.

117. Wang Yusheng, "Cold War 'Experts' Disappointed Again," *Liberation Army Daily*, November 24, 2003, FBIS-CHI-2003-1124, November 28, 2003.

118. Liao Ya-meng, "The Second Sino-Indian Normalization," *Wen Wei Po*, June 20, 2003, FBIS-CHI-2003-0620, June 23, 2003.

119. "China Values Military Ties With Neighboring Countries," *Xinhua*, March 2,2004, at *www.chinaembassy.org.au/eng/wgc/t80309.htm*, accessed on June 8, 2005.

120. See Tao Deyan and Zhang Binyang, "*Zhuanjia zonglun Zhongguo heping jueqi jinglue*" ["Experts Discuss China's Peaceful Rise Concept"], *Zhongguo Zhengzhi Xue*, May 18, 2004 (originally published in *Guoji Xianqu Daobao*, at *www.cpd.org.cn*, accessed on July 23, 2005).

121. "*Zhongguo ying xuanze daguo zhanlue: Fang Zhongguo Renmin daxue jiashou Gu Haibing*" ["China Needs to Adopt a Great Power Strategy: Interview with Chinese People's University Professor Gu Haibing"] *Zhongguo Zhengzhi Xue*, June 29, 2004, at *www.cp.org.cn* accessed on July 23, 2005 [article originally published *China Economic Times*].

122. Hu Xin, "*Guoji liliang 'duozhong jueqi' shiye xia de Zhongguo jueqi zhilu*" ["The Pathway of Chinese Rise in View Of 'Multiple Rises' in International Power"], *Zhongguo Zhengzhi Xue*, May 18, 2004 (originally published in *Guoji Xianqu Daobao* [*International Herald Guide*]).

123. Samina Yasmeen, "Sino-Pakistan Relations and the Middle East," *China Report*, Vol. 34, Nos. 3 and 4, 1998, pp. 327-343. For the geo-political link with Pakistan, see Lin Liangguang, *et. al.*, 2001, p. 114.

124. See John W. Garver, *Protracted Contest: Sino-Indian Rivalry in the Twentieth Century*, New Delhi: Oxford University Press, 2001; Mohan Malik, "The China Factor in the India-Pakistan Conflict," Occasional Paper Series, Asia-Pacific Center for Security Studies, Honolulu, Hawaii, November 2002; Shao Zhiyong, "India's Big Power Dream," *Beijing Review*, April 12, 2001, p. 10.

125. See An Qiguang, *"Zhonghua renmin gongheguo yu Bajisitan guanxi"* ["PRC and Pakistan Relations"], Tang Jiaxuan ed., *Zhongguo Waijiao Ci Indian* [*Dictionary of China's Diplomacy*], Beijing: World Knowledge Publications, 2000, pp. 552-553, p. 552.

126. See "Dhaka Airstrip Used by CIA for Covert Operation," *Independent* (Dhaka), April 23, 1999.

127. See Samina Yasmeen, "China and Pakistan in a Changing World," K. Santhanam and Srikanth Kondapalli, eds., *Asian Security and China 2000-2010*, New Delhi: Shipra Publications & IDSA, 2004, pp. 309-19.

128. John Garver, "Sino-Indian Rapprochement and the Sino-Pakistan Entente," *Political Science Quarterly*, Vol. 111, No. 2, 1996, pp. 323-347, cited on pp. 324 and 345.

129. Yu cited "Pakistan President Meets Chinese Military Delegation," *Xinhua*, May 06, 1997, FBIS-CHI-97-126, May 7, 1997.

130. See "The Solid Foundation For Sino-Pakistani Friendship: High Level of Mutual Trust," *International Strategic Studies*, Beijing, No. 1, Serial 71, January 2004, pp. 25-27 [*emphases* added].

131. For this revelation by Jiang himself, see "President Jiang Zemin Met with Pakistan Chief Executive Officer Pervez Musharaf," September 10, 2000, at *www.fmprc.gov.cn/eng/5116.html* [downloaded on August 10, 2002].

132. "Jiang Backs Pakistan Role Afghan Peace Aims," *China Daily*, January 17, 2002, p. 1.

133. This is based on Chinese Foreign Ministry Policy Research Division's *Zhongguo Waijiao 2003 nianban* [*China's Foreign Affairs 2003* edition], Beijing: World Knowledge Publication, 2003, p. 240.

134. See "China Tilts Toward India on Kargil Conflict" at *www.strafor.com*, June 16, 1999. See also He Chong, "The Historical Roots of the 'Kashmir Conflict' Between India and Pakistan," *Zhongguo Tongxun She*, June 14, 1999, FBIS-CHI-1999-0615, June 16, 1999.

135. See Lin Liangguang, *et. al.*, 2001. Wang Taiping, writing for the Ministry of Foreign Affairs history during the 1970s, termed the Sino-Pakistan objective as "common struggle" [*gongtong touzheng*]. See Wang Taiping, ed., *Zhonghua renmin gongheguo wiajiaoshi 1970-1978* [*PRC's Diplomatic History 1970-1978*], Beijing: World Knowledge Publications, 1999, p. 110.

136. For details about the Chinese advice, see General Mohammad Musa, *My Version: India Pakistan War 1965*, Wajidalis, Lahore, Pakistan, 1983, as quoted

Ahmad Faruqui, "China's Defence Policy and Its Implications for Pakistan," *www. defencejournal.com/2001/feb/china-defence.htm*. Marshal Chen Yi reportedly advised Pakistan, during his visit to Karachi on September 4, to occupy Aknoor Fort first and deny India the advantages the war. Altaf Gauhar's account of this period as well recounts Zhou Enlai's and Chen Yi's advice to visiting President Ayub Khan September 1965 on the need to wage a protracted warfare, raising people's militia, etc. See Gauhar as cited "Chinese Wisdom for Pakistan's Benefit," *The Dawn*, reprinted *The Asian Age*, July 26, 1999.

137. "Chinese Government Leaders Condemn Indian Expansionism And Aggression Against Pakistan," *Beijing Review*, No. 38, September 17, 1965, pp. 10-11 (Zhou cited on p. 10).

138. "Chairman Liu Shao-chi [Shaoqi] Visits Pakistan," *Beijing Review*, No. 14, April 1, 1966, p. 3. During this occasion, President Ayub acknowledged the Chinese support "in that hour of trial." *Ibid.*, p. 4.

139. "Chairman Liu Shao-chi's Speech," *Beijing Review*, No. 14, April 1, 1966, p. 5 [*emphases* added].

140. "China-Pakistan Joint Communiqué," March 31, 1966, *Beijing Review*, No. 15, April 8, 1966, p. 6.

141. See Wang Taiping, 1999, *op.cit.*, p. 110.

142. See Faruqui, *op. cit.* During the secret conclave between U.S. Secretary of State Henry Kissinger and Chinese Permanent representative to the UN Huang Hua on December 10, 1971, at New York, the latter, after listening to the imminent fall of West Pakistan in the 1971 War, asserted, "China would never stop fighting as long as it had a rifle in its armory; it would surely increase its assistance to Pakistan." However, no direct and active Chinese support to Pakistan was forthcoming. As explained by Zhou Enlai to Kissinger in Beijing during Nixon's visit, "Of course, we don't interfere in other's internal affairs, but Yahya really did not lead his troops in East Pakistan. Even though we assisted with armaments, we didn't send a single military personnel, who the Soviet Union calls military adviser. We only sent people to train in the use of the planes and guns we sent and afterwards brought those people back." Zhou cited in "Chinese Wisdom for Pakistan's Benefit," *The Dawn*, reprinted *The Asian Age*, July 26, 1999.

143. See Tang Jiaxuan, ed., *Op.cit.*, 2000, p. 552.

144. Zafar Iqbal Rao, "China and the Muslim World — A Glance at Military Relations," Rawalpindi *Nawa-i-Waqt*, August 16, 2001, FBIS-CHI-2001-0817, August 20, 2001. He also adds that China has set up a nuclear reactor in Algeria, supplied chemical weapons to Libya, sold medium range ballistic missiles to Saudi Arabia, transferred nuclear technology to Iraq, Libya, and Syria, and signed a 10-year agreement with Iran on supply of nuclear weapons in 1990. See also "China Helping Pakistan Build Missiles: Report" at *www.dawn.com/2000/07/03/top5.htm*; and "China Increased Missile Sales to Pakistan: US," at *www.dawn.com/2000/08/10/top8.htm* that cited reports from the United States.

145. See "China, Pakistan Sign Secret Pacts: Military Agreements Raise Concerns Over Nuke Technology" at *www.worldnetdaily.com/news/article.asp?ARTICLE_ID=26907* accessed on March 20, 2004. This report cites U.S. intelligence sources as mentioning transfers recently of not only F-8 fighters, but also ballistic missile materials for Pakistan's *Shaheen*-1 and *Shaheen*-2 types of missiles.

146. Muhammad Saleh Zafir, "Pakistan, China Agree to Enhance Defense Cooperation," *Rawalpindi Jang*, September 7, 2001, FBIS-CHI-2001-0913, September 14, 2001.

147. "PN Allowed to Negotiate Purchase of Chinese Frigates," *The News*, February 21, 2003, FBIS-CHI-2003-0221, February 24, 2003.

148. Azim Zaidi, "Pakistan Has Produced Modern Jet Fighter Aircraft Super Seven with China's Cooperation," *Khubrain*, May 30, 2003, FBIS-CHI-2003-0530, June 2, 2003.

149. "China Offers to Sell F-7MG Aircraft to Pakistan," Editorial at Rawalpindi's *Nawa-i-Waqt*, June 4, 2000, FBIS-CHI-2000-0607, June 8, 2000.

150. See Ihtashamul Haque, "POF Will Manufacture T-80 Tank Shells: China To Transfer Technology," at *www.dawn.com/2001/06/02/top3.htm*.

151. Brigadier Retd A. R. Siddiqi, "HIT: Rebuild to Manufacture," *The Nation*, August 1, 2001, FBIS-CHI-2001-0801, August 2, 2001.

152. Hsiao Peng, "China Sells Sophisticated Weapons To Help Pakistan Deal With War," *Sing Tao Jih Pao*, October 26, 2001, FBIS-NES-2001-1026, October 29, 2001. Hsiao adds that these LY-60N medium-to-low range all weather missile systems were developed and produced by the Shanghai Space Technology Research Institute. It can track and follow 40 targets and its interception capability stretches between 30 and 1200 meters.

153. Zheng Hong, "The Thick Nuclear Haze is Flowing in the Sky of South Asia," *Liberation Army Daily*, June 3, 2002, FBIS-CHI-2002-0603, June 6, 2002.

154. Zha Chunming, "*Zhongba haijun shouci haishang soujiu yanxi*" ["Sino-Pakistan First Naval Search and Rescue Operation at Sea], *Bingqi Zhishi*, Issue 194, December 2003, pp. 28-29.

155. Qian Xiaohu and Ding Zengyi, "Building a Sea to Sky 'Life Channel' — Witnessing the Sino-Pakistani Joint Maritime Search and Rescue Exercise," *Liberation Army Daily*, October 23, 2003, FBIS-CHI-2003-1023, October 27, 2003; and Zha Chunming, "*Zhongba haijun shouci haishang soujiu yanxi*" ["Sino-Pakistan first Naval Search and Rescue Operation at Sea"] *Bingqi Zhishi*, Beijing, Issue 194, December 2003, pp. 28-29. China reportedly did not send its fleet to the Indian Fleet Review 2001, citing the absence of the Pakistan Navy in the event. Nevertheless, subsequently Chinese ships visited Mumbai. This has been a far cry from the 1986 Chinese naval visits to Chittagong, Colombo, and Karachi, skipping Indian ports.

156. "China Cooperates with Others to Combat Non-Traditional Security Threats," *PLA Daily*, December 27, 2004.

157. Wang Zhanliang, *"Bajisitan yu fangong zhanzheng"* ["Pakistan and Counterterrorism"] *Xiandai Bingqi*, Issue 311, November 2004, pp. 2-4.

158. See Xiong Guangkai, "The Global Counterterrorism Campaign: Current Situation and Future Prospects" in his *International Strategy and Revolution Military Affairs*, Beijing: Qinghua University Publications, 2003, p. 146. Xiong stated that East Turkistan proponents launched 260 terrorist attacks in China since 1990, killed 170 and wounded 440. *Ibid.*, p. 145.

159. This is based on Chinese Foreign Ministry Policy Research Division's *Zhongguo Waijiao 2003 nianban* [*China's Foreign Affairs 2003* edition], Beijing: World Knowledge Publication, 2003, p. 92.

160. "China Assures Help to Modernise Defence Forces," *Daily Star* (Dhaka), May 19, 1993.

161. See Hao Fusheng, "China: Bangladesh's Foreign Minister Meets PLA Delegation," *Xinhua Domestic Service*, November 5, 1998, FBIS-CHI-98-309, November 6, 1998.

162. Fu cited at "Fu Quanyou Meets With Bangladeshi Military Leader," *Xinhua*, May 7, 1999, FBIS-CHI-1999-0507, May 10, 1999.

163. "Zhang Wannian Meets Bangladesh Guest, Spoke on Taiwan Issue," *Xinhua Domestic Service*, March 29, 2000, FBIS-CHI-2000-0329, March 30, 2000. Zhang thanked Bangladesh for its position on Taiwan, Tibet, and the human rights issue.

164. "Khaleda China-Bound for Defence Agreement," *PTI* report, December 22, 2002, cited at *www.telegraphin India.com/1021223/asp/foreign/story_1508248.asp*, accessed on April 6, 2005.

165. See "Bangladesh to Acquire Eight Chinese Fighter Planes," *Daily Star*, April 8, 2000.

166. See "Dhaka Considering Chinese Offer of F-7MB Jets," *Daily Star*, December 28, 2000. The delay procurement of these aircraft was traced to internal differences in Bangladesh politics between the Awami League and the Bangladesh Nationalist Party. See "Beijing Unaware of Dhaka's Plan To Buy War Planes," *Daily Star*, June 21, 2000; and "Govt Deviating from Self-Reliant Defence Policy: BNP," *Independent* (Dhaka), September 1, 2000.

167. "Vice President Hu Jintao Meets Nepalese Military Leader," *Xinhua*, December 9, 1999, FBIS-CHI-1999-1209, December 10, 1999. The Nepalese Army Chief said that his army would not allow any activity in Nepal that "splits" China. Chi Haotian, during his meeting with the Nepalese army chief, said that "Support for a so-called "independence of Tibet" by some foreign forces which harbor evil intentions is unacceptable, and it will, beyond any doubt, be resolutely opposed by the entire Chinese people, including the people of Tibet." See "Defense Minister Chi Haotian Meets Nepalese Army Chief," *Xinhua*, December 9, 1999, FBIS-CHI-1999-1209, December 10, 1999.

168. This is based on Keshab Poudel, "Chi's Visit: Security Concerns?" *Nepal News*, Vol. 20, No. 33, March 2-8, 2001, at *www.nepalnews.com/contents/englishweekly/ spotlight/2001/mar/mar02/national1.htm*.

169. See Nischal Nath Pandey, "Nepal's Foreign Policy vis-a-vis India and China: The Security Imperatives," Paper presented on April 9, 2003, at Banaras Hindu University, at *www.ifa.org.np/article/article10.php*, accessed on April 6, 2005.

170. "Nepal Announces Bus Services to Tibet," *Indo-Asian News Service*, August 2, 2004, at *www.123bharath.com/in India-news/index.php?action=fullnews&id=5273*, accessed on August 2, 2004.

171. See "Direct Passenger Bus to Open between China and Nepal in May," *People's Daily*, March 29, 2005, at *english.peopledaily.com.cn/200503/28/eng20050328_ 178434.html*, accessed on April 1, 2005.

172. Chen Anning, "Nepalese King Meets PRC Military Delegation" *Xinhua Hong Kong Service*, June 18, 1999, FBIS-CHI-1999-0618, June 21, 1999.

173. "Nepali King Meets With China's Fu Quanyou," *Xinhua*, April 10, 2000, FBIS-CHI-2000-0410, April 11, 2000.

174. Liu cited at "Nepal PM Says Committed To Enhancing Friendship With China." *Xinhua*, September 4, 2001, at FBIS-CHI-2001-0904, September 6, 2001. A day earlier, the Royal Nepalese Army Chief reiterated Nepal's position that "any activities detrimental to China's security interests will not be allowed within its territory" — a euphemism to Tibetan activities. See "Nepali Army Chief Reaffirms Support for One-China Policy," *Xinhua*, September 3, 2001, at FBIS-CHI-2001-0903, September 4, 2001.

175. "Nepali Army Chief Reaffirms Support For One-China Policy," *Xinhua*, September 16, 2002, FBIS-CHI-2002-0916, September 17, 2002.

176. "Tibet-Nepal Trade Drops After Chinese Police Assaults," June 26, 1997, at *www.tibetinfo.net/news-updates/nu260697.htm* accessed on June 6, 2004. This reportly indicated that bribery and violence is a common feature with the Chinese armed police, but these demonstrations were termed "unprecedented."

177. See "Chinese Border Police Misbehave with Nepalis," *Kathmandu Post* Report, October 22, 2000, at *www.nepalnews.com.np/contents/englishdaily/ ktmpost/2000/oct/oct23.htm*. This report indicated that the Chinese police often use harsh words, drag, beat, or even employ Nepalese in their personal work.

178. See V. Suryanarayan, "Sri Lanka's China Policy-Legacy of the Past and Prospects," Paper presented at the Department of Chinese and Japanese Studies, University of Delhi, September 17-18, 1993.

179. See, for details, "China Seeks Sri Lanka Support at Human Rights Meet," *Sunday Times* (Colombo), February 26, 1995; and "Business with Taiwan Despite One-China Policy," *Island* (Colombo), March 3, 1995. For the displeasure of the Tibetan community at the refusal of the Sri Lankan government to allow entry to the Dalai Lama, see "Refusal to Okay Dalai Lama Visit to Lanka Decried," *Sunday Leader* (Colombo), August 15, 1999.

180. See the "Joint Communiqué between the People's Republic of China and the Republic of Sri Lanka, 1972," at *www.fmprc.gov.cn/eng/4989.html*.

181. "PLA General Logistics Department Starts Up Emergency Military Aid Mechanism," *PLA Daily*, January 6, 2005, at *english.chinamil.com.cn/site2/columns/2005-01/07/content_106699.htm*.

182. See "Sri Lanka's Main Military Equipment Deal Under Cloud," *Sunday Times*, August 20, 1995; "Armed Forces Acquiring Equipment To Meet Tiger Threat," *Island*, September 13, 1995; and "Rs 2.5 Billion Sino-Lankan Arms Deal," Sunday Times, September 17, 1995.

# CHAPTER 10

# CHINA AND SOUTHEAST ASIA: BUILDING INFLUENCE, ADDRESSING FEARS

## Larry M. Wortzel

The People's Republic of China (PRC) has undertaken a diplomatic strategy of moderation and reassurance in Southeast Asia over the past decade. The objectives of this strategy have been to ease fears of China as a military threat to the region; to build Chinese influence in the region and within its major multilateral organization, the Association of Southeast Asian Nations (ASEAN); and to lessen U.S. influence in response to earlier American containment strategies in Southeast Asia. The People's Liberation Army (PLA) has been a factor influencing and supporting this strategy, but has not been the major actor in articulating the strategy.

Beijing's diplomatic strategy in Southeast Asia has political, economic, and military or security components. In this sense, China is exercising all of the instruments of national power in executing the strategy; these are political, diplomatic, economic, military, social, and cultural.[1] The Foreign Ministry and the Chinese Communist Party (CCP), including its liaison and propaganda organs, have been major architects of the strategy and agents of its articulation. China's military organs have played a supporting role in articulating the strategy, but a role that clearly has been subordinate to the Foreign Ministry. However, unlike the situation in the 1960s and 1970s, there is no strong ideological component in today's strategy. Even though the CCP maintains friendly party-to-party relations with the Communist parties in the region, especially those of Vietnam and Laos, the Foreign Ministry plays the main role in articulating the strategy.

Although the PLA is not the major instrument through which China addresses its goals in the region, it, nonetheless, has an important role in advancing the strategy. The PLA provides the backdrop of military power and that makes the nations in the region consider China's security interests as a factor in their policies. One of the most active actors in advancing China's strategy in Southeast Asia has been the Central Communist Party School. For the most part, the Central Party School has acted through its surrogate, the China Reform Forum. The major goal of China's activities in the region is to reassure Southeast Asian nations that China's long-term intentions are benign. This played to the very nature of ASEAN. ASEAN is a body for the discussion of political, economic, and security matters through mutual consultation, as is its ASEAN Regional Forum (ARF). By actively engaging the ARF and ASEAN, China's has played to ASEAN's goals through careful diplomacy.

**The Historical Record.**

Security always has been a major component of the policies of the PRC in Southeast Asia. In the 1950s and 1960s, China's support for Communist insurgencies in the region and its actions in providing weapons to indigenous Communist parties created deep concern about China's long-term intentions among Southeast Asian nations. The active support and presence of PLA forces in Vietnam and Laos during the U.S. war in Southeast Asia exacerbated fears of China in the region. China's seizure of the Paracel Islands, its expansive territorial claims in the South China Sea, and its aggressive rate of military growth increased concerns within Southeast Asia over China's long-term intentions. A naval clash with Vietnam in the Spratly Islands only increased fears of China, as did its 1979 attack into Vietnam. Indeed, it was these concerns about the PLA that led to the creation of the ASEAN ARF.[2] The Chinese seizure of Mischief Reef claimed by the Philippines after the withdrawal of U.S. forces from Clark Air Force Base and Subic Bay was another factor that created the perception of a threat from China.

China's policies toward overseas Chinese also complicated diplomacy and security perceptions in the region. There are significant Chinese populations throughout Southeast Asia, and for a long time, Beijing treated all of the Diaspora as "overseas Chinese" (*Huaqiao*), ignoring their citizenship and claiming that their ethnicity made them citizens of China. In a couple of instances claims that

Beijing has an obligation to protect ethnic Chinese citizens in other countries (in Vietnam in 1975 and Indonesia in 1995) exacerbated concerns over China's military intentions. Over the past 5 decades, there have been explicit attempts by Beijing to put such fears among Southeast Asian governments to rest, the first of which took the form of a charm offensive in Indonesia.

## China's First Charm Offensive in Southeast Asia.

Zhou Enlai, China's Foreign Minister, represented China at the Afro-Asian Conference in Bandung, Indonesia, April 18-24, 1955. At that time, Zhou advanced China's policy of peaceful coexistence in an attempt to address concerns among Asian nations that China was a threat to the internal security of those nations. Beijing also was working to counter U.S. containment strategy by seeking to establish a nonaggression pact with the Philippines, ease concerns in Thailand, and address concerns about a Communist fifth column in Indonesia.[3] Indeed, at the time, there were concerns throughout Southeast Asia about the Chinese population in those nations, and Beijing's attempts to support the spread of communism in the region. This affected China's relations with Thailand, Malaysia, the Philippines, and Indonesia.

The "peace offensive" did not last long, however. By 1963, China sought to place itself at the center of a worldwide movement to spread socialist revolution, strengthening anti-Chinese policies in Southeast Asia and the American network of alliances designed to contain Communism in the region. The beginnings of the ideological split between Beijing and Moscow fed the CCP's efforts in the region. However, the CCP was not successful in all cases. The United States provided significant covert and overt help to the Philippine government in its effort to suppress the indigenous, but Beijing-supported, Communist rebellion in the Philippines. The same is true in Laos. In Malaya, the British government was instrumental in suppressing the mainly ethnic-Chinese Communist insurgency. In this period, China's ideological and military aid to Southeast Asian insurgencies increased. Beijing supported Indonesian President Sukarno's confrontation with Malaysia. A tipping point came in

Indonesia, when in 1965 a coup broke out with radical military officers attempting to overthrow the anti-Communist senior leadership of the Indonesian Army. Beijing had supported the Communist Party of Indonesia (PKI) with encouragement, money, and some 100,000 small arms.[4] When the PKI and Communist sympathizers in the Army tried to take over the government, there was a bloodbath as the Indonesian armed forces went after not only the insurgents, but also ethnic Chinese in general. Even today, in Beijing one can meet surviving members of the Indonesian, Philippine, and Malayan Communist Party (or their children) who fled to China to escape death in anti-Communist counterinsurgency operations in their home countries. In addition, of course, the American involvement in Vietnam strengthened, while the PLA poured money, equipment, and some 50,000 troops in engineer, armor, and air defense units into North Vietnam and Laos.

## Why it Matters for the United States.

The United States has important interests in Southeast Asia. These interests include freedom of navigation through the region and ensuring protection of the sea and air lines of communication; keeping the area open to free trade and investment; promoting the rule of law and values such as democratic institutions of government, human rights, and religious freedom; and supporting America's treaty allies and friends in the region.[5] In pursuing these national interests, "the United States has followed a strategy to promote a stable, peaceful, and prosperous Asia-Pacific Region."[6] From the standpoint of diplomatic engagement and military security engagement this means promoting regional stability and nurturing friendships and alliances designed to keep another power or group of powers from dominating the region. In addition to military contacts and relations, the United States exercises diplomatic and political strategies designed to avoid being excluded from influence in the region by another power or group of powers.[7] Nonetheless, there is room for China as a strong power in the American strategy for the region. In a speech in China in 2004, then U.S. Trade Representative (and now Deputy Secretary of State) Robert Zoellick told an audience ". . . the United States and others need to work with China to integrate its rising power into regional and global security, economic, and political arrangements. For its part, China warrants respect, but needs to be careful not to trigger fears."[8]

There should be no mistake that in recent years this mention of preventing the domination of the region by other powers is principally a concern about China. China's influence in Southeast Asia is strong, its economic influence is growing, and its history in security relations over the 56 years the PRC has been in existence primarily has been one of excluding American and Russian (earlier Soviet) influence. India more recently has expressed its own concerns about the security of Southeast Asia, but has not acted to pursue those interests in a way that affects U.S. interests negatively. Australia and Japan both have important interests in the region. The interests of these strong U.S. allies, however, are complementary to those of the United States.

The same is not true of China. China's previous actions in the region: its support for indigenous revolutionary groups, its expansive maritime claims in the South China Sea, its muscular claims to be the protector of citizens of other countries who are ethnic Chinese, its pursuit of oil and natural gas resources, and its military build-up create security concerns in the region.[9] Naturally, given its own interests, the United States has responded to those concerns by strengthening its own diplomacy in the region, tying Southeast Asian states into the general war on terrorism, stationing more military forces in the region (primarily in Guam), and reinvigorating security assistance.

China has responded as well. In the world of ideas, scholars speaking for the Communist Party and the government in Beijing have articulated a strategy by which China would rise as a major power and do so peacefully. At the same time, the PLA has worked with the Foreign Ministry to create confidence-building measures through the ASEAN ARF. In 2002, the PRC signed the Declaration on the Conduct of Parties in the South China Sea, with ASEAN outlining a code of conduct for nations with competing territorial claims in that area. This resulted in enough good will that in August 2005, a Chinese state-owned oil company, China Oilfield services, won a contract from the Philippine National Oil Company and

PetroVietnam (both state owned) to do seismic exploration for oil and gas in the Spratly Islands.[10] The PLA also has worked on security assistance programs in the region. These will be covered in more detail later in this chapter, but these actions include providing military equipment to Burma and developing an anti-ship cruise missile with the Indonesian Armed Forces.

## A New Security Concept.

Beijing sought to reassure the rest of the world of its peaceful intentions in 2002 with the "new security concept." Aimed primarily at calming fears in the Asia-Pacific region after the seizure of Mischief Reef in 1995, the firing of missiles over Taiwan, and the arrival of a U.S. fleet off the Taiwan Strait in 1996, China's leaders called for a "new security concept" based on "mutual trust, mutual benefit, equality, and coordination."[11] The "Concept" emphasized confidence building and a multi-lateral security dialogue as a means to resolve international problems. Of course, Beijing still reserved the right to use force against Taiwan, which it views as an internal problem. In this paper, Beijing lauded the resolution of border disputes with Russia and noted the establishment of the Shanghai Cooperative Organization (SCO). Addressing Southeast Asia specifically, Beijing emphasized its active participation in the ASEAN Regional Forum, seeking "cooperation and dialogue over confrontation." In the economic sphere, Beijing emphasized its participation in the "10+3 cooperation in East Asia." While this was a move toward calming fears of China in Southeast Asia, other scholars in China associated closely with the Central Communist Party School moved further with a more comprehensive theory to address concerns over China's rise as a great power.

There was a division of labor among ministries and agencies in China. The PLA handled the military-to-military portion of a general package of diplomatic and economic initiatives. While PLA officers reassured regional neighbors about China's benign intentions at various regional fora, the PLA Navy ventured further into the region and built its own strength. This conveyed the point that while China's intentions might be benign, the nation was prepared to protect its interests with force.

## China's Peaceful Rise.

The earlier themes designed to reassure China's neighbors evolved into a full- blown effort to reassure the world that China has peaceful intentions.[12] In April 1998, four of China's national security scholars published a book discussing the concept of a peaceful rise for China as an international power.[13] The focus of the book, as outlined by its main author in the introduction, is to examine how the rise of China as a world power (or superpower) can take place in such a way as to avoid war and another cold war.[14] The authors began their work on the theory in 1994 and, through the China Philosophy Society, began further research on the topic. With respect to Southeast Asia, Yan Xuetong explained that the strategists who developed the theory of China's peaceful rise designed it to respond to the "China Threat Theory" advanced at the time by Lee Kuan-yew of Singapore and Prime Minister Mahathir of Malaysia.[15]

The Central Communist Party School has been the major actor in promulgating this theory internationally. In a speech to the Center for Strategic and International Studies of the United States on November 13, 2003, Zheng Bijian, as he retired from his work at the Central Communist Party School in China, explained the concept of China's peaceful rise. American scholars, who argued that the rise of great powers usually creates instability in the international system, particularly when those powers are nondemocratic states, challenged him. The Americans specifically mentioned the cases of Germany and Japan in the lead-up to World Wars I and II. In response, in a 2004 issue of the China Reform Forum journal, Zheng responded with a new formulation: "our [China's] path is different from both the paths of Germany in World War I and Germany and Japan in World War II, when they tried to overhaul the world political landscape by way of aggressive wars. Our path is also to be different from that of the former U.S.S.R. [Union of Soviet Socialist Republics] during the reign of Brezhnev, which relied on a military bloc and arms race in order to compete with the United States for world supremacy."[16]

As the Chairman of the China Reform Forum, a position he assumed after his retirement from the Central Party School, he advanced the "Peaceful Rise" theory at the Bo'ao Forum on Hainan

Island in 2003.[17] Indeed, he may be its most active international proponent for China, including publishing a version of his popular "China's Peaceful Rise" speech in the U.S. Council on Foreign Relations magazine, *Foreign Affairs*.[18] The "Peaceful Rise" thesis is an interesting one. The thesis suggests that China's rise as a great power is inevitable, and that the different interests of a rising power and an existing superpower in the same region will create friction. Implicit in the "Peaceful Rise" theory, however, is the suggestion that it is up to the United States, as the lone superpower in the world, to accommodate China's rise.[19]

It was not only CCP intellectuals that put forth the formula. On December 10, 2003, not long after Zheng Bijian's speech, Premier Wen Jiabao told an audience at Harvard University in Boston that, as a developing country, China would seek to rise peacefully as it resolves its natural resource and energy problems.[20] Sixteen days later, celebrating the 110th anniversary of Mao Zedong's birth, Hu Jintao told the audience that China would "develop along its own socialist course . . . and would follow a peaceful road to development."[21] Hu repeated the formulation on February 23, 2004, to a politburo study meeting of senior CCP leaders, telling them that the peaceful development path would also follow a policy of self-reliance.[22] In addition, to complete the set of new senior leaders that repeated the formulation, on March 14, 2004, Wen Jiabao echoed the formula, telling a session of the National People's Congress in Beijing that, although China's peaceful rise would take a long time, it would not depart from the general interests of the world.[23]

The CCP did not accept the "Peaceful Rise" formulation without some internal debate. In a meeting of senior PLA Air Force officers in May 2004, Jiang Zemin suggested that perhaps the formulation should be set aside, since the thesis potentially limited China's military development and modernization. This objection by Jiang was both a manifestation of friction between Jiang and Hu Jintao in the transfer of power from Jiang to Hu and a demonstration of genuine concern within the PLA that it could continue to modernize and strengthen.[24] In the end, after some period of debate, the CCP arrived at the position that "there is no contradiction between military modernization or military strength and China's peaceful rise."[25] China's policymakers in the PLA and the CCP see military development as complementing China's peaceful rise, and accommodating this rise requires an adjustment in attitude by the United States and Southeast Asia. [26]

There are unspoken elements in the "Peaceful Rise" formulation. Some of China's security thinkers suggest that it is a sign of hostility if the United States or other powers try to prevent China's rise. Some in Beijing interpret the debate between the United States and the European Union (EU) over Brussels lifting arms sales sanctions against China as a sign of hostility on the part of Washington.[27] There is also some resentment among security specialists in China over the continued imposition of high technology export controls by the United States.

An analogy that illustrates Beijing's attitude on the "Peaceful Rise" debate is to imagine yourself walking down the middle of a wide street when someone else turns the corner and walks in your direction on an intersecting path. That person does not deviate his or her course, but expects another to shift its own course to accommodate the new arrival's route. Failure to accommodate the new arrival could be interpreted as hostile and to directly challenge the new arrival is clearly hostile. Moreover, since the path of the new arrival is not shifting, any failure to adjust your route could result in a clash. Thus, the "Peaceful Rise" thesis may not be quite as benign as Beijing's security thinkers suggest. That said, in Southeast Asia, the thesis has been successful and has won Beijing increased influence and diplomatic influence.

A more recent formulation of the "Peaceful Rise" formula takes into consideration China's "comprehensive national power" (*zonghe guoli*). In an article in *Guoji Zhengzhi Kexue* (The Science of International Politics), Yan Xuetong argues that there is a defined position (standing) of actual strength for China in the international community.[28] He argues that, in terms of overall national strength, China is now the number two nation in the world, second to the United States. Moreover, according to Yan, China can maintain this position and even grow in comprehensive national power peacefully without coming into conflict with the United States. The theme of comprehensive national power is an integral part of grand strategy in China today. Strategic thinkers are consumed by computations of what China's rightful place in the world should be based on, using mathematical equations representing elements of power (economic, social-cultural, scientific/technical, military, and political), with the objective of creating a "scientific" justification for China's rise, while the Foreign Ministry argues that the rise will not upset the international order.[29]

The PLA has been part of the action. The first security policy conference of the ASEAN Regional Forum was held in Beijing on November 4-6, 2004, with the goal of "expanding the channel for dialogue on security issues between high ranking officials in the Asia-Pacific region.[30] This latest effort represents a stage of a longer-term policy in the PLA, and by China, to interact with and engage the member states of ASEAN.

## China's Multilateral Activities in Southeast Asia.

Over the decades since the establishment of the PRC, there has been an evolution of policy toward participation in multilateral institutions. If China was not able to lead a multilateral body, such as the nonaligned movement, Beijing generally treated such institutions as potential threats to China's sovereignty that could limit the foreign policy options open to China's diplomacy.[31] China's diplomats also knew that ASEAN originally developed the ARF, in part, to respond to fears of China's military activities and expansion into Southeast Asia, especially in the Spratly Islands. Gradually, however, Beijing participated in multilateral institutions in Southeast Asia, albeit grudgingly. In addition, in the past 4 to 5 years, as U.S. policy shifted to focus on fighting the war on terror and countering the proliferation of weapons of mass destruction (WMD), China is perceived in Southeast Asia as a positive and effective player in multilateral institutions in the region.[32]

China is now active in security-related multilateral matters in the ASEAN Regional Forum.[33] In Track II, nongovernmental (or quasi-governmental) organizations, China participates in the Council for Security and Cooperation in the Asia Pacific (CSCAP), the Northeast Asia Security Cooperation Dialogue (NEACD), and the Asia-Pacific Roundtable.[34] In the economic realm, China is an active participant in the Bo'ao Forum for Asia and the Asia-Pacific Economic Cooperation (APEC) forum, and has negotiated an ASEAN-China Free Trade Agreement.[35] Meanwhile, in Northeast Asia, China has gone from being a mere "concierge" for the six-party talks with North Korea to being an active facilitator and negotiator.

These activities by China are consistent with the broader foreign policy orientation in Beijing of trying to achieve a multipolar world order.[36] They are effective means of countering fears that China means to dominate the region and have helped Beijing achieve its broader international goals.[37] These policies toward Southeast and Northeast Asia have not been carried out in isolation. Beijing also has worked hard to create the Shanghai Cooperative Organization, a multilateral institution aimed at cementing security policy and relations in Central Asia and with Russia. Indeed, China's *Defense White Paper* says that "China supports regional security dialogue and cooperation at different levels, through various channels, in different forms and in a step-by-step manner pursuant to the principles of participation on equal footing and reaching consensus through consultation in the spirit of seeking common ground while reserving differences," a comfortable formulation for ASEAN states.[38] Writing in the *Far Eastern Economic Review*, Murray Heibert assessed China's actions as "subtle," but aimed at "diluting American influence" and reducing American strategic dominance in the region.[39] Meanwhile, ASEAN increasingly is willing to cooperate with China, especially as the United States has been preoccupied with other security problems.[40]

China's activities with ASEAN have been effective in bringing about acceptance of Beijing as a center of power and balancer in the Asia-Pacific region.[41] China is seen in the region as a positive actor, especially after the Asian financial crisis. The Philippines has accepted security cooperation with China, softening its attitudes since the occupation of Mischief Reef in 1995. Indonesia, whose armed forces have been held at arms length by the United States for human rights violations in East Timor and Aceh, is cooperating with China on the development of a naval cruise missile. For years, the United States refused to work with Indonesian industry on any form of missile development on nonproliferation grounds. Nonetheless, while China has gone from a skeptical attitude toward ASEAN, there is still concern in the region over China's long-term intentions, particularly in view of its military buildup and the development of a blue-water navy.[42]

In the last year, China hosted an ARF security policy conference, workshops on alternative development, and on increasing cooperation in the field of nontraditional security issues (such as disaster relief). According to Chinese Foreign Minister Li Zhaoxing, "in the next year China will co-host with Brunei an Inter-sessional Meeting on counterterrorism and international crime, and with the United States and Singapore will host a seminar on nonproliferation of WMD."[43] Li also expressed Beijing's willingness to co-host an intersessional meeting with Indonesia.

China's active diplomacy and confidence-building measures in the security realm have gone a long way to improve Beijing's image in the region. This has been a coordinated effort across the government and the CCP. The PLA has been an active player in these activities, even if it is not the primary agent for engaging Southeast Asia. The combination of strategy conferences PLA officers attend and diplomacy emphasize the point that the rise of China is in the interests of Southeast Asian nations. China's diplomacy also stresses that China's goal is not to "push the United States out of the region," but given the way that the United States exercised its military power in Iraq, some military hedge to American hegemony is a valuable tool in Asia.

**Specific Actions in Southeast Asia.**[44]

During the 2-year period between January 2001 and January 2003, there were 21 bilateral military-diplomatic visits between leaders of the PLA and Southeast Asian military leaders.[45] The year 2001 opened with a visit by the Philippine Defense Minister to China in January, while in February the Chinese Defense Minister took a PLA delegation to Vietnam, Laos, and Cambodia. The numbers of visits into China from Southeast Asia was about two to three times the number of visits by Chinese officials overseas. This is consistent with the author's experience in dealing with China as a military attaché, from the staff of the office of the Secretary of Defense, and on the Department of the Army staff. Simply put, the PLA has a finite annual budget for overseas visits as well as to receive foreign visitors. The PLA distributes its budget for international activities around the world, with an emphasis on specific geographical regions or countries, depending on broader policy considerations.[46] If there are a significant number of visits by a specific country to China, the PLA accepts the visiting delegation if that country foots the bill for the visit.[47]

With respect to arms sales policies, the PLA is also an important actor and can shape regional policy. Arms sales decisions, foreign military cooperation, and foreign military assistance come under the purview of the General Armaments Department of the PLA. Officers from this department participate in policy decisions across the government and can shape foreign policy.[48]

## Vietnam.

China's relations with Vietnam are "normal" and regular, but not particularly friendly. Vietnam's security planners see all of Southeast Asia at some risk in the face of China's size and strength. Nonetheless, physical proximity alone requires close contact.

The senior leaders of China visited Vietnam in April 2001, September 2001, February 2002, and October 2004. These visits, however, were either Communist Party-to-Party visits or government-to-government visits. They were not specific military delegations. In most cases, however, the Chinese delegation included a military official responsible for improving military-to-military contacts.[49]

In November 2001, the guided missile frigate *Yulin* made a port call to Ho Chi Minh City as part of a friendship visit. This was billed as a way to "increase military understanding between the two countries."[50] A PLA delegation also visited Vietnam in September 2003, led by the inspector general for discipline of the PLA General Political Department (GPD). During the visit, Major General Ye Wanbi visited the tunnels of Cu Chi, most likely an opportunity to emphasize the bilateral China-Vietnam military effort against the United States during the Vietnam War.[51] Later the same year, Chinese Vice President Zeng Qinghong visited Vietnam in October and paid a call on the Chief of the General Staff of the People's Army of Vietnam (PAVN), Phung Quang Thanh.[52]

The Deputy Chief of the General Staff Department (GSD) of the PLA, Lieutenant General Qian Shugen, visited Vietnam in March 2004, as part of a good will, training, and military education visit. Qian met with Defense Minister General Pham Van Tra.[53] Later the same year, there were economic delegation visits and even a visit by Premier Wen Jiabao. But there were only passing references to the Spratly Islands during the Wen visit.[54] The PLA GDP followed this up with a visit by GPD vice director Lieutenant General Tang Tianbao in December 2004, another Party-to Party visit that emphasized cooperation against the United States.[55]

In 2005, a major delegation of Vietnam military officials visited China in April, meeting with General Xiong Guangkai, CMC Vice Chairman Xu Caihou, and PLA Chief of the General Staff Department General Liang Guanglie.[56] There were the obligatory expressions of a "desire for friendly cooperation between the two armed forces," but no substantive agreements came from the visit. Later the same year, in July 2005, the PAVN Chief of the General Staff met with his Chinese counterpart in a confidence-building visit.[57] In addition to these military delegations, there were a number of trade, border demarcation, and Foreign Ministry related visits. There are still no close relations between the two nations, although efforts are being made to ensure balanced, friendly relations. In the military sphere, using the GSD as the main agent to make or sponsor visits between the two militaries demonstrates a tepid relationship. Considering that during the U.S. war in Vietnam there were 50,000 Chinese troops operating in that country, the level of cooperation today between the PAVN and the PLA is relatively low. The contacts reflect the reality of a smaller nation overshadowed by a more powerful military and a stronger economy. In addition, there probably is still some restraint on both sides, given the Chinese attack into Vietnam in 1979 and the ensuing years of combat.

**Laos.**

During the American war in Vietnam, the PLA was building roads through Laos and had air defense forces stationed there. One road system almost reached the border with Thailand. Today, those roads are functional but devoted to civil trade. Vietnam is Laos' dominant security partner, and China does not dispute this limited sphere of influence for Vietnam. The Laotian military is relatively small and is equipped with a mix of older United States and Soviet-bloc weapons. China could supply parts or ammunition for many of these weapons, but there is no major military trade or activity between the two countries.

The Chinese Defense Minister visited Laos in February 2001 as part of a swing through Southeast Asia that included Vietnam, Cambodia, and Nepal. His Laotian counterpart made a return visit in December of the same year, spending about 2 weeks in China. In 2003, PLA Chief of the GSD General Liang Guanglie met with the Deputy Chief of the General Staff of the People's Army of Laos.[58] They discussed unspecified "military exchanges," but Laos remains a relatively low priority for China today. In May 2005, in connection with attending a security policy meeting of the ASEAN Regional Forum in Vientiane, Deputy Chief of the PLA GSD General Xiong Guangkai met with Prime Minister Buongnang Volachit and Deputy Defense Minister Major General Douangchai Pichit.[59] Relations between Laos and China are cordial, with Laos supporting China on its Taiwan policy.[60]

## Cambodia.

China maintains a correct but distant relationship military relationship with Vietnam and good but not deep relations with Laos. The long-standing relationship between King (Prince) Sihanouk and Beijing has been the focus of China's aid and friendship for years. Relations with Cambodia, on the other hand, are strong, backed by foreign aid and military assistance, and aimed at building a strategic relationship in Southeast Asia and in the Indian Ocean.[61] There are parallels in the way that China treats Cambodia and the way that Beijing approaches relations with Thailand and Burma.

China supported Pol Pot during his reign in Cambodia with the Khmer Rouge. Beijing also actively worked to undermine Vietnam's influence there, supporting an insurgency after Vietnam's invasion of Cambodia. There are military aid packages in the millions of dollars each year for Cambodia, including the reconstruction of Kampong

Chhnang Air Base. The 2003 aid package from China to Cambodia was some $30 million.[62] *The Wall Street Journal* quotes Cambodian Army Major General Bun Song as saying, "The U.S. helped us open the door to democracy, but then they flew away. So we have no choice right now but to rely on China."[63] Former Cambodian Ambassador to the United States Roland Eng, who spent years in Beijing with Prince Sihanouk, tells of thousands of Chinese merchants and families moving to Cambodia to set up businesses.[64] Nor is China's interest solely in the ports along the Indian Ocean. Beijing is cultivating relations with Cambodia (and Thailand) because of their strategic location on the Mekong River as part of Beijing's relationship with the Greater Mekong Subregion.[65]

**Myanmar.**

During the 1990s, Myanmar (Burma) received as much as $3 billion in weapons from China.[66] Analyzing the bilateral relationship, the *Financial Times* characterized Myanmar as China's "client state." Beijing is putting shelters for ships in the Mergui archipelago in the Andaman Sea while supplying tanks, patrol boats, fighters, and air force training to Myanmar.[67] Still, Myanmar seems to seek some balance in its relations, also purchasing jet aircraft from India and Moscow. When Jiang Zemin visited Rangoon (Yangyon) in late 2001, China and Myanmar signed six agreements on the economy and border security.[68] In 2003, China's Vice Premier Li Lanqing offered Myanmar debt relief and $200 million in new loans, which propped up the military and its rule.[69]

If one doubted the relationship between China and Myanmar, the old Burma Road, a muddy track during and after World War II, is now a paved, multimodal highway, supplementing rail and river transport systems.[70] Thus, while using China for a security anchor, Myanmar has managed to turn isolation by the United States into a strong position in ASEAN and Southeast Asia.[71] Still, while there are strong security considerations in China's relations with Myanmar, the PLA is not a direct actor in a range of political, economic, and security relations. This allows China to be in a position to export from its southwest region, allows access to the sea from the southwest part of China, and provides a set of places from which China can monitor India.

**Indonesia.**

No security relationship in Southeast Asia has seen greater improvement in the past 5 years than that between China and Indonesia. Yet U.S.-Indonesian security relations should be close. Between 1950 and 1993, 8,065 Indonesian officers trained at U.S. military institutions. The United States also provided about $200 million in military assistance to Indonesia and $400 million in loans and credits for military purchases.[72] The President of Indonesia, Susilo Bambang Yudyohono, is a 1991 graduate of the U.S. Army Command and General Staff College in Fort Leavenworth, Kansas. However, the U.S. Congress cut off security assistance to Indonesia in 1992 after extrajudicial killings and atrocities by the Indonesian armed forces in Dili, East Timor.

It is fair to say that China has taken advantage of the end of U.S. military assistance to improve its own relations with Jakarta. Still, Indonesian military leaders always have tried to avoid direct alignment with any powers. Even when American military assistance was flourishing, there was still a Soviet military mission in Indonesia. One can go to the naval base in Surabaya and see Soviet PT-76 amphibious tanks entering the water off the ramps of U.S. landing ships. Before 1965, China provided arms and assistance to Indonesia. Although China established diplomatic relations with Indonesia on April 13, 1950, those relations were suspended on October 30, 1967, in the wake of the November 30, 1965, coup attempt and the subsequent anti-Chinese riots and suppression in Indonesia.[73]

Beijing used loans at concessional rates and a series of bilateral visits to repair relations with Jakarta over the period 1990 to 2002.[74] Of course, given the close association of Li Peng with the Tiananmen Massacre, China was not critical of the role of the Indonesian armed forces in suppressing civil liberties. When PRC Defense Minister Chi Haotian visited Indonesia in September 2002, he met with then Coordinating Minister for Politics and Security (now President) Yudyohono to discuss cooperation in counterterrorism. Chi praised Indonesia's domestic and international counter-terrorist programs.[75]

Beijing also has taken advantage of the end of U.S. military assistance cooperation to improve relations with Indonesia. There have been traditional concerns in the United States over missile development and proliferation around the world. When the United States sold high-speed computers to Indonesia's aircraft manufacturer, IPTN, in the 1980s, Washington placed restrictions on the software applications that could run on the computer and refused to allow the computer to network with military research institutes working on air-to-air missiles.[76] China has no such proliferation concerns. Indonesian Minister Juwono Sudarsono noted in November 2004 that Indonesia needed alternative sources of military equipment and expertise because of the U.S. embargo, and that China was one nation that could supply such equipment.[77]

China and Indonesia reportedly have signed agreements to develop missiles together and a strategic partnership agreement.[78] Together, China and Indonesia will develop a ballistic missile with a range of 150 kilometers in accordance with an agreement initialed by Defense Minister Jurwono Sudarsono in August 2005, and they will work together on naval cruise missiles with ranges of 9-19 miles. These defense ties are important inroads for China in Southeast Asia, and are one way that Chinese diplomacy has flanked the United States, with its neuralgia for cooperation with the Indonesian armed forces.

Beijing secured its new relationship with Jakarta through low interest loans ($300 million), relief assistance (about $2 million), and a strategic partnership agreement.[79] One defense-related web site in India claims that China will build a submarine base in Indonesia as a means to help secure the Malacca Strait; however, no reliable independent source has confirmed this information.[80] Thus far, on the Chinese side, the defense cooperation between the two nations has involved North China Industries (NORINCO), which was established originally by the equipment department of the PLA GSD.[81] Indonesian Defense Minister Sudarsono noted, "Within 2 years, military relations will make up 40 percent of our bilateral relations" with China.[82]

**Philippines.**

Philippine-China security relations were at their recent nadir after the 1995 seizure of Mischief Reef by China. Originally, Chinese fishermen detained Philippine fishing boats. By early February 1995, however, the PLA Navy was involved, and China reiterated its claims to the Spratly Islands and the South China Sea.[83] By 1996, the two countries had exchanged military attachés at their respective embassies. China built two concrete structures there that appeared to have military use. In October 1998, two PLA navy frigates blocked passage to the reef by a Philippine naval ship carrying journalists.[84] Chinese diplomacy and Beijing's actions in the ARF, however, have done much to improve the situation with the Philippines and in the South China Sea in general.

Beijing and Manila agreed on a bilateral framework for cooperation on May 16, 2000.[85] In addition to agreeing to scientific, technical, legal, and economic cooperation, the two governments committed to "peace and stability in the South China Sea." Thus, having handed Manila a fait accompli by its actions on Mischief Reef, Beijing got Manila to agree that neither side would "take actions that might complicate or escalate the situation." This is effective diplomacy backed up by the naval presence of the PLA. China made its commitments to the government in Manila firmer in 2002 when Beijing signed the 2002 ASEAN-China Declaration on the Conduct of Parties in the South China Sea.[86] There also have been a series of military contacts aimed at confidence-building. In October 2000, Philippine Chief of the General Staff Angelo Reyes paid a visit to China. He visited again as Secretary of Defense in April 2002. PLA General and Minister of Defense Chi Haotian paid a return visit to the Philippines in September 2002, and in 2004 two Philippine defense officials, Armed Forces Chief of Staff Narcisco Abaya and Secretary of Defense Avelino Cruz, visited China.[87] Manila and Beijing also opened formal defense and security consultations between the PLA and the Philippine armed forces, the first of which was when PLA General Xiong Guangkai visited Manila between May 22 and 25, 2005. Beijing will train five Filipino soldiers in China in the future, and Xiong donated 80 million pesos of equipment to the Philippine armed forces.[88] In the future, the two countries will hold annual defense talks.[89]

**Malaysia.**

Malaysia has shown some interest in diversifying its sources of military equipment. In the past, Malaysia has bought short-range air defense systems from the United States, Pakistan, and Russia, but Malaysian armed forces are exploring purchases from China. China Precision Machinery Import and Export Corporation, a state-owned major producer of missiles, signed a memorandum of understanding with two Malaysian companies on the purchase of short-range missiles and co-production in Malaysia of the FN-6 short-range, shoulder-launched anti-aircraft missile. This has an engagement capability of about 6 kilometers. Malaysia also has explored the purchase of the KS-1A medium-range surface-to-air missile from China.[90] In addition, in the general area of science and technology cooperation, China is willing to share satellite and space technology with Malaysia. Such technology has both civil and military application.[91] These overtures aside, there has been no substantive action between the two countries, and no arms deal is expected before 2006, if at all.

**Singapore.**

Of all the nations in Southeast Asia, Singapore has made the strongest commitments to the United States. Notwithstanding the security agreements between the United States and Thailand and the renewed U.S.-Republic of Philippines security agreement, Singapore has taken substantive action to provide facilities for U.S. forces. The naval base at Sembawang houses a U.S. Navy logistics and support group, a pier was built there to permit a U.S. aircraft carrier to berth, and Changyi Airfield can accommodate two squadrons of U.S. fighter aircraft. Still, the PLA is making some inroads in Singapore.

As part of a "show the flag" trip around the world, a PLA Navy task force stopped in Singapore in 2002. The guided missile destroyer, *Qingdao*, and a fleet support/ depot ship, *Taicang*, made a 3-day call in Singapore where China's North Sea Fleet commander, Ding Yiping, embarked.[92] Singapore Navy ships already had visited China twice on good-will voyages in the past. However, there have really been no direct military initiatives between Singapore and China. Instead, there have been a series of diplomatic confidence-building measures, most of which involved the ARF.

## Thailand.

When the People's Army of Vietnam was poised on the Thai-Cambodian border in 1980, its guns and artillery had greater range than the howitzers the United States had provided to Thailand. The Royal Thai Army remedied that problem with the purchase of Chinese 130 millimeter guns. In addition, China perhaps sealed a new security relationship with Thailand when as many as five main force PAVN divisions withdrew from the Cambodian-Thai border to reinforce the Vietnam-China border in the aftermath of Beijing's February 16-March 16, 1979, attack into Vietnam.

Beijing has been a good security partner for Thailand. The Royal Thai Army inventory includes 50 Type-69 Tanks. Today these are in storage or used for training, but in the 1980s, they were in the active inventory. Thai officers complained about the durability of the tracks, but the tanks were serviceable and of use in the event of an attack by Vietnam. Thailand also has 450 Type-85 armored personnel carriers from China, 15 130 millimeter Type-59 towed guns, Type-85 multiple rocket launchers, and 24 57 millimeter anti-aircraft guns. The Thai Navy has two PRC *Jianghu-III* class frigates, designated the *Chao Phraya* class in Thailand and two *Jianghu-IV* frigates, designated the *Kraburi* class.[93] In a 2004 interview, Chinese Minister of Defense General Cao Gangchuan described Sino-Thai military relations as "comprehensive, deep, and high-level." [94] Cao repeated these remarks on the 30th anniversary of the establishment of Sino-Thai diplomatic ties on July 4, 2005.[95]

## Brunei.

The PLA's exchanges with Brunei and military relations in general have developed more slowly than in other places in Southeast Asia. The first Memorandum of Understanding on Military Exchanges was signed on September 12, 2003, committing both countries to bilateral exchanges, attendance at military courses, visits, sports, and cultural exchanges.[96] Later the same year, two PLA Navy ships made a port call at Muara en-route to a friendship cruise that also stopped in Singapore and Guam.[97] In 2004, Shenyang Military Region Commander Qian Guoliang, Guangzhou MR deputy political commissar Ma Guowen, and staff from both military regions visited the Brunei Ministry of Defense and the commander of the Royal Brunei armed forces.[98] The attention to Brunei rounds out generally good relations between the PLA and other armed forces in Southeast Asia.

## Conclusions.

In their 1999 study, Kenneth Allen and Eric McVadon said that the PLA has had a role in "shaping and implementing" China's foreign policies by pursuing the following goals:

- To shape the international security environment in support of key Chinese national security objectives;
- To improve political and military relations with foreign countries;
- To enhance China's military and defense industry modernization;
- To provide military assistance to countries in the developing world; and,
- To acquire knowledge in modern military doctrine, operations, training, military medicine, administration, and a host of noncombat related areas.[99]

The PLA has not been the principal actor in China's relations with Southeast Asian nations. Southeast Asian nations, meanwhile, hedge their security interests by maintaining good relations with China, but would not want to exclude the United States or Australia from the region. Nor would Southeast Asian nations "buy into" an American-led containment policy against China. The peaceful rise of China and its economic strength is consistent with the interests of Southeast Asian states and Australia. The hedge is needed, however, because the PLA is the backup for the legal claims of China in the

South China Sea. Thus, China's public diplomacy is successful, but its military power is enough of a latent threat that Southeast Asian nations still hedge their security.

Therefore, it is fair to say that there has been a strong security component to all relationships in the region. Beijing has been skillful in exercising a range of relations using the "comprehensive national power" of China, ensuring contacts in the political, diplomatic, cultural, trade, and economic spheres around the region. However, the growing military power of China and its increased ability to send its Navy around the region have been a factor in ensuring good relations. The PLA's activity has consisted mainly of high-level visits and military diplomacy, except, of course, for Thailand. The backdrop of regional security has been a major factor in promoting the way that China has behaved in the region. Thus, the PLA may not be leading in all relations, but it can certainly see itself as a major factor behind China's improved standing in Southeast Asia.

## ENDNOTES – CHAPTER 10

1. Yan Xuetong, "Heping Jueqi de Yan Guan Jiao" (Research Perspectives on Peaceful Rise), *Zhanlue Guancha* (*China Strategic Review*) Vol. 6, 2005, pp. 70-77, Published by the China Reform Forum.

2. Larry M. Wortzel, *The ASEAN Regional Forum: Asian Security Without an American Umbrella*, Carlisle, PA: Strategic Studies Institute, 1995.

3. John W. Garver, *Foreign Relations of the People's Republic of China*, Englewood Cliffs, NJ: Prentice-Hall, Inc., 1993, pp. 49, 122. China's Five Principles of Peaceful Coexistence are 1) mutual respect for territorial integrity and sovereignty; 2) mutual nonaggression; 3) mutual noninterference in internal affairs; 4) equality and mutual benefit; and 5) peaceful coexistence. These principles were enumerated in a Sino-Indian agreement on April 29, 1954, and repeated in Bandung by Zhou Enlai on April 19, 1955. The principles are mentioned in full in the 1972 Sino-U.S. Communiqué and in Hu Yaobang's September 1, 1982, report to the 12th National People's Congress.

4. Garver, p. 150.

5. Bruce Vaughn, *China-Southeast Asia Relations: Trends, Issues, and Implications for the United States*, CRS Report for the Congress, CRS RL32688, February 8, 2005, p. 4. See also Michael McDevitt, "U.S. Strategy in the Asia-Pacific Region: Southeast Asia," in W. Lee, R. Hathaway, and W. Wise, eds., *U.S. Strategy in the Asia-Pacific Region*, Washington, DC: Woodrow Wilson Center for International Scholars, 2003, p. 44.

6. This quote is from the U.S. National Security Strategy. See the statement of Richard Ellings, President, National Bureau of Asian Research, Committee on International Relations, House of Representatives, Hearing on "The United States and Asia: Continuity, Instability and Tradition," March 17, 2004.

7. Wortzel, *The ASEAN Regional Forum: Asian Security without an American Umbrella*.

8. The Office of the U.S. Trade Representative/Home/Document Library/ USTR Zoellick Speeches/2004/02/25/04/China Trade. *China and America: Power and Responsibility*, 02/24/2004.

9. See the table on diverging and converging U.S. and Chinese interests in Southeast Asia in David Shambaugh, "China Engages Asia: Reshaping the Regional Order," *International Security*, Winter 2004/2005, p. 64.

10. *Taipei Times*, August 28, 2005, p. 1.

11. China's Position Paper on the New Security Concept," August 6, 2002, *www.chinaembassy.org.tr/eng/xwdt/t61685.htm*.

12. Information Office of the State Council of the People's Republic of China, *China's Peaceful Development Road*, Beijing, December 22, 2005, issued as a *White Paper on Peaceful Development*, *www.chinadaily.com.cn/english.doc/2005-12/22/content_505678.htm*.

13. Yan Xuetong, Wang Zaibang, Li Zhongcheng, and Hou Ruoshi, *Zhongguo Jueqi: Guoji Huanjing Pinggu (The International Environment for China's Peaceful Rise)*, Tianjin: Tianjin Renmin Chubanshe, 1998.

14. *Ibid*. p. 2.

15. *Ibid*. pp. 234-235.

16. The Center for Strategic and International Studies (CSIS) in Washington, DC, maintains a regular program of exchanges with the Central Communist Party School of China and its China Reform Forum. A compilation of Zheng Bijian's speeches on "China's Peaceful Rise" can be found on the CSIS web site, *www.csis.org*. See also Zheng Bijian, "Zhongguo Heping Jueqi Fazhan Daolu You Liyu Zhong-Mei Guanxi" ("China's Peaceful Rise is Conducive to the Sino-U.S. Relationship"), *Luntan Tongxun (China Reform Forum Newsletter*, 9/2004), September 28, 2004, pp. 3-6.

17. Xinhua, October 29, 2003, in *www2.chinadaily.com.cn/en/doc/2003-10/29/content_276497.htm; www.adb.org/Documents/Events/2003/Boao_Fourm_Asia/default.asp*. Zheng Bijian, "Zhongguo Heping Jueqi Fazhan Daolu You Liyu Zhong-Mei Guanxi," pp. 3-6.

18. Zheng Bejian, "China's Peaceful Rise," *Foreign Affairs*, Summer/Fall 2005.

19. Discussion with Zheng Bijian, Beijing, August 23, 2005.

20. See *news.xinhuanet.com/zhengfu/2004-03/26/content_1386611.htm*, in Chinese.

21. *Ibid*. Hu Jintao, Speech in celebration of the 110th anniversary of Mao Zedong's birth, December 26, 2003.

22. *Ibid.*

23. *Ibid.*

24. Discussion between the author and PLA officers in May 2004 and August 2005.

25. Discussion with Zheng Bijian, August 23, 2005.

26. Larry Wortzel, "China's Peaceful Rise," *The Asian Wall Street Journal,* September 5, 2005, p. A9.

27. Meetings with the Chinese Academy of Social Sciences, the China Reform Forum, and at Qinghua University, Beijing, August 22-23, 2005.

28. Yan Xuetong, "Zhongguo Jueqi de Shili Diwei" ("China's Overall Strength and Its Peaceful Rise"), *Guoji Zhengzhi Kexue, (Science of International Politics)*, Vol. 2, 2005, pp. 1-25, see especially p. 23.

29. See Huang Shifeng, ed., *Zonghe Guoli Lilun, (The Theory of Comprehensive National Power)*. Beijing: Chinese Academy of Social Sciences Press, 1993, pp. 1, 10-14, and 104-105. See also Liu Zhongmin, "Pondering Non-traditional Security Threat in the Maritime Space After the Indian Ocean Tsunami," *Zhongguo Zhanglue Guacha*, Vol. 1, January 26, 2005, pp. 55-65.

30. Xinhua News Agency, Beijing, 1418 GMT, December 20, 2004, in BBC Monitoring International Reports.

31. Kuik Cheng-Chee, "Multilateralism in China's ASEAN Policy: Its Evolution, Characteristics, and Aspiration," *Contemporary Southeast Asia*, Vol. 27, No. 1, April 2005, p. 102.

32. Discussions with journalists in Hong Kong, August 28, 2005.

33. In addition to the 10 ASEAN states (Brunei, Cambodia, Indonesia, Laos, Malaysia, Myanmar, the Philippines, Singapore Thailand and Vietnam), the ARF is comprised by Australia, Canada, China, the European Union, India, Japan, Mongolia, New Zealand, North Korea, Papua New Guinea, Pakistan, Russia, South Korea, East Timor, and the United States. See *vietnamnews.vnagency.com.vn/showarticle.php?num=02POL290705.*

34. See Yan Yang and Chu Dao, "The Security Problems in the Asia-Pacific Region and the Security Problems of Parties Concerned," *Xiandai Guoji Guanxi (Contemporary International Relations)*, Vol. 7, 1994, pp. 2-7; Eric Teo, "Solidifying China's Regional Partnerships," *China Daily*, May 15, 2005; and Wang Yizhou, *Quanqiu Zhengzhi he Zhongguo Waijiao (Global Politics and China's Foreign Policy)*, Beijing: Zhijie Zhishe Chubanshe, 2003.

35. John Wang and Sarah Chan, "China-ASEAN Free Trade Agreement: Shaping Future Economic Relations," *Asian Survey*, Vol. 43, No. 3, May/June 2003, pp. 507-526.

36. *Ibid.* p. 297.

37. "Deals and Diplomacy: China's Influence in Southeast Asia is Growing as its Trade and Investments Boom," *Time International,* Asia Edition, May 30, 2005, p. 14.

38. *China's National Defense in 2000,* Xinhua, October 16, 2000.

39. Murray Heibert, "How China is Building an Empire," *Far Eastern Economic Review,* November 20, 2003, p. 30.

40. David Shambaugh, "Beijing Charms its Neighbors," *The International Herald Tribune,* May 14, 2005, p. 6; Michael R. J. Vatikiotis, "Catching the Dragon's Tail: China and Southeast Asia in the 21st Century," *Contemporary Southeast Asia,* Vol. 25, No. 1, April 2003, p. 65.

41. Alice D. Ba, "China and ASEAN: Reinvigorating Relations for a 21sr Century Asia," *Asian Survey,* Vol. 43, No. 4, July/August 2003, pp. 622-674.

42. Ba, "China and ASEAN," p. 646; "China looks to flex ASEAN muscle," TV New Zealand, July 25, 2005, *tvnz.co.nz/view/page/411366/599871.*

43. "China to forge security cooperation in Asia-Pacific region: FM," *People's Daily Online, english.people.com.cn/200507/29/eng20050729_199142.html.*

44. For a comprehensive look at China's military diplomacy in the region in from the time of the establishment of the PRC until 1999, see the monograph by Kenneth W. Allen and Eric A. McVadon, *China's Foreign Military Relations,* Washington, DC: The Stimson Center, October 1999.

45. See *www.chinamil.com.cn/sitel/wdwjdlsl/wdwjdlsl.htm.*

46. Discussions with PLA foreign affairs office staff, 1999, 2002.

47. In the case of incoming U.S. visitors, this is often the case because the U.S. Government funds such visits as part of its own internal engagement planning, and the PLA tends to use the money from such visits to fund its own international operations. Thus, the PLA will often accept more visits than it makes.

48. The author owes this point to discussion from the floor at the 2005 PLA conference, Carlisle, PA, September 23-25, 2005. See also David Shambaugh, *Modernizing China's Military: Progress Problems and Prospects,* Berkeley, University Of California Press, 2002, pp. 143-146.

49. See *vn.chineseembassy.org/chn/zygx/t177232.htm.*

50. "First PLA Navy Visit to Vietnam," *Jane's Defense Weekly,* November 28, 2001, p. 16.

51. BBC Monitoring Service, September 30, 2003, from Vietnam News Agency, September 29, 2003.

52. BBC Monitoring Service, October 28, 2003.

53. BBC Monitoring Service, March 6, 2004.

54. *SCMP.com,* October 6, 2004.

55. BBC Monitoring Service, December 7, 2004.

56. BBC Monitoring Service, April 11, 3005.

57. *People's Daily Online*, July 0, 2005.

58. World News Connection (hereafter WNC) NTIS, U.S. Department of Commerce, August 27, 2003.

59. BBC Monitoring Service, May 28, 2005.

60. *People's Daily Online*, July 27, 2005; Vietnam News Agency, July 28, 2005.

61. Karby Leggett, "Beyond the Wall: China Looks Abroad, Challenging the US for Influence in Asia," *Wall Street Journal*, June 7, 2001, p. A.1.

62. Sothea, "China Seen as 'Real Cause' of Current Political 'Turmoil' in Cambodia," *Foreign Broadcast Information Service*, FBIS-SEP20040518000092, May 13, 2004.

63. Legget, "Beyond the Wall, " June 7, 2001.

64. Interview, September 2004, Washington, DC.

65. "Cambodian PM to attend GMS Summit in China," *www.chinaview.com.cn*, 2005-07-03, 10:20:09.

66. Amy Kazin and James Kynge, "A Tussle for Asia," *Financial Times*, June 27, 2001, p. 20.

67. "Burma's Reliance on China, BBC, December 11, 2001, 23:38 GMT; Peter Kammerer, "China India Hold Key to Burma," *South China Morning Post*, June 20, 2003, p. 8.

68. See *interactive.wsj.com/archives/retrieve.cg?id-BT-CO20011212-001537.djm*.

69. Amy Kazin, "China Throws Burma a Financial Lifeline," *Financial Times*, January 17, 2003; *Washington Post*, September 28, 2003, p. B7.

70. *Asia Times*, September 23, 2003.

71. Helen James, "Myanmar's International Relations Strategy," *Contemporary Southeast Asia*, No. 3, Vol. 26, December 1, 2004, p. 530.

72. Dana R. Dillon, *Democratic Indonesia as a Security Partner*, Heritage Backgrounder 1800, Washington, DC: The Heritage Foundation, September 24, 2004.

73. See *www.chinaembassy-indonesia.or.id/eng/4360.html*.

74. Tan Hongwei, "Roundup on NPC Chairman Li Peng's Fruitful Found-Day Visit to Indonesia," *Zhongguo Xinwenshe*, 0250GMT, September 12, 2002, *FBIS-CPP20020912000017*.

75. Jakarta TVRI 1 Television, 2300 GMT, September 18, 2002, *FBIS-SEP200209919000025*.

76. Author's experience with security review visits to Indonesia in 1987.

77. "Indonesia Explores Arms Purchases from China," BBC Monitoring Service, November 6, 2004; "Indonesia to Pursue Military Cooperation with Russia and China," BBC Monitoring Service, November 25, 2004.

78. *Yeguang Xinwen, latenews.com,* June 13, 2005, 08:36:20; and BBC Worldwide Monitoring, August 5, 2005.

79. "China and Indonesia Seal Strategic Pact, *International Herald Tribune,* April 26, 2005.

80. *India-defence.com, srirangan.net/india-defence/node/241/print.*

81. Murie Dickie and Shawn Donnan, "Jakarta in Missile Deal with Beijing," *Financial Times,* August 1, 2005, p. 7.

82. *Ibid.*

83. Terry McCarthy, "Reef Wars," *Time,* March 8, 1999.

84. See *www.subcontinent.com/sapra/world/w_1999-21.html.*

85. See *ph.china-embassy.org/eng/zfgx/zzgx/t183269.htm.*

86. See *ph.china-embassy.org/eng/zfgx/zzgx/t183270.htm.*

87. Gilbert Felongo, "Manila and Beijing Agreee to Set up Mechanism for Annual Defence Talks," *Financial Times,* November 19, 2004.

88. "Beijing Expands Influence, Woos RP," *Manila Times,* "Newsbites," May 24, 2005.

89. Volt Contreras, "Chinese Envoy Allays Fear of Stronger RP-Sino Ties," *Philippine Daily Inquirer,* July 27, 2005.

90. "Malaysia to Buy PRC Surface to Air Missiles," *Kuala Lumbpur Bernama,* July 20, 2004, in *FBIS*-SEP20040720000095.

91. *The Star Online,* September 16, 2003, *allmalysiainfo.com.*

92. *People's Daily Online, english.peopledaily.com.cn,* May 24, 2002.

93. Institute for International Strategic Studies, *The Military Balance, 2004-2005* London: Oxford University Press, 2005, pp. 190-192.

94. BBC Monitoring service, March 22, 2004, from Xinhua News Agency, 1257 GMT March 21, 2004, pp. 2—4.

95. BBC Monitoring service, July 4, 2005, from Xinhua News Agency, 0628 GMT, July 4, 2004.

96. BBC Monitoring Service, September 13, 2003, from Borneo Bulletin, Bandar Seri Begawan, September 13, 2003.

97. BBC Monitoring Service, October 30, 2003.

98. BBC Monitoring Service, November 28, 2004

99. Allen and McVadon, *China's Foreign Military Relations*, p. iv.

# ABOUT THE CONTRIBUTORS

PAUL H. B. GODWIN is a Senior Fellow at the Foreign Policy Research Institute, Philadelphia, Pennsylvania. He retired as professor of international affairs, the National War College, Washington, DC, in the summer of 1998. In the fall of 1987, he was a visiting professor at the Chinese National Defense University. His teaching and research specialties focus on Chinese defense and security policies. Dr. Godwin's most recent publications are "Change and Continuity in Chinese Military Doctrine: 1949-1999," in Mark A. Ryan, David M. Finkelstein, and Michael A. McDevitt, eds., *Chinese Warfighting: the PLA Experience Since 1949* (Armonk, New York: M.E. Sharpe, 2003); "China's Defense Establishment: The Hard Lessons of Incomplete Modernization," in Laurie Burkitt, Andrew Scobell, and Larry Wortzel, eds., *The Lessons of History: The Chinese People's Liberation Army at 75* (Carlisle, PA: U.S. Army War College, Strategic Studies Institute, 2003); *Preserving the PLA's Soul: Civil Military Relations and the New Generation of Chinese Leadership*, CAPS Papers No. 33 (Taipei, Taiwan, Republic of China: Chinese Council of Advanced Policy Studies, October 2003); and "China as Regional Hegemon?" in Jim Rolfe, ed., *The Asia-Pacific Region in Transition* (Honolulu, Hawaii: Asia-Pacific Center for Security Studies, 2004). Dr. Godwin graduated from Dartmouth College with a degree in International Relations, and received his Ph.D. in Political Science from the University of Minnesota.

LONNIE D. HENLEY is Defense Intelligence Officer for East Asia and Pacific, in the Defense Intelligence Agency. He is a retired Army China Foreign Area Officer, and has worked in a variety of China and Korea-related positions. He is the author of *China's Capacity for Achieving a Revolution in Military Affairs* , U.S. Army War College, Strategic Studies Institute (1996); "The RMA After Next," *Parameters*, Winter 1999-2000; and other publications dealing with Chinese military capabilities, Asian security issues, and the future of warfare. He was educated at West Point, Oxford, Columbia, and the Defense Intelligence College.

ELLIS JOFFE is Professor of Chinese Studies at the Hebrew University of Jerusalem and a Senior Fellow at the Truman Research Institute at that university. Among Dr. Joffe's works are *Party and Army: Professionalism and Political Control in the Chinese Officer Corps, 1949-64* (1965), *The Chinese Army After Mao* (1987), and many articles in journals and books. He was educated in Jerusalem, Hong Kong, and at Harvard University.

SRIKANTH KONDAPALLI is a Research Fellow at the Institute for Defence Studies & Analysis, New Delhi. He has completed two research projects at IDSA - "China's Armed Forces" and "China's National Defence Strategy"; was Post-Doctoral Visiting Fellow at People's University, Beijing, in 1997-98; qualified in the Chinese language test of Beijing Language & Culture University, 1996-97; was an Honorary Fellow at the Institute of Chinese Studies, Delhi; and is a Member of the Indian Council for Asia Pacific Studies. Dr. Kondapalli's current project is Security Initiatives in Enhancing National Power: China in Asia. His latest publications include *China's Naval Power* (New Delhi: Knowledge World & IDSA, 2001), *A Great Leap Forward Modernisation: China's Armed Forces in 2003* (Taipei: Centre for China Studies, 2005), and "China's Political Commissars and Commanders: Trends & Dynamics," (Singapore: Institute for Defence and Strategic Studies, University of Nanyang, Working Paper, 2005). Dr. Kondapalli received his Ph.D. in Chinese Studies at the Centre for East Asian Studies, School of International Studies, Jawaharlal Nehru University, New Delhi.

JAMES R. LILLEY is Senior Fellow in Asian studies at the American Enterprise Institute. Mr. Lilley was the U.S. Ambassador to the People's Republic of China from 1989 to 1991 and to the Republic of Korea from 1986 to 1989. He served as Assistant Secretary of Defense for International Security Affairs from 1991 to 1993. Mr. Lilley wrote the forewords for the AEI publications *Chinese Military Modernization, Over the Line,* and *China's Military Faces the Future.* He is also the coeditor of *Beyond MFN: Trade Beyond MFN: Trade with China* and *American Interests and Crisis in the Taiwan Strait.* He is the author most recently of: *China Hands: Nine Decades of Adventure, Espionage, and Diplomacy in Asia,* with Jeffrey Lilley (New York: Public Affairs, 2004).

FRANK MILLER is currently the Army Attaché to the U.S. Embassy in Beijing. As a Special Forces Officer assigned to First Special Forces Group and as a China Foreign Area Officer, he has served throughout East Asia, including tours in Okinawa, Hong Kong, and Hawaii as the J5 Country Manager for China, Taiwan, Hong Kong, and Mongolia. His previous tour was as the Defense and Army Attaché to the Socialist Republic of Vietnam in Hanoi. Colonel Miller is a graduate of the U.S. Military Academy, Naval Postgraduate School, and the U.S. Army War College.

SUSAN M. PUSKA retired from the U.S. Army on February 1, 2005. As a military logistician, she served in various command and staff positions in Germany; Korea; Fort Hood, Texas; and Aberdeen Proving Ground, Maryland. Her last position prior to retirement was Political-Military

Advisor, Bureau of Asian and Pacific Affairs, Department of State. Prior to this she served as the Army Attaché, U.S. Embassy, Beijing, during 2001-03. During 1999-2000, Colonel Puska was the Director of Asian Studies, Department of National Security and Strategy, U.S. Army War College. Between 1996 and 1999, she served as the China Political-Military Desk Officer, Office of the Deputy Under Secretary of the Army, International Affairs. During 1992 to 1994, she was an Assistant Army Attaché at the U.S. Embassy, Beijing. Her publications include "SARS 2002-2003: A Case Study in Crisis Management," in *Chinese Crisis Management* (Carlisle, PA: Strategic Studies Institute, 2005); "The People's Liberation Army General Logistics Department: Toward Joint Logistics Support," in *PLA As Organization* (Santa Monica, California: RAND, 2002); editor of *People's Liberation Army After Next* (Carlisle, Pennsylvania: Strategic Studies Institute, 2000); and *New Century, Old Thinking: The Dangers of the Perceptual Gap in U.S.-China Relations*, (Carlisle, Pennsylvania: Strategic Studies Institute, 1999). She studied Mandarin Chinese at the Defense Language Institute, Monterey, California, and The John Hopkins-Nanjing University Center for Chinese and American Studies, Nanjing, PRC. Colonel Puska has a BA from Michigan State University, an M.A. from the University of Michigan, and is a 1997 graduate of the U.S. Army War College, Carlisle, Pennsylvania.

ANDREW SCOBELL is an Associate Research Professor at the Strategic Studies Institute, U.S. Army War College, and Adjunct Professor of Political Science at Dickinson College. Prior to his current position, he taught at the University of Louisville, Kentucky, and Rutgers University, New Jersey. Dr. Scobell's research focuses on political and military affairs in the Asia-Pacific Region. He is the author of *China's Use of Military Force: Beyond the Great Wall and the Long March* (Cambridge University Press, 2003). Dr. Scobell earned a Ph.D in political science from Columbia University.

ROBERT G. SUTTER became a Visiting Professor in the School of Foreign Service at Georgetown University in August 2001. Dr. Sutter specialized in Asian and Pacific Affairs and U.S. foreign policy in a U.S. Government career of 30 years. He held a variety of analytical and supervisory positions with the Library of Congress for over 20 years, and he also worked with the Central Intelligence Agency, the Department of State, and the Senate Foreign Relations Committee. After leaving the Library of Congress, where he was for many years the Senior Specialist in International Politics for the Congressional Research Service, Dr. Sutter served for 2 years as the National Intelligence Officer for East Asia and the Pacific at the U.S. Government's National Intelligence Council. He has held adjunct faculty positions with Georgetown, George Washington, and Johns Hopkins Universities and the University of Virginia. He has published 12 books, numerous articles and several hundred government reports dealing with contemporary East Asian and Pacific countries and their relations with the United States. Dr. Sutter received a Ph.D. in History and East Asian Languages from Harvard University.

JOHN J. TKACIK, JR. is Senior Research Fellow in Asian Studies at The Heritage Foundation with a research focus on U.S. policies toward China (including Hong Kong and Macao), Taiwan, and Mongolia. Mr. Tkacik is a retired diplomat who served overseas with the U.S. Foreign Service in Taiwan, Iceland, China and the former British Crown Colony of Hong Kong, as well as in the Department of State in Washington, DC, where he was Chief of China Analysis in the Bureau of Intelligence and Research (INR). After Mr. Tkacik's retirement, he worked in Hong Kong as vice president for external relations for R.J. Reynolds Tobacco International. He joined The Heritage Foundation in 2001. Mr. Tkacik is the Editor and main contributor to "Rethinking One China," a book published by The Heritage Foundation in 2004. He has a master's degree from Harvard University and a bachelor's degree from Georgetown University.

LARRY M. WORTZEL is a commissioner on the U.S.-China Economic and Security Review Commission, a Congressionally appointed body. He is also a fellow with The Heritage Foundation, where he previously was Vice President for Foreign Policy and Director of the Asian Studies Center. Dr. Wortzel was a career Army officer, retiring as a colonel after 32 years of military service in 1999. He spent 7 years as an infantryman. He has long experience as a counterintelligence officer and foreign intelligence collector for the Defense Department. In 1971-72, while assigned in Southeast Asia, he collected communications intelligence on Chinese forces in Laos and Vietnam. He was an intelligence analyst on China at the U.S. Pacific Command from 1978-82. Dr. Wortzel served as a military attaché in China from May 1988 to June 1990 and June 1995 to December 1997. He also served as a strategist on the Department of the Army staff. His last military position was Director of the Strategic Studies Institute, U.S. Army War College. Dr. Wortzel is the author of two books on military history and political issues in China and has edited and contributed chapters to five other books on the Chinese armed forces. He has been quoted widely on these subjects in newspapers and on wire services. He studied at the Chinese Language and Research Centre of the National University of Singapore in 1982-83. A graduate of the Armed Forces Staff College and the U.S. Army War College, Dr. Wortzel earned his B.A. from Columbus College, Georgia, and his M.A. and Ph.D. from the University of Hawaii.